DIVINE ACTION IN
HEBREWS

DIVINE ACTION IN
HEBREWS
AND THE ONGOING
PRIESTHOOD OF JESUS

Gareth Lee Cockerill, Craig G. Bartholomew,
and Benjamin T. Quinn, editors

ZONDERVAN
ACADEMIC

ZONDERVAN ACADEMIC

Divine Action in Hebrews
Copyright © 2023 by the Kirby Laing Centre for Public Theology in Cambridge

Requests for information should be addressed to:
Zondervan, *3900 Sparks Dr. SE, Grand Rapids, Michigan 49546*

Zondervan titles may be purchased in bulk for educational, business, fundraising, or sales promotional use. For information, please email SpecialMarkets@Zondervan.com.

Library of Congress Cataloging-in-Publication Data

Names: Quinn, Benjamin T., editor. | Bartholomew, Craig G., 1961- editor. | Cockerill, Gareth Lee, editor.
Title: Divine action in Hebrews : and the ongoing priesthood of Jesus / Benjamin T. Quinn, Craig Bartholomew, Gareth Lee Cockerill.
Description: Grand Rapids : Zondervan, 2023. | Series: The new scripture collective
Identifiers: LCCN 2023016768 (print) | LCCN 2023016769 (ebook) | ISBN 9780310139102 (paperback) | ISBN 9780310139119 (ebook)
Subjects: LCSH: Bible. Hebrews--Criticism, interpretation, etc. | God (Christianity) | BISAC: RELIGION / Biblical Commentary / New Testament / General Epistles | RELIGION / Biblical Criticism & Interpretation / New Testament
Classification: LCC BS2775.52 .D58 2023 (print) | LCC BS2775.52 (ebook) | DDC 227/.8706--dc23/eng/20230629
LC record available at https://lccn.loc.gov/2023016768
LC ebook record available at https://lccn.loc.gov/2023016769

Scripture quotations marked CEB are taken from the Common English Bible. Copyright © 2011 Common English Bible. ● Scripture quotations marked CEV are taken from the Contemporary English Version. Copyright © 1991, 1992, 1995 by American Bible Society. Used by permission. ● Scripture quotations marked ESV are taken from the ESV® Bible (The Holy Bible, English Standard Version®). Copyright © 2001 by Crossway, a publishing ministry of Good News Publishers. Used by permission. All rights reserved. ● Scripture quotations marked KJV are taken from the King James Version. Public domain. ● Scripture quotations marked NIV are taken from The Holy Bible, New International Version®, NIV®. Copyright © 1973, 1978, 1984, 2011 by Biblica, Inc.® Used by permission of Zondervan. All rights reserved worldwide. www.Zondervan.com. The "NIV" and "New International Version" are trademarks registered in the United States Patent and Trademark Office by Biblica, Inc.® ● Scripture quoted by permission. Quotations designated (NET©) are from the NET Bible® copyright ©1996–2017 by Biblical Studies Press, L.L.C. http://netbible.com All rights reserved. ● Scripture quotations marked NRSV are taken from the New Revised Standard Version Bible. Copyright © 1989, Division of Christian Education of the National Council of the Churches of Christ in the United States of America. Used by permission. All rights reserved. ● Scripture quotations marked NRSVue are taken from the *New Revised Standard Version Updated Edition*, copyright © 2021 National Council of the Churches of Christ in the United States of America. Used by permission. All rights reserved worldwide. ● Scripture quotations marked RSV are taken from the Revised Standard Version of the Bible. Copyright © 1952 [2nd edition 1971] by the Division of Christian Education of the National Council of the Churches of Christ in the United States of America. Used by permission. All rights reserved. ● Scripture quotations marked TNIV are taken from the Holy Bible, Today's New International® Version TNIV®. Copyright © 2001, 2005 Biblica, Inc.® Used by permission of Zondervan. All rights reserved worldwide. "TNIV" and "Today's New International Version" are trademarks registered in the United States Patent and Trademark Office by Biblica, Inc.®

Any internet addresses (websites, blogs, etc.) and telephone numbers in this book are offered as a resource. They are not intended in any way to be or imply an endorsement by Zondervan, nor does Zondervan vouch for the content of these sites and numbers for the life of this book.

Cover Design: Tammy Johnson
Cover photos: © *"Christ Enthroned," Kelly Latimore, 2020*
Interior design: Sara Colley

Printed in the United States of America

23 24 25 26 27 28 29 30 31 32 /TRM/ 15 14 13 12 11 10 9 8 7 6 5 4 3 2 1

Dedicated to William J. Abraham (1947–2021) for his lifetime of Christian scholarship and his recent, magisterial work on divine action. He is sorely missed.

Contents

Part IV: The Ongoing Priesthood of Jesus

Part V: Divine Action and Hebrews Today

Part VI: Concluding Reflections

Abbreviations

AB	Anchor Bible
AYBRL	Anchor Yale Bible Reference Library
BBR	*Bulletin for Biblical Research*
BDAG	W. Bauer, F. W. Danker, W. F. Arndt, and F. W. Gingrich, *Greek-English Lexicon of the New Testament and Other Early Christian Literature.* 3rd ed. Chicago: University of Chicago Press, 1999.
Bib	*Biblica*
BJS	*Brown Judaic Studies*
BR	*Biblical Research*
BSac	*Bibliotheca Sacra*
BU	Biblische Untersuchungen
BZNW	Beihefte zur Zeitschrift für die neutestamentliche Wissenschaft
CBQ	*Catholic Biblical Quarterly*
CBQMS	Catholic Biblical Quarterly Monograph Series
CCSS	Catholic Commentary on Sacred Scripture
CEV	Contemporary English Version
CO	John Calvin, *Ioannis Calvini opera omnia quae supersunt.* Edited by G. Baum, E. Cunitz, and E. Reuss. 59 vols. Brunsvigae: C. A. Schwetschke, 1863–1900.
CTQ	*Concordia Theological Quarterly*
CTR	*Criswell Theological Review*
CTS	*Calvin's Commentaries.* Calvin Translation Society edition [1843–1855]. 26 vols. Reprint, Grand Rapids: Baker, 1989.
CUA	Catholic University of America
CUP	Cambridge University Press
ESV	English Standard Version
HBT	Horizons in Biblical Theology
JBL	*Journal of Biblical Literature*

JRT	*Journal of Reformed Theology*
JSHJ	*Journal for the Study of the Historical Jesus*
JSNTSup	Journal for the Study of the New Testament: Supplement Series
JTI	*Journal of Theological Interpretation*
JTS	*Journal of Theological Studies*
KEK	Kritisch-exegetischer Kommentar über das Neue Testament (Meyer-Kommentar)
KJV	King James Version
LNTS	Library of New Testament Studies
LXX	Septuagint
MT	Masoretic Text (Standard Hebrew Old Testament)
NAB	New American Bible
NASB	New American Standard Bible
NICNT	New International Commentary on the New Testament
NICOT	New International Commentary on the Old Testament
NIGTC	New International Greek Testament Commentary
NIV	New International Version
NovT	*Novum Testamentum*
NovTSup	Supplements to Novum Testamentum
NPNF	*Nicene and Post-Nicene Fathers*
NRSV	New Revised Standard Version
NRSVue	New Revised Standard Version Updated Edition
NRTh	*Nouvelle Revue Théologique*
NT	New Testament
NTL	New Testament Library
NTS	*New Testament Studies*
NTT	New Testament Theology
OT	Old Testament
OUP	Oxford University Press
PG	Patrologia Graeca [Patrologiae Cursus Completus: Series Graeca]. Edited by J.-P. Migne. 161 vols. Paris, 1857–1866.
PIBA	*Proceedings of the Irish Biblical Association*
RSV	Revised Standard Version
SAH	Scripture and Hermeneutics
SBJT	*Southern Baptist Journal of Theology*
SJT	*Scottish Journal of Theology*
SNTSMS	Society for New Testament Studies Monograph Series
STDJ	Studies on the Texts of the Desert of Judah
StTh	*Studia Theologica*

SwJT	*Southwestern Journal of Theology*
TDNT	*Theological Dictionary of the New Testament*. Edited by G. Kittel and G. Friedrich. Translated by G. W. Bromiley. 10 vols. Grand Rapids: Eerdmans, 1964–1976.
TJ	*Trinity Journal*
T/NIV	Today's New International Version/New International Version
TNIV	Today's New International Version
TNTC	Tyndale New Testament Commentaries
TynBul	*Tyndale Bulletin*
UBS	United Bible Societies
WBC	Word Biblical Commentary
WTJ	*Westminster Theological Journal*
WUNT	Wissenschaftliche Untersuchungen zum Neuen Testament

Preface

The present volume attends to the portrayal of divine action in the letter to the Hebrews. Inspired in part by William Abraham's four-volume work on divine action (OUP, 2017–2021), the contributors to this volume explore important biblical, theological, moral, and practical themes informed by God's ongoing activity in the world, not least in relation to the ongoing priesthood of Jesus. While each contributor was afforded considerable freedom, the editors have worked hard to ensure overall coherence and continuity of engagement with the theme of divine action, between chapters in this volume, with content from the eight-volume Scripture and Hermeneutics Series published by Zondervan Academic between 2000 and 2015, and with the first volume in our new Scripture Collective series, *The Scripture and Hermeneutics Seminar: Retrospect and Prospect*.

As this volume was being planned, Billy (William) Abraham delightfully agreed to contribute an introductory essay outlining the history of scholarship on divine action, the state of this conversation, a summary of his own view, and the importance of the book of Hebrews in this discussion. Craig met Billy in Chicago while serving as a senior research fellow at the Carl Henry Center at Trinity International University. In a paper he gave there, Billy commented, evoking Wittgenstein, that our theological work on divine action must return to the "rough ground" of the Bible;[1] i.e., it needs to attend to actual examples of divine action. This volume aims to do just that with its attention to Hebrews.

Sadly, Billy passed away unexpectedly in the fall of 2021 before completing his essay. We consequently approached Fellipe do Vale, one of Billy's last PhD students, about writing the introductory essay for this volume, both in Billy's

---

1. The Wittgenstein quote is, "We have got on to slippery ice where there is no friction and so in a certain sense the conditions are ideal, but also, just because of that, we are unable to walk. We want to walk: so we need *friction*. Back to the rough ground!" Ludwig Wittgenstein, *Philosophical Investigations*, trans. G. E. M. Anscombe (Oxford: Blackwell, 1997), section 109.

honor and as an engagement with his thought. Fellipe obliged, and we are glad to have his rich essay opening this volume.

The content for this volume began as a two-year focus by the Scripture and Doctrine Seminar (SADS), one of four Scripture Collective seminars of the Kirby Laing Centre for Public Theology in Cambridge, UK (KLC). Many of the papers presented during that two-year focus are included in this volume, with additional chapters added to fill out and further the conversation.

The volume is comprised of five parts: Introductory Issues, Hebrews and the Doctrine of God, Divine Action in Hebrews, The Ongoing Priesthood of Jesus, and Divine Action and Hebrews Today. Contributors range from biblical scholars to theologians, historians, philosophers, and ethicists, as we have sought to engage Hebrews from multiple angles and perspectives.

Ultimately, our hope is fourfold. First, we hope that the current volume stimulates further discussion about the importance of divine action in the whole of Scripture, not just in Hebrews. Second, we hope that this volume serves as an example of the fertility of engagement between theologians and biblical scholars. This, after all, is the aim of SADS as articulated on the KLC's website, namely:

> SADS focuses on the intersection of Scripture and Doctrine. Historically doctrine has developed as the church needed to give an account of what it believed and to protect itself from heresy. SADS explores the move from Scripture to the formulation of doctrine, and how doctrine and tradition illuminate our reading of the Bible. Insofar as doctrine captures the message of the Bible it also provides an indispensable lens through which to read Scripture and informs our faithful witness to Christ in His world.[2]

Third, we hope this volume honors the important work and legacy of Dr. William Abraham. And, finally, we hope this volume serves well both academics and practitioners of the faith so that they might think better about and attend more closely to God's active work, especially the ongoing priesthood of Jesus in Hebrews. May the contributions of this volume enhance their reading, hearing, teaching, and living of the Bible.

We remain very grateful to Katya Covrett and her colleagues at Zondervan Academic for the marvellous opportunity this series presents. We are also grateful to Istine Rodseth Swart for her editorial help and to Daniel Saxton for his exemplary work as our copyeditor. The KLC is committed to intellectual

---

2. "The Kirby Laing Centre's Scripture and Doctrine Seminar," The Kirby Laing Centre for Public Theology in Cambridge, 2022, https://kirbylaingcentre.co.uk/scripture-collective/the-scripture-and-doctrine-seminar/.

community rooted in deep spirituality, and we invite you, the reader, to become part of our community. You will find the details of our work on our website: www.kirbylaingcentre.co.uk.

Insofar as we have accomplished our fourfold aims, we give praise to Christ our Great High Priest.

On behalf of the editors,
Benjamin T. Quinn, October 2022

PART I

Introductory Issues

CHAPTER 1

Divine Action, Theological Method, and Scripture's Narrative

Fellipe do Vale

INTRODUCTION

Divine action is beginning to enjoy something of a renaissance within contemporary theology. However, the direction, purpose, and content of this rebirth are still difficult to discern. Renewed interest in, for instance, divine action and the laws of nature[1] or the human mind[2] have proved to be valuable advances in research, along with reorientations to the question of the compatibility between divine and human action.[3] While salutary, these studies nevertheless run the risk of confining divine action to parochial spheres focused upon its compatibility with other commitments, such as the natural sciences. A volume such as the present one, which intends to conceive of divine action as a theologically basic concept, distributed amongst and foundational to the full range of the Christian confession, must avoid this risk.[4] The best means for doing so, moreover, is to articulate a clear account of how divine action relates to theological method and

---

1. See Jeffrey Koperski, *Divine Action, Determinism, and the Laws of Nature* (New York: Routledge, 2020).

2. See Sarah Lane Ritchie, *Divine Action and the Human Mind* (New York: CUP, 2019).

3. John M. G. Barclay and Simon J. Gathercole, *Divine and Human Agency in Paul and His Cultural Environment*, LNTS 335 (London: T&T Clark, 2006).

4. On the notion of a doctrine's "distribution," see John Webster, "On the Theology of Providence," in *God without Measure: Working Papers in Christian Theology*, vol. 1, *God and the Works of God* (New York: Bloomsbury T&T Clark, 2016), 128–29.

its accountability to Scripture, simultaneously releasing divine action from its constraints and allowing for the range of actions presented in Scripture (in this case, the book of Hebrews) to be taken seriously and on their own terms.

No one has done more to advocate for this approach to divine action than William J. Abraham (1943–2021), whose four-volume work *Divine Agency and Divine Action* has paved the way for a recalibrated understanding of divine action that constitutes it as intrinsic to the work of theology. For Abraham, "divine action is constitutive of Christianity,"[5] to the extent that if divine action is compromised, Christian theology would be too. Therefore, Christian theology is dependent upon a sufficiently flexible concept of divine action. These are claims that reorient the basic contours of theological work, and my intent for this chapter is to exposit and defend them.[6] I shall do so first by surveying Abraham's reasons for identifying divine action as that which makes theology distinctive as an intellectual enterprise. While I take his project to be substantially correct, more needs to be said for it to comprise a full-fledged theological method. I supplement it, therefore, with additional considerations about how divine action ought to be *organised*, namely, into a coherent narrative about what God is doing to create, redeem, sustain, and perfect creatures, otherwise known as the divine *economy*.[7] That economy, finally, is disclosed in Scripture, that "true *story of the whole world*."[8] Jointly, I shall claim that divine action constitutes a robust theological method by commending ontological commitment to the Christian story understood as an economy and disclosed in Scripture, a story whose truth or falsehood depends upon whether God has actually acted in the ways it claims.

The method I am proposing has the advantage of clarifying what makes theological interpretations of Scripture in fact *theological*. If divine action is constitutive of theological method such that it is necessary for any maximally theological enterprise to succeed, then approaches to Scripture that attend to it can also be considered theological. Many potential avenues are thereby opened into the epistle to the Hebrews, all responding to the psalmist's invitation to

---

5. William J. Abraham, *Divine Agency and Divine Action*, vol. 1, *Exploring and Evaluating the Debate* (Oxford: OUP, 2017), 175.

6. An earlier and somewhat more expansive version of this argument can be found in Fellipe do Vale, "Divine Action Is Constitutive of Theology: William Abraham, John Webster, and Theological Theology," *Irish Theological Quarterly* 86, no. 4 (2021): 388–403.

7. I shall have more to say about the finer points of what constitutes an economy, but see, initially, Eph 1:9–10, 3:2, 3:9, and 1 Tim 1:4 for Paul's characteristic usage of the term.

8. Craig G. Bartholomew and Michael W. Goheen, *The Drama of Scripture: Finding Our Place in the Biblical Story*, 2nd. ed. (Grand Rapids: Baker Academic, 2014), 20. Unless otherwise noted, the emphasis is in the original throughout this chapter.

"Come and see what God has *done*: he is awesome in his *deeds* among mortals."[9] I shall conclude with some methodological desiderata for interpreting Scripture theologically.

UNSHACKLING DIVINE ACTION: ABRAHAM AND OPEN CONCEPTS

"The deep and abiding significance of divine action in the Christian tradition is made visible in this," claims Abraham, "when its central claims about divine action are attacked from within, the whole tradition is in deep trouble. Divine action cannot be confined to the mighty acts of God in history; but if even these are undermined the very future of Christianity is at stake."[10] For Abraham, Christianity, and the work of Christian theologians, stands or falls with divine action; if the latter is compromised in some way, the former likewise falls. This is because Christians confess belief in something God has actually *done*; the earliest creeds and rules of faith are full of action predicates, such as creating, suffering, dying, resurrecting, ascending, and judging. If such claims cannot be made – whether because of methodological presuppositions or metaphysical restrictions – then ordinary Christian belief, and the work that follows from it, cannot succeed.

In the first volume of his work on divine action, Abraham takes stock of the recent literature on this topic by philosophers, theologians, and scientists and maintains that it runs the risk of truncating divine action to the point where the characteristic actions comprising the Christian faith cannot be considered in theological work, with some writers even going as far as stating that God is not an agent who acts.[11] Unifying these various approaches is a "standard strategy," argues Abraham: first, adopt a concept of action with individually necessary and jointly sufficient conditions, usually derived from ideal instances of human action; second, apply such conditions to divine action; finally, observe which divine actions remain coherent or possible on the other side.[12] This standard strategy depends upon action being a "closed concept," which "is governed by a definitive set of necessary and sufficient criteria which correspond to a definitive

---

9. Ps 66:5 NRSV, emphasis added.

10. Abraham, *Divine Agency and Divine Action*, vol. 1, 32.

11. See, for instance, Brian Davies, "Letter from America," *New Blackfriars* 84 (2003): 371–84.

12. Cf. Abraham, *Divine Agency and Divine Action*, vol. 1, 84–88. Abraham's argument here parallels the one he makes against standard strategies in the epistemology of religion. See William J. Abraham, *Crossing the Threshold of Divine Revelation* (Grand Rapids: Eerdmans, 2006), 8.

set of necessary and sufficient properties."[13] Contemporary treatments of divine action have all operated according to this standard strategy, and their search for a closed concept of action has resulted in attritional accounts of the kinds of actions befitting God.

Abraham, out of a motivation to "let God set the agenda for what he does," directs two arguments against this standard strategy.[14] First, the necessary and sufficient conditions proffered by the authors he surveys often omit intuitively obvious instances of action.[15] Actions simply seem to be diverse, variable, context-dependent, and different in kind, so much so that any attempt to provide conditions free of specificity "simply looks bleak."[16] It is therefore "best to conclude that there are no necessary conditions for the proper use of the concept of action."[17] Second, on the supposition that necessary and sufficient conditions could be found for what counts as action, such conditions would leave us "at such a level of generality that we do not know what to say about the specific acts or activity of God that is more than minimally illuminating, if even that."[18] That is, such conditions would be *theological inutile* – what would we actually know about what God has done if all we knew was that God exercised an intention, or set a goal, or acted in ways informed by reasons? A concept of divine action, if it is going to be theologically serviceable, must do more than this. Abraham summarises the two arguments by saying, "On the one hand, much of the discussion assumed that we could have a closed concept of action. Over against this hasty presumption, we have seen that it is far from easy to secure a closed concept even of intentional action. Worse still, no concept of action will provide the resources to spell out what God really did."[19] Divine action has therefore been held captive by a quixotic pursuit for conditions that cannot be found, conditions that could not promise anything of substance even if they were discovered.

Abraham's constructive solution, alternatively, is to approach "action" as an open, rather than a closed, concept. Whereas a closed concept is one with individually necessary and jointly sufficient conditions, for an open concept

---

13. Abraham, *Divine Agency and Divine Action*, vol. 1, 95. Abraham locates the classic iteration of this strategy in G. E. M. Anscombe's *Intention* (Oxford: OUP, 1957), for whom a necessary condition for an action is the exercise of an intention.

14. Abraham, *Divine Agency and Divine Action*, vol. 1, 209.

15. For the omissions, see Abraham, *Divine Agency and Divine Action*, vol. 1, 97. For instance, Charles Taylor maintains that actions must be goal directed (cf. his *The Explanation of Behavior* [New York: Humanities Press, 1964]). But such an account would preclude actions like sneezing and doodling, for reasons that are not apparent.

16. Abraham, *Divine Agency and Divine Action*, vol. 1, 96–97.

17. Abraham, *Divine Agency and Divine Action*, vol. 1, 102.

18. Abraham, *Divine Agency and Divine Action*, vol. 1, 103.

19. Abraham, *Divine Agency and Divine Action*, vol. 1, 209.

"there are no substantial or informative necessary conditions."[20] Drawing on his particularist epistemology,[21] Abraham maintains that it is sufficient to rely on intuitive and natural means of detecting actions in the world: "We generally know perfectly well how to use the concept of action and deploy it with ease in the host of ways that show up in ordinary discourse. We intuitively and naturally know the strata to which a particular usage may belong; and we can informally follow the rules governing its varied usage across a rich tract of predication."[22] We may not be able to indicate with a great amount of specificity *why* an action counts as an action, but this is not required to use the concept adequately, even for theological reflection. We cannot articulate the necessary and sufficient conditions for a variety of concepts we employ with constant regularity ("gender," "human," "matter"), yet this does not prevent us from employing them successfully. Perhaps, suggests Abraham, the entire search for necessary and sufficient conditions for contested concepts is wrongheaded at a fundamental level.[23] Divine action, contested as it is, should be the kind of concept philosophers and theologians should be content to use without having secure conditions in place.[24]

The flexibility Abraham wishes to retain for conceptual analyses of action are all intended to smoothen the path for theological work. As he confesses, "My ultimate goal is unapologetically theological."[25] How does an adaptable and pliable concept of action lend itself to unhindered theological work? Here, I suggest, is Abraham's most impressive insight: *when we operate with a sufficiently broad concept of action, we can consider thoroughly those elements of divine activity that compose theology.* For Abraham, theology *just is* sustained reasoning about divine action in all of its particularity, for it "succeeds insofar as it captures who God is and what God has done."[26] The work of a theologian is to give a faithful answer, derived from Scripture and the rich canonical resources of the Christian tradition,[27] to the question "Tell me what God has

---

20. Abraham, *Divine Agency and Divine Action*, vol. 1, 96.

21. For which see his *Crossing the Threshold of Divine Revelation*, 30–35.

22. Abraham, *Divine Agency and Divine Action*, vol. 1, 102–3.

23. In fact, this conviction is representative of his broad approach to philosophical theology. For a representative articulation of this, see William J. Abraham, "Turning Philosophical Water into Theological Wine," *Journal of Analytic Theology* 1, no. 1 (May 2013): 1–16.

24. I have objected to and reconfigured this point in Abraham's argument in do Vale, "Divine Action Is Constitutive of Theology," 393–94.

25. Abraham, *Divine Agency and Divine Action*, vol. 1, 14.

26. Abraham, *Divine Agency and Divine Action*, vol. 1, 146.

27. For Abraham's (admittedly idiosyncratic) use of "canonical," see William J. Abraham, *Canon and Criterion in Christian Theology: From the Fathers to Feminism* (New York: OUP, 1999); William J. Abraham, Jason E. Vickers, and Natalie B. Van Kirk, eds., *Canonical Theism: A Proposal for Theology and the Church* (Grand Rapids: Eerdmans, 2008). His main claim is that "canon" cannot serve as an epistemic criterion but must instead denote the vast array of resources available to Christians for their spiritual nourishment.

actually done."[28] Theology's object differs from that of other disciplines to the degree that it takes divine action as its central focus. Or, in the words of John Webster, "The distinctiveness of Christian theology lies . . . in its invocation of God as agent in the intellectual practice of theology. In order to give account of its own operations, that is, Christian theology will talk of God and God's actions."[29] Only if action is sufficiently malleable can it serve such a distinguished role in theological work. Having an open concept of action allows theology to attend to its proper object, namely, "the extraordinary deposit of description and reflection on the activity of God."[30]

DIVINE ACTION AND THEOLOGICAL METHOD: FINDING THE ORDER

"Divine action involves serious, detailed speech about what God has done. This is simply another description for theology proper."[31] As we have seen, for William Abraham theological work stands or falls with divine action. The work of the theologian is not to confine divine action by searching for necessary and sufficient conditions, thereby precluding God from performing the actions Scripture proclaims him to have done. Rather, her task is to rely on fairly dependable epistemic capacities for detecting actions, even if she cannot provide such conditions. Rather than becoming derailed by the conceptual analysis of a contested concept, she should be far more concerned with the deep exploration of the actual deeds of God.

In his third volume, in which he treats the traditional loci of systematic theology, Abraham expatiates further on the method by which one arrives at theological conclusions from considerations about divine action. He considers theology to be "an exercise in university-level, post-baptismal Christian instruction" which has as its content "a deep, contemporary articulation of the Christian faith in terms that focus on divine agency and divine action."[32] Abraham proposes four stages along which a theologian proceeds to arrive at such a rich account of theology. First, she must treat divine action as an open concept, as argued in Abraham's first volume. Second, she must consider these actions as an

---

28. Abraham, *Divine Agency and Divine Action*, vol. 1, 199.
29. John Webster, "Theological Theology," in *Confessing God: Essays in Christian Dogmatics II* (London: Bloomsbury T&T Clark, 2005), 25.
30. Abraham, *Divine Agency and Divine Action*, vol. 1, 224.
31. Abraham, *Divine Agency and Divine Action*, vol. 1, 108.
32. William J. Abraham, *Divine Agency and Divine Action*, vol. 3, *Systematic Theology* (Oxford: OUP, 2019), 9.

ingredient to the gospel, which Abraham claims is identical to the inauguration of the kingdom of God in the life, death, and resurrection of Jesus of Nazareth.[33] Third, she must inhabit a Christian community whose central liturgical acts and instruction display "the core elements of Christian teaching that are spelled out succinctly in the creeds," elements adequate to provide "a definite vision of faith that makes available the identity of the God of the kingdom, together with other immediate matters essential for getting our intellectual bearings."[34] Finally, once she has discerned the distinct divine actions that constitute the gospel exhibited by the creeds within an appropriate community, she is in a suitable place to develop systematic loci from those very creeds, for theological loci are nothing other than those tools that "allow us to identify and articulate a network of divine actions neatly summarised in terms of creation, freedom, fall, redemption, and consummation."[35] These four stages ostensibly take the theologian from a sufficiently flexible understanding of divine action to full-fledged theological loci, and for Abraham they adequately display the method befitting a theologian concerned to "tell us what God has actually done."

For the most part, I consider Abraham to be correct. Commitment to the gospel, the creeds, and the loci indicate that there is some order and coherence to the actions Christians confess God to have performed. My contention, however, is not that Abraham's account is incorrect but that it is *incomplete*, because in both the theological loci and in theological interpretations of Scripture we are not dealing *exclusively* with divine actions. An obvious case of a theological locus that *is* a divine action would be the doctrine of creation – it is a sustained investigation into what God has done. But other loci are not as straightforward; the doctrine of sin, for instance, *cannot* be an investigation into what God does, for God cannot sin. It is, rather, an investigation into creaturely action within an economy that has been established by God. Or, again, the doctrine of the Trinity is not obviously about divine action; traditionally, there has been a distinction been God *ad intra* and the operations God exercises *ad extra*, and while both are crucial for this doctrine, only the latter is about God's operations or acts. Additionally, while Abraham's efforts to allow the gospel and the creeds to structure theological work are correct, such a focus can narrow the aperture of divine action too strictly if not rightly qualified. Famously, the doctrine of the atonement is not a creedally attested doctrine, yet it is certainly a theologically relevant divine action. Such counterexamples indicate that not enough has been

---

33. Abraham, *Divine Agency and Divine Action*, vol. 3, 26.

34. Abraham, *Divine Agency and Divine Action*, vol. 3, 30.

35. Abraham, *Divine Agency and Divine Action*, vol. 3, 23.

said to establish Abraham's stronger conclusion, namely, that divine action constitutes theology.

The right qualification needed to arrive at that conclusion, I argue, is a more precise articulation of divine action *organised into a recognizable or meaningful form*. Theology is indeed meant to capture what God has done, but with an appropriate attention to the order and structure in which those actions have been performed and the narrative they compose as a result. Put succinctly, theology's focus ought to be God's activity understood as an *economy*: a coherent narrative with sources, means, and ends.[36] Only then, I will conclude, can divine action act as a foundation for a theological method serviceable for systematic theology and theological interpretation.

To begin to see why a narrative construal is necessary, consider a recent argument made by Sameer Yadav on what it means to engage in Christian doctrine. Yadav begins with a distinction between an enquiry being *minimally* theological and it being *maximally* theological. To be minimally theological, an enquiry must meet conditions for what it means to do theology *at all*, independent of its quality; these are "norms that tell us what counts as engaging in the dogmatic task *simpliciter* – norms that someone has to satisfy in order to count as engaging the task of dogmatics at all, whether well or badly."[37] To be maximally theological, however, further conditions are provided for carrying on the task with excellence or superlatively; these are "norms that tell us what counts as engaging in the dogmatic task *properly*, in doing it well rather than badly."[38] The conditions for being minimally theological differentiate theology from other disciplines like literature or history, but not all minimally theological enterprises will be maximally theological, or even maximally theological in the same way. All maximally theological work, conversely, must be minimally theological.

Yadav proposes that what makes something minimally theological is that

---

36. Abraham was himself always of two minds about making the transition to narrative. Thus, he recognises that the "emphasis on divine agency and divine action is often expressed by saying that Christianity operates as a story that runs from creation to final consummation in the life to come. I do not reject this theme but it too readily becomes a kind of mantra that masks more than it reveals. Thus, it evades, for example, radical questions about the truth of the story and how it is to be defended intellectually" (Abraham, *Divine Agency and Divine Action*, vol. 3, 2). In his most recent fourth volume, the ambivalence toward an economy-style construal of divine action is retained, even if the door is still left open. See William J. Abraham, *Divine Agency and Divine Action*, vol. 4, *A Theological and Philosophical Agenda* (Oxford: OUP, 2021), 60 n. 11.

37. Sameer Yadav, "Christian Doctrine as Ontological Commitment to a Narrative," in *The Task of Dogmatics: Explorations in Theological Method*, ed. Oliver D. Crisp and Fred Sanders (Grand Rapids: Zondervan, 2017), 74.

38. Sameer Yadav, "Christian Doctrine as Ontological Commitment to a Narrative," 74.

it is "engaged in the task of making explicit some sense in which Christians are ontologically committed to a narrative of creation and redemption. To formulate Christian doctrine, I claim, is at a minimum, to formulate and commend ontological commitment to a narrative."[39] Ontological commitment is here understood as some account that there is "something (some things) that makes that [narrative] true."[40] Yadav intends this to be a wide tent able to house a variety of theologians with divergent commitments. More classically orientated theologians will claim that the narrative is true if the events of the narrative did in fact happen; others who identify as constructive or revisionist theologians may opt to articulate the truth of the narrative in terms of an individual's affective states or existential decisions.[41] While the objects of their ontological commitment may differ, both types of theologians are doing *theology*, at least in a minimal sense.

In order to be maximally theological, further details must be specified about the two conditions for doing minimal theology, sharpening each in order to define what it means to display theological virtue. In other words, what is the nature of the narrative beyond mere assertions of creation and redemption? What exactly makes it true? We must be attentive to the economy of divine action here. As Thomas Tracy indicates, "the story we tell about God as an agent of intentional actions not only introduces God as a subject of reference but also provides individuating relations that connect God to the events and individuals that populate our world. The theistic story seeks to broaden and complete our field of reference by describing the ultimate context in which we live our lives."[42] It is not precise enough to focus only on divine actions, claims Tracy, because what we need is a sensitivity to the ways those actions relate to one another so a coherent narrative reflective of the story of Christianity is constituted.[43] God is acting to create, redeem, sustain, and perfect all creatures, and these acts create a coherent narrative ecosystem for theological reflection.

---

39. Sameer Yadav, "Christian Doctrine as Ontological Commitment to a Narrative," 75–76.

40. Sameer Yadav, "Christian Doctrine as Ontological Commitment to a Narrative," 76. Yadav defends a view where the truthmaker of a claim is its ontological commitment first set forward by Bradley Rettler, "The General Truthmaker View of Ontological Commitment," *Philosophical Studies* 173 (2016): 1405–25. Notice that such a move avoids Abraham's worry that transitioning to narrative obscures questions about the truth of the narrative. Here some account of the truth of the narrative is integral to the method.

41. For one reading that sees Friedrich Schleiermacher as one such theologian, see Andrew Dole, "Schleiermacher's Theological Anti-Realism," in *Analytic Theology: New Essays in the Philosophy of Theology*, ed. Oliver D. Crisp and Michael C. Rea (New York: OUP, 2009), 136–54.

42. Thomas F. Tracy, *God, Action, and Embodiment* (Grand Rapids: Eerdmans, 1984), 79.

43. For his specific proposal on how to do that, see Thomas F. Tracy, "Narrative Theology and the Acts of God," in *Divine Action: Studies Inspired by the Philosophical Theology of Austin Farrer*, ed. Brian Hebblethwaite and Edward Henderson (Edinburgh: T&T Clark, 1990), 173–96.

A theologically apposite designation for that narrative labels it as an *economy*. Originally meant as a term for how a household ought to be arranged, this word was used by St. Paul to describe the arrangement of all human history, the "plan [*oikonomian*, or 'economy'] for the fullness of time" (Eph 1:10). Elaborating on this insight, John Webster understood the divine economy to be central to his account of maximally theological work, and he summarised it as the "historical form of God's presence to and *action upon* creatures."[44] He goes on to elaborate the economy in greater detail:

> The history of holy love, the *economy* of God's works, is *divine* history (and therefore really is holy, really loving, really the creature's rock of defence) because it is willed by God the Father, rooted in his eternal act of self-consecration. Moreover, it is a history of comprehensive scope, *gathering up all of God's acts toward the creature*. Yet at the centre of this all-embracing series of divine acts lies a particular history, the history of Israel, and – as the centre of the centre, so to speak – the history of Jesus, the Son of God in whom God's holy love overcomes its opposite and in whom, therefore, holiness is perfectly triumphant.[45]

For Webster, the divine economy is divine history, the sum total of all of God's actions in time coalesced and arranged into a narrative of redemption. The economy *is* what God has actually done. It is the broad story of Christian confession, beginning with God's act of creation and ending with God's act of consummation.

In hand, therefore, we have a more specific account of the narrative to which Christians are committed, namely, an arrangement of divine action whose distinct components come together to weave a history in which creatures are created, redeemed, sustained, and perfected. What, however, is the nature of the ontological commitment on this account? What, in other words, makes this narrative *true*? At the risk of oversimplification, it can be nothing other than whether or not these divine actions have in fact been performed. Abraham asserts this with remarkable candor, and his words are an extension of his commitment to the fact that defeaters to divine action entail defeaters to Christian theology and the Christian faith: "If not just this or that special action of God is in trouble, but the very idea of divine action itself turns out to be unworkable, then the disease is fatal."[46] If the story of Christianity is a story composed of

---

44. John Webster, "Biblical Reasoning," in *The Domain of the Word: Scripture and Theological Reason* (London: Bloomsbury, 2012), 117. Emphasis added.
45. John Webster, "The Holiness and Love of God," in *Confessing God: Essays in Christian Dogmatics II* (London: Bloomsbury, 2005), 125. Emphasis added.
46. Abraham, *Divine Agency and Divine Action*, vol. 1, 52.

divine actions, then those very divine actions must serve as the truthmakers for the narrative. If God cannot and did not act in the way described by the economy, to put it bluntly, the story is compromised.

A summary is in order. Recall that we are in search of a method enabling us to state that divine action is constitutive of theology. Abraham's model got us quite far, but it did not go far enough. The open character of divine action for which he advocates is indeed necessary to keep the theologian from precluding herself from the full range of divine actions in Scripture, liberating her to investigate those actions deeply and without qualification. However, the lack of structure and relationship amongst those actions prevent it from being a complete theological method. With recourse to Yadav's distinction between conditions necessary for doing theology as such (minimal) and doing theology well (maximal), I have argued that (1) the Christian narrative to which theological work must be accountable is an economy of divine actions jointly arranged into a history of creation, redemption, sustenance, and perfection; and (2) what makes that narrative true is whether God has in fact performed these actions. In the space that remains, I shall conclude with some suggestions about how theological work can proceed along those lines, making special reference to theological interpretation and the ways it can guide an enquiry into Scripture, as will be exemplified with the book of Hebrews throughout this volume.

DIVINE ACTION AND THEOLOGICAL EXEGESIS

The theological interpretation of Scripture has received a remarkable amount of renewed interest, both critical and affirming, over the last thirty years or so. Though itself a contested concept, it typically names a method of exegesis that employs theologically informed skills for interpretation that yield theologically substantive conclusions.[47] If the preceding argument is successful, then what makes the theological interpretation of Scripture *theological* is the degree to which it is *attentive to* and *evaluable under* the divine economy, particularly as it assumes that the acts predicated of God in Scripture have actually been performed.[48] Interpreting Scripture ought to be the kind of practice that sheds

---

47. Though the literature is vast, one account of theological interpretation to which I find myself attracted is found in Grant Macaskill, "Identifications, Articulations, and Proportions in Practical Theological Interpretation," *JTI* 14, no. 1 (2020): 3–15.

48. Of course, all of the appropriate caveats relevant to good exegetical practice will need to be in place here, such as sensitivity to genre, grammatical detail, and the like. The claim being made is intended to be precise: to the extent that Scripture asserts that God performed a certain action (something determined by exegetical practice), then God has in fact performed such an action.

light on the economy by enriching our understandings of how God has acted. Abraham's question applies just as forcefully here with regard to Scripture's attestation: "Tell me what God has done."

I suggest that there are at least two ways in which the exegete can answer such a question well. First, she will display "canonical sensitivity."[49] Exegetical approaches that neglect the broader canonical context in which any particular passages are situated (or worse, sever those passages from the canon in the interest of historical particularity) are not demonstrating a commitment to the economy, for the economy is disclosed in the canon.[50] So theological interpretation has the additional duty of *situating* the text under study within that broader narrative, taking the canon as a determinative context. What role does the text being studied have within the broader narrative? To which divine actions does it point, and how do these actions constitute important fibers within the broader tapestry of the biblical story? How does the text testify to particular characters or settings within that story and their particular indexing within the economy?

This brings me to the second recommendation for theological interpretation of Scripture, namely, that divine action calls us to read *doctrinally*. Doctrines arise *from* the economy as distillations of its various moments and their conceptual connections; or, as Stephen Holmes has articulated it, doctrines are "an underlying set of conceptions and distinctions that allows the whole of Scripture to be taken seriously without resort to hermeneutical gymnastics."[51] Serene Jones similarly describes doctrines as providing "the basic outline of theological drama within which the Christian life unfolds ... doctrines construct an imagistic and conceptual terrain within which people of faith locate and interpret their lives and the world around them."[52] Doctrines are attempts to provide organised models of the main contours of the divine economy, and this enables them to possess an organic connection to divine action. They do not, therefore, need to have a one-for-one correspondence with *particular* divine actions (just as I

---

49. A term I borrow from Kevin J. Vanhoozer, "A Drama-of-Redemption Model," in *Four Views on Moving beyond the Bible to Theology*, ed. Gary T. Meadors (Grand Rapids: Zondervan, 2009), 151–99.

50. Webster is clear that Holy Scripture is both an element within the divine economy *and* God's chosen means to disclose that economy to creatures. Thus, Holy Scripture is both "that creaturely instrument inspired and appointed by God to serve God's self-presentation" *and* that which announces "the reality of the gospel" (John Webster, *Holiness* [Grand Rapids: Eerdmans, 2003], 17–18, 20). Ultimately that is because of his account of revelation, which is the same as Abraham's: "Revelation ... is a way of talking about those *acts* in which God makes himself present" (John Webster, *Holy Scripture: A Dogmatic Sketch* [Cambridge: CUP, 2003], 13).

51. Stephen R. Holmes, "Scripture in Liturgy and Theology, " in *Theologians on Scripture*, ed. Angus Paddison (New York: Bloomsbury T&T Clark, 2018), 117.

52. Serene Jones, *Feminist Theory and Christian Theology: Cartographies of Grace*, Guides to Theological Inquiry (Minneapolis: Fortress Press, 2000), 16–17.

alleged against Abraham's approach), but they do arise from that economy whose existence depends on divine action. Doctrines are the basic tools of theological work, and so theological interpretation must attend to them. Wesley Hill, who has recently argued for just this approach, maintains that "approaching the task of theological interpretation armed with a particular doctrinal framework is not – or should not be – to find oneself shoehorning the Bible into an alien conceptual apparatus but is rather to find oneself searching out (1) how that framework may have arisen from exegesis itself and (2) how it may best be understood as an effort to *enable* ongoing exegesis in turn."[53] Doctrines therefore have a fitting compatibility with theological interpretation, and I am suggesting that this is because of divine action. We can therefore read the text with robust christological categories in mind,[54] or in an attempt to identify speakers corresponding to persons of the Trinity.[55] Doctrines arise from the economy whose existence depends on divine action, the same divine action that has revealed the economy in the canon of Scripture. They therefore *empower* exegesis, not hinder it.

Of course, this is to gesture and assert rather than to demonstrate, but I shall leave the demonstrations to the concrete engagements with the book of Hebrews and the doctrine of Christ's ongoing priesthood found in this volume. What I hope has been shown is that divine action is integral to what makes theology and its interpretative methods unique. With a sufficiently open approach to what God has done, as Abraham suggests, we are enabled to turn to the text rich with expectation. What God has done is indeed awesome, as the psalmist attests, and this awe lies precisely in the integrated economy that discloses our creation and salvation, the proper object of theological investigation.

SELECT BIBLIOGRAPHY

Abraham, William J. *Canon and Criterion in Christian Theology: From the Fathers to Feminism.* New York: OUP, 1999.

———. *Crossing the Threshold of Divine Revelation.* Grand Rapids: Eerdmans, 2006.

———. *Divine Agency and Divine Action.* Vol. 1, *Exploring and Evaluating the Debate.* Oxford: OUP, 2017.

---

53. Wesley Hill, "In Defense of 'Doctrinal Exegesis': A Proposal, with Reference to Trinitarian Theology and the Fourth Gospel," *JTI* 14, no. 1 (2020): 22.

54. An example of which is "partitive exegesis." For a discussion, see John Behr, *The Nicene Faith* (Crestwood, NY: St. Vladimir's Seminary Press, 2004), 349.

55. Or, as it is better known, prosopological exegesis. For an application of such a strategy to the book of Hebrews, see Madison N. Pierce, *Divine Discourse in the Epistle to the Hebrews: The Recontextualization of Spoken Quotations of Scripture* (New York: CUP, 2020).

———. *Divine Agency and Divine Action.* Vol. 3, *Systematic Theology.* Oxford: OUP, 2019.

———. *Divine Agency and Divine Action.* Vol. 4, *A Theological and Philosophical Agenda.* Oxford: OUP, 2021.

———. "Turning Philosophical Water into Theological Wine." *Journal of Analytic Theology* 1, no. 1 (May 2013): 1–16.

Abraham, William J., Jason E. Vickers, and Natalie B. Van Kirk, eds. *Canonical Theism: A Proposal for Theology and the Church.* Grand Rapids: Eerdmans, 2008.

Barclay, John M. G., and Simon J. Gathercole. *Divine and Human Agency in Paul and His Cultural Environment.* LNTS 335. London: T&T Clark, 2006.

Bartholomew, Craig G., and Michael W. Goheen. *The Drama of Scripture: Finding Our Place in the Biblical Story.* 2nd ed. Grand Rapids: Baker Academic, 2014.

Behr, John. *The Nicene Faith.* Crestwood, NY: St. Vladimir's Seminary Press, 2004.

Dole, Andrew. "Schleiermacher's Theological Anti-Realism." In *Analytic Theology: New Essays in the Philosophy of Theology*, edited by Oliver D. Crisp and Michael C. Rea, 136–54. New York: OUP, 2009.

Hill, Wesley. "In Defense of 'Doctrinal Exegesis': A Proposal, with Reference to Trinitarian Theology and the Fourth Gospel." *JTI* 14, no. 1 (2020): 20–35.

Holmes, Stephen R. "Scripture in Liturgy and Theology." In *Theologians on Scripture*, edited by Angus Paddison, 105–118. New York: Bloomsbury T&T Clark, 2018.

Jones, Serene. *Feminist Theory and Christian Theology: Cartographies of Grace.* Guides to Theological Inquiry. Minneapolis: Fortress Press, 2000.

Macaskill, Grant. "Identifications, Articulations, and Proportions in Practical Theological Interpretation." *JTI* 14, no. 1 (2020): 3–15.

Pierce, Madison N. *Divine Discourse in the Epistle to the Hebrews: The Recontextualization of Spoken Quotations of Scripture.* SNTSMS 178. New York: CUP, 2020.

Rettler, Bradley. "The General Truthmaker View of Ontological Commitment." *Philosophical Studies* 173 (2016): 1405–25.

Tracy, Thomas F. *God, Action, and Embodiment.* Grand Rapids: Eerdmans, 1984.

———. "Narrative Theology and the Acts of God." In *Divine Action: Studies Inspired by the Philosophical Theology of Austin Farrer*, edited by Brian Hebblethwaite and Edward Henderson, 173–96. Edinburgh: T&T Clark, 1990.

do Vale, Fellipe. "Divine Action Is Constitutive of Theology: William Abraham, John Webster, and Theological Theology." *Irish Theological Quarterly* 86, no. 4 (2021): 388–403.

Vanhoozer, Kevin J. "A Drama-of-Redemption Model." In *Four Views on Moving beyond the Bible to Theology*, edited by Gary T. Meadors, 151–99. Grand Rapids: Zondervan, 2009.

Webster, John. "Biblical Reasoning." In *The Domain of the Word: Scripture and Theological Reason*, 115–32. London: Bloomsbury, 2012.

———. *Holiness*. Grand Rapids: Eerdmans, 2003.

———. "The Holiness and Love of God." In *Confessing God: Essays in Christian Dogmatics II*, 109–30. London: Bloomsbury T&T Clark, 2005.

———. *Holy Scripture: A Dogmatic Sketch*. Cambridge: CUP, 2003.

———. "On the Theology of Providence." In *God without Measure: Working Papers in Christian Theology*. Vol. 1, *God and the Works of God*, 127–42. New York: Bloomsbury T&T Clark, 2016.

———. "Theological Theology." In *Confessing God: Essays in Christian Dogmatics II*, 11–32. London: Bloomsbury T&T Clark, 2005.

Yadav, Sameer. "Christian Doctrine as Ontological Commitment to a Narrative." In *The Task of Dogmatics: Explorations in Theological Method*, edited by Oliver D. Crisp and Fred Sanders, 70–86. Grand Rapids: Zondervan, 2017.

CHAPTER 2

Hebrews and Historical Theology:
The Contours

Steven E. Harris

INTRODUCTION

Pivotal moments in the history of theology tend to be associated in the popular imagination with Romans, not Hebrews. When Augustine heard the voice in the garden saying, *"Tolle, lege,"* he turned to Romans.[1] In reading Romans, Luther (re-)discovered the doctrine of justification by faith.[2] And when Barth dropped a bombshell on the playground of the theologians, that bombshell was his volume on the *Römerbrief.*[3] Hebrews does not hold quite so visible a place in the history of theology, yet it is arguably of equal importance. To take a prominent example, the christological controversies of the fourth century onward circled around various passages from this letter.[4]

---

1. The event is narrated in Augustine, *Confessions* 8.12.29, trans. Henry Chadwick (Oxford: OUP, 1991), 152–53.

2. At least, this is the story Luther tells at the end of his life: see "Preface to the Complete Edition of Luther's Latin Works" (1545) in *Luther's Works*, eds. Jaroslav Pelikan and Helmut I. Lehman, 55 vols. (St. Louis: Concordia Publishing, 1955–86), 34:336–37. Scholars are now generally agreed he came to his understanding of justification by faith not in his lectures on Romans (1516), but already in those on the Psalms (1513–15). See, for example, Wilhelm Pauck, "Introduction," in Martin Luther, *Lectures on Romans*, ed. Wilhelm Pauck (Louisville, KY: Westminster John Knox Press, 2006 [1961]), xxxvi–xxxviii.

3. The famous comment comes from Karl Adam, "Die Theologie der Krisis," *Hochland* XXIII (1926): 271–86; quoted in Colin Gunton, *Revelation and Reason: Prolegomena to Theology*, ed. P. H. Brazier (London: T&T Clark, 2008), 164 n. 7.

4. Rowan A. Greer, *The Captain of Our Salvation: A Study in the Patristic Exegesis of Hebrews* (Tübingen: J. C. B. Mohr [Paul Siebeck], 1973).

18

This chapter examines how the letter to the Hebrews has contributed to the history of theology, and conceptions of divine action in Christian theology, by focusing mainly on five figures.[5] Each was a model interpreter of Hebrews in his own distinctive way and a significant theologian in his own time. The first is John Chrysostom (*c.* 347–407), the "golden-mouthed" preacher of Constantinople in the fourth and fifth centuries amid the emerging christological debates. The second, Thomas Aquinas (*c.* 1225–1274), was one of the most gifted exegetes at the height of the Middle Ages. The third figure is John Calvin (1509–1564), the leader of the Genevan reformation and a prodigious biblical commentator. The fourth is John Owen (1616–1683), a nonconformist English theologian from the period of Protestant orthodoxy who contested Socinian theologies. The fifth and final figure is John Wesley (1703–1791), a tireless preacher and one of the fathers of evangelicalism.

While all these figures approached Hebrews in ways appropriate to their historical moment, they also each found in the letter essential teaching about Christ as humanity's high priest in this period of the divine economy. Their discoveries overlap with one another and, indeed, occasionally conflict with one another. Instead of attempting to give an overview of the whole of these figures' interaction with Hebrews, this chapter focuses mainly on their exegetical works – whether a series of homilies, a biblical commentary, or notes on the text. It first details their distinctive method before concentrating on their "exegetical theology" – the theology which emerges from their interaction with the biblical text.[6]

---

5. Excerpts from a broad collection of historical commentators can be found in Erik M. Heen and Philip D. W. Krey, eds., *Hebrews*, Ancient Christian Commentary on Scripture: New Testament X (Downers Grove: IVP Press, 2005) and Ronald K. Rittgers, ed., *Hebrews, James*, Reformation Commentary on Scripture: New Testament XIII (Downers Grove: IVP Academic, 2017). Philip Edgcumbe Hughes, *A Commentary on the Epistle to the Hebrews* (Grand Rapids: Eerdmans, 1977) is particularly attentive to the history of interpretation. A thorough bibliography of historical commentary is found in Ceslas Spicq, *L'Épître aux Hébreux*, 2 vols. (Paris: J. Gabalda, 1952), 1:379–407.

For broad scholarly treatments of Hebrews in the history of biblical interpretation, see Jon C. Laansma and Daniel J. Treier, eds., *Christology, Hermeneutics and Hebrews: Profiles from the History of Interpretation* (London/New York: T&T Clark, 2012); for the Greek tradition, Greer, *The Captain of Our Salvation*; for the Latin tradition, Eduard Riggenbach, *Die ältesten lateinischen Kommentare zum Hebräerbrief: Ein Beitrag zur Geschichte der Exegese und zur Literaturgeschichte des Mittelalters* (Leipzig: Deichert, 1907); and Matthew Fox, "Alcuin's *Expositio in epistolam ad Hebraeos*," *Journal of Medieval Latin* 18 (2008): 335–36, for a brief overview of the Carolingian period. Bruce Demarest, *A History of Interpretation of Hebrews 7,1–10 from the Reformation to the Present* (Tübingen: J. C. B. Mohr [Paul Siebeck], 1973) is, despite the limited passage under discussion, quite valuable for the past five centuries as a whole. Kenneth Hagen, *Hebrews Commenting from Erasmus to Bèze 1516–1598* (Tübingen: J. C. B. Mohr [Paul Siebeck], 1981) is of interest only to specialists, focusing largely on the *argumenta* (introductions) to the commentaries.

6. I thus use the term in the same way as Brian Brock, *Singing the Ethos of God: On the Place of Christian Ethics in Scripture* (Grand Rapids; Cambridge: Eerdmans, 2007), ch. 5; cf. John Webster, "Biblical Reasoning," in *The Domain of the Word: Scripture and Theological Reason* (London: T&T Clark, 2012), 130–31.

In looking at these figures, we will attend particularly to themes that appear in this volume: God's speech in the OT and the NT, including the letter to the Hebrews itself; divine action in and through Christ in creation and redemption; Christ's existence and work as the great High Priest of his people; and, especially, Christ's ongoing priesthood and its relation to the church's present ministry. I do not cover all of these for each author, but I do touch on the most prominent themes. A picture will emerge across these five figures of significant and suggestive *topoi* in a Christology of high priestly divine action from exegetical engagement with the letter to the Hebrews.

GREEK COMMENTARY IN THE CHRISTOLOGICAL DEBATES: JOHN CHRYSOSTOM

The church's understanding of the mystery of God becoming flesh in Christ grew gradually through the patristic period. The early- to mid-fifth century, in particular, saw debates over the proper way of articulating the relationship of Christ's divinity to his humanity. Following the Arian controversy, in which the Son was acknowledged as fully God in every way, lesser in no respect, the question of how one who could not change, suffer, or die could "become flesh" (John 1:14) in Jesus took on new urgency.[7]

The interpretation of Hebrews took a central place in these debates. Hebrews speaks of Christ both as God's "Son" (1:2), "the same yesterday and today and forever" (13:8), and as the one who became "like [his brothers], fully human in every way" (2:17) and "Son though he was, he learned obedience from what he suffered" (5:8). Just how to interpret the letter to the Hebrews, then, played a decisive role in the development of Christology and, consequently, theologies of divine and human action. For instance, is it right to say that God can "suffer" or "learn"? Do some passages of Scripture refer to Christ's divinity only, or humanity only?[8]

Amid the debates' early stage, John Chrysostom (*c.* 347–407) was a moderate figure. His hermeneutical commitments were similar to others associated with the influential city of Antioch, but he was never condemned by later

---

7. Lewis Ayres notes the artificiality of sharply distinguishing between "earlier" Trinitarian debates between the councils of Nicaea (325) and Constantinople (381) and "later" christological ones around Ephesus (431) and Chalcedon (451), emphasising that christological questions emerged in the context of debates about the Trinity, and so, the nature of divinity. See Ayres, "Articulating Identity," in *The Cambridge History of Early Christian Literature*, ed. Frances Young, Lewis Ayres, and Andrew Louth (Cambridge: CUP, 2004), 447.

8. See, further, Greer, *The Captain of Our Salvation*.

councils as others, such as Theodore of Mopsuestia (352–428) and Nestorius (c. 386–450), were.[9] Chrysostom was archbishop of Constantinople for most of the last ten years of his life. During his forced exile in 406, shortly before his death, he preached thirty-four homilies on the letter to the Hebrews, which he took to be by the apostle Paul.[10]

These homilies evidence Chrysostom's typical lengthy moral application, but also, importantly for our purposes, his view of Scripture's inspiration. All five figures we will examine receive Scripture as the Word the Spirit gives to his church, the set of divine actions in the economy by which human beings come to know the narrative coherence of God's works in creating, sustaining, redeeming, and perfecting. Hear Chrysostom's exclamation:

> O! the wisdom of the Apostle! or rather, not the wisdom of Paul, but the grace of the Spirit is the thing to wonder at. For surely he uttered not these things of his own mind, nor in that way did he find his wisdom. . . . But it was from the working of God.[11]

In speaking about divine action in Hebrews, then, the first thing to note is that the letter itself comes to us by the "working of God," by divine speech.[12]

Chrysostom's homilies also evidence his explicit exposition of the text in line with Nicene orthodoxy. In commenting on the "radiance of his glory" in Heb 1:3, Chrysostom glosses the phrase with the Nicene Creed's "Light from Light."[13] But how this orthodoxy is further worked out in relation to Christ's becoming human does not clearly line up on either side of the christological debates.[14] In relation to the person and work of Christ, Chrysostom suggests that Paul continually leads his readers from lower to higher matters, then back

---

9. There has been significant debate around to what extent theologians associated with Antioch constitute a common "school." As a good starting point, see Donald Fairbairn, "Patristic Exegesis and Theology: The Cart and the Horse," *WTJ* 69 (2007): 1–19. On our topic, see Ashish J. Naidu, "John Chrysostom's Homilies on Hebrews: An Antiochene Christological Commentary?," *Perichoresis* 6/1 (2008): 85–108.

10. For context, see Greer, *The Captain of Our Salvation*, 264–66, and Charles Kannengiesser, "'Clothed with Spiritual Fire': John Chrysostom's *Homilies on the Letter to the Hebrews*," in *Christology, Hermeneutics and Hebrews*, 74–77.

11. Chrysostom, *Homilies on the Epistle to the Hebrews* 1.3 (*NPNF* 1/14:367; PG 63:15–16). John Webster highlights this passage in a discussion of theological interpretation of Scripture that introduces his own reading of the prologue to Hebrews: "One Who Is Son: Theological Reflections on the Exordium to the Epistle to the Hebrews," in *The Epistle to the Hebrews and Christian Theology*, ed. Richard Bauckham, Daniel R. Driver, Trevor A. Hart, and Nathan MacDonald (Grand Rapids/Cambridge: Eerdmans, 2009), 69–70.

12. See Nick Brennan's essay in this volume on the Son's speech as divinely powerful: "Divine Power and the Priestly Abilities of the Son," 77.

13. Chrysostom, *Homilies* 2.2 (*NPNF* 1/14:371; PG 63:22).

14. See, further, Greer, *The Captain of Our Salvation*, 282–91.

to the lower. In the exordium (1:1–4), he starts with Christ as "heir," a "humble" thought, before mentioning the "higher step" of Christ's making of the worlds. Only then does he refer to "the brightness of His glory, and the express image of His person." Chrysostom accordingly states, "Truly he has led them to unapproachable light, to the very brightness itself. And before they are blinded see how he gently leads them down again," touching on the "lowly" incarnation and his purification for sins.[15] This movement, according to Chrysostom, is the apostle teaching about both the "economy" of the Son's condescension and Christ's "incorruptible nature" as the divine Word.[16] *This One* acts in creation, incarnation, and atonement.

In this movement, Chrysostom perceives Paul deftly cutting off every heretical suggestion. On Heb 1:3, "by whom also He made the worlds," Chrysostom boasts, "Where are those who say, 'There was when He was not?',"[17] referencing the infamous Arian dictum about the Son. In reading the epistle, the preacher also follows a pro-Nicene rule utilised by Augustine in a different way in *De trinitate* (written between 400 and 427): Chrysostom distinguishes between things said of Christ "according to the flesh" and those said according to his divinity.[18] In doing so, heresy regarding both natures is prevented. For example, when Hebrews says that Christ "obtained a more excellent name" than the angels (1:4), this was spoken "according to the flesh," since as "God the Word" he eternally possesses this name.[19] Such partitive exegesis carefully identifies the nature to which particular actions of the incarnate Christ relate. The exaltation of the (now human) Son is also significant given the impotence of humanity generally, and the Levitical priesthood in particular, in Hebrews.[20]

Chrysostom, finally, develops a theme that is prominent to this day in Orthodox theology, namely, that in the liturgy the church participates in the worship of heaven. Commenting on the "heavenly things" of Heb 8:5, he states:

> For although [these things] are done on earth, yet nevertheless they are worthy of the Heavens. For when our Lord Jesus Christ lies slain, when the Spirit is with us, when He who sitteth on the right hand of the Father is here, when sons are made by the Washing, when they are fellow-citizens of those in

15. Chrysostom, *Homilies* 1.3 (*NPNF* 1/14:367–68; PG 63:16).

16. Chrysostom, *Homilies* 1.3 (*NPNF* 1/14:368; PG 63:17).

17. Chrysostom, *Homilies* 1.3 (*NPNF* 1/14:367; PG 63:15).

18. Augustine, *On the Trinity* 1.3.14, trans. Edmund Hill, O.P. (New York: New City Press, 1991), 74–75.

19. Chrysostom, *Homilies* 1.3 (*NPNF* 1/14:368; PG 63:16–17).

20. See Nick Brennan's essay in this volume: "Divine Power and the Priestly Abilities of the Son," 75–83.

Heaven, when we have a country, and a city, and citizenship there, when we are strangers to things here, how can all these be other than "heavenly things"? But what! Are not our Hymns heavenly? Do not we also who are below utter in concert with them the same things which the divine choirs of bodiless powers sing above? . . . [F]or the Church is heavenly, and is nothing else than Heaven.[21]

By the Spirit's divine presence to act, and in the sacramental divine and human co-action by which children are adopted by the washing and the slain Lord is made present in bread and wine, the church in its liturgy is rendered participant in heaven. These themes will reemerge in different forms in Thomas Aquinas and John Calvin, both of whom had read and refer to Chrysostom.

CHRIST IN THE HIGH MEDIEVAL PERIOD: THOMAS AQUINAS

For Thomas Aquinas (*c.* 1225–1274), all of Scripture is a single, albeit highly differentiated Word because it has one primary author, namely, God. Aquinas utilises a scholastic technique of biblical exegesis called the *divisio textus*, a logical tool which views the whole canon of Scripture as one, complexly articulated statement.[22] To situate Hebrews: Thomas accepts the traditional ascription of Hebrews to Paul and thus classes it with his other letters about the power of grace.[23] Among Paul's fourteen letters, then, nine speak of grace working in the body of Christ (Rom–2 Thess), four of the power of grace in church leadership (1 Tim–Phlm), and one of the power of grace in Christ himself, the head of the body; this final letter is Hebrews.

This way of situating Hebrews in the canon singles it out as the crown of Paul's letters. The subject of Hebrews is the power of grace as we find it in

---

21. Chrysostom, *Homilies* 14.3 (*NPNF* 1/14:434; PG 63:111, 112).

22. On the *divisio textus*, see John F. Boyle, "The Theological Character of the Scholastic 'Division of the Text' with Particular Reference to the Commentaries of Saint Thomas Aquinas," in *With Reverence for the Word: Medieval Scriptural Exegesis in Judaism, Christianity and Islam*, ed. Jane Dammen McAuliffe, Barry D. Walfish, and Joseph W. Goering (Oxford: OUP, 2003), 276–83; idem, "Authorial Intention and the *Divisio textus*," in *Reading John with St. Thomas Aquinas: Theological Exegesis and Speculative Theology*, ed. Matthew Levering and Michael Dauphinais (Washington, D.C.: Catholic University of America Press, 2005), 3–8; and Timothy F. Bellamah, *The Biblical Interpretation of William of Alton* (Oxford: OUP, 2011), 15–20.

23. Though he is not unaware of challenges to its authenticity: Thomas Aquinas, *Super Epistolam B. Pauli ad Hebraeos lectura*, prooemium 5, in *Super Epistolas S. Pauli Lectura*, ed. Raphael Cai, 8th ed., 2 vols. (Turin/Rome: Marietti, 1953), 2:335–506. I have made use of the English translation of Fabian Larcher, O.P., alongside this Latin edition, available on corpusthomisticum.org.

Christ himself, the head of his body. Or, as Aquinas puts it in his *prooemium* to his commentary, Hebrews treats the "preeminence of Christ" (*excellentiam Christi*).[24] Another feature of the *divisio textus* will specify this "preeminence" more closely. Aquinas takes Ps 86:8 (Vulg.) as the theme of the letter: "There is none like you among the gods, O Lord, nor are there any works like yours." This verse from the Psalms displays the twofold preeminence of Christ: first, Christ is unique among the "gods" – angels, prophets, and priests – and, second, he is distinguished by his works, including his works of creation, illumination, and justification.[25] Because Hebrews deals so centrally and fully with Christ's person and work, which are foreshadowed under the old covenant, Aquinas claims that "almost all the mysteries of the Old Testament are contained in this epistle."[26]

Aquinas, first, demonstrates a complex view of divine speech, and its relation to Christ, in Heb 1:1–2. The one Word of God, he argues, was only conceived by God once, yet it was expressed three ways in the divine economy.[27] The first was "in the production of creatures, namely, when the conceived Word, existing as the likeness of the Father, is also the likeness according to which all creatures were made: 'God said: Be light made. And light was made' (Gen. 1:3)."[28] Thus, every creature that God speaks out is a different likeness of the divine speech. Second, God spoke in the minds of holy people by revelations "in many and various ways" (1:1). This includes different subjects (divine realities and future events); different figures (e.g., a stone, a lion); three kinds of prophetic vision (ocular, imaginary, and intellectual);[29] and either plain or obscure speech from God.[30] And, third, God spoke by assuming flesh in Jesus Christ. This third form of divine speech is, according to Aquinas, the reason for the NT's superiority to the Old: God "speaks more perfectly in the New, because in the Old he speaks in human minds, but in the New through the Son's Incarnation." In the Old, that is, God speaks by means of human emissaries; in the New, Christ's words are God speaking "in His very person."[31]

---

24. Aquinas, *Super Epistolam B. Pauli ad Hebraeos lectura*, prooemium 1.

25. Aquinas, *Super Epistolam B. Pauli ad Hebraeos lectura*, prooemium 2–3. Cf. Thomas G. Weinandy, "The Supremacy of Christ: Aquinas' *Commentary on Hebrews*," in *Aquinas on Scripture: An Introduction to His Biblical Commentaries*, ed. Thomas G. Weinandy, Daniel A. Keating, and John P. Yocum (London/New York: T&T Clark, 2005), 224.

26. Aquinas, *Super Epistolam B. Pauli ad Hebraeos lectura* 13.3.772: "In ista enim epistola fere omnia mysteria veteris testamenti continentur." Cf. Weinandy, "The Supremacy of Christ," 224 n.5, who cites this as "almost all the mysteries of the *New* Testament" (emphasis added), being waylaid by Larcher's faulty English translation at this point.

27. Aquinas, *Super Epistolam B. Pauli ad Hebraeos lectura* 1.1.15.

28. Aquinas, *Super Epistolam B. Pauli ad Hebraeos lectura* 1.1.15.

29. Cf. Aquinas, *Summa theologiae* 2a2ae.171–175 on prophecy, esp. 173.3 and 174.3.

30. Aquinas, *Super Epistolam B. Pauli ad Hebraeos lectura* 1.1.9.

31. Aquinas, *Super Epistolam B. Pauli ad Hebraeos lectura* 1.1.15.

This leads us to a brief discussion of the Christology of the commentary. For Aquinas, following John of Damascus (675/6–749), "the humanity of Christ is like an instrument of the divinity."[32] The divine Word is the active subject making use of the humanity, yet this is a true humanity such that the Word is the subject of its experiences. This can be seen particularly in relation to Thomas's discussion of Christ's suffering and intercessory prayer. In relation to suffering, Christ knew obedience by "simple knowledge" as God, yet he still "learned obedience from what he suffered" (Heb 5:8) – that is, in the way that human beings learn obedience by hard experience. This is how God, who cannot suffer, yet truly and mysteriously suffered. Thomas's Christology thus elucidates how God can act in ways that seem contrary to his nature, namely, suffering and dying.

In relation to prayer, the manner of Christ's prayer, "with loud cries and tears" (Heb 5:7), shows this true humanity. Christ was affected by natural human fears and inhibitions; he thus "shrank from death" as any would. "It was under these influences," Aquinas states, "that He prayed and thus showed Himself true man."[33] But our intercessor Christ also prays for us as the one who has experienced this fear and suffering. Christ's prayer, Thomas stresses, is perfect, since the one who prays effectively has two things: fervent love, expressed by the "loud cries" of Heb 5:7, and "internal groans." In this, Christ had preeminent piety. The same desire he has for our salvation – what Thomas calls "the desire of his most holy soul" – he expresses in his continuing intercessory prayer on our behalf.[34] Christ's present heavenly exercise of his high priesthood, thus, is characterised by the ongoing hypostatic union, in which all his work is divine-human action.

Like Chrysostom, Thomas connects themes of priesthood to the liturgical life of the church. Christ's priesthood, which is ongoing because he lives forever, is connected to the daily ritual offering of bread and wine by the Catholic priesthood. In the mass, Christ himself presides: "Christ alone is the true priest," Aquinas states; "others are His ministers."[35] This both relates and distinguishes the instrumentality of divine agency in the self-offering of the incarnation and the ritual offering of the mass. In the former, God offers himself as priest by the humanity of Christ; in the latter, this true priest offers himself through the separate but cooperating human agency of the church's priests. More succinctly, in the incarnation one divine-human person is the sole agent; in the mass, the

---

32. Aquinas, *Super Epistolam B. Pauli ad Hebraeos lectura* 8.1.382: "Humanitas enim Christi est sicut organum divinitatis." This is a citation of John of Damascus, *On the Orthodox Faith* 3.15.

33. Aquinas, *Super Epistolam B. Pauli ad Hebraeos lectura* 5.1.257.

34. Aquinas, *Super Epistolam B. Pauli ad Hebraeos lectura* 5.1.256. Though note that Gareth Cockerill denies that the Son's ongoing intercession is petition of the Father, rather than the distribution of mercy and grace to humanity: see in this volume, "The Present Priesthood of the Son of God," 223–24.

35. Aquinas, *Super Epistolam B. Pauli ad Hebraeos lectura* 7.4.368.

divine-human Christ acts by means of other human agents, yet Christ's action alone brings about the efficacy of the ritual act.

PRIESTHOOD IN THE REFORMATION: JOHN CALVIN

John Calvin (1509–1564) will take this same theme of Christ's sole true priesthood in quite a different direction in his Hebrews commentary.[36] Michael Allen calls Calvin "the theologian of this Epistle to the Hebrews," arguing that "his greatest achievements are rooted there."[37] The commentary is, indeed, the source of a great number of creative – though not innovative – theological insights.[38] Calvin, as a humanist, approaches Hebrews not with the *divisio textus*, but with the rhetorical tool of the *argumentum*. The "argument" lays out the rhetorical progression of the text, identifying the centre of Hebrews's message and its major themes. While Calvin rejects the traditional ascription of Pauline authorship to Hebrews, the *argumentum* shows that he forefronts several Pauline themes in his interpretation, including, especially, the "abrogation of ceremonies" and Christ as "the end of the law" (Rom 10:4).[39] Hebrews's canonical embeddedness thus allows Calvin to see Christ's action in the divine economy in a broader Pauline theological scope.

In commenting on the exordium, Calvin gives voice to two of his common

---

36. For background, see R. Michael Allen, "The Perfect Priest: Calvin on the Christ of Hebrews," in *Christology, Hermeneutics and Hebrews*, 120–34, and Gary Neal Hansen, "Calvin as Commentator on Hebrews and the Catholic Epistles," in Donald K. McKim, ed., *Calvin and the Bible* (Cambridge: CUP, 2006), 257–81.

37. Allen, "The Perfect Priest," 120, 134. Allen sees in Calvin's commentary three particular developments in his Christology: (i) a focus on the historical course of Christ's life and the historical progression of the covenants, drawn from Hebrews; (ii) a construal of Christ's full divinity as *autotheos*, God himself; and (iii) a construal of Christ's full humanity as one that came to gradual perfection through suffering, mirroring the gradual progression of revelation.

38. Allen wants to downplay the role of Romans in Calvin's theology, both architectonically in his *Institutes* and as a marker of his individual creativity (see "The Perfect Priest," 120–21, 125 n. 21). I judge this unnecessary to what Allen does successfully demonstrate, which is the central role the epistle to the Hebrews plays in Calvin's Christology in particular.

39. John Calvin, *Commentaries on the Epistle of Paul* [sic] *to the Hebrews* (Edinburgh: Calvin Translation Society, 1853), xxvi, hereafter CTS; *Commentarius in epistolam ad Hebraeos*, in vol. 55 of *Ioannis Calvini opera quae supersunt omnia*, ed. G. Baum, E. Cunitz, and E. Reuss, 59 vols. (=Corpus Reformatorum 29–87; Brunswick: Schwetschke, 1863–1900), 5, hereafter CO with volume number. There is a newer English translation in Calvin's New Testament Commentaries, ed. David W. Torrance and Thomas F. Torrance, 12 vols.: *Hebrews and 1&2 Peter*, trans. William B. Johnston, vol. 11 (Grand Rapids: Eerdmans, 1994). Anthony N. S. Lane calls the CTS translation "less than adequate in places" ("Guide to Recent Calvin Literature," *Vox Evangelica* 17 [1987]: 37); Richard A. Muller, by contrast, prefers them to the newer, which are "less than satisfactory" (*The Unaccommodated Calvin: Studies in the Foundation of a Theological Tradition* [New York: OUP, 2000], ix). I have used the CTS translation, comparing it against the Latin of the CO.

themes. First, that "God has spoken to us in the Son" (1:2) means we need to listen to Christ our teacher and be "satisfied with [his teaching] alone," not search for new revelations beyond it.[40] Hebrews starts here, Calvin argues, because we must first learn to view Christ as teacher before we can fruitfully "learn from his mouth, and in his school, what is the benefit of his priesthood, and what is its use and end."[41] Christ's work as a whole is communicative – is speech. Second, everything Hebrews says about Christ is about Christ "for us," *pro nobis*. Calvin is wary of speculations about divinity abstracted from the economy. Thus, where Hebrews quotes Ps 2:7, "You are my Son; today I have begotten you," he states, "Christ doubtless is the eternal Son of God, for he is wisdom, born before time; but this has no connection with this passage, in which respect is had to human beings, by whom Christ was acknowledged to be the Son of God after the Father had manifested him."[42]

This second theme comes to the fore in Calvin's treatment of Christ's priesthood. And he stresses this *everything* strongly. These are his comments on Heb 7:25, "he always lives to make intercession for them":

> What sort of pledge and how great is this of love towards us! Christ liveth *for us*, not for himself! That he was received into a blessed immortality to reign in heaven, this has taken place, as the Apostle declares, *for our sake*. Then the life, and the kingdom, and the glory of Christ are all destined *for our salvation* as to their object; nor has Christ *any thing*, which may not be applied *to our benefit*; for he has been given *to us* by the Father once for all on this condition, that *all* his should be *ours*. He at the same time teaches us by what Christ is doing, that he is performing his office as a priest; for it belongs to a priest to intercede for the people, that they may obtain favor with God. This is what Christ is ever doing, for it was for this purpose that he rose again from the dead.[43]

Everything that is Christ's, and that Christ himself is, is ours by faith. All his divine action is purposed for our benefit. This is clear from Christ's continuing intercession on our behalf, which is the very reason he rose from the dead.

As our living High Priest, Christ is also the one to whom the whole creation will become subject and in whom it will be renewed as the end of the divine

---

40. Calvin, *Commentarius in epistolam ad Hebraeos* 1:1–2 (CTS, 31; CO 55:9).

41. Calvin, *Commentarius in epistolam ad Hebraeos* 4:14 (CTS, 106; CO 55:53).

42. Calvin, *Commentarius in epistolam ad Hebraeos* 1:5 (CTS, 42; CO 55:15). Cf. *Commentarius in epistolam ad Hebraeos* 4:15: "he does not speak of what Christ is in himself, but shews what he is to us" (CTS, 108; CO 55:54: "quia non disputat qualis sit in se Christus, sed qualem se nobis ostendat").

43. Calvin, *Commentarius in epistolam ad Hebraeos* 7:25 (CTS, 175; CO 55:94), emphasis added. I remark here that in this chapter all emphasis is original unless otherwise noted.

economy. Commenting on the citation of 2 Sam 7:14 in Heb 1:5 ("I will be to him a father"), Calvin notes that this was originally spoken of Solomon's temporal kingship, but is a fitting type, "for the empire (*imperium*) of the whole world is destined for the Son mentioned there, and perpetuity is also ascribed to his empire."[44] Yet even now Christ is reigning and renewing all things. On the "world to come" of Heb 2:5, Calvin writes, "the world to come is not that which we hope for after the resurrection, but that which began at the beginning of Christ's kingdom; but it will no doubt have its full accomplishment in our final redemption."[45] The same creation that came into being through the Son, and over which he has been appointed heir (Heb 1:3), also finds its renewal from corruption and decay in him.[46]

Part of that renewal of Christ's kingdom is his ongoing work as minister to his people. This reemerges in Calvin's view of the relationship of Christ's heavenly ministry to the church's pastoral work. Commenting on the citation of Ps 22:22 in Heb 2:12, "I will declare Your name to my brothers," he writes, "the office which Christ assumes" is that of proclaiming the gospel, which Christ himself did in his earthly work and "is now done daily by the ministry of pastors." Thus, when we hear a sermon "we ought not so much to consider men as speaking to us, as Christ by his own mouth." But since the gospel always leads to gratitude, Calvin, commenting now on the second half of the Psalm quotation ("in the assembly I will sing your praises"), states that it "may lead us most fervently to praise God, when we hear that Christ leads our songs, and is the chief composer of our hymns."[47] Whereas Aquinas highlighted Christ's divine-human agency in the Eucharist, Calvin attends to his agency in sermon and song.

PROTESTANT ORTHODOXY AGAINST THE SOCINIANS: JOHN OWEN

The Puritan theologian and church leader John Owen (1616–1683) wrote a lengthy and diffuse commentary on Hebrews, originally in four volumes (1668–84).[48] In the commentary Owen is arguing extensively against theology deriving from Faustus Socinus (1539–1604), which was anti-Trinitarian, viewed Christ

---

44. Calvin, *Commentarius in epistolam ad Hebraeos* 1:5 (CTS, 42; CO 55:15–16).

45. Calvin, *Commentarius in epistolam ad Hebraeos* 2:5 (CTS, 58; CO 55:24–25).

46. As Brennan says, "[the Son] is no mere eschatological agent of God" ("Divine Power," 77).

47. Calvin, *Commentarius in epistolam ad Hebraeos* 2:12 (CTS, 66–67; CO 55:29).

48. For background, see Kelly M. Kapic, "Typology, the Messiah, and John Owen's Theological Reading of Hebrews," in *Christology, Hermeneutics and Hebrews*, 134–54.

as only an extraordinary human being, absorbed his priesthood into his kingship, and argued that his sacrifice was properly performed only in heaven rather than on the cross.[49] Several of Owen's preliminary exercitations involve Christ's high priesthood; they are primarily concerned with the origin of this priesthood in the eternal counsel of the Trinity, its prefiguration in the OT, and Christ's high priestly acts in his self-sacrifice and intercession.[50] Our brief exposition will focus on Christ's ongoing exercise of his priesthood and, therefore, turns to Owen's commentary proper.

It is worth lingering over Owen's "observations" on Heb 7:25, "Wherefore he is able also to save them to the uttermost that come unto God by him, seeing he ever liveth to make intercession for them" (KJV). With the perpetual exercise of Christ's priesthood, Owen contends, we come to the very heart of the gospel. His commendation of Hebrews's teaching on this theme is emphatic. Christ's ongoing possession and discharge of this office is, Owen writes, "the foundation of all the benefits which are received by Christ, – that is, of the spiritual and eternal salvation of the church"; it is "the first cause, the root and spring, of all spiritual blessings unto us"; it is "the fundamental article of faith evangelical" and "the first ground of all friendship between God and [human beings]."[51]

It is not just that the risen Christ holds this office in perpetuity, Owen argues; it is its enactment, the "discharge of this office for the church in his own person, throughout all generations," that "is the glory of it." In this regard Owen develops some remarkable and moving reflections on Christ's ongoing high priestly work, worth quoting at length. The very being of the church, according to Owen, depends on the exercise of Christ's high priesthood, and this is stated in three ways. Divine action is thus fundamental to ecclesiology.

First, the church's *"preservation* and *stability"* depend on Christ's high priesthood:

> There is neither a ceasing nor any the least intermission of that care and
> providence, of that interposition with God on its behalf, which are required
> thereunto. Our high priest is continually ready to appear and put in for us on
> all occasions. And his abiding for ever manifests the continuance of the same

---

49. There was a commentary on Hebrews written prior to Owen by the Socinian theologian Jonas Schlichting (1592–1661) with the aid of Jan Crell (1590–1631). See, further, Demarest, *A History of Interpretation of Hebrews 7,1–10 from the Reformation to the Present*, 20–24. See Cockerill's essay in this volume for engagement with the contemporary revival of this last Socinian theme in David Moffitt's *Atonement and the Logic of Resurrection in the Epistle to the Hebrews*.

50. John Owen, *The Works of John Owen, D.D*, ed. William H. Goold, 24 vols. (London/Edinburgh: Johnstone and Hunter, 1850–55), 19:1–259. The Hebrews commentary takes up volumes 18 through 24.

51. Owen, *Works*, 22:524.

care and love for us that he ever had. The same love wherewith, as our high priest, he laid down his life for us, doth still continue in him.

For Socinus, Christ becomes a priest only at the ascension and exercises it only for those still on earth. Owen, by contrast, sharply emphasises that Christ is a High Priest "forever," eternally constant in his active care for his own.

Second, the "*union* and *communion* of the church with itself in all successive generations" depend on Christ's high priesthood. In other words, the communion of the saints is not a self-subsisting reality but one mediated by the living Christ, our High Priest. This has implications for Owen's doctrine of the saints, or the church triumphant. He writes:

> For whereas he is their head and high priest, in whom they all centre as unto their union and communion, and hath all their graces and duties in his hand, to present them unto God, they have a relation unto each other, and a concernment in one another. We that are alive in this generation have communion with all those that died in the faith before us.... For all the prayers of the church from first to last are lodged in the hand of the same high priest, who abides for ever; and he returns the prayers of one generation unto another. We enjoy the fruits of the prayers, obedience, and blood of those that went before us; and if we are faithful in our generation, serving the will of God, those shall enjoy the fruits of ours who shall come after us.

Against the Socinians, Owen again contends that Christ's priesthood encompasses both those saints still battling through life and those already in his presence in heaven. This exercise of his priestly office firmly guarantees their unity in the body of Christ.

Third, the church's "*consolation*" also depends on Christ's high priesthood.

> Do we meet with troubles, trials, difficulties, temptations, and distresses? hath not the church done so in former ages? ... [B]ut all their preservation and success, their deliverance and eternal salvation, depended merely on the care and power of their merciful high priest. It was through his blood, "the blood of the Lamb," or the efficacy of his sacrifice, that they "overcame" their adversaries, Rev. xii. 11. By the same blood were "their robes washed, and made white," chap. vii. 14. From thence had they their righteousness in all their sufferings. And by him had the church its triumphant issue out of all its trials.[52]

---

52. Owen, *Works*, 22:520–21.

Owen is well cognizant that Christians only make their "triumphant issue" out of suffering by the ongoing, contemporary work of Jesus, his "care and power."

PREACHING CHRIST'S HIGH PRIESTHOOD: JOHN WESLEY

The fifth and final interpreter of Hebrews in our survey is John Wesley (1703–1791). Wesley preached from the letter to the Hebrews more than any other biblical book – an astounding statement, considering that for more than fifty years of his life, Wesley preached two or three times a day.[53] Yet rather than draw on his sermons, here I draw on Wesley's *Explanatory Notes Upon the New Testament* (1754). During a time of convalescence following a serious illness, Wesley drew up his *Notes* "chiefly for plain, unlettered Men, who understand only their Mother-Tongue, and yet reverence and love the Word of GOD, and have a Desire to save their Souls."[54]

This last phrase signals the evangelical character of the notes. Following in the train of the humanist emphasis on rhetorical simplicity treasured by the Protestant Reformers,[55] Wesley wants his preaching and writing to be readily understandable by the masses, and, therefore, as he himself puts it, "as short as possible" and "as plain as possible."[56] We will focus on Wesley's view of the "ages," their beginning and consummation, and the work of Christ and the Trinity

53. Joel B. Green, *Reading Scripture as Wesleyans* (Nashville: Abingdon, 2010), ch. 8.

54. John Wesley, *Explanatory Notes Upon the New Testament*, 2nd ed. (London, 1757), iii. Cf. John Wesley, "Preface to the Sermons," in *Wesley's Standard Sermons*, ed. Edward H. Sugden, 2 vols. (Nashville: Lamar & Barton, 1920), 1:30.

55. See esp. Erika Rummel, *The Humanist-Scholastic Debate in the Renaissance and the Reformation* (Boston: Harvard University Press, 1998) and Kirk Essary, *Erasmus and Calvin on the Foolishness of God: Reason and Emotion in the Christian Philosophy* (Toronto: University of Toronto Press, 2017).

56. Wesley, *Explanatory Notes Upon the New Testament*, iv. For the same reason, Wesley states that though he has drawn many of his notes – either verbatim or in abridged form – from others, he has not cited his borrowing in the text. Those he names are Johann Albrecht Bengel, *Gnomon Novi Testamenti*, 3rd ed., 2 vols. (Tübingen: Ludov. Frid. Fues., 1836 [1742]); John Heylyn, *Theological Lectures at Westminster-Abbey, With an interpretation of the Four Gospels* (London: J. and R. Tonson and S. Draper, 1749); John Guyse, *The Practical Expositor, Or, An Exposition of the New Testament*, 5th ed., 6 vols. (Edinburgh: Ross & Sons, 1797 [3 vols., 1739–52]); and Philip Doddridge, *The Family Expositor* (London: Frederick Westley and A. H. Davis, 1831 [6 vols., 1739–56]) (iv–v).

While this may seem like a reason for discounting the value of Wesley's *Explanatory Notes*, a study of it can show, first, how Wesley was a vehicle for the transmission of Lutheran pietism to England; and, second, where and how Wesley chose to use his sources. Similar justifications can be made, for example, for studying the medieval *Glossa ordinaria* or Greek catenae. See, for example, Tia M. Kolbaba, "Byzantine Orthodox exegesis," in *The New Cambridge History of the Bible*, vol. 2, *From 600 to 1450*, ed. Richard Marsden and E. Ann Matter (Cambridge: CUP, 2012), 485–504, esp. 488–93. I have tracked down Wesley's usage of prior

therein; the evangelical call to conversion and sanctification; and Christ's role in leading the church's praise.

According to Wesley, the "Scope" of the letter to the Hebrews is to "confirm their faith in *Christ*. And this he does, by demonstrating his Glory."[57] In his division of the letter, Heb 1:1–2:5 describes the glory of the Son of God; from 2:6 onward, it describes the glory of the Son of Man, beginning briefly with his "Humiliation" but more "copiously after his Exaltation: As from hence the Glory He had from Eternity, began to be evidently seen," alluding to John 17:5.[58] The glory, or majesty, of the Son of God is thus the central matter of the letter to the Hebrews. The author's display of this glory is meant to confirm his readers' faith in the Son.

In the exordium (1:1–4), then, the Son's "Majesty" is in view, both as he possesses it in himself and as he enacts it towards his creation. The opening of Hebrews displays the Son's majesty, first, "Absolutely, by the very Name of Son, v. 1," and, second, "by three glorious Predicates, *whom he hath appointed, by whom he made, who sat down*; whereby he is described, from the Beginning to the Consummation of all Things, v. 2, 3."[59] Christ's glorious work thus spans the whole creation, from its introduction into existence to its renovation by his self-offering on the cross. For, as Wesley writes, commenting on "the consummation of the ages" (Heb 9:26), "The Sacrifice of Christ divides the whole Age or Duration of the World into two Parts."[60] The most fundamental distinction in the series of divine acts in the economy is before and after Christ's death. The new age has begun in Christ's high priestly work, and he carries on this work until his return.

The glorious Son's work is also indivisible from that of the Father and the Spirit. Wesley thus attends to the Trinitarian shape of divine action.

---

sources where possible. The *Explanatory Notes* will make up volumes 5 and 6 of the Bicentennial Edition of the Works of John Wesley, 35 vols. projected (Nashville: Abingdon, 1984–).

57. Wesley, *Explanatory Notes Upon the New Testament*, 589. This is from Bengel, *Gnomon Novi Testamenti*, 2:391: "Totus in id incumbit, ut fratrum *fidem* in Jesum Christum *confirmet*, cap. 13, 8.s. Confirmat autem eam per demonstrationem *Gloriae* ipsius."

58. Wesley, *Explanatory Notes Upon the New Testament*, 590–1. This is from Bengel, *Gnomon Novi Testamenti*, 2:395: "Gloriam Christi, ita potissimum, ut est Filius DEI, hoc capite describit; deinceps, Gloriam Christi hominis. c. 2, 6. Ipsam gloriam filii DEI, ante exinanitionem, summatim commemorat; post exaltationem, copiosissime. nam ex hac demum evidentissime conspici coepta est Gloria, quam habebat ab aeterno."

59. Wesley, *Explanatory Notes Upon the New Testament*, 590. This is from Bengel, *Gnomon Novi Testamenti*, 2:394: "Hujus Filii Majestas *PROPONITUR* 1) *absolute*, a) per ipsum *Filii* nomen: v. 1. b) per tria gloriosa praedicata, totidem verbis finitis cum pronomine *qui* expressa: *quem posuit; per quem fecit; qui consedit*: quo pacto Ejus quasi cursus ab initio rerum omnium usque ad Ipsius metam describitur.: v. 2. 3."

60. Wesley, *Explanatory Notes Upon the New Testament*, 609–10. This is from Bengel, *Gnomon Novi Testamenti*, 2:443: "Sacrificium Christi totam mundi aetatem in duas secat partes."

Commenting on Heb 9:14, on Christ, "who through the eternal Spirit offered himself without spot to God," he writes:

> The Work of Redemption being the Work of the whole Trinity. Neither is the *Second Person* alone concerned even in the amazing Condescension that was needful to compleat [sic] it. The *Father* delivers up the Kingdom to the *Son*: And the Holy Ghost become the Gift of the Messiah, being, as it were, *sent* according to his good Pleasure.[61]

Such a Trinitarian construal is, remarkably, one of Wesley's particular insights. While others interpreted the "eternal Spirit" of Heb 9:14 as Christ's own eternal deity or, at most, the Spirit's anointing of the Son, Wesley extends his vision to the work of all three Persons in redemption.[62]

This work in human beings enacts their justification and sanctification. In this Wesley shows his character as a preacher of the gospel. On the "today" of Heb 3:13, for instance, Wesley writes, "This *to-day* will not last for ever. The Day of Life will end soon, and perhaps the Day of Grace yet sooner," with a knowing glance, it almost seems, towards his reader.[63] On the promise of God in Heb 6:17, Wesley admonishes, "Thou that hearest the Promise, dost thou not yet believe?"[64]

The citation of Jer 31:31–14 in Heb 8:8–12 leads Wesley to a short consideration of the *ordo salutis*, the process of salvation as God ordinarily enacts it in each individual. He writes, "This therefore is GOD's Method. First a Sinner is pardoned: Then, he knows GOD, as gracious and merciful. Then GOD's Laws are written on his Heart: He is GOD's, and GOD is his."[65] This writing of God's laws on one's heart distinguishes the new covenant from the old, and so marks out the superiority of the Christian dispensation over that of Israel. Since Israel's sacrifice could not perfect those who offered them (Heb 10:1), "the Attainments of David" cannot be "the proper Measure of Gospel-Holiness." No, "*Christian*

---

61. Wesley, *Explanatory Notes Upon the New Testament*, 608. Remarkably, the words are Wesley's own, as far as I can uncover.

62. See Hughes, *A Commentary on the Epistle to the Hebrews*, 358–60.

63. Wesley, *Explanatory Notes Upon the New Testament*, 596. The first sentence is from Bengel; the second seems a paraphrase of Guyse. Bengel, *Gnomon Novi Testamenti*, 2:414: "Non erit hoc *hodie* perpetuum"; Guyse, *The Practical Expositor*, 5:290: "Attend to this as your present duty, while the day of life is continued, and the day of gospel-grace lasts, which will soon come to a period at death, and will do so, particularly to the *Jews*, at the approaching destruction of *Jerusalem*."

64. Wesley, *Explanatory Notes Upon the New Testament*, 602. This is from Bengel, *Gnomon Novi Testamenti*, 2:428: "Adhuc non credis, auditor promissionis?"

65. Wesley, *Explanatory Notes Upon the New Testament*, 607–8. This seems to be Wesley's own.

Experience" has to rise higher.[66] And this because Christians have a greater High Priest, *"the author and finisher of our faith* – Who begins it in us, carries it on, and perfects it."[67] Just as Christ's work, then, encompasses the beginning and the consummation of the ages, it also encompasses the beginning and the perfection of the Christian's faith.

Finally, Wesley too has a vision of Christ's high priestly activity in the church's life of worship. Commenting, like Calvin, on the quotation of Ps 22:22 in Heb 2:12, "In the midst of the church will I sing praise unto thee," Wesley writes:

> This he did literally, in the Midst of his Apostles, on the Night before his Passion. And as it means, in a more general Sense, setting forth the Praise of GOD, he has done it in the Church, by his Word and his Spirit, he still does, and will do it, throughout all Generations.[68]

To which a fitting conclusion may simply be: Amen.

CONCLUSION

There are many more suggestive theological insights we could draw upon from the history of the interpretation of Hebrews regarding a Christology of high priestly divine action, not least from the five exegetes surveyed in this chapter. But to allow one example from elsewhere: Cyril of Alexandria (*c.* 376–444), a generation younger than Chrysostom, quotes the opening of Hebrews to suggest the elevated place of the four gospels within the canon. In the words of Jesus in the four gospels we hear directly from "the Son" in whom God has spoken to us in these last days.[69] The congregation standing for the reading of the gospels in certain liturgical traditions is a visible display of this conviction regarding contemporary divine action.

This being said, we have canvassed several important themes that will

---

66. Wesley, *Explanatory Notes Upon the New Testament*, 610. Wesley may be drawing here on Heylyn, *Theological Lectures*, 42–44, on the natural, Jewish, and Christian dispensations as a progression of three moral states.

67. Wesley, *Explanatory Notes Upon the New Testament*, 617. This is a slight paraphrase of Guyse, *The Practical Expositor*, 5:419.

68. Wesley, *Explanatory Notes Upon the New Testament*, 594. This is a slight paraphrase of Guyse, *The Practical Expositor*, 5:280.

69. Matthew R. Crawford, *Cyril of Alexandria's Trinitarian Theology of Scripture* (Oxford: OUP, 2014), ch. 4.

reemerge in this volume in various forms: the status of Christ as both divine and human, and so the need to parse his divine-human action; his differentiated works across the economy, from creation through redemption to consummation; that everything Christ is and does is "for us"; and, finally, the way in which each of Christ's high priestly works impinge on the life of the church today.

This has only been a brief sketch of a few themes from the history of biblical interpretation, which is, in large measure, but another name for the history of theology. After all, much of the church's theology has arisen from its reading of Scripture. Rowan Greer, in his unsurpassed study of Greek patristic exegesis of Hebrews, contends that theology, though "largely indistinguishable" from exegesis in the early church, also came to shape interpretation of the letter. It did so by virtue of the questions posed by the theological debates about the nature of Christ in the fourth and fifth centuries, often crystallizing around key texts in Hebrews.[70] Theology, in important ways, determined the results of exegesis.

Yet this is not strictly true. That theology emerged first as a reading of Scripture which, in turn, shaped the way Scripture was read. It seems best to think of the relationship of theology and exegesis not unidirectionally, the former directing the latter, but as a kind of virtuous – rather than vicious – circle. Greer himself comes to this conclusion: "The theological traditions, *derived themselves from Scripture*, determine the questions asked of the text."[71] Theology develops as human beings hear the Word of God and go on to speak it to others; this new understanding, in turn, shapes the way in which the Word is subsequently heard and interpreted.

Such a view, true as it may be, may be a source of further anxiety: if different theologies emerge and go on to influence exegesis, how do we adjudicate between them? By what human method may we lay hold of the truth? There is no method *as such*, I suggest, that guarantees the truth of our interpretation. Our theology and exegesis, as everything else, is caught between sin and redemption, and this will not cease until Christ comes a second time, bringing salvation to those who are waiting for him (Heb 9:28). Let us simply, then, return to Scripture again and again to hear the voice of the living Christ. For our great High Priest is not dead but alive, and intercedes for us before the throne of grace. As Calvin reminds us, "But the blood of Christ cries out, and the atonement made by it is heard daily."[72]

---

70. Greer, *The Captain of Our Salvation*, 2, 5, 64, et passim.

71. Greer, *The Captain of Our Salvation*, 357, emphasis added. Cf. Fairbairn, "Patristic Exegesis and Theology," 12.

72. Calvin, *Commentarius in epistolam ad Hebraeos* 12:25 (CTS, 335; CO 55:184).

SELECT BIBLIOGRAPHY

Adam, Karl. "Die Theologie der Krisis." *Hochland* XXIII (1926): 271–86.

Aquinas, Thomas. *Super Epistolam B. Pauli ad Hebraeos lectura.* In *Super Epistolas S. Pauli Lectura.* 8th ed., edited by Raphael Cai, 2:335–506. 2 vols. Turin/Rome: Marietti, 1953.

Augustine. *Confessions.* Translated by Henry Chadwick. Oxford: OUP, 1991.

———. *On the Trinity.* Translated by Edmund Hill, O.P. New York: New City Press, 1991.

Ayres, Lewis. "Articulating Identity [ca. 300–450]." In *The Cambridge History of Early Christian Literature,* edited by Frances Young, Lewis Ayres, and Andrew Louth, 414–63. Cambridge: CUP, 2004.

Bellamah, Timothy F. *The Biblical Interpretation of William of Alton.* Oxford: OUP, 2011.

Bengel, Johann Albrecht. *Gnomon Novi Testamenti.* 3rd ed. 2 vols. Tübingen: Ludov. Frid. Fues., 1836 [1742].

Boyle, John F. "Authorial Intention and the *Divisio textus.*" In *Reading John with St. Thomas Aquinas: Theological Exegesis and Speculative Theology,* edited by Matthew Levering and Michael Dauphinais, 3–8. Washington, D.C.: CUA Press, 2005.

———. "The Theological Character of the Scholastic 'Division of the Text' with Particular Reference to the Commentaries of Saint Thomas Aquinas." In *With Reverence for the Word: Medieval Scriptural Exegesis in Judaism, Christianity and Islam,* edited by Jane Dammen McAuliffe, Barry D. Walfish, and Joseph W. Goering, 276–83. Oxford: OUP, 2003.

Brock, Brian. *Singing the Ethos of God: On the Place of Christian Ethics in Scripture.* Grand Rapids/Cambridge: Eerdmans, 2007.

Calvin, John. *Commentaries on the Epistle of Paul to the Hebrews.* Edinburgh: Calvin Translation Society, 1853.

———. *Commentarius in epistolam ad Hebraeos.* Vol. 55 of *Ioannis Calvini opera quae supersunt omnia,* edited by G. Baum, E. Cunitz, and E. Reuss, 1–198. Brunswick: Schwetschke, 1896.

———. *Hebrews and 1&2 Peter.* Translated by William B. Johnston. Vol. 11 of Calvin's New Testament Commentaries, edited by David W. Torrance and Thomas F. Torrance. Grand Rapids: Eerdmans, 1994.

Chrysostom, John. *Homilies on the Epistle to the Hebrews.* NPNF 1/14.

Crawford, Matthew R. *Cyril of Alexandria's Trinitarian Theology of Scripture.* Oxford: OUP, 2014.

Demarest, Bruce. *A History of Interpretation of Hebrews 7, 1–10 from the Reformation to the Present*. Beitrage zur Geschichte der biblischen Exegese. Tübingen: J. C. B. Mohr (Paul Siebeck), 1973.

Doddridge, Philip. *The Family Expositor*. London: Frederick Westley and A. H. Davis, 1831 [1739–56].

Essary, Kirk. *Erasmus and Calvin on the Foolishness of God: Reason and Emotion in the Christian Philosophy*. Toronto: University of Toronto Press, 2017.

Fairbairn, Donald. "Patristic Exegesis and Theology: The Cart and the Horse." *WTJ* 69 (2007): 1–19.

Fox, Matthew. "Alcuin's *Expositio in epistolam ad Hebraeos*." *Journal of Medieval Latin* 18 (2008): 326–45.

Green, Joel B. *Reading Scripture as Wesleyans*. Nashville: Abingdon, 2010.

Greer, Rowan A. *The Captain of Our Salvation: A Study in the Patristic Exegesis of Hebrews*. Tübingen: J. C. B. Mohr (Paul Siebeck), 1973.

Gunton, Colin. *Revelation and Reason: Prolegomena to Theology*. Edited by P. H. Brazier. London: T&T Clark, 2008.

Guyse, John. *The Practical Expositor, Or, An Exposition of the New Testament*. 5th ed. 6 vols. Edinburgh: Ross & Sons, 1797 [1739–52].

Hagen, Kenneth. *Hebrews Commenting from Erasmus to Bèze 1516–1598*. Tübingen: J. C. B. Mohr (Paul Siebeck), 1981.

Hansen, Gary Neal. "Calvin as Commentator on Hebrews and the Catholic Epistles." In *Calvin and the Bible*, edited by Donald K. McKim, 257–81. Cambridge: CUP, 2006.

Heen, Erik M., and Philip D. W. Krey, eds. *Hebrews*. Ancient Christian Commentary on Scripture: New Testament X. Downers Grove: IVP Press, 2005.

Heylyn, John. *Theological Lectures at Westminster-Abbey, With an interpretation of the Four Gospels*. London: J. and R. Tonson and S. Draper, 1749.

Hughes, Philip Edgcumbe. *A Commentary on the Epistle to the Hebrews*. Grand Rapids: Eerdmans, 1977.

Kolbaba, Tia M. "Byzantine Orthodox Exegesis." In *The New Cambridge History of the Bible*. Vol. 2, *From 600 to 1450*, edited by Richard Marsden and E. Ann Matter, 485–504. Cambridge: CUP, 2012.

Laansma, Jon C., and Daniel J. Treier, eds. *Christology, Hermeneutics and Hebrews: Profiles from the History of Interpretation*. London/New York: T&T Clark, 2012.

Lane, Anthony N. S. "Guide to Recent Calvin Literature." *Vox Evangelica* 17 (1987): 35–47.

Luther, Martin. *Luther's Works*. Various translators. 75 vols. projected. St. Louis: Concordia/Minneapolis: Fortress Press, 1957–.

———. "Preface to the Complete Edition of Luther's Latin Works." In *Luther's Works* 34:336–37.

Muller, Richard A. *The Unaccommodated Calvin: Studies in the Foundation of a Theological Tradition*. New York: OUP, 2000.

Naidu, Ashish J. "John Chrysostom's Homilies on Hebrews: An Antiochene Christological Commentary?" *Perichoresis* 6/1 (2008): 85–108.

Owen, John. *The Works of John Owen, D.D.* Edited by William H. Goold. 24 vols. London/Edinburgh: Johnstone and Hunter, 1850–55.

Pauck, Wilhelm. "Introduction." In Martin Luther, *Lectures on Romans*, edited by Wilhelm Pauck, xvii–lxvi. Louisville, KY: Westminster John Knox Press, 2006 [1961].

Riggenbach, Eduard. *Die ältesten lateinischen Kommentare zum Hebräerbrief: Ein Beitrag zur Geschichte der Exegese und zur Literaturgeschichte des Mittelalters*. Leipzig: Deichert, 1907.

Rittgers, Ronald K., ed. *Hebrews, James*. Reformation Commentary on Scripture: New Testament XIII. Downers Grove: IVP Academic, 2017.

Rummel, Erika. *The Humanist-Scholastic Debate in the Renaissance and the Reformation*. Boston: Harvard University Press, 1998.

Spicq, Ceslas. *L'Épître aux Hébreux*. 2 vols. Paris: J. Gabalda, 1952.

Webster, John. "Biblical Reasoning." In *The Domain of the Word: Scripture and Theological Reason*, 115–32. London: T&T Clark, 2012.

———. "One Who Is Son: Theological Reflections on the Exordium to the Epistle to the Hebrews." In *The Epistle to the Hebrews and Christian Theology*, edited by Richard Bauckham, Daniel R. Driver, Trevor A. Hart, and Nathan MacDonald, 69–94. Grand Rapids/Cambridge: Eerdmans, 2009.

Weinandy, Thomas G. "The Supremacy of Christ: Aquinas' *Commentary on Hebrews*." In *Aquinas on Scripture: An Introduction to His Biblical Commentaries*, edited by Thomas G. Weinandy, Daniel A. Keating, and John P. Yocum, 223–44. London/New York: T&T Clark, 2005.

Wesley, John. *Explanatory Notes Upon the New Testament*. 2nd ed. London, 1757.

———. *Wesley's Standard Sermons*. Edited by Edward H. Sugden. 2 vols. Nashville: Lamar & Barton, 1920.

PART II

Hebrews and the Doctrine of God

CHAPTER 3

"No One Greater"

Classical Christian Theism and Hebrews

R. Lucas Stamps

INTRODUCTION

The essays that form the core of this volume were spawned during a two-year reflection hosted by the Scripture and Doctrine Seminar on this topic: "Divine Action and Hebrews: The Ongoing Priesthood of Christ." This is, indeed, not one topic but several – a cluster of interrelated biblical and theological issues concerned, first, with whether and how God, as classically understood, can act as a personal agent on the stage of creation and redemption; second, how the fertile soil of the epistle to the Hebrews can help resource this theological reflection; and, third, what specific relevance the ongoing priesthood of Christ – the crucified, resurrected, and ascended God-Man – bears upon our accounting of divine action.

This chapter touches on each of these components of the question but is principally concerned with the theological preconditions for conceiving of divine action, given the commitments of what has come to be known as "classical Christian theism." Several texts and themes from the book of Hebrews will be highlighted, but we will home in on one particularly illuminating passage in Hebrews 6, which speaks of God's unchanging promise to Abraham, grounded in the immutability of God's own essence: "For when God made a promise to Abraham, since he had no one greater by whom to swear, he swore by himself" (Heb 6:13).[1] In one of the most lucid treatments of divine action from a systematic-theological perspective, the late Christoph Schwöbel laid down the necessity of "giving clear conceptual expression" to divine action and of "trying to offer a conceptual reconstruction of discourse about divine action."[2] And that is precisely what this chapter seeks to do: to provide a theological accounting for how we may speak meaningfully of God's action in the world, especially in light of the classical attribute of God's absolute immutability. As we will see, some who have reflected on the possibility of divine action have found the God of classical Christian theism to be particularly problematic in this regard. So, after a brief explanation of what is meant by "classical Christian theism," I will examine the ways in which divine action is potentially problematised by God's absolute immutability and will then turn to the history of interpretation to see how several classic scriptural exegetes have dealt with this text (namely, Hebrews 6:13–20). Three interpreters will be consulted for their representative perspectives in three different eras: the fourth- and fifth-century Greek father John Chrysostom, the medieval doctor Thomas Aquinas, and the seventeenth-century English theologian John Owen. I will conclude by suggesting a few theological principles for thinking about how Scripture relates to these perennial problems.

CLASSICAL CHRISTIAN THEISM

So, what exactly do we mean when we speak of classical Christian theism (CCT)? I admit to some ambivalence about this term;[3] it seems to suffer from two main weaknesses. First, it appears to have been coined by process theists, who sought to reject the concept. Charles Hartshorne, for example, critiques "the traditional and still widely accepted form of theology (which I call 'classical theism')" and puts in its place "a revised form of theism which some call 'process theology' and I call 'neoclassical theism.'"[4] According to Hartshorne, the classical model of God as immutable and omnipotent is too immobile and too focused on "static being." The process view seeks to remedy this classical conception by emphasising God's "becoming" in relation to the

---

1. All Scripture translations in this chapter are from the ESV unless noted otherwise.

2. Christoph Schwöbel, *God: Action and Revelation* (Kampen: Kok Pharos, 1992), 25, 27.

3. Recently, Steve Duby published a book with "classical theism" in the title but still expressed some hesitancy about the term as an "imprecise" phrase that he has "no particular interest in defending." Still, the term expresses for Duby a "broadly cohesive" though not uniform "set of exegetical and theological resources that will prove fruitful in contemporary Christology." Steve Duby, *Jesus and the God of Classical Theism* (Grand Rapids: Baker Academic, 2022), xiii.

4. Charles Hartshorne, *Omnipotence and Other Theological Mistakes* (Albany, NY: SUNY Press, 1984), ix.

world.[5] To accept the moniker "classical theism," then, is to meet the process theist on his own terms, so to speak, and to risk tacitly accepting his characterisations (and mischaracterisations) of traditional views on the divine attributes. A second reason why we might be hesitant to embrace CCT is the tendency to elide important distinctions within the tradition itself. There are significant differences, for example, between Thomas Aquinas and Duns Scotus on the doctrine of divine simplicity. One scholar has observed eight main definitions of the doctrine of divine impassibility and four different applications of it to the various aspects of a person (nature, will, knowledge, and feelings), producing a dizzying number of possibilities.[6] Even if we were to simplify and consolidate such a list, some diversity in the tradition is not terribly difficult to demonstrate.

So why stick with a label that was not chosen by its own proponents and may run the risk of oversimplifying a fairly diverse tradition? On the first point, the utility of a term is not always determined by its origin. Even if process theists coined the term, it has also taken on a life of its own and has been explicitly embraced by its adherents in recent years.[7] In that way, it is not entirely dissimilar from the term "Christian" itself (Acts 11:26). Language changes and develops. Provided proponents of CCT make their own definitions clear, the origin of the term in process theism is not a fatal blow to its contemporary usage. On the question of diversity within the classical tradition, these variations should not be dismissed or too hastily harmonised. But diversity exists in any intellectual tradition. As Alasdair MacIntyre has argued, a tradition is "an historically extended, socially embodied argument, and an argument precisely in part about the goods which constitute that tradition."[8] So, contested understandings of the doctrines that fall under the rubric of CCT need not count against seeing it as a basically coherent tradition. Indeed, there is a discernible consensus (though not a stale uniformity) on the key doctrines that fly under the banner of CCT, especially the divine attributes and the traditional conception of the doctrine of the Trinity.[9]

---

5. Hartshorne, *Omnipotence and Other Theological Mistakes*, 10.

6. Richard E. Creel, *Divine Impassibility: An Essay in Philosophical Theology* (Cambridge: CUP, 1986), 9–12.

7. For example, see Brian Davies, *Introduction to the Philosophy of Religion*, 3rd ed. (Oxford: OUP, 2004), 2. See also Craig A. Carter, *Contemplating God with the Great Tradition: Recovering Trinitarian Classical Theism* (Grand Rapids: Baker Academic, 2021). Recently, a "Center for Classical Theology" has been founded by the evangelical publication *Credo*. Another project, the *Journal for Classical Theology*, launched in the fall of 2022. In full disclosure, I serve on the editorial board for this journal.

8. Alasdair MacIntyre, *After Virtue: A Study in Moral Theory*, 2nd ed. (Notre Dame, IN: Notre Dame University Press, 1981), 222.

9. On this consensus and how it contrasts with the modern trinitarian "revival," see Stephen R. Holmes, *The Quest for the Trinity: The Doctrine of God in Scripture, History, and Modernity* (Downers Grove: IVP Academic, 2012).

Perhaps another term will do (traditional theism? Catholic theism?). The term itself is less important than the substance.[10]

So, what exactly is the substance of CCT? In one sense, framing a doctrine of God as "classical" obviously requires a foil – an alternative that seeks modifications to the traditional view. And there is certainly no lack of alternatives in contemporary theology, with process theism, open theism, and what Brian Davies has termed "theistic personalism" among the traditional view's chief rivals.[11] Perhaps we should begin by noting that not all forms of classical theism are *Christian* in their particulars. The basic commitments of classical theism regarding the attributes of God and God's causal relationship to the world have also been embraced in the classical traditions of Judaism and Islam. But, certainly, a Christian theist will wish to maintain the Trinitarian distinctives that mark our faith uniquely and more adequately ground the principal commitments of the classical view. Putting those considerations aside, we can speak about CCT in two main ways. First, CCT commits one to a particular view of God's relationship to creation. God creates all that is not God by his Word and Spirit from nothing (*creatio ex nihilo*). As Creator, God does not occupy the same metaphysical space as the created order. Proponents of CCT often point out that God is not just another being in the world, albeit the greatest. In one sense, we might say that God is not so much *a being* as he is "being itself subsisting" (*ipsa essentia subsistens*).[12] Though God is personal – indeed, tripersonal! – his personhood is not univocally the same as that of men and angels. He is not a superhuman or a demigod; he is the Lord of heaven and earth, the source and cause of all that exists. Thus, the doctrine of creation *ex nihilo* (and the Creator-creature distinction that it entails) is not merely a matter of origins, but of causal dependency.[13] All that is not God is entirely dependent upon God moment by moment for its existence. Therefore, all forms of interdependence and mutuality such as we find in process theism, for example, are ruled out.

---

10. "Canonical theism," as espoused by the late Billy Abraham and others, represents an important recent alternative to classical theism, among other "theisms." See William J. Abraham, Jason E. Vickers, and Natalie B. Van Kirk, eds., *Canonical Theism: A Proposal for Theology and Church* (Grand Rapids: Eerdmans, 2008). Abraham also wrote an impressive multivolume monograph series on the other major theme we are discussing: divine agency and action. See William J. Abraham, *Divine Action and Agency*, 4 vols. (Oxford: OUP, 2018–2021).

11. Davies, *Introduction to the Philosophy of Religion*, 2.

12. Thomas Aquinas, *Summa Theologiae*, translated by Fathers of the English Dominican Province, 2nd ed., 21 vols. (London: Burns Oates & Washbourne, 1920–1935), 1.4.2.

13. Robert Sokolowski refers to this insistence that God is not a being in the world as "the Christian distinction" that demarcates the Christian religion from all forms of paganism and polytheism. Robert Sokolowski, *The God of Faith and Reason: Foundations of Christian Theology* (Washington, D.C.: CUA Press, 1995).

The second characteristic of CCT concerns a particular understanding of the nature of God and his attributes, especially the so-called metaphysical or incommunicable attributes. In the classical view, God is metaphysically simple, not composed of parts, such that all that is in God simply *is* God.[14] Any distinctions we can draw between the divine attributes exist in our understanding or in the effects of God's activity in the world, but they do not constitute real distinctions in the undivided essence of God. The God of CCT is also *a se*, from himself, and is in no sense dependent upon his creation for anything whatsoever. God is also conceived of in CCT as timelessly eternal, existing entirely outside of time; though he creates time and effects changes within it, God himself does not enter into time and is not composed of temporal parts.[15] Finally, the God of CCT is also conceived of as absolutely immutable and impassible. He is not modified in any way by his creation, and he is not "causally modified" by any outside agent.[16] Strictly speaking, God cannot and does not suffer. In Aristotelian language, God is pure act, and possesses no potentialities; he is all that he is wholly and entirely in the plenitude of his eternal Triune life.[17] Each of these divine attributes is identical with the divine essence and therefore identical with each of the divine persons, who are only distinguished from one another by their eternal relations of origin or their modes of subsistence as the one true God.

Now, there are many finer points we could make in this portrait of CCT. And we would need a fuller account to explore the diversity within the tradition on some of these points. But this brief description of CCT should suffice as a launching point for considering some of the critiques levelled against CCT vis-à-vis divine action.

One further note: closely related to CCT but not coterminous with it is the "perfect being theology" associated with Anselm of Canterbury.[18] We can distinguish perfect being theology from CCT in that the former is more concerned with a particular mode of theologizing than it is with the precise content of that theologizing. Theoretically, some today might use the Anselmian method in

---

14. For a defense of this doctrine, see James E. Dolezal, *God without Parts: Divine Simplicity and the Metaphysics of God's Absoluteness* (Eugene, OR: Pickwick, 2011).

15. See Paul Helm, *Eternal God: A Study of God without Time*, 2nd ed. (Oxford: OUP, 2010).

16. Davies, *Introduction to the Philosophy of Religion*, 5. For a fuller defense of impassibility, see Ronald S. Baines, Richard C. Barcellos, James P. Butler, Stefan T. Lindblad, James M. Renihan, eds., *Confessing the Impassible God: The Biblical, Classical, and Confessional Doctrine of Divine Impassibility* (Palmdale, CA: Reformed Baptist Academic Press, 2015).

17. For an excellent summary of the biblical case for each of these divine attributes, see Duby, *Jesus and the God of Classical Theism*, 22–32.

18. For one exemplar of this approach, see Thomas V. Morris, *Our Idea of God: An Introduction to Philosophical Theology* (Vancouver: Regent College Publishing, 1997).

order to *disprove* certain features of the classical view. But certainly the two categories have significant overlap in the Christian tradition itself.

THE PROBLEMATIZING OF DIVINE ACTION

As I have noted, CCT is not without its detractors in contemporary theology. The challenges to CCT fall on the spectrum of more to less radical modifications to the traditional view. On the more radical end, we should certainly make mention of the process theism of Hartshorne and others, as well as the proposals of "openness" theology (Clark Pinnock, John Sanders, and others).[19] Another fairly radical proposal has been put forward by Keith Ward in his impressive work, *Divine Action: Examining God's Role in an Open and Emergent Universe.*[20]

But we should also be aware of proposals that seek a more mediating position – that is, theologies that wish to preserve the best of the classical view while nuancing and adapting it to ameliorate its allegedly problematic features. Here, again, we can take note of the view that Davies refers to as "theistic personalism." This perspective, espoused by philosophers such as Alvin Plantinga and Richard Swinburne, often entails a rejection or else a radical redefinition of the classical doctrine of divine simplicity, as well as significant modifications to the doctrines of immutability and impassibility. According to this view, God is to be conceived of primarily as a "person without a body," where "person" indicates a being possessed of mind and will. At the risk of oversimplification, we can say that rather than the simple, atemporal, absolutely immutable and impassible cause and ground of being, as in classical theism, theistic personalists conceive of God as one agent or being – albeit the greatest being – among others. For theistic personalists, classical theism yields a God who would be effectively immobile, unable to act and interact with his creation. Appeal is often made to the biblical storyline, which envisions a God who is highly interactive with his creation, who even changes his mind, relents of previous decisions, and appears for good and ill to be affected by his creatures' actions. CCT's notable apophaticism when it comes to describing the essence of God and its appeal to analogical,

---

19. For an introduction to open theism, see Clark Pinnock, Richard Rice, John Sanders, William Hasker, and David Bassinger, *The Openness of God: A Biblical Challenge to the Traditional Understanding of God* (Downers Grove: IVP Academic, 1994). Open theism sparked an intense controversy within North American evangelicalism in the 1990s and 2000s. For a rebuttal of the view, written during that controversy, see John Piper, Justin Taylor, and Paul Kjoss Helseth, eds. *Beyond the Bounds: Open Theism and the Undermining of Biblical Christianity* (Wheaton: Crossway, 2003).

20. Keith Ward, *Divine Action: Examining God's Role in an Open and Emergent Universe* (West Conshohocken, PA: Templeton, 2007).

metaphorical, and anthropomorphic language about God are often dismissed by theistic personalists as biblically and theologically deficient. If the kind of divine action we see in Scripture is problematised by the vision of God emphasised in CCT, then it is the latter that must be either jettisoned or modified to make room for the former. Even here, there are more and less radical versions of theistic personalism, and, to speak of my own tribe, even within evangelical Protestantism there have been several recent attempts to find a mediating position between CCT and these theistic personalist accounts. James Dolezal provides a lucid rebuttal of these revisionist theisms within evangelicalism in his book *All That Is in God*.[21]

What I would like to focus on here is one of the more sophisticated examples of this kind of modification to CCT that aims to make room for a more robust accounting of divine action – the treatment of these issues by the late Christoph Schwöbel in his important 1992 work *God: Action and Revelation*. Schwöbel maintains that there is a "fundamental dilemma in Christian discourse about God."[22] He sees this dilemma as a "structural problem" in Christian thought. In other words, it isn't a problem that manifests itself in some specific proposals, but is endemic to the entire enterprise of traditional Christian theology. What is the dilemma? Schwöbel states it plainly:

> The dilemma seems to be clear: either we hold fast to the traditional interpretation of the metaphysical attributes of God in philosophical theology, and then we cannot talk about divine action as personal intentional action; or we remain faithful to discourse about divine agency in biblical traditions and in Christian faith, and take leave of the traditional interpretation of the metaphysical attributes of God in philosophical theology.[23]

Now, to be sure, Schwöbel is not suggesting that we should jettison the classical attributes altogether; instead, it is the "traditional interpretation" of those attributes that problematises divine action. So Schwöbel seeks to reconceive the traditional divine attributes in a manner that is ordered towards the picture of divine action we find in Scripture. For Schwöbel, this means we must accept a kind of "self-limitation of the exercise of God's power."[24] Personal agency is Schwöbel's starting point; the metaphysical attributes simply serve as qualifiers

21. James Dolezal, *All That Is in God: Evangelical Theology and the Challenge of Classical Christian Theism* (Grand Rapids: Reformation Heritage Books, 2017).

22. Schwöbel, *God*, 52.

23. Schwöbel, *God*, 53.

24. Schwöbel, *God*, 38.

on God's personal action, the ways in which divine action is different from crea-turely action. So, for Schwöbel, we must reject an atemporal interpretation of God's eternity: "However if God's agency is seen as the necessary condition of all worldly occurrences, then divine eternity cannot be interpreted as atempo-rality, strictly beyond time."[25] Thus, God's knowledge of the future is just that – a knowledge of states of affairs that are future, even to God. God's immuta-bility, likewise, must be modified to make room for meaningful divine action. Schwöbel writes, "Contrary to the concept of the immutability of God in philo-sophical theology, the biblical notion of the constancy of God, which underlies his faithfulness, presupposes God's free intentional agency which includes his capacity for change."[26] So, in Schwöbel's view, if CCT and divine action (con-ceived of as intentional personal agency) conflict, CCT must give way or else undergo significant modifications. If Scripture presents God as involved in interpersonal relationships and engaged in intentional action and change, then our conceptions of God must adapt to the biblical data. Our understanding of divine personal agency must be significantly similar to human personal agency in order to be meaningful. Hence Davies's category for this family of views: the-istic personalism. In this vein, Schwöbel seeks for a modified theism on each of the classical metaphysical attributes. Just as immutability is redefined as con-stancy, so also omnipotence understood as the power to do all that is logically possible (Thomas's view) must be re-conceived as a "self-restriction of power" qualified by God's other attributes.[27] Likewise, God's omniscience must be set within certain limitations: "This implies that God's knowledge is self-limited through the free actions of his creatures in such a way that God knows the future not as eternal presence, but as the future, as the sum of all possibilities which are given in the world at a particular moment in time."[28] In sum, the clas-sical metaphysical attributes must be interpreted in "mutual qualification" with the personal attributes of God.[29]

So, how can the defender of CCT respond to these charges? Does the God of CCT render divine action impossible? Has the proponent of CCT left the Scriptures behind in favor of what Schwöbel calls the "cultural compromise of Christianity with Greek metaphysics"?[30] As an initial response, before we explore some relevant themes in Hebrews, we need to acknowledge that some

---

25. Schwöbel, *God*, 39.
26. Schwöbel, *God*, 39.
27. Schwöbel, *God*, 60.
28. Schwöbel, *God*, 39.
29. Schwöbel, *God*, 60.
30. Schwöbel, *God*, 47.

methodological questions are being begged here. All versions of Christian theism, not just the classical ones, affirm that in some sense God transcends the space-time universe he has created. In other words, at least in some sense, God is a supra-historical being. If this is the case, then it raises some important questions as to whether and how we appeal to the narrative and anthropomorphic portions of Scripture in developing a theology proper. Dolezal states the matter baldly: "[I]t seems to me that biblical theology with its unique focus on historical development and progress, is not suited for the study of theology proper. The reason for this is that God is not a historical individual, and neither does his intrinsic activity undergo development and change."[31] Dolezal is not suggesting that the *Bible* has nothing to say regarding our theology proper – far from it – but rather that *biblical theology* with its focus on historical development is not the best foundation on which to build an understanding of God's essence *in se*. It seems to me that CCT demands, at some level, the privileging of the straightforward teaching of Scripture concerning the otherness of God when developing our theology proper and interpreting the narrative/anthropomorphic portions in that light.[32]

READING HEBREWS FOR CLASSICAL THEISM TODAY

There is no doubt some truth in Harold Attridge's claim that the book of Hebrews "does not provide a systematic analysis of what 'God' language might mean and only seems to treat 'God' incidentally to its focus on the person and work of Christ." But it is also true, as Attridge goes on to argue, that God is "the indispensable horizon within which discussion of a heavenly high priest makes sense."[33] In other words, Hebrews's doctrine of atonement requires some antecedent doctrine of God.

What, then, does Hebrews have to teach us about theology proper, our understanding of God's being and works? Attridge considers the epistle "a kind of catechetical summary of first-century Christian theism."[34] It compels

---

31. Dolezal, *All That Is In God*, xv.

32. Jamieson and Wittman suggest a strategy for interpreting anthropomorphic passages in a "Godfitting" way, that is, in light of what the whole canon plainly states about the distinction between the Creator and the creature. See R. B. Jamieson and Tyler R. Wittman, *Biblical Reasoning: Christological and Trinitarian Rules for Exegesis* (Grand Rapids: Baker Academic, 2022), 77–90.

33. Harold W. Attridge, *Hebrews: A Commentary on the Epistle to the Hebrews*, Hermeneia (Minneapolis: Fortress Press, 1989), 95.

34. Attridge, *Hebrews*, 96.

its readers to believe that God "exists and that he rewards those who seek him" (11:6). It speaks of God as the one who creates the universe by his word such that "what is seen was not made out of things that are visible" (11:3; a difficult and fascinating locution that may imply *creatio ex nihilo* or could be alluding to debates within Hellenistic Judaism about the creation of the world from the realm of ideas).[35] God is also the sovereign and providential Lord over his creation – for him and by him all things exist (2:10). He is the "builder of all things" (3:4). He is omniscient; no creature is hidden from his sight, "but all things are naked and opened unto the eyes of him with whom we have to do" (4:13 KJV). God is also spoken of in Hebrews as "the living God" (10:31) whose word is "living and active" (4:12), the "Father of spirits" (12:9), and a "consuming fire" who is preparing an unshakable kingdom (12:28, 29). The book of Hebrews also exhibits a rich theology of divine action, ascribing many action verbs to God. God is the one who creates, rests, witnesses, testifies, calls, reveals, promises, saves, disciplines, warns, and judges. So, whatever Hebrews has to say in defense of classical theism cannot be at the expense of a robust account of divine action. And, in what is perhaps the most fascinating element of Hebrews's theology, the writer places Jesus – without any diminution of his humanity or his oneness with his brothers – on the divine side of the ledger. Christ is also spoken of as the one who creates, upholds, saves, and judges. He is spoken of as the χαρακτήρ of God's ὑπόστασις – the exact imprint of the Father's being (1:3).[36] The risen Christ is said to have the "power of an indestructible life" (7:16), and his immutable character is brought forward as an encouragement to remain faithful: "Jesus Christ is the same yesterday and today and forever" (13:8).

Any one of these texts or themes could provide fodder for a discussion of classical Christian theism. But I want to focus on one text in particular, which, as I said earlier, is particularly rich in its theological implications: Hebrews 6:13–20:

> [13] For when God made a promise to Abraham, since he had no one greater
> by whom to swear, he swore by himself, [14] saying, "Surely I will bless you
> and multiply you." [15] And thus Abraham, having patiently waited, obtained
> the promise. [16] For people swear by something greater than themselves,

---

35. For a discussion of the possible influence of Platonism on the book of Hebrews, see Gareth Lee Cockerill, *The Epistle to the Hebrews*, NICNT (Grand Rapids: Eerdmans, 2012), 28–33.

36. So, hypostasis may not mean here precisely what it meant in the later tradition, especially as associated with the Cappadocian Fathers. In that latter context, the word was co-opted as a descriptor for the three divine persons: not the one being of God but three personal modes of being. On the Cappadocian usage of hypostasis, see Khaled Anatolios, *Retrieving Nicaea: The Development and Meaning of Trinitarian Doctrine* (Grand Rapids: Baker Academic, 2011), 23–24.

and in all their disputes an oath is final for confirmation. [17] So when God desired to show more convincingly to the heirs of the promise the unchangeable character of his purpose, he guaranteed it with an oath, [18] so that by two unchangeable things, in which it is impossible for God to lie, we who have fled for refuge might have strong encouragement to hold fast to the hope set before us. [19] We have this as a sure and steadfast anchor of the soul, a hope that enters into the inner place behind the curtain, [20] where Jesus has gone as a forerunner on our behalf, having become a high priest forever after the order of Melchizedek.

Now, of course, there is more here than we could possibly treat in this chapter, but I want to make a few observations of this text that I think imply (or are at least highly consistent with) a classical Christian theist understanding of God, and then I want to highlight some relevant observations from three historical interpreters of Hebrews: Chrysostom, Aquinas, and Owen.

THREE OBSERVATIONS

First, consider the claim in v. 13 that God had "no one greater" by whom he might swear an oath. Now, this claim could perhaps be rendered in a quantitative sense: God is one being among others who just so happens to have more great-making properties than all other beings. But the statement is more categorical than that: God *had* no one greater (οὐδενὸς εἶχεν μείζονος). It is not difficult to see how a text like this lends support to the Anselmian notion that God is the greatest conceivable being. The logic of the oath is that it invokes one with absolute knowledge and power. In the case of God, as improper as oath-taking appears to be for an infinite Being, there is no other candidate by which God might swear but God himself.

Second, consider how the language of immutability is leveraged in this text and to what end. On a first reading, one of the most puzzling aspects of this text is the unspecified pair of "unchangeable things" by which the faithful may have strong encouragement. What are these two immutable things? From the earliest centuries, commentators on this text have identified these two things (δύο πραγμάτων) as the promise of God and the oath that supplements it. These are said to be immutable because they are grounded in the immutability of God himself, which, again, is the only recourse God could have as a proper object of his swearing. And the immutable promise and oath, grounded in the absolute and categorical immutability of God himself, are marshaled as evidence for the trustworthiness of God's word to Abraham and by extension to the heirs of that promise: those who have fled to this God for refuge. As theologian Peter Sanlon puts it,

"The perfection of God is, according to Hebrews 6:13, the grounds upon which we are invited to rest our confidence in the gospel promise given to Abraham."[37]

Third, consider the clause appended to these two immutable things in v. 18: "in which it is impossible for God to lie." At first blush, this phrase almost appears to be a throwaway line or at least a redundancy. But, again, the point the writer is underscoring here is that the immutability of God's promise is grounded in the nature of God himself. This statement – "it is impossible for God to lie" – is making a modal claim about God's perfection. God is not only trustworthy and true but he is so necessarily, not contingently. It also raises the question of how best to understand the attribute of omnipotence, as we noted in the section dealing with Schwöbel. God's power is not to be understood as the ability to do anything whatsoever, but to do all that is consistent with his nature and purpose – or, as Aquinas has it, the ability to do all that is logically possible (which is to say the same thing). There are some things God cannot do, not because he is lacking in any causal power that renders him impotent, but because his will is ordered towards his mind. Thus, it is not difficult to see where the writer of Hebrews would side in the late medieval debates between intellectualism and voluntarism.

With these observations in place, let us now consider some germane sections from the commentaries of our representative interpreters. Again, there is much in these works that I cannot address, so our focus will be on those places where Chrysostom, Aquinas, and Owen address the theological implications of this text.

JOHN CHRYSOSTOM

What is so striking about John Chrysostom's homily on Hebrews 6:13–20 is just how thoroughly christological it is. Chrysostom sees the oath being uttered to Abraham (by the angelic messenger in Genesis 22) as spoken by Christ himself: "Well, who then is He that swore unto Abraham? Is it not the Son?"[38] He finds evidence for this christological reading in Jesus's formulaic phrase from the Gospels, "truly, I say unto you." Chrysostom understands this locution as a kind of self-referential divine oath. "So when he [the Son] swears the same oath, Verily, verily I say unto you, it is not plain that it was because he could not swear by any greater? For as the Father swore, so also the Son swears by himself, saying, Verily, verily I say unto you."[39] This christological reading of Hebrews

---

37. Peter Sanlon, *Simply God: Recovering The Classical Trinity* (Nottingham, UK: IVP UK, 2014).

38. John Chrysostom, *Homilies on the Gospel of John and the Epistle to the Hebrews*, 11.2, trans. Frederic Gardiner (*NPNF* 1/14).

39. Chrysostom, *Homilies on Hebrews*, 11.2.

6 (and Genesis 22 behind it) allows Chrysostom not only to affirm the true deity of the Son, but also to position the Son in a mediatorial role between God and Abraham (and his heirs). He even suggests that the word for "confirmed" or "guaranteed" in v. 17 (ἐμεσίτευσεν) should be literally rendered "mediated."[40] For Chrysostom, swearing is properly "unworthy" of God; it is only because of God's infinite condescension to humanity in his Son that he chooses to take an oath in order to "impart full assurance" to his people.[41] Chrysostom also picks up on the implicit perfect being theology taught in Hebrews 6:18. He writes, "For he by whom men swear, by him also God swore, that is by himself. They indeed as by one greater, but he not as by one greater. And yet he did it. For it is not the same thing for man to swear by himself, as for God. For man has no power over himself."[42] This last line suggests that God, unlike man, in some sense *does* have power over himself – in other words, that God is *a se*, from himself, and uniquely so, independent of any need or prompting from the creature. As Chrysostom says, the oath was "not of [Abraham's] patient endurance," but was initiated by God in order to show that "the whole was of God."[43] God acts independently and gratuitously out of his own unique and unparalleled perfection, and he does so preeminently in the condescension and suffering of his Son. In sum, Chrysostom provides a reading of Hebrews 6 that is consistent with the emerging Trinitarian and christological orthodoxy of the fourth century and also with the classical conception of God's aseity.

THOMAS AQUINAS

Thomas's commentary on the epistle to the Hebrews comes to us in the form of a *reportatio*, essentially a transcript from his lectures on the book. Because of this format, the commentary is succinct, discursive, and somewhat choppy. Thomas offers a close reading of the literal sense of the text, but also stops to make observations on some of the letter's theological and ethical dimensions. He even includes an excursus on the biblical legitimacy and dangers of oath-taking. Concerning the classical conception of God, Thomas's commentary makes an important distinction that demonstrates how the classical theist tradition understands some of the particularities of the biblical narrative. On the immutability of God's promise, he writes:

---

40. In a recent commentary, Gareth Cockerill also makes note of the use of "mediated" but suggests that the term "carries the significance of 'guaranteed.'" Cockerill, *The Epistle to the Hebrews*, 287.

41. Chrysostom, *Homilies on Hebrews*, 11.2.

42. Chrysostom, *Homilies on Hebrews*, 11.2.

43. Chrysostom, *Homilies on Hebrews*, 11.2.

But it must be shown that in those things which proceed from God two things are to be considered: the very procession of things, and the counsel of God by which such a procession is caused. Now, the counsel of God is altogether immovable. Is. 46:10: "My counsel shall stand, and all my will shall be done." But the disposition is quite mutable, for the Lord sometimes pronounces something according to what the order and procession of things demands, as is clear from [several biblical passages].[44]

Among the biblical proofs for this distinction, Thomas cites the threat against Hezekiah's life in Isaiah 38, the warning against the Ninevites in Jonah 3, and the general warning against unrepentant nations in Jeremiah 18. In each of these cases, the promise of judgement is not necessarily and in every case carried out. Why? Because these threats come with an implicit or explicit condition: if there is no repentance, then judgement will fall. But these are examples of Thomas's first category: the actual procession of things in history, which, taken together, are simply the external outworking of the immutable divine counsel. These conditional and temporal outworkings are not to be confused with the absolute and immovable counsel of God itself, which is immutable. And it is this second category – the immutable divine counsel – that is spoken of in Hebrews 6 and Genesis 22. In his *Summa Theologiae*, Thomas says something similar: "To change the will is one thing; to will that certain things be changed is another."[45] God's will is eternal and immutable, but the object of his will contains all of the mutable events that God has immutably willed shall come to pass. Thomas also employs the distinction of John of Damascus between the antecedent and consequent will of God. God has antecedently willed, for example, that all humans shall be saved. But he has also willed consequently that some humans will suffer eternal punishment in consequence of their sin and God's judgement. Again, the immutable God immutably wills, but the objects of his will take mutable shape in the sequence of events. Thus, in Thomas's reckoning, we need not choose between a God who is absolutely immutable and a God whose will can have diverse effects in their actual procession in the experience of creatures.

JOHN OWEN

John Owen's exposition of the letter to the Hebrews is overwhelming. In the Banner of Truth edition, it comes in seven volumes and is exhaustive in

44. Thomas Aquinas, *Commentary on the Epistle to the Hebrews*, trans. Chrysostom Baer, O.P. (South Bend, IN: St. Augustine's Press, 2006), 322 (p. 138).
45. Thomas Aquinas, *Summa Theologiae*, 1.19.7.

its detail, dealing with every word and syntactical structure along with the theological and even pastoral implications of the text. Owen speaks in four tongues, as it were: his native English, the Greek text of the epistle itself, the Hebrew text of its OT citations, and at times the Latin rendering of both. For our purposes, I just want to point out a couple of ways in which Owen reads this text through the lens of the classical divine attributes. In his discussion of God swearing by himself, Owen digresses to consider several other examples of divine swearing in the OT. God and other actors in the biblical drama sometimes swear by God himself and at other times by his holiness, his right hand, the arm of his strength, his great name, his soul, or his excellency. Owen concludes that these diverse biblical oaths amount to the same thing, precisely because of the doctrine of divine simplicity. All of these oaths refer to "himself only," Owen writes, "for all the holy properties of God are the same with his nature and being."[46] This is a classical statement of divine simplicity. All that is in God is one with God's essence. This reading serves as an instructive example of a kind of theological interpretation of the whole Bible: reading Hebrews 6 and its cross-references in light of the doctrinal deliverances of canonical interpretation.

When Owen comes to the nature of God's oath in Hebrews 6, he considers two conditions that must be met in the object of any swearing. First, the one invoked must possess "absolute omnisciency, or infallible knowledge of the truth or falsehood of what we assert."[47] Second, the one invoked must possess a "sovereign power over us, whence we expect protection in case of right and truth, or punishment in case we deal falsely and treacherously."[48] Given these conditions, only one being is capable of serving as the object of an oath, even for God. As Owen writes, "It is because, as to infinite omniscience, power, and righteousness – the things respected in an oath – God is that essentially in and unto himself which he is in a way of external government unto his creatures."[49] Note the similarity to Thomas: a distinction is made between what God is essentially in and unto himself, on the one hand, and the external government (or procession, in Thomas's language) of God's purposes for his creatures, on the other. In short, Owen argues that the certainty of God's promise and oath is grounded in God's own essence: his simplicity, omniscience, omnipotence, righteousness, and immutability.

46. John Owen, *An Exposition of the Epistle to the Hebrews*, vol. 5 (Edinburgh: J. Ritchie, 1814), 259.
47. Owen, *An Exposition of the Epistle to the Hebrews*, 259.
48. Owen, *An Exposition of the Epistle to the Hebrews*, 259.
49. Owen, *An Exposition of the Epistle to the Hebrews*, 260.

THEOLOGICAL CONCLUSIONS

To conclude, I want to point to a few principles that emerge from these classical commentators that may guide how we appeal to the Bible in defense of classical Christian theism. First is what we might call the *apophatic principle*. Defenders of CCT have long been reticent to speak too definitively about the essence of God himself. In Calvin's words, the divine essence is rather to be adored than inquired into.[50] Distinctions must be made between God as he is in himself and the ways in which God has ordered the world and his purposes for it. The divine essence and the divine counsel are shrouded in mystery, not only because of our creaturely finitude (which could in theory be transcended if we possessed greater capacities) but also because of a qualitative distinction between Creator and creature. Again, Sokolowski refers to this as *the* Christian distinction. In the classical mode, we mainly speak of God's essence in negative terms, the so-called *via negativa*: God is not finite, not material, not temporal, not changeable, not passible, not composed of parts, and so on. Revisionist complaints against the classical conception of God seem to find this reticence to speak of God's essence especially problematic. According to revisionist accounts, it seems that we must be able to speak of divine action in ways that are immediately intelligible to us as creatures. If God has the freedom to act, we are told by the revisionists, then he *cannot* possess the attributes of CCT.[51] If divine action is to be rendered intelligible, then God *must* modify, qualify, or self-limit his immutability, omnipotence, and so on. But how would finite creatures be in an epistemic position sufficient to be able to discern with such confidence what the infinite Creator *cannot* or *must* do? The classical tradition seems comfortable with a kind of apophatic silence on these matters – indeed, as Gregory of Nazianzus argues in another context, we honor the divine mystery precisely by our silence.[52]

A second principle that is assumed in these classic commentaries without always being made explicit is what we might call the *analogical principle*. While swearing is unworthy of God in the strict sense, he condescends to offer oaths to his people in the outworking of his immutable divine counsel. But this language, like all divine predication, is uttered in a kind of improper sense. Because

---

50. John Calvin, *Institutes of the Christian Religion*, trans. Ford Lewis Battles, ed. John T. McNeill (Louisville, KY: Westminster John Knox Press, 1960), 1.5.9.

51. Schwöbel writes, "Agency in the sense expressed in the biblical traditions and in the discourse of Christian faith cannot be ascribed to the God who is presented in the conception of the metaphysical attributes." That's why, for Schwöbel, we must "modify" the metaphysical attributes in "mutual qualification" with the personal attributes. Schwöbel, *God*, 52.

52. Gregory of Nazianzus, *Select Orations*, 29.8, trans. Charles Gordon Browne and James Edward Swallow (*NPNF* 2/7).

of the qualitative distinction between Creator and creature, our language about God is always by way of analogy. It is neither univocal nor equivocal but occupies this important middle space as adequate and divinely sanctioned but at the same time accommodated revelation. God is not just another being in the world participating in being alongside creatures, only to a greater degree. Instead, God is "being itself subsisting," and creatures exist to the degree that they participate in his being. Because of this qualitative distinction between the Creator and the creature, our language about God is only fitly spoken in an analogical register.[53]

A third principle, and one that emerges especially in Chrysostom's homily, is the *christological principle*. There are places in the biblical narrative that speak of God deigning to perform actions that seem suitable only to human creatures. God walks with his people; he changes his mind; and (most relevant for our purposes) he swears an oath. One possible explanation for these texts is to appeal to metaphor and anthropomorphism, to analogy and accommodation. That appears to be the approach of Thomas and Owen. But another alternative open to the Christian interpreter (when appropriate) is a christological reading. Chrysostom is especially interested in the fact that the divine promise from Genesis 22 is uttered by the messenger of the Lord, which he takes as a prefiguration of the Son of God. Even if one does not take this alternative reading in Hebrews 6, it remains a valid option elsewhere. Interestingly, Schwöbel seems to assume that a "Christocentric" approach to theology would run in the other direction: that to see Jesus as the definitive revelation of God's love entails that we cannot transform God's revelation into a "transhistorical metaphysical . . . principle" (contrast this with Dolezal's point about the limitations of a strictly historical approach to the doctrine of God).[54] But keep in mind that the Christology which emerges in the earliest centuries, as Christians are grappling with the NT revelation, is a *two-natures* doctrine. The one person of Christ has two natures: the one simple divine essence that he eternally is (along with the Father and Spirit) and the discrete human nature that he took to himself in the incarnation. So, texts that speak of the Son must be read *partitively* – that is, according to the respective sense in which the Son is being addressed. Some texts speak of the Son of God as such, while others speak of him under the aspect of his status as the Mediator. If one were to see Genesis 22 (and Hebrews 6) as an utterance of the Son in his preincarnate role as the Mediator, as Chrysostom does, then it would require no modifications to the absolute immutability of the divine essence, which renders swearing, properly speaking, "unworthy"

---

53. Thomas gives one of the definitive explanations of analogical divine predication in his *Summa Theologiae*, 1.13.5–6.

54. Schwöbel, *God*, 14.

of God. I take note of this principle, not because I think it is the only or most plausible rendering of Hebrews 6, but only because it demonstrates the necessity of accounting for the incarnation in treatments of divine action.[55]

I think that ideas about what "must be the case" in order for God to act should be tempered by these three principles. Claims to God-as-personal-agent must be understood in analogical terms that preserve God's ineffability and absolute immutability. Schwöbel seems to argue the exact opposite – namely, that the metaphysical attributes must be modified and qualified by the attributes of personal agency.[56] But the classical theistic tradition runs the other way, assuming that the so-called metaphysical divine attributes describe (in negative terms) the truest but most metaphysically modest truths we can know about the divine essence, which in turn can only be known by means of God's self-revelation in his incarnate Son, Jesus Christ. As Michael Horton suggests, if there is a univocal core to God's consistently analogical self-revelation, it is the God-Man himself, who, as Hebrews reminds us, is both one with God (the exact imprint of the Father's hypostasis) and one with us (made like his brothers in every respect).[57] In Christ, the impassible God has joined himself to passible humanity in order to serve as a sure and steadfast anchor for all who flee to him. In the words of the Fathers, without ceasing to be what he was – the immutable God – he has become what he was not – mutable man – so that he might suffer and die and be raised and ascend into heaven and enter beyond the veil as our great hope and forerunner and High Priest. To him be glory forever and ever. Amen.

SELECT BIBLIOGRAPHY

Abraham, William J. *Divine Agency and Divine Action*. Vol. 1, *Exploring and Evaluating the Debate*. Oxford: OUP, 2017.

———. *Divine Agency and Divine Action*. Vol. 2, *Soundings in the Christian Tradition*. Oxford: OUP, 2017.

———. *Divine Agency and Divine Action*. Vol. 3, *Systematic Theology*. Oxford: OUP, 2018.

———. *Divine Agency and Divine Action*. Vol. 4, *A Theological and Philosophical Agenda*. Oxford: OUP, 2021.

---

55. For more on these themes, see Duby, *Jesus and the God of Classical Theism*.
56. Schwöbel, *God*, 38.
57. Michael S. Horton, *Covenant and Eschatology: The Divine Drama* (Louisville, KY: Westminster John Knox Press, 2002), 65.

Abraham, William, Jason E. Vickers, and Natalie B. Van Kirk. *Canonical Theism: A Proposal for Theology and the Church*. Grand Rapids: Eerdmans, 2008.

Anatolios, Khaled. *Retrieving Nicaea: The Development and Meaning of Trinitarian Doctrine*. Grand Rapids: Baker Academic, 2011.

Aquinas, Thomas. *Commentary on the Epistle to the Hebrews*. Translated by Chrysostom Baer. South Bend, IN: St. Augustine's Press, 2006.

———. *Summa Theologiae*. Translated by Fathers of the English Dominican Province. 2nd ed. 21 vols. London: Burns Oates & Washbourne, 1920–1935.

Attridge, Harold W. *The Epistle to the Hebrews: A Commentary on the Epistle to the Hebrews*. Minneapolis: Fortress Press, 1989.

Baines, Ronald S. *Confessing the Impassible God: The Biblical, Classical, & Confessional Doctrine of Divine Impassibility*. Palmdale, CA: Reformed Baptist Academic Press, 2015.

Calvin, John. *Institutes of the Christian Religion*. Translated by Ford Lewis Battles. Edited by John T. McNeill. Louisville, KY: Westminster John Knox Press, 1960.

Carter, Craig A. *Contemplating God with the Great Tradition: Recovering Trinitarian Classical Theism*. Grand Rapids: Baker Academic, 2021.

Chrysostom, St. *Homilies on the Gospel of John and the Epistle to the Hebrews*. Translated by Frederic Gardiner. *NPNF* 1/14.

Cockerill, Gareth Lee. *The Epistle to the Hebrews*. NICNT. Grand Rapids: Eerdmans, 2012.

Creel, Richard E. *Divine Impassibility: An Essay in Philosophical Theology*. Eugene, OR: Wipf and Stock, 2005.

Davies, Brian. *An Introduction to the Philosophy of Religion*. Oxford: OUP, 2020.

Dolezal, James E. *All That Is in God: Evangelical Theology and the Challenge of Classical Christian Theism*. Grand Rapids: Reformation Heritage Books, 2017.

———. *God without Parts: Divine Simplicity and the Metaphysics of God's Absoluteness*. Eugene, OR: Wipf and Stock, 2011.

Duby, Steven J. *Jesus and the God of Classical Theism: Biblical Christology in Light of the Doctrine of God*. Grand Rapids: Baker Academic, 2022.

Hartshorne, Charles. *Omnipotence and Other Theological Mistakes*. Albany, NY: SUNY Press, 1984.

Helm, Paul. *Eternal God: A Study of God without Time*. Oxford: OUP, 2010.

Holmes, Stephen R. *The Quest for the Trinity: The Doctrine of God in Scripture, History and Modernity*. Downers Grove: IVP Academic, 2012.

Horton, Michael Scott. *Covenant and Eschatology: The Divine Drama*. Louisville, KY: Westminster John Knox Press, 2002.

Jamieson, R. B., and Tyler R. Wittman. *Biblical Reasoning: Christological and Trinitarian Rules for Exegesis*. Grand Rapids: Baker Academic, 2022.

MacIntyre, Alasdair C. *After Virtue*. London: A&C Black, 2013.

Morris, Thomas V. *Our Idea of God: An Introduction to Philosophical Theology*. Vancouver, BC: Regent College Publishing, 2002.

Gregory of Nazianzus. *Select Orations*.Translated by Charles Gordon Browne and James Edward Swallow. *NPNF* 2/7.

Owen, John. *An Exposition of the Epistle to the Hebrews*. Vol. 5. Edinburgh: J. Ritchie, 1814.

Pinnock, Clark H., Richard Rice, John Sanders, William Hasker, and David Basinger. *The Openness of God: A Biblical Challenge to the Traditional Understanding of God*. Downers Grove: IVP Press, 1994.

Piper, John, Justin Taylor, and Paul Kjoss Helseth. *Beyond the Bounds: Open Theism and the Undermining of Biblical Christianity*. Wheaton: Crossway, 2003.

Sanlon, Peter. *Simply God: Recovering the Classical Trinity*. Nottingham, UK: IVP UK, 2014.

Schwobel, Christoph. *God: Action and Revelation*. Kampen, The Netherlands: Peeters, 1992.

Sokolowski, Robert. *The God of Faith and Reason: Foundations of Christian Theology*. Washington, D.C.: CUA Press, 1995.

Ward, Keith. *Divine Action: Examining God's Role in an Open and Emergent Universe*. West Conshohocken, PA: Templeton Foundation Press, 2007.

CHAPTER 4

Divine Power and the Priestly Abilities of the Son

Nick Brennan

One goodness, wisdom, justice, providence, power, incorruptibility,
– all other attributes of exalted significance are similarly predicated
of each, and the one has in a certain sense His strength in the other;
for on the one hand the Father makes all things through the Son,
and on the other hand the Only-begotten works all in Himself,
being the Power of the Father.
—*Gregory of Nyssa, Contra Eunomium VII.3 (NPNF 2/5:197)*

Bringing about all things by his powerful word . . .
—*Hebrews 1:3[1]*

INTRODUCTION

Hebrews has long been recognised as encoding an understanding of the Son
of God which, perhaps in the whole NT, most approaches the kind of two-
natures Christology of Chalcedon, in which the Son is presented as both *vere
homo* and *vere Deus*.[2] In regard to this latter aspect of the Son's divine status,

---

1. Unless noted, Scripture translations are my own.
2. Gareth Lee Cockerill, *The Epistle to the Hebrews* (NICNT; Grand Rapids: Eerdmans, 2012), 129;
Luke Timothy Johnson, *Hebrews: A Commentary* (NTL; Westminster John Knox Press, 2006), 50; Oscar

Divine Action in Hebrews

modern readers of Hebrews have often wanted to affirm the material continuity between the teaching of Hebrews and Chalcedon whilst also arguing for a fundamental difference of idiom.[3] This often relies on a frequently unargued assumption that the nature of the NT writers' thought world and locutions are formally incommensurate with the more overtly philosophical tone of later patristic theology. Whilst there is certainly some truth to this statement, it frequently fails to account for the extent to which the conceptualities and language of NT authors exercised a real pressure on patristic writers in their exegetical development and theological formations.[4] One fruitful area that deserves more reflection than it has received is the connection of the language and nature of the Son's attributes which frequently connects the texture of the NT writings and the thought world of patristic theologians. As part of an attempt to explore such connections, in this chapter I will briefly outline the way in which the concept of power and power language form a real bridge between the thought world of one patristic reader of Scripture, Gregory of Nyssa, and the role that the Son as God's power plays in the thought of Hebrews. In order to pursue this, it is helpful first to reflect on the way in which power language played an important part in the world of pro-Nicene Christology and also finds its roots in the NT, not least in the epistle to the Hebrews.

Cullmann, *The Christology of the New Testament* (Philadelphia: Westminster Press, 1959), 97. On the patristic side see Rowan A. Greer, "The Jesus of Hebrews and the Christ of Chalcedon," in *Reading the Epistle to the Hebrews: A Resource for Students*, ed. Eric Farrel Mason and Kevin B. McCruden (Atlanta: SBL Press, 2011).

3. Richard Bauckham, "Monotheism and Christology in Hebrews 1," in *Early Jewish and Christian Monotheism*, ed. Loren T. Stuckenbruck and Wendy E. S. North (London; New York: T&T Clark, 2004), 185. This, of course, stands alongside others who have seen either real and material tensions between the christological position of Hebrews and that of later creedal Christology (e.g., Harold W. Attridge, *The Epistle to the Hebrews: A Commentary on the Epistle to the Hebrews* [Hermeneia; Philadelphia: Fortress Press, 1989], 55; John Knox, *The Humanity and Divinity of Christ: A Study of Pattern in Christology* [Cambridge: CUP, 1967], 35–37), or have altogether seen these later patristic developments as a betrayal, misrepresentation, or misapprehension of the teaching of the NT authors, including Hebrews (e.g., D. Friedrich Büchsel, *Die Christologie des Hebräerbriefs* [Gütersloh: C. Berterlsmann, 1922], 177–84; Silviu N. Bunta, "The Convergence of Adamic and Merkabah Traditions in the Christology of Hebrews," in *Searching the Scriptures: Studies in Context and Intertextuality*, ed. Craig A. Evans and Jeremiah J. Johnston, LNTS 543 [London; New York: Bloomsbury, 2015], 285).

4. Frequently the sense in which this could be the case has arisen from an assumed and inherent tension between philosophical articulation and scriptural reception, with an underlying conviction that the attempted integration in the Fathers evidenced a "hellenization [that was] . . . a betrayal of the purity of the gospel." (Johannes Zachhuber, *The Rise of Christian Theology and the End of Ancient Metaphysics: Patristic Philosophy from the Cappadocian Fathers to John of Damascus* [Oxford; New York: OUP, 2020], 2) Such an assumption fails to grapple with the extent to which the theology of the patristic period can be seen as itself an attempt to articulate a truly Christian theology/philosophy within the world of ancient metaphysics, one which stood substantially on its own feet. On which see the recent arguments of Zachhuber's monograph.

62

ON DIVINE POWER IN PATRISTIC
THOUGHT AND IN HEBREWS

The popular retelling of the rise, and eventual triumph, of Nicene Christology frequently concentrates on the language of the Son's consubstantiality with the Father as decisive at the Council of AD 325. However, recent historical work has not only demonstrated that this represents a radical simplification of the development of christological thought,[5] but also that other ways of describing the Son's relation to God were equally important in contemporary and subsequent patristic discussion.[6] One significant example, that of power language, has been traced at length by Michel Barnes.[7] Both before, and significantly after, Nicea the Son's relation to God's power frequently played a key role in Nicene and pro-Nicene theology in response to homoian or anti-Nicene interlocutors.[8] Initially this relation took the form of equating the Son with God's power, often via appeal to key texts like Wis 7:25; Heb 1:3, and 1 Cor 1:24.[9] This often stood alongside another stream of patristic thought, in which the Son was described as equally sharing in the singular divine power with the Father; this latter articulation was particularly evident in the writing of Gregory of Nyssa.[10] Gregory's understanding of the common power of Father and Son situates it in an ordered set of connections, of φύσις to δύναμις to ἐνέργεια to ἔργον.[11] In application to the Son, the significance of this set of connections means that the works (ἔργον) of the Son demonstrate a divine activity (ἐνέργεια) reliant on unique divine power (δύναμις), which itself arises uniquely from the divine nature

---

5. "The Christian imagination has tended to portray the Nicene council as ushering in the victory of Athanasian 'orthodoxy' over 'the Arian heresy' with the inspired confession of the homoousios. However, the reception of Nicaea was a far more convoluted process than such a rendering suggests." Khaled Anatolios, *Retrieving Nicaea: The Development and Meaning of Trinitarian Doctrine* (Grand Rapids: Baker Academic, 2011), 18. Significant accounts of this process can be found in Lewis Ayres, *Nicaea and Its Legacy: An Approach to Fourth-Century Trinitarian Theology* (Oxford: OUP, 2004). Anatolios, *Retrieving Nicaea*, and John Behr, *The Way to Nicaea*, The Formation of Christian Theology, vol. 1 (Crestwood, New York: St. Vladimir's Seminary Press, 2001).

6. Ayres, *Nicaea and Its Legacy*, 43–52. Even where the language of divine being is well accepted, there was still a tendency for "language for naming and imaging God [to come] primarily from Scripture" (Anatolios, *Retrieving Nicaea*, 46).

7. Michel R. Barnes, *The Power of God: Dunamis in Gregory of Nyssa's Trinitarian Theology* (Washington, D.C.: CUA Press, 2001).

8. Anatolios, *Retrieving Nicaea*, 17, 18. On the ante-Nicene and Nicene eras, see Barnes, *Power of God*, 125–72. On post-Nicene development, see Barnes, *Power of God*, 167–221.

9. The common use of these texts may in part reflect the importance of Origen's influence on various sides of the debate. So Barnes, *Power of God*, 111.

10. The argument from common power with respect to the Son's divinity pervades many of Gregory's writings, but particularly significant is its role in his *Contra Eunomium, De Hominis Opificio, Ad Ablabium*, and *Ad Eustathium*.

11. Barnes, *Power of God*, 303–4.

(φύσις) which he possesses. In this way of thinking, Gregory argued for the oneness of God's being and power which could be equally predicated of both Father and Son.[12] In his earlier writings in opposition to Eunomius, this idea tends to be applied as "an argument for the unity of nature based on the single Power common to the Persons," though in later writings it evolves towards "an argument for the unity of nature based on multiple operations common to the Persons."[13] This latter concept, perhaps more associated with Augustine, speaks of the inseparability of divine operations *ad extra*, in which God's works *ad extra* are a fundamental unity in which Father, Son, and Spirit are all equally operative.[14]

Gregory's schematic relation of φύσις–δύναμις–ἐνέργεια–ἔργον, in which concepts of Hellenistic philosophy and medicine are reshaped in service of Gregory's Christian theology,[15] is not merely of historical interest but, I would argue, provides a significant resource for thinking about divine action in both theology and exegesis.[16] The relation may be parsed in either direction of the chain. On the one hand, the divine being possesses certain proper abilities, resolving into certain activities which, in turn, enable and produce the resultant work or product. In this direction, each link in the chain metaphysically grounds the next. On the other hand, to follow work backward to activity, to power, and thereby to nature, is to trace the logic of revelation, in which the divine works ultimately reveal the divine nature through the abilities and realised activities proper to that nature. This is the path of revelation.

In this respect, Gregory's chain provides an interesting point of comparison to modern accounts of divine action. As Fellipe do Vale notes in his opening essay, William Abraham certainly was right to stress divine action as a substantial element of what is accounted for in the theological task; however, as do Vale also notes, the divine works *simpliciter* should not be taken as a total description

---

12. Barnes, *Power of God*, 260–307.

13. Barnes, *Power of God*, 299.

14. For a recent theological account of this concept, see Adonis Vidu, *The Same God Who Works All Things: Inseparable Operations in Trinitarian Theology* (Grand Rapids: Eerdmans, 2021).

15. Barnes, *Power of God*, 21–93.

16. My intent here resonates both with those aligned with the Theological Interpretation movement who stress the church as the natural locus of scriptural reception (Robby Holt and Aubrey Spears, "The Ecclesia as Primary Context for the Reception of the Bible," in *A Manifesto for Theological Interpretation*, ed. Craig G. Bartholomew and Heath A. Thomas [Grand Rapids: Baker Academic, 2016]) and with theologies of retrieval that seek to "treat [...] pre-modern Christian theology as resource rather than problem" (John Webster, "Theologies of Retrieval," in *The Oxford Handbook of Systematic Theology*, ed. John Webster, Kathryn Tanner, and Iain Torrance [Oxford: OUP, 2009], 585) A grasp of the theology of Hebrews integrates both concerns in understanding that the church to whom God continually speaks (3:7) is not bounded by the present horizon (3:5, 6), and that saints of the past are to be remembered (13:7), still speak (11:4), and in fact are not even really "past" (12:1, 22, 23).

of theology. As Katherine Sonderegger puts it, in the revelation of God "all is not soteriology;"[17] nor, one might add, is all creation, or any other act of God. The divine works are neither the sum total of revelation,[18] nor does theology as a description of the divine works quite satisfy Gregory's conception of the way that works reveal and lead us to a knowledge of the divine persons. Nor would such an understanding do justice to the texture of Scripture itself, which sometimes speaks in a more unabashedly metaphysical fashion.[19]

Though do Vale recognises this, his move to conceive of divine action in Scripture as narrative perhaps reopens the can of worms he is trying to shut. Though one might relate much of the canon's contents in narrative form, the canon of Scripture is not straightforwardly narrative. It itself consists of a multiplicity of genres which cannot be reduced to a single one. Even at the narrative level, one must ask whether movements towards articulating Scripture as a single narrative are not in fact a reduction of even its narrative passages. Scripture itself frequently presents parallel accounts which the canonical process has not reduced to a single narrative.[20] From the opening creation narrative, which replays the action twice with different emphases, to the parallel accounts of Kings and Chronicles, to the canonising of a fourfold gospel, rather than a single gospel or compound Diatesseron-like gospel, "the narrative" is frequently not single. The choice to position the Bible as narrative or story moves from the multiple genres of Scripture to identify the macro-genre of Scripture with one of its aspects. Certainly, there are benefits to this approach, which have been frequently noted.[21] An approach to Scripture as containing, or being, a single narrative can help greatly in articulating the unity of the Bible, the unfolding epochal nature of God's work in it, and how the whole is directed towards and filled up in Christ. But the decision itself is not as obvious, un-value-laden, or "biblical," as many seem to assume. Why not promote another of Scripture's genres to the place of macro-genre, whether law, wisdom saying, apocalypse,

---

17. Katherine Sonderegger, *Systematic Theology*, vol. 2 (Minneapolis: Fortress Press, 2020), 33.

18. For the way in which the revelation of God *ad extra* leads us to a knowledge of a God who is more than his works, see the discussion of Steven J. Duby, *God in Himself: Scripture, Metaphysics, and the Task of Christian Theology* (London: Apollos, 2019), 11–26.

19. Matthew Levering, "God and Greek Philosophy in Contemporary Biblical Scholarship," *JTI* 4 (2010): 73–85.

20. Mark A. Seifrid, "The Narrative of Scripture and Justification by Faith," *CTQ* 72 (2008): 33–35; Craig G. Bartholomew and Michael W. Goheen, "Story and Biblical Theology," in *Out of Egypt: Biblical Theology and Biblical Interpretation*, SAH Series 5, ed. Craig G. Bartholomew, Mary Healy, Karl Möller, and Robin Parry (Grand Rapids: Zondervan, 2004), 159.

21. Bartholomew and Goheen, "Story and Biblical Theology"; sim. N. T. Wright, *The New Testament and the People of God*, Christian Origins and the Question of God, vol. 1 (Minneapolis: Fortress Press, 1992), 132.

parable, or poetry? And is it straightforward, having made this move, to reintegrate other scriptural genres into the chosen macro-genre to which they seem less straightforwardly related?[22]

Part of the problem of identifying narrative as Scripture's macro-genre is a resultant equivocation between the concepts of God's revelation taking place in history, the interpretation of Scripture against a reconstructed historical narrative (both of which are to my mind unobjectionable), and the identification of Scripture as a narrative or story *simpliciter*.[23] Though exponents argue that the last concept finds roots in pre-critical theologians,[24] the results of this identification lead to theological moves that problematise this connection. Systematic theology must then by nature be seen as a poorer cousin, for it must source an extraneous organising principle through which to articulate its results.[25] This is not a potential issue – it has been played out in circles particularly devoted to biblical theology.[26] Furthermore, this identification has tended to contribute to a divide between special and general revelation in recent Protestant theology. Such a divide can be seen when the Christian pursuit of truth is "locate[d] ... in the story of God's deeds and words in history" in contrast to the "classical humanist" pursuit of "truth in timeless ideas that can be accessed by human thought."[27] If this contrast is an articulation of revelation against rationalism,

---

22. As Allen notes, where concepts of Scripture as story result in "a single minded focus on redemptive history [it] can narrow the canonical form of holy scripture and, in so doing, not only miss key elements to which systematic theology might alert us but also mangle exegesis of passages and books (even genres such as the wisdom literature) that do not fit the narrative mold" ("Systematic Theology and Biblical Theology – Part Two," *JRT* 14 [2020]: 353).

23. This seems to me the difference between Stroup writing that "At the centre of Scripture is a set of narratives and these narratives are a frame around which the whole of Scripture is constructed" (*The Promise of Narrative Theology: Recovering the Gospel in the Church* [Atlanta: John Knox Press, 1981], 145) and simply saying that Scripture is a narrative or story. Cf. Bartholomew and Goheen, "Story and Biblical Theology," 160.

24. Appeals are made to Irenaeus and Calvin (Bartholomew and Goheen, "Story and Biblical Theology," 153), among others. One might equally appeal to the typological nature of Ephrem the Syrian's hymns, or, at least in some ways, the *Theologoumena Pantodapa* of John Owen, which traces the theme of true theology through the various biblical epochs.

25. This can be seen in the way that biblical theology can be described, by Vos, as paying attention to "both the form and the contents of revelation" (Geerhardus Vos, ed., *Redemptive History and Biblical Interpretation: The Shorter Writings of Geerhardus Vos*, ed. Richard B. Gaffin [Phillipsburg, NJ: P&R, 2001], 8). One is left asking the question why one would need systematic theology if biblical theology articulates both form and content in a more immediately biblical fashion. In fact, Vos articulates biblical theology as structured by a principle "given in the divine economy of revelation itself" rather than systematics which does so as "a human work ... according to logical principles." In the choice between a divinely revealed principle and logic, surely the former takes precedence. See the comments of Michael Allen, "Systematic Theology and Biblical Theology – Part One," *JRT* 14 (2020): 55, 56, and particular his recognition that "the vast majority of governing principles in systematic theology are overtly intracanonical categories" (Allen, "Systematic Theology and Biblical Theology – Part One," 61), which does not seem well attended to in such discussions.

26. See the overview of Allen, "Systematic Theology and Biblical Theology – Part One," 52–72.

27. Bartholomew and Goheen, "Story and Biblical Theology," 150.

then the point stands. But it is hard not to see it as equally a contrast between history and metaphysics or revealed and natural theology. Both these trajectories seem entirely foreign to the thought of the theologians who are appealed to as pre-critical exemplars of biblical theology. The trajectories do, however, sit rather well in a post-Enlightenment world in which Heraclitus roundly triumphs over Parmenides.[28] Such questions of positioning the nature of Scripture as a whole are also not without impact on theology proper. A canon reduced to "story" may well fit with the storied God of some post-Barthian theology, or of theology as an account only of God's works, but any sense that the latter is an undue truncation of the doctrine of God, as Vale indeed suggests, must result in a more complex understanding of the former.[29]

To return to Gregory of Nyssa against this backdrop, I would argue, is to find a theologically thick description of the relation of divine being and action, mediated by concepts of power and activity. It provides a significant resource, both theologically and exegetically. Indeed, in reflecting on the text of Hebrews and its account of divine action, one may note immediately that the epistle reflects not only an account of the work of God but also of the powers and abilities which relate to that divine work. In fact, Gregory's mediate concept of divine power significantly draws his christological discussion close to the language and conceptualities of the NT text, perhaps more so than the small set of texts frequently applied to suggests.

Though talk of the quiddity of divine nature is not absent from the NT,[30] it is certainly less close to the surface than the manifest interest in the works of God in history, most importantly and recently brought to a head in the advent, incarnation, and career of Jesus of Nazareth. But part of this witness certainly concerns not only the works of the Son as the works of God, but also a correlate language of the power or ability of the Son, which stand behind and enable his distinct and proper works in the NT. These abilities, though predicated of a man, push the careful reader to recognise the identity of Jesus as far more than an ordinary human.[31]

---

28. This at times is articulated via the von Harnack-like opposition of the Hebrew and Greek mindset (Allen, "Systematic Theology and Biblical Theology – Part One," 57). It can also be seen where biblical theology in its attention to history is viewed as "concrete and thus practical, real, pertinent" unlike the "cold formalism" of systematics (Allen, "Systematic Theology and Biblical Theology – Part One," 65).

29. For the tendencies of configuring theology narrativally to generated a "storied" doctrine of God, see chapter 1 of Francesca Aran Murphy, *God Is Not a Story: Realism Revisited* (Oxford; New York: OUP, 2007).

30. E.g., Rom 1:20; Col 2:9; 2 Pet 1:3.

31. This seems to be one of the elements that to me is most lacking in the modern revival of divine Christology, in which focus on the works of God in history seems not to be attended by equal reflection on the attributes of God and their application to Jesus as part of the witness to his divinity in the NT.

Harnessing this concept of Gregory regarding the significance of unique divine power as arising from the divine nature, my aim in this chapter is to reflect on the way in which the power and abilities of the Son in Hebrews form an important part of the epistle's Christology. In particular, I want to focus on how these situate him in relation to who and what God is, and, further, how these are involved in portraying the Son as the true locus of God's action. This concept of the Son's power and ability can be immediately recognised at the bare level of lexis in Hebrews, he being described as acting "by his powerful word" (1:3), but is also encoded in several important auxiliary uses of δύναμαι in describing the ongoing ministry of the Son to his people (2:18; 4:15; 7:25). The significance of this lexis is equally strengthened by noting the lexical antonyms of inability and inefficacy, which characterise humanity in the epistle and connect to the Levitical cult's failure to realise God's good purposes for humanity (2:14, 15; 7:18; 9:9; 10:1, 11). These lexical elements only form one slight aspect of this theme, buttressed by how the Son is portrayed as pivotal in realising the divine purposes, which have languished due to the inability of other agents in Hebrews. In the rest of this chapter, then, I want to explore this concept of the Son as God's power, or sharer in the proper divine power, as it works its way out in the surprising priestly abilities of the Son. Despite both his clearly human and priestly identities, these abilities demonstrate an efficacy which stands in stark contrast to other humans and priests and are thus indicative of his divine nature as God. The argument involves, first, evaluation of the epistle's portrayal of the weakness and inability which characterise humanity, as a backdrop to the second concept: the abilities and powers of the Son, which are reflective of his divine status. Before moving to these two concepts, however, it is helpful to briefly discuss something which is important for both elements, namely, the depiction of God as powerful agent in Hebrews in his past relation to his people.

THE POWER OF GOD IN HEBREWS

Whilst certainly the epistle touches on divine power, it obviously does not represent a treatise on this subject. Because of the pastor's commitment to old covenant revelation, the letter assumes much about the portrait and character of God contained therein. In this sense, it is obviously not creating a view of God's character and attributes from whole cloth, but is rather assuming that the God who revealed himself diversely and at length in the prophets is the same God of whom the pastor speaks (1:1). Thus, old covenant portrayal of God's power forms an important latent understanding for the epistle. Here, then, we may briefly note the way in which the pastor's Scriptures locate divine power specially around the twin themes of creation and redemption.[32] The God of the patriarchs, and of Israel, is the one who made the world and everything in it (Gen 1:1; 14:19; Exod 20:11). He stands transcendently above it, ruling over it from his divine throne (Is 66:1; Ps 11:4), and yet this transcendence is not conceived of as a removed distance from it (Ps 139). The creation not only came into existence by God's power, but continues in dependence on it. Though the psalmists surely understood some aspects of the natural processes at work in the world, Yhwh is described as intimately and directly involved in all aspects of creational life and its preservation, the natural world "look[ing] to him" (Ps 104:27) at every point for its own upholding as God renews and enlivens it by his Spirit.[33]

Alongside the sphere of creation, divine power is equally, if not even more, stressed with regards to redemption, and perhaps no place more than in the relation to the archetypal redemptive events of the exodus.[34] Yhwh's deliverance of his covenant people from Egypt represents an essential "power struggle" between Pharaoh, his magicians, and his forces,[35] and the powers of Yhwh are evident in connection to his man, Moses, the series of plagues/wonders, and the climactic deliverance via the plague on the firstborn (Exod 1–12). The final act within the narrative stresses the power(s) of Yhwh, in which he delivers Israel through the Red Sea, acting alongside their commanded inactivity (Exod 14:13, 14), and the consequent deliverance hymn which reflects on and praises Yhwh as a mighty man of war (Exod 15:1–18) who has delivered Israel to bring them near to him for priestly service at a prototypical temple established by his very hand (Exod 15:17).[36] This whole complex of events is effectively summarised by the central purpose statement of Yhwh, that he raised up Pharaoh to "show to [him] my power, and that my name might be proclaimed in all the earth" (Exod 9:16).

---

32. Intertestamental Jewish literature certainly bears witness to the continued importance of these twin themes in conceiving who and what the God of Israel was, especially sharpened by the non-Israelite contexts of the exile and subsequent life under Roman rule. Richard Bauckham, *Jesus and the God of Israel: God Crucified and Other Studies on the New Testament's Christology of Divine Identity* (Grand Rapids: Eerdmans, 2009), 7–11. On connections between creation and redemption in the epistle see Angela Costley, *Creation and Christ: An Exploration of the Topic of Creation in the Epistle to the Hebrews*, WUNT 2/527 (Tübingen: Mohr Siebeck, 2021), 94–105, and Cockerill, *Hebrews*, 97n54, who notes the connection between "making the ages" and the pleonastic use of ποιέω in "making purification" in 1:3. Heb 1:1–4 in general also spans and unites the themes (William L. Lane, *Hebrews 1–8*, WBC 47a [Nashville: Thomas Nelson, 1991], 12).

33. For further reflection on the foundational nature of God's creative work in relation to God's subsequent action in Scripture, see the discussion of Bartholomew in his chapter in the present volume.

34. The centrality of Exodus can be seen in the way in which subsequent promises of salvation become tinged with the language and concepts of Exodus. So, e.g., Isa 4:5, 6 and the extensive discussion of Bryan D. Estelle, *Echoes of Exodus: Tracing a Biblical Motif* (IVP Press, 2018).

35. Walter Brueggemann, *An Introduction to the Old Testament: The Canon and Christian Imagination* (Louisville, KY: Westminster John Knox Press, 2003), 56.

36. מכון לשבתך פעלת יהוה מקדש אדני כוננו ידיך (Exod 15:17b).

This was a proclamation of the irresistible power of Yhwh exercised on behalf of his people and his own glory.

Israel's piety reflects this pervasive power of Yhwh in its stress on dependence, which spans every aspect of Israel's canon. This is already reflected in the exodus events as a response to Israel's cries for help (Exod 2:23–25), but is perpetuated in the historical and prophetic books, in which Israel is consistently called to look to and rely on Yhwh for deliverance rather than to the promises of alliances with foreign powers, the strength of horse and chariot, and the security of wealth.[37] But no part of the old covenant Scripture is perhaps more marked by the interplay of Yhwh's power and the people's dependence than the Psalter. Here the psalmists as representative and model frequently appeal to the action of Yhwh as their only hope in the midst of trials and enemies beyond their own strength.[38] What especially draws together the dependence of the psalmists and the history of God's dealing with Israel, is the frequent depiction of Yhwh's hoped for action in terms which call to mind both creation and exodus.[39] The God in whom the psalmists hope, and Israel is to hope, is frequently referred to as king by virtue of creation (Ps 24:1, 2; 29:10), and his royal throne guarantees the establishment of justice for the needy and poor (Ps 9:4; 11:4). As Creator and God of the exodus, he may also act powerfully within his creation for the deliverance of his people (Ps 18:7–19).

With the preceding in mind, where Hebrews touches in passing on the power and activity of God, it is not surprising that the shape of the pastor's thought closely follows these lines as a reception and development of God's speech "of old." The pastor continues to characterise God as the one who made the world (1:2; 2:10; 3:4; 11:3) and who rescued Israel from Egypt (3:7–11, 16–19; 11:23–29).[40] Important in this narrative of God's past dealings is his status as the living God (3:12; 9:14; 10:31; 12:22), a term frequently adduced to contrast Yhwh with idols in their inability to do anything.[41] Because he is living, he is able to both accomplish his plans of blessing for his people and bring his enemies into judgement. Thus, appeals to the past judgements of God for those who ignore his words (3:16–19) establish the sober reality of encountering God as a consuming fire, into whose hands one may fall (10:31). His ongoing

---

37. One can see, for example, these themes coalesce in a particularly clear way in Isaiah 7–10.

38. E.g., Ps 34; 35; 54–59; 120.

39. On remembrance of the exodus in the Psalter and especially its relation to Book 4 and the situation of exile, see Susan E. Gillingham, "The Reception of the Exodus Tradition in the Psalter," in *The Reception of Exodus Motifs in Jewish and Christian Literature: "Let My People Go!"*, ed. Beate Kowalski and Susan E. Docherty (Leiden; Boston: Brill, 2021), 50–55.

40. Further notes the allusion to miracles of the exodus in the language of 2:1–4 (Cockerill, *Hebrews*, 122).

41. E.g., Deut 5:10.

ability to judge and punish in Hebrews forms a smaller part of his ability to bring the whole world into judgement by the shaking of his voice.[42] As Creator of all, he is able to bring all things into eschatological judgement. He stands over all things as πεποιημένα (12:27).[43] However, though God's ongoing purposes, plans, and power can bring about repayment of judgement, they also ground the possibility of the repayment of reward (10:35; 11:6, 26). He stands as the sender of divine rains on the covenant community, which have brought them to share in the Spirit and taste the powers of the coming age (6:4–7).[44] Just as God's powers accompanied the exodus and threatened the wilderness community, they attended the opening proclamation of the Lord's words (2:3, 4) and continue in the life of the epistle's hearers.[45] This bridge of expectation between God's past, present, and future power for the community is perhaps nowhere more clearly expressed than in chapter 11. Here the focus and trust of the many OT saints is on the power of God which vitiated the powers of death and loss that consistently threatened them.[46] By faith they lived as subjects of promise and trusted in God's power to look to a future beyond their present suffering.[47] Though this hope focused on the future (11:7, 13–16, 39), by faith some "received power" in the present and "were strengthened" (11:11, 34). The exhortative result for the pastor, in calling for a faith in his audience like those of chapter 11, in which they continue to look to the Son, is that his readers too may have confidence in God's power both to overcome death in the future and strengthen his people in the present.[48]

Reinforcing this concept of God's ongoing powerful activity is the concept of mediators in Hebrews, which is reliant on OT concepts. The letter appeals in its opening chapter to the exalted angels as created instruments at the divine

---

42. Note the use of κτίσις and πάντα in 4:13, which call the created sphere to mind (Cockerill, *Hebrews*, 218).

43. Edward Adams, *The Stars Will Fall from Heaven: Cosmic Catastrophe in the New Testament and Its World*, LNTS 347 (London; New York: T&T Clark, 2007), 190, 91. Pace Paul Ellingworth, *The Epistle to the Hebrews: A Commentary on the Greek Text*, NIGTC (Grand Rapids: Eerdmans, 1993), 688, it is the rights of God as Creator over the whole scope of "made things," rather than their inferiority, which motivates the phrase ὡς πεποιημένων in 12:27. Again note the ties to the concept of the Son's right to "change" heaven and earth based on his eternality as Creator in 1:12 and thus the mutuality of Father and Son in final judgement and restoration.

44. Lane, *Hebrews 1–8*, 141, 142.

45. For a very helpful discussion of the interplay of God's ongoing action present in the community and held out in salvation, with the issues of response raised in the warning passages, see the chapter by Peeler in the present volume, in particular in its demonstration of the priority of God's action and the dependence of human response on it in the epistle.

46. Cockerill notes the connection between death as fearful power here and in 2:14–18 (*Hebrews*, 146, 47).

47. See the comments of Hughes on 11:13, 14 in Philip Edgcumbe Hughes, *A Commentary on the Epistle to the Hebrews* (Grand Rapids: Eerdmans, 1977), 477, 478.

48. 12:1–17.

disposal (1:7, 14). As they featured in the past, they continue as spiritual minis-ters sent out by God to serve the inheriting sons as instruments of God's action towards his people. More developed in Hebrews is the concept of the hyposta-tised Word of God as an instrument of divine activity.[49] Its description as a word "living and active," able to bring all into judgement, acts as a hypostatised rep-resentation of the divine power itself.[50] Thus, just as God creates by his word (11:3) and judges by his word (4:12, 13), so also he saves by it (6:13–20), which is especially revealed in God's promises effecting the realities of which they speak. So, for example, not only does the divine promise speak of the new covenant in Jer 31:31–34, but for the pastor the very act of God's locution "new" "ages" the old (8:13). Similarly, the divine word is no mere commentary on other things, but powerfully and effectively prevents the wilderness community from entering the promised land yet guarantees the entry of others (3:11, 15; 4:1). In essence, as a representation of word as powerful action, all of God's history in both the old and new ages can be summed up in speech terms: God having spoken of old has now spoken in these last days.

THE LACKING POWER OF HUMANITY AND THE INEFFICACY OF THE LEVITICAL CULT

With this portrayal of God's power in mind, we may turn to the depiction of humanity generally in Hebrews, in which God's people are frequently portrayed as the objects and, hence, recipients of this power.[51] So, for example, Sarah in the face of divine promises of childbearing "by faith received power to conceive,"[52] the implication being that she received power by faith from the power of God. This explicit description in Hebrews thus segues into the description of the faithful past saints who, by faith, conquered and survived the onslaught of ene-mies.[53] Thus, God's power is not merely, here, his own distinct attribute focused

---

49. 4:12, 13. Craig R. Koester, *Hebrews: A New Translation with Introduction and Commentary*, AB 36 (New York: Doubleday, 2001), 97. The common attributive participle ζῶν ties God and Word together (3:12; 4:12; 9:14; 10:31; 12:22).

50. Attridge, *Hebrews*, 134.

51. Cockerill, *Hebrews*, 521.

52. 11:11. The issues surrounding exactly who received power here, whether Abraham or Sarah, are complicated both by textual and syntactic issues. However, the presence of the explicit third person pronoun seems difficult to fit with the reading of Abraham as subject, and outweighs the tendency for the meta-phor to refer to the male role in conception. For a full discussion, see Ellingworth, *Hebrews*, 586, and Erich Gräßer, *An die Hebräer*, vol. 2 (Zürich: Neukirchener Verlag, 1990), 131, 132. My point here is independent of which way one sees the issue falling out.

53. Note the concentration of power language in 11:33–35.

in the divine nature and proper to God, but is also a resource, a gift, which his people receive by faith, and through which they may themselves triumph.

However, this reception of power by the faithful also presupposes the depiction of humanity in Hebrews as themselves powerless, a feature particularly on display in 2:6–11. Here both language and concepts around weakness, enslavement, fear, and lack of power come to a particular head in Hebrews, in a way that is perhaps only matched in the discussion of the Levitical system in chapters 7–10. Though God's intention for humanity generally, as revealed in Psalm 8, is that they would reign over creation with an absolute dominion in which nothing was left "unsubjected" to them,[54] in this age this is "not what we now see" (2:8b).[55] Sin and the devil have rendered humanity weak, particularly via the reality of death, the signal example of the "unsubjected" that lords it over them.[56] Humanity's lot involves the devil wielding death's power over them,[57] rendering them servile and in fear throughout life. This blanket description of the enslaved nature of humans "through the whole of life"[58] clearly connotes an inability to escape or overrule such power for humanity as a whole.[59] It is only the possibility of ἱλασμός ("atoning sacrifice") that holds out hope to deal with the dominating power of sin, death, and the devil, a ἱλασμός that humans cannot provide. The Son's work answering and overcoming the power wielded by Satan over enslaved humanity positions his action in relation to power language, thus suggesting that the salvific language predicated of the Son, of releasing and destroying, is to be understood in terms of the exercise of divine power.[60] The previous mention of the Son as ἀρχηγός ("champion") only confirms this.[61]

---

54. οὐδὲν ἀφῆκεν αὐτῷ ἀνυπότακτον (2:8).

55. I here assume a mixed reading of the referent, seeing in the appeal to Ps 8 an explanation of the Son's coming to fulfill the destiny of human sons, as viceregents over creation. Thus, the immediate horizon of Ps 8 is the creation of humanity, a theological commentary on Gen 2, which becomes predictive of the necessary "being made lower" of the Son in incarnation in order to complete human destiny in the flesh. For a defense of this mixed reading, see David M. Moffitt, *Atonement and the Logic of Resurrection in the Epistle to the Hebrews*, NovTSup 141 (Leiden; Boston: Brill, 2011), 121–29, and also the discussion of Costley, *Creation and Christ*, 214–22, and Koester, *Hebrews*, 221, 222.

56. In other words, it is death as "unsubjected" to humanity which is the particular interest of what is "not now seen" (Lane, *Hebrews 1–8*, 61). See also I. Howard Marshall, "Soteriology in Hebrews," in *The Epistle to the Hebrews and Christian Theology*, ed. Richard Bauckham, Daniel R. Driver, Trevor A. Hart, and Nathan MacDonald (Grand Rapids: Eerdmans, 2009), 257.

57. Lane, *Hebrews 1–8*, 49, 50.

58. διὰ παντὸς τοῦ ζῆν (2:15).

59. Thus, "life" here becomes the sphere of human weakness in contrast to the Son's "life," which connotes his intrinsic saving power. See the comments later, especially on 7:16.

60. Attridge notes that the collocation of ἀρχηγός and ἀπαλλάσσω calls to mind the language of Exodus (*Hebrews*, 91–93).

61. Though certainly the predominant Septuagintal usage leans towards a chief or captain (Ceslas Spicq, *L'Épître aux Hébreux*, vol. 2 [Gabalda, 1953], 38, 39), the issues of power and rescue contextually would also favour a translation more like "champion." So Lane, *Hebrews 1–8*, 53, 56, 57.

Parallel to the description of the weakness of humanity in Hebrews is the weakness and inability of the Levitical system, in spite of its God-given legitimacy (8:9). The parallels of language are neither accidental nor merely formal, for the inadequacy of the law is tied inextricably to the human nature of the priests involved in its administration, not simply to God's provisional purposes in it. Thus, though the structure of the priesthood requires a like-for-like representation (5:1, 2),[62] a human standing in the place of humanity, this representative necessity is, at the same time, its very liability.[63] The weakness, which in part enables the priests, also at the same time disables them (5:2, 3).[64] The description of the Levitical system as "weak and ineffective" (7:18) and as unable to realise God's purposes – that is, perfection (7:11) – are at least in part rooted in the weakness of the priests themselves.[65] This outline of the failure of the priesthood in general in 7:11–19 is connected to the priests themselves in 7:20–28, rather than simply to issues of system. Just as death hamstrings human destiny in general, so in particular it "prevents"[66] the priests from continuing in ministry and thus prevents the realisation of its goal (7:11, 18, 19).[67] Their weakness subjects them to a fatal necessity (5:5; 9:27), and the consequent necessity of physical descent, required because of death, is the very point of contrast with the power language present in 7:16.[68] The potential for the law to realise God's plan is thus evacuated by humanity at every turn. It appoints human priests in their weakness (7:28) to try to deal with a weakness, death, to which they themselves are subject.[69]

A second element of critique of the Levitical ministry, which also pertains to inability, seems initially to diverge from this line of argument: that Levitical ministry is problematised not only via the nature of the priests but also via the offerings prescribed. Though the sacrificial system aims at forgiveness, the

---

62. Spicq rightly sees the stress on the necessary humanity of priests in 5:1–10 (*Hébreux*, 105).

63. Here, already weakness is forged as a connection between priest and people (Lane, *Hebrews 1–8*, 116) that will be more fully explored in Heb 7. Though 5:1–10 trades on Christ fitting the outline of priestly identity, his superiority is already hinted at (Ellingworth, *Hebrews*, 273).

64. Here it seems Spicq goes astray in assuming that weakness also applies to the Son because of the pattern of moving from the priestly outline in 5:1–5 to the shape of the Son's ministry as priest (Spicq, *Hébreux*, 104, 5). But though Hebrews is explicit that the Son can sympathise with the weak (4:15), the term "weakness" is never predicated of the Son and is in fact contrasted with his state of perfection (7:28).

65. Attridge, *Hebrews*, 140; Cockerill, *Hebrews*, 233–37.

66. διὰ τὸ θανάτῳ κωλύεσθαι παραμένειν (7:23).

,67. Note the several explicit uses of ἄνθρωποι for the priests in contexts in which substantive participles would have sufficed (7:8, 28) and the explicit connection in 7:28 of the priestly context with the language of weakness.

68. Note the balanced parallelism of οὐ κατὰ νόμον ἐντολῆς σαρκίνης ... ἀλλὰ κατὰ δύναμιν ζωῆς ἀκαταλύτου (7:16). On which see the following content.

69. Attridge, *Hebrews*, 144, 203; Ellingworth, *Hebrews*, 367; Gräßer, *Hebräer*, 45.

purification of the people, and the cleansing of the holy places (9:6–10), and though bloodshed is crucial to this process (9:22), the blood of the animals prescribed is "unable to perfect the conscience of the worshipper" (9:9; sim. 10:1) because the blood of such is "unable to remove sin" (10:4).[70] Thus, the frequentative shape of the Levitical ministry is itself a signal of its own inefficacy (10:1–3). What initially appears as a separate line of argument, however, turns on the relationship to the priests themselves. The offering of animal blood in the Levitical system relates to the offering of the blood of "another,"[71] which in turn is necessitated because the priests need to make offerings for themselves, that is, their own sins (5:3; 9:7).[72] The movement from the impossibility of atonement via animal blood (10:1–5) into the self-offering of Christ as both priest and victim (10:6ff.) thus highlights that the problem of the victim is equally an issue of human weakness. Human priests could not offer themselves because though "like us in every way" they were not "without sin" nor "separated from sinners."[73] Thus, the Levitical ministry unduly separated priest and victim in a way that demonstrated that the εἰκών had not yet come, but it also implicitly critiqued the sinful priests as unworthy victims. This ministry can neither offer fitting sacrifices objectively nor can it carry on the ongoing and necessary intercession which might correct the wayward and ignorant. In this way language of failure and weakness spans both humanity in general and the Levitical cult in particular, because the latter entails both the involvement and inabilities of the former.[74]

THE POWERS AND ABILITIES OF THE PRIESTLY SON

Against the background of the previous depiction of divine power, human inability, and Levitical weakness, the abilities of the Son in Hebrews are particularly

---

70. Note the repetition here of ability language: μὴ δυνάμεναι κατὰ συνείδησιν τελειῶσαι τὸν λατρεύοντα (9:9); οὐδέποτε δύναται τοὺς προσερχομένους τελειῶσαι (10:1); and ἀδύνατον γὰρ αἷμα ταύρων καὶ τράγων ἀφαιρεῖν ἁμαρτίας (10:4). Each significantly connects inability to key aims of perfection and forgiveness, which are central to the realisation of the new covenant and God's eschatological purposes in Hebrews.

71. ἐν αἵματι ἀλλοτρίῳ (9:25).

72. Thus, they cannot offer themselves as the required ἀμίαντος sacrifice (7:26).

73. Cf. 4:15; 5:1; 7:26. Separation here is frequently taken in a spatial direction. This may be an aspect of it, but if taken this way *in toto* it would represent a tautology with the phrase that follows "exalted to the heavens." The ascension element itself parallels and is dependent on the moral purity of Christ's separation from sin, pace Lane, *Hebrews 1–8*, 192, 93. Gräßer, *Hebräer*, 69 better integrates the sinlessness of Christ and spatial notes in his discussion.

74. Cockerill, *Hebrews*, 326.

striking. That he is human, and indeed participates in all that belongs to human-ity, makes him "like us in every way" (4:15). And yet not. For balancing all the inability of humanity broadly, and the Levitical system in particular, is the Son who acts decisively and with power. The Son nowhere in Hebrews seeks to, attempts to, or tries to save or atone. Nor does he merely make salvation possible. Rather, everywhere he is the one who rescues (2:15), helps (2:18), sanctifies (2:11; 10:10), perfects (10:14), saves, and intercedes (7:25), *simpliciter* and without qualification.[75]

This portrait of the powerful Son in Hebrews, like the OT portrait of God's power in general, spans both the creative and the redemptive spheres.[76] The positioning of the Son as agent of creation in 1:2, 3 is significant against the old covenant revelation of God's unique and supreme role in the same, and comprises two related parts. That the term "ages,"[77] rather than more standard terms for the world,[78] is used to describe what the Son created not only witnesses to his creating power, but also introduces a clearly temporal element to the Son's work. He has not merely created all reality but all of history, thus suggesting that the Son who made the "ages" will be key to the resolution of the purpose of the "ages" in history in the eschatological realisation of God's plans.[79] With regards to the second creational statement in 1:3, concerning his φέρων of all things, here the Son's ongoing work with respect to creation explicitly introduces the language of power. The meaning of this action is generally taken to depict the Son as providentially sustaining all things, taking φέρω as something like "bear" or "carry."[80] However, the semantic range of φέρω is wider than simply "bear," and in contexts which relate to the language of created elements the sense of "effecting," or "bringing about," all reality tends to be activated, a sense evident in extrabiblical usage.[81] Important in the move from 1:2 to 1:3 is the progression

---

75. The only point of question is whether the hearers will themselves "maintain their hold on [their] confidence and hopeful boasting" (3:6). But even here the realities of the new covenant and the effectiveness of Christ's sustaining priestly help provide reasons for confidence (6:9; 10:32–39).

76. Erich Gräßer, *An die Hebräer*, vol. 1 (Zürich: Neukirchener Verlag, 1990), 57.

77. τοὺς αἰῶνας 1:3.

78. E.g., Κόσμος, τὰ πάντα, οἰκουμένη, all of which are used in Hebrews elsewhere.

79. This need not be taken to mean that "ages" is exclusively eschatological pace K. R. Harriman, "'Through Whom He Made the Ages': A Salvation-Historical Interpretation of Heb 1:2c," *NovT* 61 (2019). For a more balanced handling, see Costley, *Creation and Christ*, 109–34.

80. On the exegetical possibilities here, see Koester, *Hebrews*, 181. It is common to simply see the bear-ing as a general act of sustaining creation, e.g., Jean Calvin, *Commentaries on the Epistle of Paul the Apostle to the Hebrews* (Edinburgh: Calvin Translation Society, 1853), 37, and frequently in the exegesis of 1:3 in the patristic period.

81. E.g., Philo, *Who Is the Heir?*, 36; *On the Change of Names*, 192, 256. Attridge's point that this would make the statement redundant in the face of 1:2c fails to note that the change of how the agency is construed differs and that "bring about" may include effecting of all God's purposes, which would be a wider state-ment than creation only (*Hebrews*, 45.)

from God's instrumental action through his Son to the positioning of the Son himself as the subject of "bringing about" created reality. Comparing this shift with the similar way in which the Son is taken to be the Lord of Psalm 102 who "in the beginning made the heavens and the earth," alongside the instrumental language of God as the one "through whom is all" in 2:10, demonstrates that Christ is no mere agent of God or even "chief agent."[82] He is no mere servant, but Son (1:1; 3:1–5). Indeed, the creation through the Son is, in essence, the creation of God through God's self (1:2; 2:10).[83] This language of creation brackets and, in part, explains the status of the Son as ἀπαύγασμα τῆς δόξης κτλ (1:3).[84] The Son's coming forth from the Father, and bearing the stamp of his substance, stands behind, and is illustrated in, the Son's creational power.[85] Further, the "bringing about of all things through the word of [the Son's] power" portrays him in a manner of speech that plays with the language of Wisdom but also moves beyond it.[86] That the Son himself has his own powerful word, by which he effects the divine purpose, suggests that his state and being as Son represents a reduplication of the divine nature rather than simply identifying the Son as mere instrument or hypostatised attribute.[87]

If the focus of the epistle seems straightforwardly salvific, however, we might well ask why the author focuses on the involvement of the Son in creation in the opening chapters. Part of the explanation is that this relation of the Son to creation clarifies that he is no mere eschatological agent of God. Though in the order of time the Son follows the prior divine speech and can be said to

---

82. Cf. Larry W. Hurtado, *One God, One Lord: Early Christian Devotion and Ancient Jewish* (London: T&T Clark, 1988).

83. Attridge, *Hebrews*, 82; Cockerill, *Hebrews*, 136.

84. On the grammatical ties here, see Costley, *Creation and Christ*, 94.

85. Aquinas comments on the power language of 1:3:

> But is it not also by the Father's power? It is also by His power, because the power of both is identical. He works, therefore, both by His own power and by the Father's power, because His power comes from the Father. Yet the Apostle does not say, 'by His power', but by his word of power, in order to show that just as the Father produced all things by the Word: "He spoke and they were made: He commanded and they were created" (Ps. 32:8), so the Son by the same Word that He is, made all things. By these words, therefore, the Apostle shows the strength of His power, because He has the same power as the Father: for the power by which the Father acts is the same as the power by which the Son acts. (Thomas Aquinas, *Commentary on the Letter of Saint Paul to the Hebrews*, Latin/English Edition of the Works of St Thomas Aquinas, trans. Fabian R. Larcher [Lander, WY: Aquinas Institute for the Study of Sacred Doctrine, 2012], 16)

86. The tendency to simply see Wisdom language as standing behind such statements (e.g., Attridge, *Hebrews*, 43) fails to reckon with the christological reworking involved. Christ was not merely identified as "Wisdom" unreconstructed, but rather prior Wisdom language was refracted through the revelation of Christ in the last days. See Koester, *Hebrews*, 188.

87. Pace Koester's identification of Jesus with the Word of God in 1:3 (*Hebrews*, 105) and sim. Gräßer, *Hebräer*, 59.

follow or fulfill it (1:3; 3:5b; 7:15), the protological portrayal of the Son clarifies that he is himself the exclusive locus of all divine action.[88] The acting of the Father in power, through the Son as power, extends through the whole work of God. In other words, the scope of the Son's work which spans both creation and redemption, both proton and eschaton, makes it clear that there is no acting of the Father without the acting of the Son.

This is further highlighted through the ways in which lines of continuity are drawn in the epistle between acts of creation and redemption. The way in which God saves through his Son is "fitting" for the God for and through whom all came into existence.[89] The glory of the Son in the construction of the redemptive house(hold) of God (3:3, 4) fits with the Son's worth in relation to the divine action of building all things. This development of the Son as the extensive and exclusive locus of the Father's actions thus sets the stage for the portrayal of the Son's priestly abilities in the letter, the inarguably dominant note. As the exclusive locus of divine action, he is the effector of God's plans.[90]

This reality is most fully explored at the level of priestly redemption in the epistle, and can be seen both in explicit lexis and at a conceptual level, especially in comparison to the inability of humanity and the Levitical system as detailed previously.

First, at the level of lexis, the redemptive abilities of the Son already appear in 2:18, where the Son is spoken of as "able to help those being tested" because of the suffering tests through which he has himself already passed.[91] This provision of needed help, given to sustain those undergoing tests, goes to the heart of the needs of the pastor's audience, whom he exhorts to persevere in the face

---

88. Commenting on 1:3, Harriman notes that the description of the Son portrays him as "the embodiment and executor of God's will and purpose ..." ("'Through Whom He Made the Ages'," 45). On issues of relating creation to eschatology, see the stimulating outline of proposals in Bartholomew, "Creation, Divine Action, and Hebrews," 151–64 in the present volume. Focusing on issues of exactly how this world (10:5) and the coming world (2:5) relate can become mired in difficulty, but the discussion might in part be helped by attending to the unity and continuities of action in and through God's self rather than focusing on the continuities or discontinuities of created order(s). In spite of all the differences outlined even within this world in God's work, the fundamental unity is found in God as Actor – "God, having spoken, ... has spoken." (1:1).

89. See the discussion on the relation between God and the Son's glory in 3:1–6 in Nick Brennan, *Divine Christology in the Epistle to the Hebrews: The Son as God*, LNTS 656 (London; New York: T&T Clark, 2021), 82–87. See also Costley's analysis of the interpenetration of creational and redemptive metaphors here (*Creation and Christ*, 239–60).

90. Hence language of causing or bringing into being is often predicated of the Son in Hebrews, e.g., the frequent ἀρχ- root lexemes (2:3, 10; 12:2), language around securing or initiating (9:12; 10:6, 20; and especially 10:9), and the following discussion of αἴτιος.

91. The concept of the Son as helper is closely parallel to the OT's stress on God as helper (Gen 49:25; Exod 15:2; Deut 33:26; 1 Sam 7:12), especially in the Psalter (Ps 20:2; 22:19; 27:9 et passim). This becomes even more stressed in the OG Psalter as many Hebrews metaphors for God (e.g., Rock, Fortress, Shield) are reified into the Greek language of "help." E.g., Ps 7:11; 9:9; 17:3.

of flagging faith.[92] In returning to the same concept, we find in 4:14–16 that the divine throne has become conditioned as a place of help for petitioners by the work and identity of the Son. Here the pastor returns to ability language, using litotes to stress that the Son "is not unable to sympathise with our weakness" (4:15).[93] In this way, the Son already flags his identity as positively and beneficially like "every priest" (5:1), yet without the liabilities inherent in the weaknesses of others.[94]

This line of initial argument around Christ's legitimate and efficient priestly identity and ministry culminates in 5:9, 10 in which the Son is termed the αἴτιος σωτηρίας αἰωνίου. This language of αἴτιος, I would argue, similarly inhabits the same semantic domain of power and ability as the more obvious lexemes. In English translations of Heb 5:9, αἴτιος is often translated as "source."[95] BDAG suggests a primary meaning of "cause/source," suggesting a certain ambiguity with respect to the semantic range.[96] However, when considering the range of meanings for αἴτιος in the Greek corpus, though the gloss "source" may be possible in certain examples,[97] "cause" is necessary in a much wider number of occurrences and can equally serve in verses in which "source" is possible.[98] Further, to see the semantic core of αἴτιος as "cause" better explains the extended uses of αἴτιος both outside and within the NT.[99] Without, the most common usage by far surrounds contexts in which one designated as αἴτιος is the one who has caused some harm, death, or evil to befall others and is thus "culpable" or "blameworthy," with the lexeme at times approaching a meaning similar to ὑπόδικος. By a common semantic process, that of extension, the three other occurrences of αἴτιος in the NT are easily handled: αἴτιος is the "grounds" or "evidence" for a charge of culpability in a legal situation. Thus, against many English translations of 5:9, the phrase αἴτιος σωτηρίας αἰωνίου ought to be seen

---

92. Gräßer, *Hebräer*, 248.

93. On the language of help tying 2:18 and 4:16 together, see Attridge, *Hebrews*, 96n197. Spicq recognises that 4:14–16 in essence responds to what might have been the hearers' natural reaction to the Son's session "tout puissant au ciel," to question "peut-il s'intéresser aux épreuves et aux misères de Chrétiens?" (*Hébreux*, 92).

94. Cf. 4:15 "without sin"; 5:2 "weakness." Cockerill sees the movement from 5:1–5 to Christ as a contrast of "effectiveness" (*Hebrews*, 231).

95. NIV, NRSV, NASB, ESV. KJV, on the other hand, has "Author."

96. BDAG s.v. αἴτιος.

97. E.g., Josephus, *Jewish Antiquities* 3.64, 4.4.

98. See, e.g., Aristotle, *Rhetoric* 2.6; Demosthenes, *On the Chersonese* 8.30; Herodotus, *Histories* 1.45; Josephus, *Jewish Antiquities* 1.211; 2:8, 198, 255; 4:99; Philo, *On Agriculture* 96; *On the Life of Abraham* 261; *On the Special Laws* 1.252. See, further, Attridge, *Hebrews*, 153n209; sim. "Auteur" (Spicq, *Hébreux*, 109). Gräßer translates as "Urheber... Ursächer" and notes the similar expression to Heb 5:9 in OG Isa 45:17 Ισραηλ σῴζεται ὑπὸ κυρίου σωτηρίαν αἰώνιον· (*Hebräer*, 310). Pace Cockerill, who supports "source" arguing that it better captures the ongoing role of the Son as Saviour (*Hebrews*, 249).

99. E.g., Luke 23:4, 14; 23:22.

as designating the Son as the "cause" or "author" of the eternal salvation that comes to his followers. This is a striking locution, considering the way in which the Father is clearly the initiator of salvation in the epistle, leading the many sons to glory (2:10) via his designation and perfection of the Son as Melchizedekian priest (5:10), the vocation of which is both clearly from God (5:4, 5) and relates to the enactment of his salvific plan (10:7, 10). That the Son is then described as the "cause" of salvation, even alongside the primacy of the Father in the taxis of Father and Son, suggests that the Father's primacy does not relegate the Son to a mere agent in the economy but preserves the Son's equal responsibility for divine salvation with the Father.

Second, though certain lexemes are significant, it is really the wider conceptual world of ability and inability that stresses the power and ability of the Son in Hebrews. This is frequently encoded in acts of syncrisis, in which the pastor moves from the inefficacy, or typological nature, of the Levitical offerings to the eschatological and efficacious action of the Son. The former itself raises the language of power and ability, but it always does so in order to deny that it can be found within human agency or the Levitical system. By such contrasts, the stress on Christ's singular and effective achievement, even where it lacks explicit language of power and ability, still connotes issues of power because of its comparison to the inability and weakness of other alternatives.

The heart of this syncrisis of "powers" is particularly felt through Hebrews 7–10. Here the pastor repeatedly moves from the inadequacies of the Old to the efficacy of the New. So, in 7:18 we are told that the former commandment, instituting the Levites, has been set aside because it is "weak and useless." In its place a better hope has been introduced, through which access to God has been made possible. This better hope is one that Jesus himself has both inaugurated and guaranteed, he thus securing what the Levitical priests could not. Contextually 7:18, 19 raise this contrast through the use of two important other lexemes: the language of "better"-ness and "perfection." The former is what is associated with the New explicitly.[100] But the fact that the latter was not realised through the law's commands, tied to the statement earlier in 7:11, makes it clear that perfection is indeed what Christ achieves in the New.[101] Thus, the key terms of "better"-ness and "perfection," both of which portray the goal of God's realised purposes, are clearly enacted in and through the Son, and are done so in contrast to the powerlessness of the preceding types and shadows, consequently stressing

---

100. The language of what is "better" is introduced in 1:4 and 6:9, and by 7:7 begins to be decisively connected to the "better hope" and thus "better covenant" realised by the Son (7:22; 8:6; 9:23).

101. Further, the language of perfection is the antithesis of the weakness of the Levitical system, so Cockerill, *Hebrews*, 325.

the powerful nature of the Son's work in realising them.[102] That this concept of power is at play is clarified immediately following in 7:16. Here the two orders, the Levitical and Melchizedekian, are contrasted in a carefully balanced pair of noun phrases which syntactically match.[103] Whilst the former priesthood is implicitly portrayed as coming about "according to the law of fleshly command," the Melchizedekian priest inhabits his ministry "according to the power of an indestructible life."[104] Here the syncrisis follows the opposite pattern to those which precede. Power language this time is explicitly associated with the basis and ground of the Son's priestly office, in connection to his indestructible life. This explicit use of power language, positively predicated of the Son, thus paints the old order of law, flesh and command, as one implicitly powerless, dead, and perishable.[105] The language of destruction, which is negated with regards to the Son, calls to mind how death destroyed the ministry of the Levitical priests, thus necessitating a fleshly law of bodily succession. Thus the Son's ministry, founded in indestructible life, clarifies not only that this divine life carried him through death,[106] unable to be destroyed by it, but also that the power of this life is the basis for its operative efficacy.[107]

These same patterns, of power language featuring on one side of the syncrisis, by implication raising questions of power and powerlessness in the other side of the comparison, continue into chapters 8–10. The gifts and sacrifices of the Levitical arrangement "could not perfect the conscience of the worshipper" (9:9), thus granting them access into the presence of God. But, in contrast, Christ has "entered once for all into the holy places, . . . by means of his own blood, thus securing an eternal redemption" (9:12), securing with it the cleansing that the former order lacked. This former order "was never able to perfect those who approach," for it was "impossible" for the blood it offered to remove sins (10:1, 4). This goal, however, of perfection, interpreted in chapters 8 and 9 as both cleansing and forgiveness, was exactly what the self-offering of the Son

102. On the better quality of the new covenant connoting efficacy, see Lane, *Hebrews 1–8*, 186, 188.

103. Gräßer, *Hebräer*, 44. Though Spicq applies the concept mainly in reading 7:24–28, his contrast of the Levitical priest as "hommes faibles et pécheurs" to Christ as "Prêtre saint et tout puissant" matches much of the section (*Hébreux*, 126.)

104. 7:16; on the connotations of σάρκινος here, see Attridge, *Hebrews*, 202.

105. "In contrast to νόμος . . . δύναμις . . . connotes effectiveness" (Lane, *Hebrews 1–8*, 184).

106. On the sustaining nature of the divine life of the Son, see the comments of Spicq, *Hébreux*, 193.

107. Michael Kibbe, "'You Are a Priest Forever!' Jesus' Indestructible Life in Hebrews 7:16," *HBT* 39 (2017); Cockerill, *Hebrews*, 323, 324. Pace Moffitt, *Atonement*, 208. I failed to recognise properly in my previous discussion (Chapter 4 of Brennan, *Divine Christology*) that the very language of ἀκατάλυτος raises the horizon of death as destruction, suggesting that this life of the Son is not destroyable by death. Considering that this horizon of death can only come once (9:27), the language of indestructability thus clarifies that the Son's life cannot be simply identified with *post mortem* existence.

in human form achieved, bringing about the θέλημα of God in the sanctification and forgiveness of the people (10:10–18).

The inaugurating and establishing of the priestly ministry of the Son in power further conditions the ongoing exercise of it in the epistle.[108] He sits at God's right hand, characterising the accomplishment of objective redemption but also signalling an ongoing place of power at God's side. This place to which he has come is equally the fulfilment of the viceregency of humanity, such that he has now been "crowned with glory and honour."[109] This seat at the right hand of God is also the session in the heavenly holy of holies, the antitype of a place typologically marked not only by the language of glory but also of divine miraculous power: the tablets, the manna, and the budding staff of Aaron (9:4).[110] It represents his location not only at the seat of heavenly royal power,[111] but equally conditions this place of power as a place of resource for the people in Hebrews. Just as Israel responded to Yhwh as powerful redeemer via approach to him for the sake of help, now the divine throne is conditioned by the presence of the Son on it. His abiding presence in ongoing intercessory ministry means that he is able to save completely through his abiding intercession because he remains forever in this position.[112] The power of the Son's indestructible life, which sustained him through death, enables his eternal intercession *post mortem* in a resurrected state. This language of power in regards to place, and the means by which this eternal location at God's right hand came about, thus results in the conditioning of the divine throne as a place of help. The weakness of the people of God is not so much removed as overcome by the divine provision of a powerful Son who is able and can be approached for help (2:18; 4:15, 16; 10:19–23).[113] Thus, the language of ability, as noted before, is several times raised in connection to the help that the pastor's audience will find by approaching the Son in heaven.[114]

---

108. This, in part, can be seen from the causal nature of the participle in 7:25 ("since he always lives to intercede..."). So Ellingworth, *Hebrews*, 392.

109. 2:9.

110. For a discussion of the significance of the details of the tabernacle description in 9:1–5, see Georg Gäbel, "'You Don't Have Permission to Access This Site': The Tabernacle Description in Hebrews 9:1–5 and Its Function in Context," in *Son, Sacrifice, and Great Shepherd: Studies on the Epistle to the Hebrews*, ed. David M. Moffitt and Eric F. Mason, WUNT 2/510 (Tübingen: Mohr Siebeck, 2020), 135–74. Though there are certainly priestly elements involved here, and the privileges of Israel's past, divine miraculous powers seem to tie these three objects together, deposited in the *sanctum sanctorum*.

111. Koester, *Hebrews*, 104.

112. Cf. 4:16; 7:25; 10:19–22.

113. Cockerill, *Hebrews*, 610; Attridge rightly notes that the concept of intercession in the epistle primarily has "assistance...in view" (*Hebrews*, 212).

114. Though I have not stressed it here, it is as divine, incarnate and suffering Son that he has become source of help to his people. To be in the flesh is essential to the Son's helping ministry, but it is not a sufficient cause, for all other humans have been in the flesh. Rather, it is from him *as Son in the flesh* that divine

In this way, new covenant realities involve the Son's power, not only in the objective realisation of God's eschatological plan to save the people but also equally in the provision of divine resources, in and through the Son, which enable the audience to heed the warnings not to be conformed to the "unable" wilderness generation.[115] Through the Son they are empowered to be like the faithful of chapter 11, who were enabled by divine power to obtain the promises (11:11, 19, 33–35). Thus the Son is not only author, but perfector of the faith (12:2)[116] as one who has traversed the road of persecution, suffering, and prospective hope. He now enables the audience to walk that path after him as they "look to Jesus" (12:1, 2).

CONCLUSION

Though patristic debate on the relation of God's own power to the Son, and Gregory of Nyssa's precise articulation of the relation of the divine nature to the divine works via it, tend only to interact with Heb 1:3, their developed tendency to speak of the Son as, or possessing, the very power of God, and thus of the Son as integrally related to all of God's action in history, coheres well with the thought of the epistle in its breadth. The Son in Hebrews is portrayed as the exclusive locus of that power effecting the divine will in history from beginning to end. The explicit language of power and ability in Hebrews encodes part of this picture, but it ranges much more widely attaching to both creation and redemption, especially via the contrast of the weakness of humanity and the Levitical ministry with the effective finality of the Son's objective atonement and the ongoing efficacy of his priestly intercession. By stressing the unique power of the Son in whom the Father does all his works, the pastor christologically grounds the frequent appeals to look to and approach the Son (3:1; 4:16; 10:19–23; 12:1–3),[117] finding in him not only objective divine realities realised but also the power to persevere through their participation in the Son himself, who is "able to help" the weak (2:18; 4:16).

---

resources flow to his people. For further elaboration on this, see the helpful comments of Cockerill in the present volume. On the relation of suffering, and thus of enfleshment, to help, see Spicq's comments on the function of the ἐν ᾧ phrase in 2:18 (*Hébreux*, 49).

115. 3:19.

116. Christopher A. Richardson, *Pioneer and Perfecter of Faith: Jesus' Faith as the Climax of Israel's History in the Epistle to the Hebrews*, WUNT 2/338 (Tübingen: Mohr Siebeck, 2012), 99–101.

117. Cf. 4 Macc 17:10, in which certain pious martyrs are described as having "vindicated their nation, looking to God . . ." (Cockerill, *Hebrews*, 605.)

SELECT BIBLIOGRAPHY

Adams, Edward. *The Stars Will Fall from Heaven: Cosmic Catastrophe in the New Testament and Its World*. LNTS 347 347. London; New York: T&T Clark, 2007.

Allen, Michael. "Systematic Theology and Biblical Theology – Part One." *JRT* 14, no. 1–2 (2020): 52–72.

———. "Systematic Theology and Biblical Theology – Part Two." *JRT* 14, no. 4 (2020): 344–57.

Anatolios, Khaled. *Retrieving Nicaea: The Development and Meaning of Trinitarian Doctrine*. Grand Rapids: Baker Academic, 2011.

Aquinas, Thomas. *Commentary on the Letter of Saint Paul to the Hebrews*. Translated by Fabian R. Larcher. Latin/English Edition of the Works of St Thomas Aquinas Vol. 41. Lander, WY: Aquinas Institute for the Study of Sacred Doctrine, 2012.

Attridge, Harold W. *The Epistle to the Hebrews: A Commentary on the Epistle to the Hebrews*. Hermeneia. Philadelphia: Fortress Press, 1989.

Ayres, Lewis. *Nicaea and Its Legacy: An Approach to Fourth-Century Trinitarian Theology*. Oxford: OUP, 2004.

Barnes, Michel R. *The Power of God: Dunamis in Gregory of Nyssa's Trinitarian Theology*. Washington, D.C.: CUA Press, 2001.

Bartholomew, Craig G., and Michael W. Goheen. "Story and Biblical Theology." In *Out of Egypt: Biblical Theology and Biblical Interpretation*, edited by Craig G. Bartholomew, Mary Healy, Karl Moller, and Robin Parry, 144–71. Milton Keynes, UK: Paternoster Press, 2004.

Bauckham, Richard. *Jesus and the God of Israel: God Crucified and Other Studies on the New Testament's Christology of Divine Identity*. Grand Rapids: Eerdmans, 2009.

———. "Monotheism and Christology in Hebrews 1." In *Early Jewish and Christian Monotheism*, edited by Loren T. Stuckenbruck and Wendy E. S. North, 167–85. London; New York: T&T Clark, 2004.

Behr, John. *The Way to Nicaea*. Vol. 1 of *The Formation of Christian Theology*. Crestwood, NY: St. Vladimir's Seminary Press, 2001.

Brennan, Nick. *Divine Christology in the Epistle to the Hebrews: The Son as God*. LNTS 656. London; New York: T&T Clark, 2021.

Brueggemann, Walter. *An Introduction to the Old Testament: The Canon and Christian Imagination*. Louisville, KY: Westminster John Knox Press, 2003.

Büchsel, D. Friedrich. *Die Christologie des Hebräerbriefs*. Gütersloh: C. Berterlsmann, 1922.

Bunta, Silviu N. "The Convergence of Adamic and Merkabah Traditions in the Christology of Hebrews." In *Searching the Scriptures: Studies in Context and*

Intertextuality, edited by Craig A. Evans and Jeremiah J. Johnston, 277–96. London; New York: Bloomsbury, 2015.

Calvin, Jean. *Commentaries on the Epistle of Paul the Apostle to the Hebrews*. Edinburgh: CTS, 1853.

Cockerill, Gareth Lee. *The Epistle to the Hebrews*. NICNT. Grand Rapids: Eerdmans, 2012.

Costley, Angela. *Creation and Christ: An Exploration of the Topic of Creation in the Epistle to the Hebrews*. WUNT 2/527. Tübingen: Mohr Siebeck, 2021.

Cullmann, Oscar. *The Christology of the New Testament*. Philadelphia, PA: Westminster Press, 1959.

Duby, Steven J. *God in Himself: Scripture, Metaphysics, and the Task of Christian Theology*. London: Apollos, 2019.

Ellingworth, Paul. *The Epistle to the Hebrews: A Commentary on the Greek Text*. NIGTC. Grand Rapids: Eerdmans, 1993.

Estelle, Bryan D. *Echoes of Exodus: Tracing a Biblical Motif*. Downers Grove: IVP Press, 2018.

Gäbel, Georg. "'You Don't Have Permission to Access This Site': The Tabernacle Description in Hebrews 9:1–5 and Its Function in Context." In *Son, Sacrifice, and Great Shepherd: Studies on the Epistle to the Hebrews*, edited by David M. Moffitt and Eric F. Mason, 135–74. Tübingen: Mohr Siebeck, 2020.

Gillingham, Susan E. "The Reception of the Exodus Tradition in the Psalter." In *The Reception of Exodus Motifs in Jewish and Christian Literature: "Let My People Go!"*, edited by Beate Kowalski and Susan E. Docherty, 36–55. Leiden; Boston: Brill, 2021.

Gräßer, Erich. *An die Hebräer*. Vol. 1. Zürich: Neukirchener Verlag, 1990.

———. *An die Hebräer*. Vol. 2. Zürich: Neukirchener Verlag, 1990.

Greer, Rowan A. "The Jesus of Hebrews and the Christ of Chalcedon." In *Reading the Epistle to the Hebrews: A Resource for Students*, edited by Eric Farrel Mason and Kevin B. McCruden, 231–50. Society of Biblical Literature: Resources for Biblical Study 66. Atlanta: SBL Press, 2011.

Harriman, K. R. "'Through Whom He Made the Ages': A Salvation-Historical Interpretation of Heb 1:2c." *NovT* 61 (2019): 432–39.

Holt, Robby, and Aubrey Spears. "The Ecclesia as Primary Context for the Reception of the Bible." In *A Manifesto for Theological Interpretation*, edited by Craig G. Bartholomew and Heath A. Thomas, 72–93. Grand Rapids: Baker Academic, 2016.

Hughes, Philip Edgcumbe. *A Commentary on the Epistle to the Hebrews*. Grand Rapids: Eerdmans, 1977.

Hurtado, Larry W. *One God, One Lord: Early Christian Devotion and Ancient Jewish Monotheism*. London: T&T Clark, 1988.

Johnson, Luke Timothy. *Hebrews: A Commentary*. NTL. Louisville, KY: Westminster John Knox Press, 2006.

Kibbe, Michael. "'You Are a Priest Forever!' Jesus' Indestructible Life in Hebrews 7:16." *HBT* 39, no. 2 (2017): 134–55.

Knox, John. *The Humanity and Divinity of Christ: A Study of Pattern in Christology*. Cambridge: CUP, 1967.

Koester, Craig R. *Hebrews: A New Translation with Introduction and Commentary*. AB 36. New York: Doubleday, 2001.

Lane, William L. *Hebrews 1–8*. WBC 47a. Nashville: Thomas Nelson, 1991.

Levering, Matthew. "God and Greek Philosophy in Contemporary Biblical Scholarship." *JTI* 4 (2010): 169–85.

Marshall, I. Howard. "Soteriology in Hebrews." In *The Epistle to the Hebrews and Christian Theology*, edited by Richard Bauckham, Daniel Driver, and Trevor Hart, 252–77. Grand Rapids: Eerdmans, 2009.

Moffitt, David M. *Atonement and the Logic of Resurrection in the Epistle to the Hebrews*. NovTSup 141. Leiden; Boston: Brill, 2011.

Murphy, Francesca Aran. *God Is Not a Story: Realism Revisited*. Oxford; New York: OUP, 2007.

Richardson, Christopher A. *Pioneer and Perfecter of Faith: Jesus' Faith as the Climax of Israel's History in the Epistle to the Hebrews*. WUNT 2/338. Tübingen: Mohr Siebeck, 2012.

Seifrid, Mark A. "The Narrative of Scripture and Justification by Faith." *CTQ* 72 (2008): 19–44.

Sonderegger, Katherine. *Systematic Theology*. Vol. 2. Minneapolis: Fortress Press, 2020.

Spicq, Ceslas. *L'Épître aux Hébreux*. Vol. 2. Paris: Gabalda, 1953.

Stroup, George W. *The Promise of Narrative Theology: Recovering the Gospel in the Church*. Atlanta: John Knox Press, 1981.

Vidu, Adonis. *The Same God Who Works All Things: Inseparable Operations in Trinitarian Theology*. Grand Rapids: Eerdmans, 2021.

Vos, Geerhardus. *Redemptive History and Biblical Interpretation: The Shorter Writings of Geerhardus Vos*. Edited by Richard B. Gaffin Jr. Phillipsburg, NJ: P&R, 2001.

Webster, John. "Theologies of Retrieval." In *The Oxford Handbook of Systematic Theology*, edited by John Webster, Kathryn Tanner, and Iain R. Torrance, 583–99. Oxford: OUP, 2009.

Wright, N. T. *The New Testament and the People of God*. Vol. 1 of *Christian Origins and the Question of God*. Minneapolis: Fortress Press, 1992.

CHAPTER 5

True Knowledge as Perception of and Referral to Divine Action

Reading Hebrews in an Eastern Orthodox Epistemological Idiom

Scott Leveille

INTRODUCTION

I met William Abraham only once, at an academic conference in New York hosted by Orthodox theologians. I was in my first year of PhD studies in Toronto and was among the usual collection of student attendees at this sort of conference, both eager to make a good impression in the guild and feeling my share of imposter syndrome. As I made my way into the auditorium, a bearded man I did not recognise (but not unreminiscent of Santa Claus) seemed to sense my reticence. He smiled in my direction, waved me over to the empty seat next to him, and introduced himself: "Hi, I'm Billy." He disarmingly joked about the stuffiness and self-importance academic conferences engender. Throughout the afternoon he asked me generous questions, taking a genuine interest in my research. At a reception that evening he greeted me as a friend, introduced me to many of the conference speakers, and included me in conversations as if I belonged. And, of course, the paper he presented was characteristically insightful, challenging, and memorable.

I begin with this account, not only to honor the memory of the man to whom this book is dedicated, but to illustrate the epistemological tradition I wish to explore in the following essay. That is, true knowledge involves the ability to perceive the triune God's activity in creation and redemption, and to refer oneself along with all of reality to those divine actions. This perception and referral are rooted in a way of being, knowing, and loving, which conforms to the constraining forms of created existence revealed in God's Word and realised through the Holy Spirit. In a small but meaningful way, William Abraham embodied such a mode of knowledge in his brief interactions with me. Billy perceived what a young scholar such as myself needed in a particular time and place, related his perception of me to his understanding of God's activity, and responded to me in a way which sought to correspond to God's action. By all accounts this was quite natural to Billy, as he had cultivated a way of being and knowing throughout his life which conformed to the God he loved.

One of the fruits borne from Western interactions with Eastern Orthodox theology over the last century (which William Abraham enthusiastically participated in) is a heightened awareness of a particular connection between knowledge and divine action. While the theological epistemological tradition we will be considering in this essay is not exclusively Eastern (I am not suggesting opposition between East and West here), an Eastern stream is identifiable. We will begin by tracing in broad strokes the development of this epistemology through Eastern channels from the Greek Fathers through the Philokalian tradition. We will then turn to Hebrews, suggesting some ways this epistemology may help illuminate Christology, OT figures, and faith in the epistle.

One disclaimer before we begin: My theological commitments lie within the Reformed tradition. My interest in Orthodox epistemology comes by way of research into Vladimir Lossky's apophatic theology in relation to his theological anthropology, as well as time spent with Orthodox friends and colleagues. As such, I am approaching this Eastern stream as an outsider who has merely dipped his toe into rather deep waters. Therefore, we will be indebted along the way to more experienced guides including Khaled Anatolios and Andrew Louth, with Rowan Williams's insightful commentary.

TRACING THE TRADITION

TRINITARIAN THEOLOGY AS THE GROUND OF CHRISTIAN PROCLAMATION, LIFE, AND WORSHIP

Jesus is Lord! From its inception the church's theological reflection has (and does) centred on this fundamental apostolic proclamation which Scripture bore witness to. The crucified, risen, and ascended Jesus – a Jewish man who lived in first-century Palestine – is the Lord, the God of Israel. Whatever Jesus said and did was a divine action; God said and did those things. This not only includes the miraculous, but also those things seemingly unattributable to the divine – from the mundane elements of embodied life to suffering and death. Yet this Lord Jesus called God his Father, living out a filial relationship to God in human existence. And Jesus enables his followers to call God our Father as well. Moreover, consistent with the OT, Jesus's life and teaching revealed the Holy Spirit to be a distinct divine identity, the initiator of Jesus's followers' shared filial life with the Father and the divine presence inhabiting the church at Pentecost.

Jesus is Lord! The book of Hebrews offers a microcosm of the scriptural breadth of meaning and mystery in this phrase. The word "Lord" (*kyrios*) is used sixteen times throughout the book: sometimes referring directly to the man Jesus and sometimes referring explicitly to YHWH through OT quotations, while at other times the distinct referent is more ambiguous. But this variegation and ambiguity is intentional: while the referents may be distinguishable from one another, they are all in some sense the same. Moreover, Hebrews refers to the Holy Spirit as a divine actor in his own right. A high Christology and the fundamental unity and diversity within the Godhead are on full display throughout Hebrews.

While attesting to the Trinity, Scripture does not explicate the unity and diversity of the Triune God with the sort of conceptual precision we may desire or demand. The writers of the NT did not seem interested in explaining in a philosophically and logically satisfying way *how* it is that God is Triune; they simply described and affirmed that the Father, Son, and Holy Spirit are *who* God is. The early church did not regard the Trinity as an intellectual problem to be solved, but as the God whom they worshipped. Moreover, given the cosmic implications for Jesus's lordship revealed throughout the NT, faith in the triune God lies at the heart of a distinctly Christian interpretation of the universe. Anatolios explains that "orthodox trinitarian doctrine emerged as a kind of meta-doctrine that involved a global interpretation of Christian life and faith and indeed evoked a global interpretation of reality."[1]

Almost immediately after the church began proclaiming that Jesus is Lord, people began attempting to explain the seemingly antinomic notion that the man Jesus is God, yet he called God his Father. These explanations tended

---

1. Khaled Anatolios, *Retrieving Nicaea: The Development and Meaning of Trinitarian Doctrine* (Grand Rapids: Baker Academic, 2011), 8.

towards heterodoxy and heresy, since they were rooted in assumptions consistent with existing philosophical and religious systems of thought within the Greco-Roman world. In response to these early heresies, the church began formally to articulate what can and cannot be properly said about the Father, Son, and Holy Spirit based on God's self-revelation in Jesus Christ through the Spirit as borne witness by Scripture and experienced in the life of the church. Over time these articulations grew in conceptual clarity, often borrowing from and transforming Greek philosophical categories of thought to clarify Christian dogma (with varying degrees of success).

Now, our purpose here is not to offer a detailed account of the development of Trinitarian dogma. But I wish to emphasise two points. First, it is important to note that what was at stake during the Trinitarian debates of the first four centuries is nothing less than the church's fundamental proclamation and attendant life, worship, and piety. Indeed, it must be noted that those who espoused what became recognised as heresies did so in genuine attempts to preserve their understanding of the gospel and Christian life.[2] Second, the orthodox response to heretical and heterodox positions consciously eschewed a comprehensive conceptual grasp of the Trinity. While the pro-Nicene Fathers[3] believed we can and should make positive statements which accurately reflect the triune God, they maintained the fundamental mystery of God's divine essence.[4] These two points are foundational to pro-Nicene epistemology. Anatolios summarises:

> According to the terms of this epistemology, trinitarian doctrine does not allow us to encompass the being of God within the confines of human knowing, but it does regulate our being and knowing so as to enable us to successfully relate ourselves to God, who is really Trinity. . . . Thus, appropriating the meaning of trinitarian doctrine involves learning to think, live, and pray so as to refer to God's being as Trinity while at the same time learning to disavow a comprehensive epistemic hold on the God to whom we thus refer ourselves.[5]

---

2. See, for instance, Lewis Ayres's discussion of Arius in *Nicaea and Its Legacy: An Approach to Fourth-Century Trinitarian Theology* (Oxford: OUP, 2004), 56. Also see Anatolios, *Retrieving Nicaea*, 31; 36–38.

3. I am using this term as defined by Lewis Ayres to include "theologies recognized as orthodox by the Council of Constantinople and by subsequent imperial decrees," along with "the theologians who seem to be the direct precursors of that later orthodoxy . . ." See Ayres, *Nicaea and Its Legacy*, 239.

4. Again, many of the figures who espoused heretical and heterodox positions would have maintained the fundamental mystery of God's being. However, the pro-Nicene Fathers often attacked their opponents precisely on the grounds that they were overstating what could be said about God. See, for example, Richard Paul Vaggione's discussion in *Eunomius of Cyzicus and the Nicene Revolution* (New York: OUP, 2000), 251–57.

5. Anatolios, *Retrieving Nicaea*, 9.

As the Eastern epistemological tradition developed, it maintained this twofold commitment that God cannot be cognitively grasped yet Trinitarian doctrine does involve a way of "being and knowing" through which we may "successfully relate ourselves" to the triune God.

GOD IN MOTION: KNOWLEDGE AND DIVINE ACTION

A crucial development during the Nicene controversies involved the relationship between the divine essence and divine action. Arius had attempted to maintain a real distinction between God and creation by contending that there could not be a unity of substance or essence in the Trinity. The Father, as Unbegotten or Uncreated (*agen[n]ētos*), alone is God, while the Son was a unique creation of the Father, through whom everything else was made.[6] Eunomius further developed Arius's thought, radically asserting that the term "Unbegotten" precisely explicates the divine essence, what God is.[7] This explicitly excludes the Son, who is the "only begotten" (*monogenēs*), from sharing the divine essence. Crucially, for Eunomius action is incompatible with divine simplicity, impassibility, and eternality. Anything that God does, then – and willing is the only action proper to God – is not directly related to God's essence. As John Behr explains, "This means, finally, that the essence of God itself is both non-productive and unrelated to the willed activity of God: what he does is not related to, or derived from, what he is."[8]

The pro-Nicene Fathers attacked the Eunomian position, arguing that the divine essence is fundamentally active as evidenced by the Trinitarian relations which constitute the Godhead. Athanasius had already made this point, explaining that scriptural imagery used to describe the Son such as word, radiance of light, water from a fountain, etc., reveals a divine essence "conceived as a dynamic outgoing movement."[9] Thus, he derides the monad of the Arians: "What is to be said but that, in maintaining 'Once the Son was not,' they rob God of His Word, like plunderers, and openly predicate of Him that He was once without His proper Word and Wisdom, and that the Light was

---

6. See Arius's "The Confession of the Arians," trans. Edward Hardy, in *Christology of the Later Fathers*, ed. Edward Hardy (Louisville, KY: Westminster John Knox Press, 2006), 332–34.

7. "The 'Unbegotten' is based neither on invention nor on privation and is not applied to a part of him only (for he is without parts), and does not exist within him as something separate (for he is simple and uncompounded), and there is not something different alongside him (for he is one and only he is unbegotten), then the Unbegotten must be unbegotten essence" (Eunomius of Cyzicus, *Liber Apologeticus*, 8, in *Eunomius: The Extant Works*, text and trans. Richard Paul Vaggione [New York: OUP, 1987], 43).

8. John Behr, *The Nicene Faith, Part Two: One of the Holy Trinity* (Crestwood, NY: St Vladimir's Seminary Press, 2004), 280.

9. Anatolios, *Retrieving Nicaea*, 114.

once without radiance, and the Fountain was once barren and dry?"[10] Gregory of Nazianzus also affirmed action in the divine essence, describing Christian monotheism as "equality of nature, harmony of will, identity of action (*kinēsis*), and the convergence towards their source of what springs from unity."[11]

Gregory of Nyssa followed the other pro-Nicenes in what Anatolios calls his "kinetic conception of God."[12] Nyssa helpfully refuted the notion that divine activity would violate divine impassibility. To the contrary, if God withheld his honor and glory from his Son, then God would be jealously holding back for selfish reasons – the very definition of passibility![13] This approach to impassibility will be important for later developments regarding *apetheia* in relation to human ways of knowing.

Not only did the pro-Nicene Fathers assert activity in the divine essence, but in contrast to Eunomius they argued that the divine essence is unknowable in and of itself; it certainly cannot be cognitively grasped by a single name. Instead, it is precisely through divine action by which we have access to the knowledge of God: "We perceive, then, the varied operations (*energeiai*) of the transcendent power (*dynamis*), and fit our way of speaking of him to each of the operations known to us."[14] Anatolios explains that in Nyssa's epistemology "God is not some inert object that can be passively spied on and encompassed by a creaturely knowing but an active subject who can only be encountered in relation to his own self-presencing. . . . Ultimately, the only immanence of God to which we have access is God's self-economised immanence."[15]

Moreover, in Nyssa's notion of *epektasis*, God's self-economised immanence is inseparable from the Christian's participation in the divine economy of redemption, mediated in the church. As noted earlier, the whole point of Trinitarian dogma is to "successfully relate ourselves" to the Triune God. The implications for divine action as the source of knowledge of God involve just that. Anatolios summarises, "As God's trinitarian being is perfect interrelated

---

10. Athanasius, *Against the Arians*, I.14, trans. Henry Newman (*NPNF* 4/14:314).

11. Gregory of Nazianzus, *Theological Orations*, 29.2, trans. Lionel Wickham, in *On God and Christ: the Five Theological Orations and Two Letters to Cledonius*, ed. Lionel Wickham (Crestwood, NY: St Vladimir's Seminary Press, 2002), 70.

12. Anatolios, *Retrieving Nicaea*, 78, 239.

13. "Or does [Eunomius] tell us that the principle of perfection was never intended to apply to the one who comes from him, precisely so that the honor and glory of the one honored for his supremacy be not diminished? But who is so mean minded that he will not acquit even the divine and blessed nature of any imputation of feelings of envy?" (Gregory of Nyssa, *Contra Eunomium* I.418, trans. Stuart George Hall, in *Gregory of Nyssa: Contra Eunomium I, an English Translation with Supporting Studies*, ed. Miguel Brugarolas [Boston: Brill, 2018], 147).

14. Gregory of Nyssa, *Ad Ablabium*, trans. Cyril Richardson, in *Christology of the Later Church Fathers*, ed. Edward Hardy (Philadelphia: Westminster Press, 2006), 260.

15. Anatolios, *Retrieving Nicaea*, 230.

activity, human being consists in relating itself to the activity of divine being through its own unceasing active participation. Human existence is composed of acting into and out of inner-trinitarian activity."[16]

EVAGRIUS: DIVINE ACTION AND ANGELIC THOUGHT

Thus far, we have seen the roots of an epistemological tradition in which God cannot be cognitively grasped but can be known through his triune actions in the divine economy. This knowing involves active participation in God's triune activity as one relates oneself to those actions. As we move into the diverse landscape of the *Philokalia*, we will focus on how this epistemology develops to encompass not only the knowledge of God but knowledge of all things.

In *On Thoughts*, Evagrius Pontus identifies three categories of thoughts – three ways of knowing. The first is angelic, where "thoughts thoroughly investigate the natures of things and trace out their spiritual reasons."[17] What does he mean by "spiritual reasons"? He uses the example of gold. Angelic thoughts ask why gold is lodged in the earth, then investigates how it is mined and refined, then traces its use in the golden vessels for the tabernacle. Finally, angelic thought understands that "By the grace of Our Savior, the King of Babylon no longer drinks from those vessels, but Cleopas bears a heart burning with these mysteries."[18] Here Evagrius is alluding to Luke 24:32, where Jesus interprets the OT in reference to himself. Angelic thought sees how something like gold has ultimate meaning as a sign in relation to the divine economy and understands the reality it signifies.

Demonic thought is just the opposite. "Now the demonic thought neither knows nor understands these things, but shamelessly suggests only the possession of perceptible gold and foretells the delight and glory that will come from it."[19] Demons see only how gold relates to their own selfish desires to possess it and personally gain from it. Demonic thought is an acquisitive mode of knowledge.

Finally, human thought is a sort of neutral knowledge which "neither desires to possess gold, nor thoroughly investigates what gold is a symbol of, but simply introduces into one's thinking the simple form of gold."[20] Here Evagrius is describing the bare perception of something with the senses without yet falling

---

16. Anatolios, *Retrieving Nicaea*, 239.

17. Evagrius Ponticus, *On Thoughts*, 8, in A. M. Casiday, *Evagrius Ponticus* (New York: Routledge, 2006), 95.

18. Evagrius, *On Thoughts*, 8 (Casiday, 96).

19. Evagrius, *On Thoughts*, 8 (Casiday, 96).

20. Evagrius, *On Thoughts*, 8 (Casiday, 96).

into possessive demonic thought or rising up into angelic significance. The problem is that in a fallen world human thought always becomes diabolical. We are trapped in an acquisitive mode of knowledge and are unable to understand the significance of things as they really are, as related to the divine economy. We are beset by passions, through which we constantly refer what we perceive to our own selfish desires.

In order to rise to angelic thought, we need to be rid of these passions and arrive at a state of *apatheia*. This is not to be confused with apathy or the lack of emotion. Casiday notes that Evagrius considers positive emotions such as joy to be a barometer of spiritual progress.[21] Here is where Gregory of Nyssa's argument regarding impassibility, which I noted earlier, is apropos. There, Gregory used envy as an example of passibility. The idea that God would withhold from his Son equal honor and glory for God's own use is unthinkable. *Apatheia* is not the absence of emotion or desire, but rather the absence of desires oriented towards selfish possession and mastery – what Rowan Williams describes as "the liberty of the mind to see and respond without what we would call an 'agenda' of its own."[22] Importantly, Evagrius understands that grace is necessary for fallen humans to overcome passions. But human cooperation with grace is also required, which takes the form of ascetic practice and obedience to God's commands. This is the first stage of the spiritual life, *praktikê*.[23]

Once free of passions, one can engage in natural contemplation (*physikê*), which is "natural" in the sense that one rises to angelic knowledge, understanding the significance of the natural order. Here Evagrius employs Origen's notion of *logoi*, which Louth defines as "the principles in accordance with which everything in the cosmos was created through the Word of God, the *Logos*."[24] This is not an emanation or ontological participation in the *Logos*, but the ultimate reason for which things were created, the underlying "logic" reflective of God's wisdom.

The final phase of the spiritual life is *theologia*, or contemplation of God – pure prayer (*proseuchē*). However, Evagrius's teaching proves problematic here. Vladimir Lossky criticises that prayer for Evagrius is a state of "intellectual contemplation" in which "the mind (*nous*) acquires perfection."[25] But Evagrius sees

---

21. Casiday, *Evagrius Ponticus*, 90.

22. Rowan Williams, *Looking East in Winter: Contemporary Thought and the Eastern Christian Tradition* (London: Bloomsbury Continuum, 2021), 70.

23. For an excellent summary of Evagrius's three phases of spiritual life, which this discussion is indebted to, see Andrew Louth's insights in *Maximus the Confessor* (London: Routledge, 1996), 35–37.

24. Louth, *Maximus the Confessor*, 37.

25. Vladimir Lossky, *The Vision of God*, trans. Asheleigh Moorhouse (Crestwood, NY: St Vladimir's Seminary Press, 2013), 107.

the soul (*psyche*) in Origenist terms, "a deformation of the *nous* alienated from God and materialised. It becomes spirit (*nous*) again by way of contemplation, whose perfect phase is pure prayer."[26] Evagrius's intellectual mysticism thus ultimately ends in escape from the cosmos and from embodied existence.

MAXIMUS: KNOWLEDGE, LOVE, AND THE INCARNATION

Evagrius offers crucial insight into the nature of true knowledge, where what is perceived is understood in its significance to divine action. In this way, the knowledge of all things correlates to the way we know God. Maximus the Confessor develops this thought further, making crucial corrections to Evagrius.

Love, in short, is Maximus's corrective. Louth comments, "Whereas Evagrius's doctrine of prayer and the spiritual life is about how the soul is to regain the state of pure mind from which it has fallen, for Maximus the spiritual life is about how we love."[27] Each phase of the spiritual life (redefined by Maximus) is characterised by love. First, love is the motivation for the ascetic life. *Apatheia* does not exclude love, but holy love is "the blessed passion."[28] Second, love is also the goal of natural contemplation, which does not understand the *logoi* of creation for the sake of knowing, nor simply as the means to a higher phase of spiritual life. Rather, referring the meaning of people and things to the divine economy allows us to love as God loves them. Finally, love is the goal of *theologia*, where the encounter with God surpasses the intellect in ecstatic love: what Paul prays for the Ephesians, "to know the love of Christ that surpasses knowledge, that you may be filled with all the fullness of God" (Eph 3:19 ESV).

Crucially, this ecstatic love is not ultimately ethereal or disembodied, as in Evagrius's notion of pure prayer or contemplation. Instead, Maximus explains that ecstatic love reincorporates the intellect and body.

> For by continual participation in the divine radiance his intellect becomes totally filled with light; and when it has reintegrated its passible aspect, it redirects this aspect towards God, as we have said, filling it with an incomprehensible and intense longing for Him, and with unceasing love, thus drawing it entirely away from worldly things to the divine.[29]

Here, "worldly things" do not refer to embodied life itself but rather to the world in terms of the environment in which people and things are known only

---

26. Lossky, *The Vision of God*, 107.
27. Louth, *Maximus the Confessor*, 38.
28. Louth, *Maximus the Confessor*, 40.
29. Louth, *Maximus the Confessor*, 41.

in reference to selfish desire, "as a reservoir of objects whose significance is in their utility in satisfying an indeterminate series of desirous reactions in us."[30] Instead, the purified and reintegrated intellect and body are directed towards the divine, interpreting things as they really are in reference to the divine economy and using that understanding to love God and indeed all of creation according to the *logoi*.

Throughout his corpus, Maximus is committed to the reality of the incarnation and the Christology he defended unto his persecution and exile. God's presence among us is the means, motive, and pattern for all of redeemed life. Knowledge, for instance, is not initiated by human intellect but is a response to God's self-disclosure in the incarnate Son. The ascetic movement towards *apatheia* is rooted in Christ's kenotic emptying, which provides a pattern for divesting ourselves of selfish passions.[31] Moreover, in Maximus's restructuring of Dionysius's hierarchies, the incarnation accomplishes God's plan to "unite all things in him" (Eph 1:10b ESV). It restores humanity's original vocation as a true *mikros kosmos*, to participate in the divine activity of "drawing all created order into harmony with itself, and into union with God."[32] Maximus's emphasis on the incarnation assures that knowledge and love remain embodied, never separated from the assumed flesh of Jesus Christ.

GREGORY PALAMAS: DIVINE ENERGIES AND GOD'S SELF-CORRESPONDENCE

One theme we have not adequately explored is how God's intra-Trinitarian life relates to knowledge.[33] As noted earlier, the pro-Nicene Fathers understood that the Trinitarian relations of origin reveal that activity is proper to the divine essence. Moreover, Scripture provides analogies which denote this intra-Trinitarian activity such as the radiance of light, water from a fountain, or word of the mind. This last example has a prominence of place because of the Johannian identification of the Son as the *Logos*. Williams explains that "the elaboration of the language of *logos* in Greek Christian theology is the canonical vehicle in early Christian thought for expressing this belief: eternal reality is productive of its own reflection, inseparably moving into otherness and returning in . . . a non-dual non-identity."[34]

---

30. Williams, *Looking East in Winter*, 67.

31. See Louth, *Maximus the Confessor*, 34.

32. Louth, *Maximus the Confessor*, 71.

33. Of course, to speak of God's inner life is fraught with challenges, as someone like Karen Kilby aptly warns. See her collection of essays on this subject in *God, Evil, and the Limits of Theology* (London: T&T Clark, 2020).

34. Williams, *Looking East in Winter*, 80.

Gregory Palamas is perhaps best known for his articulation of the energies/essence distinction in God during the hesychast controversies in the fourteenth century. But Palamas's discussion of the eternal generation of the *Logos* as the grounding of the divine image in humanity has recently garnered new attention, not least in Rowan Williams's insightful analysis.[35] For this we turn to Palamas's *One Hundred and Fifty Chapters*, particularly chapters 34–40.

Palamas begins by explaining that the supreme, living, divine mind (*nous*) which is God is substantially (*ousia*) goodness. Whatever else this *nous* has (life, wisdom, eternity, etc.) is good, and so is encompassed by goodness in simplicity. To be the source of goodness is also good, so by definition God must be the source of goodness. And since God is *nous*, a Word (*logos*) is the goodness which he generates. Palamas clarifies that this is not a spoken word, either externally or internally ("discursive intellect"). Rather, it is the "word naturally stored up within our mind" or "knowledge which is always coexistent with the mind."[36] This Word is identical with God's substance, yet distinct from the *nous* which is its source. Therefore, the Word is a distinct hypostasis, a Son eternally generated by the Father.

So far, this description is in keeping with the Eastern tradition, from Origen to Athanasius, the Cappadocians, Maximus, etc. And one certainly hears echoes of Augustine here as well.[37] But Palamas's originality is his account of the Spirit's procession.

Together with the Word, the Holy Spirit proceeds from the Father. Palamas explains that this procession is not like breath which accompanies speech, nor as the inner animation of discursive intellect. Rather, the Spirit's procession is "like an ineffable love (*eros*) of the Begetter towards the ineffably begotten Word himself."[38] As Palamas develops this thought, the logic seems to be that when the Father sees his substantially (*ousia*) supreme goodness identically reflected in the distinct hypostasis of the Word, the Father expresses what is experienced analogically by humans as "insatiable desire" but which for God is perfect *eros* directed towards the reflection of infinitely divine goodness. This love is itself supreme goodness and thus consubstantial with the Father and Word, yet is

---

35. See Williams, *Looking East in Winter*, 35–45. Also see his essay "The Theological World of the Philokalia" in *The Philokalia: A Classic Text of Orthodox Spirituality*, ed. Brock Bingaman and Bradley Nassif (Oxford: OUP, 2012).

36. Gregory Palamas, *The One Hundred and Fifty Chapters*, #35, trans. Robert Sinkewicz (Toronto: Pontifical Institute of Mediaeval Studies, 1988), 121.

37. For a helpful discussion of Palamas's use of Augustine, see Reinhard Flogaus, "Inspiration–Exploitation–Distortion: The Use of St. Augustine in the Hesychast Controversy," in *Orthodox Readings of Augustine*, ed. Aristotle Papankikolaou and George Demacopoulos (Crestwood, NY: St Vladimir's Seminary Press, 2008), 63–80.

38. Palamas, #36 (Sinkewicz, 122–23).

hypostatically distinct from both. The Son experiences this love from the Father and possesses it "as proceeding from the Father together with himself and as resting connaturally in him."[39]

The image of God in humanity mirrors these divine relations, particularly "spirit as love (*eros*) in relation of the mind to the knowledge which exists perpetually from it and in it."[40] The human "insatiable desire for knowledge" is evidence of this. But since we are not supreme goodness itself, but rather derived from it, human spirit is properly love for the mind/knowledge relation as related to divine goodness. And this love is drawn out of itself towards knowledge of God who is goodness itself. Crucially, since humans are embodied souls distinct from angels, this spirit is the God-given source of life for our bodies, producing an inseparable bond between body and soul.

Adam and Eve's sin was to turn away from divine goodness, and fallen humanity now directs our spirit's erotic desire elsewhere; thus, our knowledge is distorted by interpreting reality in relation to these distorted desires. God, in his grace, does preserve the divine image in us, and our spirit continues to be the life-source of our body. But, ultimately, disordered desires "break apart the triadic and supercosmic world of his own soul," leading to death. Salvation consists of God drawing near to us and drawing our souls back to himself. Our souls are thus enabled to direct our knowledge back to divine goodness and reject our distorted desires. Each soul can then learn "more and more to love God beyond itself and its neighbor as itself."[41] Once our knowledge and love are reconnected with the source of all goodness, our souls receive eternal life and our bodies immortality in the resurrection.

The epistemological ramifications for all this are significant. In the first place, God's self-knowledge is the ground of all knowledge. As Palamas describes, the love who is the Spirit proceeds from the Father as the Father sees what he is in the reflection of the *Logos*. Williams describes this in a rather dizzying statement: "God is God as generating God's perfect reflection *and* God is God in the generativity of that reflection itself as it returns to its source – as Source and Word and Spirit simultaneously."[42] This "divine self-resonance" is expressed in the divine economy by what John's Gospel describes as "testimony"; the Word and Spirit speak truthfully about the Father and each other.[43] This divine self-testimony is the ontological basis of knowledge and truth: "God's truthful or

---

39. Palamas, #36 (Sinkewicz, 123).
40. Palamas, #37 (Sinkewicz, 123).
41. Palamas, #40 (Sinkewicz, 129).
42. Williams, *Looking East in Winter*, 80.
43. Williams refers us here to John chapters 5 and 15.

faithful correspondence with God's own divine life or act is the condition for all that we call intelligence or rationality."[44]

Furthermore, if humans reflect the Trinity through our "spirit as love in the relation of our mind to knowledge," and that spirit is what animates our bodies, then human knowledge is never separate from embodied existence and behavior. Rightly directed towards God, knowledge is not an isolated cognitive matter, but involves the entirety of human life: "Our knowing of the triune God is... not the construction of a conceptual framework, but the 'aptness' of a life that fits with the constraining and defining reality of God's being."[45]

Finally, this "apt" life is never in isolation but necessarily involves the neighbor. When our knowledge is directed towards God as the Source of goodness, we see others as connected to that Source, as reflecting supreme goodness, however imperfectly. Moreover, this knowledge perceives the *logoi* of creation in a nexus of interrelations which express the wisdom and goodness of the Creator. We are thus drawn towards others in *eros*, not in terms of mastery or possession, but as reflections of God's supreme goodness. As such, we inhabit our appropriate place in this nexus of relationships as participants in God's divine action in the universe.

EPISTEMOLOGICAL SUMMARY

In this rather long yet truncated journey, we have explored some of the major developments in the epistemological tradition of the Eastern Church. But we have not strayed far from our initial twofold foundation in the early Trinitarian debates. Namely, (1) God cannot be cognitively grasped, yet (2) Trinitarian doctrine involves a way of "being and knowing" through which we may "successfully relate ourselves" to the triune God.

First, the tradition has maintained the mystery of God. With the Eastern pro-Nicene Fathers we saw that God's essence is ineffable, but the triune relations of origin reveal that God is essentially active. God's actions in the divine economy allow us to know the "self-economised immanence" of God, even as the inner divine life remains beyond human cognition. With Evagrius we encountered angelic knowledge in which we relate the *logoi* of creation to the divine economy. With Maximus we learnt that the goal of knowledge is love, which "surpasses knowledge" and reintegrates our bodies and intellect to participate in the cosmic unification accomplished in the incarnation. Gregory Palamas showed us that the Father's self-reflection in the *Logos* and the procession of the

---

44. Williams, *Looking East in Winter*, 83.
45. Williams, *Looking East in Winter*, 91.

Spirit in love is the ontological basis for all knowledge. And as an image of the triune God, humanity reflects divine knowing in every aspect of embodied life, with our love directed towards God and neighbor.

Second, the tradition has emphasised a way of "being and knowing," which allows us to successfully relate ourselves to the triune God. With Gregory of Nyssa we learnt that human being "consists in relating itself to the activity of divine being through its own unceasing active participation." Evagrius emphasised the necessity of *apatheia*, of ridding ourselves of selfish passions, while Maximus showed us that holy love is the "blessed passion" which remains in the ascetic imitation of Christ's kenotic emptying. And Gregory Palamas taught us that knowing God is inseparable from what Rowan Williams calls "the 'aptness' of a life that fits with the constraining and defining reality of God's being."

Hopefully I have demonstrated what I suggested at the beginning – an epistemological tradition in which true knowledge involves the ability to both perceive the triune God's activity in creation and redemption and refer oneself along with all of reality to those divine actions. This perception and referral are rooted in a way of being, knowing, and loving which conforms to the constraining forms of created existence revealed in God's Word and realised through the Holy Spirit.

There are numerous applications for such an epistemology, and it is not difficult to see how modern life promotes a way of knowing and being which fundamentally interprets the world in light of one's own needs and desires. From how we consume the news to the algorithms which drive our social media feeds, from our political discourse to the advertisements directed our way, from our notions of sexuality to the way we treat our planet, it seems that every aspect of our lives would be fundamentally transformed by relating what we perceive to God's divine actions and conforming our lives accordingly. But that is not our main task here today. Interestingly, Evagrius's discussion of angelic knowledge was in the context of properly interpreting the Scripture. And we now turn to the book of Hebrews.

APPLYING THE TRADITION TO THE BOOK OF HEBREWS

CLARIFYING THE APPROACH

Before we begin our application of this epistemological tradition to Hebrews, I wish to clarify our task. I am not suggesting that an Eastern Christian epistemology offers a superior "hermeneutical key" to Scripture, nor am I attempting an Eastern Orthodox interpretation of the text. What I hope to do is explore how this epistemological tradition may be present in the text, and how reading the text in this idiom may help us see it in new and helpful ways. This is not meant to be exhaustive by any means, so we will limit our inquiry to some ways divine action relates to Christology, OT figures, and faith.

PRELIMINARY MATTERS: *APATHEIA* AND WARNING

As we turn to the text, a word of caution. A recurring theme throughout this journey thus far is that knowledge is directly related to how one lives one's life. We simply cannot expect to know the truth about anything (much less the Scripture!) if we are not actively engaged in ridding ourselves of selfish passions and moving towards *apatheia*. This may seem like an odd thing to say to modern readers, even those engaged with studying the Bible. It seems to me that theological studies (and I am including biblical studies here) as an academic discipline has largely rejected ascetic practices as necessary to theology, particularly in Protestant circles. Fasting, praying, chastity, silence, partaking of the Eucharist, even attending church regularly – none of these is a requirement for an advanced degree in theology from most universities. Yet, if our assessment of the tradition is correct, theology is inseparable from a way of "being and knowing" through which we may "successfully relate ourselves" to the triune God.[46]

The book of Hebrews highlights this approach through its many warnings, beginning in chapter two. "Therefore we must pay much closer attention to what we have heard, lest we drift away from it" (2:1).[47] What is it that we have heard? This is not simply a verbal utterance. It is what God "has spoken to us by his Son" (1:2); it is the decisive divine act of God's self-disclosure in the life and work of Jesus Christ. The exhortation is to "pay much closer attention," and the first negative consequence is "lest we drift away." This reminds us of Palamas's description of the predicament caused by the fall. In sin, we direct our love (*eros*) away from God and interpret the world according to our passions. But Christians are given the ability to direct our desire back to God, to know the Source of goodness and perceive the divine economy through which we now rightly interpret the world. We either drift away by directing our desires away from God's self-revelation in Christ, or we pay attention by directing our desire towards Jesus Christ.

The consequences for drifting away escalate. "How shall we escape if we neglect such a great salvation?" (2:3). Escape from what? Whatever is in

---

46. Cf. Craig G. Bartholomew and Robby Holt, "Prayer in/and the Drama of Redemption in Luke: Prayer and Exegetical Performance" in *Reading Luke: Interpretation, Reflection, Formation*, SAH Series 6, ed. Craig G. Bartholomew, Joel B. Green, and Anthony C. Thiselton (Grand Rapids: Zondervan, 2005).

47. Here, and throughout, I am using the ESV unless otherwise noted.

mind, it seems worse than the "just retribution" for "every transgression or disobedience" under the law (2:2) – what Bruce calls "sanctions even more awful than those which safeguarded the law."[48] This could refer to the *lex talionis* or the simple fact that punishments for disobedience were part of the law. But I think it specifically refers to disbelieving, disobedient Israel who "did not escape" (12:25), whose "bodies fell in the wilderness" (3:17). Moreover, the subsequent warnings in the epistle build on this first one, as Cockerill comments, "The exhortations that follow . . . flesh out what it means to 'pay more earnest attention,' and elaborate the nature and consequences of 'drifting away.'"[49] So "escape" here includes all that follows in the book: escape from not entering God's rest (4:1), escape from being burned like a useless crop (6:8), escape from the destruction of our souls (10:39), escape from being consumed by the fire that is God (12:29), etc.

Again, Palamas's logic helps make sense of these consequences. In sin, we direct our spirits away from the Source of goodness. Remember, according to Palamas the human spirit is what gives life to the body and what binds our bodies and souls. When we continue in sin we disintegrate, ultimately tearing ourselves apart and dying. The dire consequences described in Hebrews make sense under this logic. If we "drift away" from God's self-disclosing divine act, we disconnect ourselves from the Source of goodness and life. This inevitably leads to the death of our bodies and the disintegration of our souls. When we fail to direct our love towards God, to "pay much closer attention to what we have heard," we quite literally "fall away from the living God" (3:12) to our own demise.

Thankfully, these warnings are in the context of hope, of the great salvation accomplished by Jesus Christ. Moreover, Hebrews helpfully describes the ascetic life, the *apatheia* which is consistent with a way of "being and knowing" through which we "successfully relate ourselves" to the triune God. The ethical instruction of chapters twelve and thirteen may be thought of in this way. The ascetic struggle is summarised by "Let us also lay aside every weight, and sin which clings so closely, and let us run with endurance the race that is set before us" (12:1). The instruction which follows gives specific, practical instruction on what this looks like. But lest we think this is moralistic, it is all rooted in "looking to Jesus, the founder and perfecter of our faith" (v. 2). He is "equip[ping us] with everything good that [we] may do his will," and he is "working in us that which is pleasing in his sight" (13:21). Jesus is not simply a moral example for us to follow, but is the very source of goodness and knowledge to which he draws our love in order to know him. Thus, through him we know and love all things.

---

48. F. F. Bruce, *The Epistle to the Hebrews*, NICNT (Grand Rapids: Eerdmans, 1990), 68.
49. Gareth Cockerill, *The Epistle to the Hebrews*, NICNT (Grand Rapids: Eerdmans, 2012), 117.

Looking to Jesus is both the source and goal of the ascetic life, for "In your light do we see light" (Ps 36:9).

CHRISTOLOGY AND DIVINE ACTION

I have said that true knowledge involves the ability to both perceive the triune God's activity in creation and redemption and refer oneself along with all of reality to those divine actions. But where do we look to see divine action? Hebrews answers this question in its opening two verses with the main clause: "[God] has spoken to us by his Son" (1:2a).

Of course, God speaking is a divine action. And he has been doing this for quite some time, as the participial phrase of verse one reveals: "Long ago, at many times and in many ways, God spoke." This is contrasted with the timeframe of the main clause, "but in these last days [God] has spoken." The way God was speaking in the past is penultimate compared with now, the end times, the goal of time. And the recipients of God's speech have changed. Formerly it was "our fathers": from the patriarchs to those who tested God in the wilderness, from those who fell away in disbelief to those who persevered in faith, from every Aaronic priest who entered the Most Holy Place to all those for whom sacrificial animal blood was shed. But now God has spoken "to us": we who through Jesus enter the holy places and draw near to God, we who have faith and preserve our souls, we who are warned more sternly than our fathers, and we whose consciences have been washed clean.

Key to these verses is identifying the agent(s) through whom God has spoken. Formerly, it was the prophets – yes, the human authors of the OT, but also all those women and men through whom God revealed himself "in many ways" to his people throughout their history. Here, God's former action in speaking through these prophets is not denigrated; Ellingworth and others are right to emphasise continuity between God's self-disclosure in the OT and his final revelation in the Son.[50] But one reason the former communication was provisional and penultimate is because the divine act of speaking was mediated through non-divine agents. God's message was not compromised by these human agents, but, as Cockerill notes, "In a much more profound sense God's revelation was in the person of the Son."[51] God has spoken fully, finally, and singularly through his Son because the Son is himself divine.

What has God said in the Son? One would expect Hebrews to contain Jesus's teaching, to be filled with the proverbial red letters of my childhood Bible.

---

50. See Paul Ellingworth, *The Epistle to the Hebrews*, NIGTC (Grand Rapids: Eerdmans, 1993), 91.
51. Cockerill, *The Epistle to the Hebrews*, 90.

But, curiously, there is none of that! Instead, we see what the Son has done. This action is what God has said; it is the content of God's communication to us. So, if we apply our epistemological framework to Hebrews, this action – the Son's action – is the definitive divine action to which all our knowledge relates. All of reality is interpreted in light of the Son's action. Indeed, the Son's action constitutes reality itself. In the framework of Hebrews, my epistemological statement may be amended: True knowledge involves the ability to perceive *the Son's* activity in creation and redemption, and to refer oneself along with all of reality to *the Son's* actions. This perception and referral are rooted in a way of being, knowing, and loving which conforms to the constraining forms of created existence revealed in *the Son* and realised through the Holy Spirit.

As chapter one unfolds, the agency and action of the Son are clearly divine. First, the Son is the one through whom God created the world. Next, the Son is the "radiance of the glory of God." As we learnt from the pro-Nicene Fathers, this radiance is not static but what Athanasius called a "dynamic outgoing movement." The same is true of "the exact imprint of [God's] nature," which, according to Palamas, involves the ceaseless sharing of divine *eros* in the Spirit. Clearly, it is divine to "uphold the universe by the word of his power." Next, the passage hints at what is to come when it says, "after making purification for sins," but then we are right back to divinity as the Son "sat down at the right hand of the Majesty on high." But then the passage takes a turn. In what way did the Son *become* superior to angels? Could there ever be a time when the divine Son was less than angels? Why spend the next several verses proving the Son's superiority?

We have our answer in 2:9. "But we see him who for a little while was made lower than the angels, namely Jesus, crowned with glory and honor because of the suffering of death." Here our epistemological application to Hebrews could prove problematic; we are clearly in the realm of human actions. It is not divine to be lower than angels, and especially not to die! Right? Now we have to make a decision: Do we parse out all the human actions of Jesus from the divine actions, or is everything that Jesus does – human and divine – the action to which true knowledge refers?

We began our epistemological survey with the apostolic proclamation, "Jesus is Lord!" We return now to this fundamental truth. In Hebrews the same Lord who made a covenant with Israel (8:9) is the same Lord who physically descended from Judah (7:14), and the same Lord who promised a new covenant with Israel (8:10) is the same Lord who died and was raised (13:20). In the high Christology of Hebrews, if the Lord does something, it is divine action, even when (especially when!) the Lord is acting "in the days of his flesh" (5:7).

This is not to suggest that Jesus's human actions are not genuinely human – they certainly are. But since it is the second person of the Godhead who is acting, even Jesus's human actions may be understood as divine action. This is why the incarnation is so central for Maximus the Confessor, the great defender of Christology. We may say that for him the definitive divine action is the incarnation, that "the Creator of nature himself – who has ever heard of anything so truly awesome! – has clothed himself with our nature, without change uniting it hypostatically to himself."[52] As I explained earlier, knowledge for Maximus is a response to God's self-disclosure specifically in the incarnate Son.

Where do we look to find divine action in Hebrews, the referent for true knowledge? We look to Jesus, who we do not yet see with "everything in subjection under his feet," but he who "for a little while [was made] lower than the angels" (2:7, 8). True knowledge involves seeing Jesus's activity – things like his suffering, death, learning obedience, self-sacrifice, and priestly work – and referring ourselves and all of reality to that action. And this is perfectly consistent with Palamas's account of the Son's eternal generation. God pours all that he is into the Son without remainder, yet without depleting any of what God is. The Son does not grasp what he has been given for his own benefit, but joyfully shares the love of the Spirit in divine *eros* focused back on the Source. When the Son is "enhypostasised" in human nature, the finite expression of this eternal filial relationship continues in a way which is no less a divine person acting, but one which we now may see according to Jesus's humanity. So, referring ourselves to what we see when we "consider Jesus" (3:1) results in what Rowan Williams calls the "aptness of a life that fits with the constraining and defining reality of God's being – a knowing that is first the relation of self-forgetfulness in the face of the divine, the carrying of the cross, and the filial prayer of *Abba*. . . . a habit of faithful living."[53]

OLD TESTAMENT FIGURES AND JESUS'S DIVINE ACTION

If the definitive divine action is what "in these last days [God] has spoken to us by his Son" (1:2), and that divine action is visible to us in the incarnate Lord Jesus, then all of reality is grounded in what we see when we "pay much closer attention to what we have heard" (2:1) and when we "consider Jesus" (3:1). This has, I suggest, significant implications for how we understand Hebrews's use of OT figures, particularly the Levitical priesthood and sacrificial system.

Most interpreters agree that a major theme in Hebrews is that Jesus is

---

52. Maximus, *Letter 2: On Love*, 404C (Louth, 87).
53. Williams, *Looking East in Winter*, 91.

"better" than the old covenant and its institutions. Jesus is better than the angels, who traditionally delivered the law to Israel. Jesus is a better mediator and guarantor of the new covenant, which is better than the old. Jesus is better than the Aaronic priesthood. Jesus offers himself as a better sacrifice than those under the Levitical sacrificial system. And Jesus secures salvation, which offers better access to God for believers in the new covenant.

Importantly, all these things which Jesus is better than are not castigated as worthless or inherently bad. Jesus does not institute an alien covenant compared to the old. Rather, Jesus fulfills the old covenant. So, the tabernacle is a "copy and shadow of the heavenly things" (8:5; 9:23) but Jesus entered "into heaven itself" (9:24). The law has "but a shadow of the good things to come" (10:1) with provisional, repeated, and ultimately inadequate sacrifices. But Jesus makes a "single sacrifice for sins" in his human body through his willing obedience (10:12), which purifies not only the contamination caused by sin but also sinners themselves (9:14).

Clearly, Hebrews teaches that Jesus fulfills the old covenant along with its types and figures. But if we are not careful, we can read these fulfilled types and figures as somehow determining the divine action which Jesus must take. Yet surely this is true, in part. Someone like Ephraim Radner (if I understand him correctly) will press the point that the details of embodied life in Leviticus are the form which the life of Jesus takes up; he enters into the world constituted by the very words of Leviticus. But at the same time, the words of Leviticus are the words of the Word; Jesus himself constitutes the world which he inhabits. Radner describes the complexity of the relationship between OT figures and the life of Jesus in his discussion of time as explicated by the Levitical festivals:

> An emerging element of our reading of Leviticus is that the time that is Israel's is not only *also*, but is *first* Jesus's time. It marks his gathering up of creation. It is Israel's time only because God has first desired to walk this way. And so, if Israel's way is in fact Jesus's, the map of this way is given in the path that Jesus himself walks through time.[54]

What I am suggesting is that the definitive divine action of the incarnate Jesus not only interprets the types and figures of the OT through fulfillment, but in some way also constitutes them. For example, Jesus certainly did shed his blood in fulfillment of the animal sacrifices which foreshadowed his sacrifice.

---

54. Ephraim Radner, *Leviticus*, Brazos Theological Commentary on the Bible (Grand Rapids: Brazos Press, 2020), 245.

But, also, the divine act of shedding his blood is the very act which constituted those animal sacrifices. Jesus's divine action is the "exact image" (*eikon*) which casts the "shadow" (*skia*) that the law possesses (10:1).[55] In fact, we may venture to say that the reason blood flowed in the veins of sacrificial animals is because Jesus shed his blood. It is precisely in the act of Jesus's self-giving that the blood of animals is given "for you on the altar to make atonement for your souls" (Leviticus 17:11). If this is true, then the relationship of divine action in Jesus to true knowledge is not merely one of interpreting reality as it is. More profoundly, the divine action which Hebrews reveals in Jesus is what constitutes reality itself.

DIVINE ACTION AND FAITH

One hazard in our discussion of the relation between Jesus's divine action and true knowledge is that we can make an epistemic overstatement if we are not careful. True knowledge is grounded in God's self-revelation in Jesus, but that knowledge can never be exhaustive, especially as it relates to God himself. Yes, we are exhorted to "pay much closer attention" to what God has said in Jesus (2:1), to "consider Jesus" (3:1), and to "[look] to Jesus" (12:2). But this last reference is in relation to Jesus being the "founder and perfecter of our faith." In Hebrews, faith is not simply describing fidelity to what we have seen (although it is no less than that), but faith is also the means to knowing that which we cannot see. In fact, faith implies hiddenness, something "not seen" (11:1).

This may be where the Orthodox epistemological tradition's emphasis on God's essential hiddenness helps illuminate the notion of faith. You will recall that one of the fundamental commitments underlying the early Trinitarian debates was that "trinitarian doctrine does not allow us to encompass the being of God within the confines of human knowing" and involves "learning to disavow a comprehensive epistemic hold on the God to whom we thus refer ourselves."[56] Throughout the development of the tradition, we have noted that God's essence remains fundamentally inaccessible and that it is through God's self-economised action that we know anything about him at all.

This element of the tradition reaches a high point in the theology of Gregory Palamas in his articulation of the distinction between God's essence and energies. This has been the subject of much debate, and rightly so if we interpret it as a metaphysical claim. But at its best, this distinction is valuable as an epistemological safeguard. If what things are can be properly understood only in relation

---

55. See Ellingworth's discussion of *skia*, *The Epistle to the Hebrews*, 406.
56. Anatolios, *Retrieving Nicaea*, 9.

to God's action, then what God is (his essence) is unknowable because it stands behind his action. Rowan Williams helpfully summarises:

> To know God can only be to know him in his character as the giver of significance through his action of self-bestowing – in what is revealed of his life in Trinity and in his acts of creation and providential sustaining. The not-knowing that is central to the true contemplative enterprise is here both a "referral" of the meaning of all things to God and an acknowledgement that God's "meaning" is within himself alone.[57]

What God reveals about himself and all things through Jesus's action is really real, even as the divine essence remains hidden.

Palamas's distinction between essence and energies may be one way to understand faith in Hebrews. We might say that faith is the ability to successfully refer oneself and all of reality to that which cannot be cognitively grasped. Faith as such is grounded in divine action, and thus is not "blind" since it does include what God has spoken in the Son. Yet, simultaneously, it maintains the mystery that is inherent in God. Faith allows us to move beyond the limits of our intellect in Maximus's ecstatic love, such that we may know the God who is beyond knowledge, giving "assurance" (or "substance" – *hupostasis*) to what we "hope for" and "conviction of things not seen" (11:1), believing that the One we "draw near to" really "exists and that he rewards those who seek him" (11:6).

Faith then describes the movement towards God in true knowledge and love which exceeds knowledge – what Nyssa describes as *epektasis*, an endless reaching out and stretching forward into participation in the divine life. Khaled Anatolios summarises such a life of faith in Nyssa's thought:

> But if the trinitarian God is radically active in his own being and inaccessible apart from his self-presencing activities, then the encounter with God must stretch out toward an infinite embrace, beyond any pretensions of a comprehensive and exhaustive grasp. The proper human stance, rather, is to ceaselessly act into the infinite trinitarian divine activity, never encompassing, always traveling.[58]

Faith is essentially related to true knowledge because the God revealed in Jesus's action is infinitely beyond our grasp, yet he calls us to "draw near" in faith

---

57. Williams, *Looking East in Winter*, 16.
58. Anatolios, *Retrieving Nicaea*, 240.

to him (10:22). While the "darkness and gloom" of Sinai (12:18) no longer conceal God in the same way today, on the other side of the veil which is Jesus's flesh (10:20) the burning brightness of God is seen to be even more inexhaustible. Faith allows us to reach out in "infinite embrace" to the God whose essence is ineffable, but who has made himself known in Jesus Christ.

CONCLUSION

In this chapter, I have briefly explored how the Eastern Orthodox epistemological tradition may be a useful lens through which to view divine action in Hebrews. In doing so, I hope I have demonstrated the relationship between doctrine and Scripture which the Kirby Laing Centre's Scripture and Doctrine Seminar seeks to promote.

To truly know anything, we must perceive God's action and refer ourselves and all of reality to that activity. The book of Hebrews reveals Jesus's incarnate life and work to be divine action *par excellence*, so that true knowledge of all things involves seeing Jesus as the one Scripture bears witness to and referring ourselves and the world around us to him. This is inseparable from a way of being, knowing, and loving which conforms to the constraining forms of created existence which Jesus not only embodied but constituted by his body. By looking to Jesus we are transformed into the sort of people who by faith may know him who surpasses knowledge, and in so doing we see ourselves as we really are and the world around us as it really is.

SELECT BIBLIOGRAPHY

Anatolios, Khaled. *Retrieving Nicaea: The Development and Meaning of Trinitarian Doctrine.* Grand Rapids: Baker Academic, 2011.

Arius. "The Confession of the Arians." Translated by Edward Hardy. In *Christology of the Later Fathers*, edited by Edward Hardy, 332–4. Louisville, KY: Westminster John Knox Press, 2006.

Athanasius of Alexandria. *Against the Arians, I.* Translated by Henry Newman. *NPNF* 2/4: 303–43.

Ayres, Lewis. *Nicaea and Its Legacy: An Approach to Fourth-Century Trinitarian Theology.* Oxford: OUP, 2004.

Behr, John. *The Nicene Faith, Part Two: One of the Holy Trinity.* Crestwood, NY: St Vladimir's Seminary Press, 2004.

Bruce, F. F. *The Epistle to the Hebrews*. NICNT. Grand Rapids: Eerdmans, 1990.

Cockerill, Gareth Lee. *The Epistle to the Hebrews*. NICNT. Grand Rapids: Eerdmans, 2012.

Ellingworth, Paul. *The Epistle to the Hebrews: A Commentary on the Greek Text*. NIGCT. Edited by I. Howard Marshall and W. Ward Gasque. Grand Rapids: Eerdmans, 1993.

Eunomius of Cyzicus. *Liber Apologeticus*. Translated by Richard Paul Vaggione. In *Eunomius: The Extant Works*, 34–78. New York: OUP, 1987.

Evagrius Ponticus. *On Thoughts*. Translated by A. M. Casiday. In *Evagrius Ponticus*, 91–116. New York: Routledge, 2006.

Gregory of Nazianzus. *Theological Oration* 29. Translated by Lionel Wickham. In *On God and Christ: The Five Theological Orations and Two Letters to Cledonius*, 69–92. Crestwood, NY: St Vladimir's Seminary Press, 2002.

Gregory of Nyssa. *Ad Ablabium*. Translated by Cyril Richardson. In *Christology of the Later Church Fathers*, edited by Edward Hardy, 256–67. Philadelphia: Westminster Press, 2006.

———. *Contra Eunomium*. Translated by Stuart George Hall. In *Gregory of Nyssa: Contra Eunomium I, an English Translation with Supporting Studies*, edited by Miguel Brugarolas, 73–195. Boston: Brill, 2018.

Gregory Palamas. *The One Hundred and Fifty Chapters*. Translated by Robert Sinkewicz. Toronto: Pontifical Institute of Mediaeval Studies, 1988.

Lossky, Vladimir. *The Vision of God*. Translated by Asheleigh Moorhouse. Crestwood, NY: St Vladimir's Seminary Press, 2013.

Louth, Andrew. *Maximus the Confessor*. London: Routledge, 1996.

Maximus the Confessor. "Letter 2: On Love." Translated by Andrew Louth. In *Maximus the Confessor*, 82–90. London: Routledge, 1996.

Radner, Ephraim. *Leviticus*. Brazos Theological Commentary on the Bible. Edited by R. R. Reno. Grand Rapids: Brazos Press, 2020.

Vaggione, Richard Paul. *Eunomius of Cyzicus and the Nicene Revolution*. New York: OUP, 2000.

Williams, Rowan. *Looking East in Winter: Contemporary Thought and the Eastern Christian Tradition*. London: Bloomsbury Continuum, 2021.

CHAPTER 6

Leading Sons and Daughters from Despair to Glory

Theodicy and Divine Action in Romans 8 and Hebrews 2

Scott D. Mackie

INTRODUCTION

A number of shared features unite two of the most profound texts in the NT, Romans 8 and Hebrews 2. In them we find the early church's two greatest theologians offering panoramic presentations of the Christ event and its significance for humanity. In both texts, bleak assessments of the human condition are contrasted with effusive portrayals of Christian eschatological experience, and both bridge these disparate states by means of the Christ event. Jesus's full immersion in the human condition is accorded an instrumental role in rescuing humanity from sin, death, and despair, and conveying them into heavenly glory. Both authors contend that the certainty of that heavenly, future glory is assured by the present enjoyment of tangible and transformative foretastes of divine, heavenly love, which relate primarily to their membership in the family of God.[1]

---

1. So Colleen Shantz, *Paul in Ecstasy: The Neurobiology of the Apostle's Life and Thought* (Cambridge: CUP, 2009), 131: Rom 8 is "colored by and filled with the phenomena of religious ecstasy" and "saturated with knowledge of ecstatic religious experience." On the mysticism of Heb 2, see my essay, "'Behold! I Am with the Children God Has Given Me': Ekphrasis and Epiphany in Hebrews 1–2," in *Son, Sacrifice, and*

Participatory soteriology and Jesus's priestly ministry also are of great import to both Rom 8 and Heb 2, as well as God's providential planning and power.

Perhaps more consequential, however, are the many indications that suggest both texts were largely motivated by situations of suffering and attendant failures to understand the significance of divine action undertaken in the face of that suffering. Though operating below the surface structure of Rom 8 and Heb 2, these motivations fuel a response that is theodical in nature, which implicitly reacts and responds to concerns, questions, and complaints about God's apparent failure to act in power and love. A wide range of situations of suffering motivate theodicy: when God's people feel they are suffering unjustly, or, conversely, when they are overwhelmed by the consequences of their moral shortcomings. Adverse circumstances lead them to believe that God is no longer an ally but perhaps even an enemy, and forces of evil appear to be more powerful than God and his ability to protect his people. Divine action, or inaction, is being assessed and called into question, with special focus directed on God's power and love. Solutions to this crisis of faith vary, though among the most common are the belief that sufferings represent (1) a divine punishment for sins; (2) a test of the faith and perseverance of the sufferers; (3) a beneficial or educational "realignment" of sufferers' perception of God's nature and actions; (4) a motivation to "draw near" to God and find comfort and assistance; (5) a divine mystery that confronts the limitations of human knowledge; or (6) assurance of recompense in the afterlife. All of these solutions appear in Romans and Hebrews, though they have been reconfigured and transformed by the Christ event.

THEODICY: THE CONDITIONS AND COMPLAINTS CHALLENGING GOD'S RIGHTEOUSNESS

As practical theologians and concerned pastors, Paul and the author of Hebrews were well aware of the various conditions that threatened early Christian communities. They also would be quite familiar with the theodical complaints that had been raised by suffering and despairing Christians, and these theodical complaints appear to underlie much of the content in Rom 8 and Heb 2.

One can reasonably assume, on the basis of Romans and Hebrews, that the preeminent challenge faced by early Christians was moral in nature – specifically, the ability of sin to wreak havoc psychologically, spiritually, and socially.

Great Shepherd: Studies on the Epistle to the Hebrews, ed. Eric F. Mason and David M. Moffatt, WUNT 2/510 (Tübingen: Mohr Siebeck, 2020), 43–77.

The language of sin and transgression occur more frequently in Romans than in any other NT writing, and in Rom 8 Paul begins by comparing the epoch of sin and death with the eschatological age of Spirit and life (8:1–11). He characterises those who orient themselves towards the sinful tendencies of the "flesh" as bent on self-destruction (8:5–6) and "at enmity with God" (8:7). Though the social impact of sin is catalogued elsewhere in Romans (cf. 1:29–31; 2:21–22; 3:10–18) and the extended paraenesis of 12:3–15:13 demonstrates Paul's concern to mitigate the effects of social transgressions in the communities at Rome, in Rom 8 these effects perhaps can be inferred by Paul's emphasis on his readers' identity as the family of God (8:24–25, 28–30), which includes both Jew and Gentile, weak and strong, spiritual and fleshly.

Hebrews's preoccupation with the devastating effects of sin is nowhere more apparent than in its elaborate cultic soteriology, which depicts Jesus's death and resurrection as providing atonement for sins (1:3; 2:17; 7:27; 9:26, 28; 10:12, 17–18), purification of an unclean conscience (9:14; 10:22), sanctification (2:11; 10:10, 14, 22, 29; 13:12), and perfection (10:14). A disruption in the community's relationship with God also can be inferred by the repeated assertions of access to God (4:3, 11; 6:18–20; 7:19) and the exhortations to confidently "draw near" to his throne (4:14–16; 10:19–23; 12:22–24). Both themes are apparent in Heb 2, with Jesus described as "the one sanctifying those who are being sanctified" (2:11) and his death interpreted as "a sacrifice of atonement for the sins of the people" (2:17). And, like Paul, Hebrews's concern to establish family identity in 2:11–13 can be at least partially attributed to a desire to establish harmony and concord in the community, and to mitigate the social sins that threaten family unity (cf. 10:24–25).

The second challenge addressed by Paul and Hebrews is material, namely, the pervasive malnutrition and disease that contributed to unimaginable levels of suffering and mortality rates. While some biblical scholars appear to assume that ancient Mediterraneans led long and comfortable middle-class lives,[2] ancient historians and classical scholars paint a rather different picture, one so bleak it nearly eludes modern apprehension. Walter Scheidel contends that "throughout the Greco-Roman world, average life expectancy at birth fell in a bracket from about twenty to thirty years,"[3] resulting in vast numbers of fatherless

2. Cf. Johan Ferreira, "Reconsidering the Poor: A Fresh Translation of Matthew 5:3," in *Fountains of Wisdom: In Conversation with James H. Charlesworth*, ed. Gerbern S. Oegema, Henry W. Morisada Rietz, and Loren T. Stuckenbruck (London: T&T Clark, 2022), 107–26; Lynn H. Cohick, "Poverty and Its Causes in the Early Church," in *Poverty in the Early Church and Today: A Conversation*, ed. Steve Walton and Hannah Swithinbank (London: T&T Clark, 2019), 16–27.
3. Walter Scheidel, "Demography," in *The Cambridge Economic History of the Greco-Roman World*, ed. Walter Scheidel, Ian Morris, and Richard Saller (Cambridge: CUP, 2007), 38–86, here 39. The

children and vulnerable widows.[4] These bleak conditions clearly inform Heb 2:15, which describes a psychologically debilitating, lifelong enslavement to the "fear of death." In Rom 8 the language and imagery of life and death is pervasive,[5] and envelopes even the created order, which is drawn into the "sufferings of the present time" (8:18). In fact, the created realm sympathetically "groans in labor pains" together with Christians, and both patiently endure a presently frustrated, "futile" state (8:19–25). Though perhaps reflecting the divine curse issued in Gen 3:17–19, the "subjection" of creation to "futility" (Rom 8:20) probably should be more closely associated with the hardships attending preindustrial farming and consequently the malnutrition which was a major cause of widespread human suffering and diminished life spans.[6] The mention of "famine" in the hardship list in 8:35 is surely significant in this regard, for "hunger and the fear of starvation were omnipresent in the Roman world" and "most people had probably witnessed" and "experienced" famine, while people in the "poorest classes" "died of hunger and deprivation-related diseases at all times."[7]

The unjust persecution of early Christian communities constitutes the third significant challenge. Possible indications of persecution abound in Rom 8, with societal opposition and persecution inferred in 8:31–34 and in some of the adversities enumerated in 8:35, which include "tribulation," "distress,"

"foreignness" of these mortality rates to us moderns is apparent in cinematic (mis)representations of ancient Mediterranean city life, which are without exception predominately populated by older adults, ca. 25–60 years old.

4. Cf. Sabine R. Hübner and David M. Ratzan, "Fatherless Antiquity? Perspectives on 'Fatherlessness' in the Ancient Mediterranean," in *Growing Up Fatherless in Antiquity*, ed. Sabine R. Hübner and David M. Ratzan (Cambridge: CUP, 2009), 3–28, here 9: "a striking number of fathers died before their children reached adulthood... as many as one-third of all children in every social and economic stratum over the entire ancient Mediterranean would have lost their fathers before they reached age fifteen. Another third lost their fathers before they reached age twenty-five." Thus, "ancient fatherlessness... was pervasive and endemic."

5. The terminology used for "life" includes ζωή (8:2, 6, 10, 38), ζῳοποιέω (8:11), and ζάω (8:12–13), while death, mortality, and corruption are represented by θάνατος (8:2, 6, 38), θανατόω (8:13, 36), ἀποθῄσκω (8:13, 34), νεκρός (8:10–11 [3x]), θνητός (8:11), φθορά (8:21), and σφαγή (8:36).

6. Cf. Christian Laes, *Children in the Roman Empire: Outsiders Within* (Cambridge: CUP, 2011), 43: the "primarily vegetarian diet of the poor left them with a chronic deficiency of proteins and calories," and "this less-than-ideal nutritional situation may have resulted in general weakness and a variety of other conditions, including muscle-wasting, lack of subcutaneous fat, reduced brain mass... retarded growth, bone disorders... general apathy... skin diseases... eye diseases... and reduced resistance against infections. The impact of malnutrition in infancy on... mental function can be irreversible." In fact, Laes contends that "chronic malnutrition meant that a substantial proportion of the population was able to work for just a few hours a day." Furthermore, as Sabine R. Huebner (*The Family in Roman Egypt* [Cambridge: CUP, 2013], 164) notes, malnourishment during pregnancy led to massive increases in infant mortality and birth defects.

7. Paul Erdkamp, "Famine and Hunger in the Roman World," in *The Routledge Handbook of Diet and Nutrition in the Roman World*, ed. Paul Erdkamp and Claire Holleran (London: Routledge, 2019), 296–307, here 296.

"persecution," "peril," and "sword."[8] Equally important is Paul's quotation of Ps 44:22 in Rom 8:36, "For your sake we are being killed all day long; we are accounted as sheep to be slaughtered," a prediction which was soon fulfilled in 64 CE (Tacitus, *Annals* 15.44.2–5; Suetonius, *Nero* 16.2). Hebrews often has been thought to be at least partially motivated by conditions of persecution.[9] Though persecution may be inferred from the portrayal of Jesus's exemplary endurance of "the suffering of death" (2:9–10) and the promise that Jesus will "help those who are being tested" in the same manner in which he was tested (2:18), it is explicitly indicated in 10:32–35:

> But remember those earlier days, after you were enlightened, when you endured a hard contest with sufferings, sometimes being publicly exposed both to insults and persecution, and sometimes being partners with those thus treated. For you had compassion on prisoners, and the seizure of your possessions you accepted with joy, knowing that you yourselves have a better and more lasting possession. Therefore, do not throw away your confidence, which has great reward.[10]

Moreover, in 12:1–4, after characterising the community's struggles as an agonistic race, possibly leading to bloodshed, the author mimetically aligns them with Jesus, who "endured such hostility against himself from sinners" (12:3).

It would be surprising if these grave conditions of hardship and suffering failed to adversely affect the faith of early Christian communities, leading them to question God's power, righteousness, love, and faithfulness. In fact, a number of such concerns, questions, and complaints appear to underlie and motivate Rom 8 and Heb 2. For example, Rom 8:1–13 may be responding to common misunderstandings concerning the nature of forgiveness of sins and the extent to which sin can continue to negatively impact the Christian life. Paul perhaps had heard Christians ask, "Though we have been forgiven of our sins, why are we still under the dominion of sin and feel like we are cursed, condemned, and at enmity with God as a result?" Similarly, 8:17–18, which connects Christian

---

8. According to Robert Jewett, *Romans: A Commentary*, Hermeneia (Minneapolis: Fortress, 2006), 543: the adversities listed in 8:35 "have all been experienced by Paul and the Roman congregations."

9. Cf. Harold W. Attridge, *A Commentary on the Epistle to the Hebrews*, Hermeneia (Philadelphia: Fortress, 1989), 13; William L. Lane, *Hebrews 1–8*, WBC 47A (Dallas: Word, 1991), lvii, c; Craig R. Koester, *Hebrews: A New Translation with Introduction and Commentary*, AB 36 (New York: Doubleday, 2001), 67–71; Gareth Lee Cockerill, *The Epistle to the Hebrews*, NICNT (Grand Rapids: Eerdmans, 2012), 16–17.

10. Unless otherwise noted, all translations are mine. Cf. William L. Lane, *Hebrews 9–13*, WBC 47B (Dallas: Word, 1991), 301: "It must be stressed that the account in 10:32–34 describes an actual ordeal in the community's past."

suffering to Christ's sufferings and then unfavorably compares them to heavenly glory, may have been motivated by one of the most troubling concerns: "Are our sufferings meaningless?" Finally, in two similar texts (8:35 and 8:38–39), two of the most basic assumptions that are challenged in theodicy, God's power and love, have surely motivated Paul's assertions that neither human hardships nor existential forces are able to "separate us from the love of God in Christ Jesus."[11]

Some of these same concerns and complaints find expression in Heb 2, beginning with 2:5–9, which utilises Ps 8:4–6 to give voice to a complaint which may be paraphrased as: "If we have been destined for such great things, why are we suffering? Does God know what we are going through? And if he is watching over us, does he care?" (2:6).[12] The author's admission, in 2:8, that "all things" have not yet been subjected to Jesus's rule implicitly acknowledges a concern about the extent of God's power.[13] The remainder of the chapter then demonstrates that God's power in fact has been most powerfully expressed in the Christ event, overcoming death and all hostile forces opposed to humans and successfully atoning "for the sins of the people" (2:17). Equally significant is the author's assertions of divine love, which include a dramatically enacted divine adoption ceremony (2:12–13) as well as a warm-hearted portrayal of Jesus as a merciful and sympathetic High Priest (2:16–18).

THE SOLUTION: PAST, PRESENT, AND FUTURE DIVINE ACTIONS

In response to these perceived theodical concerns and complaints, both Paul and the author of Hebrews provide sophisticated solutions, which primarily attempt to infuse situations of suffering with deeper meaning, offer consolation, and encourage perseverance. In some instances, however, they correct "solutions" that have been adopted by their communities but are counterproductive to a relationship of trust with the God of mercy and grace. For instance, in Rom

---

11. On the centrality of these two concerns, divine power and love, see Antti Laato and Johannes C. de Moor, "Introduction," in *Theodicy in the World of the Bible*, ed. Antti Laato and Johannes C. de Moor (Leiden: Brill, 2003), vii–liv, esp. ix–xi, xx.

12. Heb 2:6: "What are human beings that you are mindful of them, or mortals that you keep watch over [ἐπισκέπτομαι] them?" Cf. Exod 4:31: "the people believed and were glad because God had been watching over [ἐπισκέπτομαι] the sons of Israel and he had seen their misery."

13. Cf. Pamela Eisenbaum, "Redescribing the Religion of Hebrews," in *"The One Who Sows Bountifully": Essays in Honor of Stanley K. Stowers*, ed. Caroline Johnson Hodge, Saul M. Olyan, Daniel Ullucci, and Emma Wasserman, BJS 356 (Providence: Brown Judaic Studies, 2013), 283–93, here 291: "Hebrews does not say to whom everything is currently subjected, but the implication is that the world is outside the authority of God."

8:1–13 Paul appears to be refuting the most common theodical solution in the Hebrew Bible, namely, that sufferings represent a divine punishment for sin.[14] The prevalence of this belief apparently convinced some early Christians to equate their sufferings with divine condemnation, coming as a just consequence of sin. Paul, instead, insists that those who are "in Christ" are not condemned by God (8:1); in fact, they have been "set free" from the sphere of sin and death through the Christ event (8:2–3) and enabled by the Spirit to inhabit the eschatological age of "life and peace" (8:4–6). However, like the existential choice placed before ancient Israelites in Deut 30:1–20, they face the choice of either orienting their "flesh" towards the Adamic age, and continuing to live under the power of sin and death (8:5–7), or orienting their lives, as those who "belong to Christ" and are indwelt by the Holy Spirit, towards the eschatological age of life and righteousness (8:9–13).[15] Since their sufferings provide an acute, heightened awareness of the eschatological consequences of Christian existence, the Christians in Rome should see them as beneficial and educative.[16] Paul's framing of the issue in Rom 8:1–13 might also convince them that they are being divinely tested. Yet, like the ancient Israelites, whose life and death choices were divinely aided by a "circumcised heart" (Deut 30:6),[17] the Christians in Rome are divinely enabled to correctly understand, choose, and live out the will of God, since they are indwelt and "led" by the same "life-giving" Spirit "who raised Christ Jesus from the dead" (Rom 8:11, 14).

As James Dunn has noted, Rom 8 is "the high point of Paul's theology of the Spirit," providing "the clearest indications of what the Spirit brings about in a human life."[18] And undoubtedly the most important expression of the Spirit's work in Rom 8 is found in Paul's portrayal of the Roman Christians' adoption into the divine family, which comes to a climax in Paul's recollection of an ecstatic experience they enjoyed: "When we cry, 'Abba! Father!' it is the Spirit of God bearing witness with our spirit that we are children of God" (8:15–16).

---

14. Cf. James L. Crenshaw, "The Shift from Theodicy to Anthropodicy," in *Theodicy in the Old Testament*, ed. James L. Crenshaw (Philadelphia: Fortress, 1983), 1–16, here 5: "the notion of reward and punishment," which places the blame for suffering entirely upon human sinfulness, "permeates the Deuteronomistic history and most of the Hebrew Bible."

15. On this, see John M. G. Barclay, *Paul and the Gift* (Grand Rapids: Eerdmans, 2015), 506.

16. A similarly positive view of sufferings is found in Rom 5:3–5: "we boast in our sufferings, knowing that suffering produces endurance, and endurance produces character, and character produces hope, and hope will not lead to shame, because the love of God has been poured into our hearts through the Holy Spirit given to us."

17. A heightened awareness of sinfulness and a corresponding need for "transformed moral organs" also is apparent in Jer 31:33; Ezek 36:26; Ps 51:10. On this, see Carol A. Newsom, *The Spirit within Me: Self and Agency in Ancient Israel and Second Temple Judaism*, AYBRL (New Haven: Yale University Press, 2021). This motif, of course, is prominent in Hebrews (cf. 8:10; 9:14; 10:16, 22).

18. James D. G. Dunn, *The Theology of Paul the Apostle* (Grand Rapids: Eerdmans, 1998), 423, 434.

Dunn further asserted that "this was where Paul rooted his and his fellow Christians' personal assurance that they were indeed God's children" and "if we can speak of a doctrine of assurance in Paul, then this is where it should start – in the experience of sonship."[19] Given the fact that most, if not all, of the Roman Christians had experienced the loss of many family members, perhaps even their entire families, this assurance of belonging to the divine family also would help assuage their sufferings and sense of loss. Misbegotten notions of a "fictive kinship" and fears that an adoption is somehow inferior to biological daughter/sonship, or even subject to possible revocation, are completely undone by Paul's reminder of this transformative, ecstatic, and embodied experience of God's fatherly love.[20] Furthermore, this knowledge and experience of divine adoption would infuse their sufferings with profound meaning and implications. Thus, the deepest and most desperate theodical cry, "Are our sufferings meaningless?", may then have motivated Paul's contention, in 8:17, that the endurance of suffering either tests or confirms the reality of their divine adoption: "if children, then heirs, heirs of God and heirs together with Christ, if/since [εἴπερ] we suffer with him so that we may also be glorified with him." The bivalence of εἴπερ, "if" or "since," affords two distinct interpretations, yet both find resolution in the same theodicy solution. The Roman Christians' sufferings either are a "test" of their family membership (if εἴπερ is ascribed a conditional sense, "if") or function as a confirmation of that identity, "since" (εἴπερ) they are presently persevering. In both cases their hardships are far from meaningless, as they provide these Christians with an opportunity to identify with Jesus and his sufferings. Since Jesus fully participated in the sufferings of human life, by sharing his sufferings they can fully participate in his life. And though Paul will shortly affirm that "God is for us" (8:31), this theodical interpretation transforms sufferings into an opportunity for Christians to prove or confirm that they "are for him"!

---

19. Dunn, *The Theology of Paul the Apostle*, 437. The presence of a similar claim in Gal 4:6, "because you are children, God has sent the Spirit of his Son into our hearts, crying out, 'Abba! Father!'", is seen by many as a clear indication of its importance to Paul's theology of adoption and its ubiquity in Pauline communities. Cf. also Jörg Frey, "Paul's View of the Spirit in the Light of Qumran," in *The Dead Sea Scrolls and Pauline Literature*, ed. Jean-Sébastien Rey, STDJ 102 (Leiden: Brill, 2014), 237–260, here 242: "We should be aware that some kind of experience, rather than theology, was at the origin of the early Christian notion of 'the Spirit,' whereas concepts, taken from the Scriptures, from early Jewish and . . . Hellenistic Jewish and Greco-Roman thought were used to describe and to understand these experiences."

20. On the origins and interrelationship of the "Abba" cry and the "adoption metaphor," Mark Wreford ("Diagnosing Religious Experience in Romans 8," *TynBul* 68, no. 2 [2017]: 203–222, here 213, 218) contends that "if the Abba cry gave expression to intuitively grasped content made available in deeply felt experiences of the Spirit which enhanced the believers' understanding of God, it did so as an unreflective, emotional outburst. On the other hand, the adoption metaphor is somewhat different: it represents a reflective attempt to adequately express the content of the spiritual experiences which inspired the Abba cry" and "which developed the recipients' understanding of what it meant for God to be their Father."

That sufferings are rewarded in the afterlife constitutes a prominent and potent theodicy solution,[21] one which comes to explicit expression in Rom 8:18 as Paul reveals that he has "carefully calculated that the sufferings of the present age are not worthy to be compared with the coming glory." We can safely speculate that the two decisive factors in this "calculation" were Paul's experiences of God's fatherly love in the midst of his hardships and his awareness of the unexpected, glorious outcome of Jesus's own endurance of suffering. That this outcome was unexpected reflects divine mystery, a mystery that Paul insists is similarly at work in the lives of the Christians in Rome, whose limited knowledge is crucially assisted by the Spirit's incomprehensible intercession (8:26–27), and for whom "all things are working together for good" (8:28). That God is firmly in control of "all things," then, is confirmed by a lengthy chain of divine planning and actions extending from the distant past to the heavenly future, to which the Roman Christians are firmly fastened in the present. They are "foreknown," "predestined," "called," "justified," and soon shall be "glorified" (8:29–30).[22] There and then, perhaps, God will reveal the details of his providential control of "all things," which have mysteriously "worked together" to lead them to heavenly glory.

Finally, two of the most basic assumptions that are challenged in theodicy, God's omnipotence and love, are defended in 8:31–39.[23] Paul first dispels any remaining doubts about God's commitment for his people by insisting that his "unsparing" "gift" of his own Son is certain proof that he is "for us" (8:31–32).[24] Then, since the forces of evil presently appear to be more powerful than God, Paul offers two lengthy lists of earthly adversities and cosmic threats including "tribulation," "distress," "persecution," "famine," "peril," "sword," "death," "angels," "rulers," "things present," "things to come," "powers," and "every kind

---

21. Cf. 4 Ezra 7:88–91: "this is the order of those who have kept the ways of the Most High, when they shall be separated from their vessel." Since "they laboriously served the Most High, and withstood danger every hour," "they shall see with great joy the glory of him who receives them, for they shall have rest" (*A Commentary on the Book of Fourth Ezra*, trans. Michael E. Stone, Hermeneia [Minneapolis: Fortress, 1990], 236).

22. See also Timo Eskola, *Theodicy and Predestination in Pauline Soteriology*, WUNT 2/100 (Tübingen: Mohr Siebeck, 1998), 166–88.

23. Thus, at its most basic level, theodicy asks, "How can a loving and all-powerful God allow bad things to happen to good people, and good things to happen to bad people?" Either God is omnipotent but not loving, or loving but not omnipotent. Divine omniscience occasionally is included as a third essential element; so James L. Crenshaw, *Defending God: Biblical Responses to the Problem of Evil* (Oxford: OUP, 2005), 16–17.

24. Cf. Jewett, *Romans*, 537–38: "'Not even to spare his own son' is the ultimate act that a father could perform in behalf of others; its pathos, especially in the ancient context, which assumed an ineradicable, emotional bond between father and son, is unmistakable. Nothing could more clearly demonstrate that 'God is for us.'"

of created thing," each of which contains matching assertions of God's omnipotence and love for his people: "nothing can separate us from the love of Christ" (8:35) and "nothing shall separate us from the love of God which is in Christ Jesus" (8:39).[25] In fact, the beleaguered Roman Christians are "in all these things more than conquerors through him who loved us" (8:37).[26]

While a number of potential theodical questions and concerns involving God's love, knowledge, power, and faithfulness are addressed in Heb 2, the most developed theodicy occurs in 2:6–11. To ensure the community of God's providential faithfulness and power, the author constructs a comprehensive temporal narrative that spans the beginning and *telos* of human history, with three pillars supporting that vast span.[27] Starting with the middle pillar, in 2:6, he utilises Ps 8:4–6 to give voice to the community's assumed complaint, which I paraphrased earlier as: "Does God know what we are going through? And if he is watching over us, does he care?" The "protological pillar" then is recounted, as the community is reminded that God's original intent for humanity was to exercise dominion over all creation, while possessing a positional status slightly below that of angels (2:7–8a). In 2:8b the author returns to the middle, present tense pillar and reengages the community's complaint, noting that the frustration of God's creational intent is painfully apparent: "But we do not yet see this exercise of human dominion" (2:8b).[28] The narrative then presses forward to its conclusion, the "teleological pillar," and by again addressing the same perceptual organ, sight, it invites the community to look into the eschaton: "But we do see Jesus, though made a little lower than angels, now crowned with glory and honor" (2:9).[29]

---

25. Cf. Tom Holmén, *Theodicy and the Cross of Christ: A New Testament Inquiry*, LNTS 567 (London: T&T Clark, 2019), 143: "the consolation offered by the teaching about God's love in Rom. 8 is, most concretely, the guarantee of belonging to God: despite their distress, Christians are his; whatever the reality would seem to suggest, they will not be condemned since they are justified by God through the death of Jesus."

26. Jewett, *Romans*, 543, 545–48, contends that Paul's rhetorical goal in 8:31–39 is to refute the pervasive theodicy which interprets suffering as a divine punishment for sin and proof that God is not "for us." This interpretation fails to fully cohere with the matched assertions in 8:35, 39, which emphasise God's power and love and show almost no interest in the equation of sin and punishment.

27. Cf. Paul Ellingworth, *The Epistle to the Hebrews: A Commentary on the Greek Text*, NIGTC (Grand Rapids: Eerdmans, 1993), 77: "no other NT writing preserves a better balance than Hebrews between the past, present, and future aspects of God's work in Christ."

28. Cf. 4 Ezra 6:53–59, which also utilises Ps 8 in theodicy.

29. This "now, but not yet" eschatological tension is presaged in Heb 1:13 and 2:8, with the juxtaposition of Ps 110 and Ps 8. Hebrews uses Ps 8 in Heb 2:8 to portray Jesus's rule as realised, while Ps 110 is enlisted in Heb 1:13 to describe a future subjugation: "Sit at my right hand until [ἕως] I make your enemies a footstool for your feet." As George H. Guthrie ("Hebrews' Use of the Old Testament: Recent Trends in Research," in *The Letter to the Hebrews: Critical Readings*, ed. Scott D. Mackie, T&T Clark Critical Readings in Biblical Studies [London: Bloomsbury, 2018], 355–375, here 363) insists, "a full interpretation of scriptural truth

Though God seems to have failed to fulfill his creation intent for humanity, and is allowing the community to suffer at the hands of "that which is not yet submitted to Jesus' lordship," Christians who exercise their spiritual sense of sight can be confident that Jesus's endurance of suffering and representative "death for all" has issued in his victorious exaltation to lordship, which will imminently be exercised over "all things" (2:9). And far from being abandoned, the "many sons and daughters" of the community are being "led" (ἄγω) through their sufferings into heavenly "glory" by the same God who "led" (ἄγω) Jesus into heaven (1:6) and the same vindicating "glory" (2:9–10). These hopes of heavenly glory are further substantiated in 2:10–11 by means of the community's mimetic alignment and participatory fusion with Jesus. The "last Adam" also is the "pioneer/forerunner" (ἀρχηγός) of their "salvation," "blazing the trail" before them into the heavenly realm (2:10). Furthermore, he is inseparably joined to them, since "those being sanctified" (i.e., the community) and "the one sanctifying" (i.e., Jesus) share the same heavenly paternal source (ἐξ ἑνὸς πάντες).[30]

To decisively quell the community's remaining fears of having been abandoned by God, in 2:11–13 the author dramatically enacts its adoption into the family of God. His initial assertion, that Jesus is "not ashamed" to identify with them as their older brother, provides further indication that the community's fears of abandonment may have been occasioned by their sins and failures or, more specifically, their hesitation to publicly identify with their shamefully crucified Saviour. Yet, despite the warning issued in Mark 8:38 that Jesus will be "ashamed" of "those who are ashamed of me and of my words," Hebrews insists that Jesus is not ashamed of them. Indeed, the short divine adoption "drama" will conclude in Heb 2:13 with the actor Jesus directly addressing the community and declaring his open-armed acceptance of them: "Behold! I am with the children whom God has given me!"

The community's divine adoption occurs in the context of a pair of confessions of familial relatedness exchanged between the Father (1:5) and the Son (2:12–13). The presence of the community in this drama is implied by the manner in which the Father and Son's declarations are presented. After the Father directly addresses the exalted Son in 1:5: "You are my Son; today I have begotten you,"

---

can only be had by reflection on both scriptural texts, which together witness to the now and not yet nature of Christ's rule over all things." The future orientation of Ps 110 is made even more explicit in Heb 10:13, where it reappears with an expanded preface: "And since then he has been eagerly waiting [ἐκδέχομαι] 'until his enemies would be made a footstool for his feet.'"

30. This family orientation also is suggested by ἀρχηγός, which is used in the LXX to describe heads of families (Exod 6:14; 1 Chron 5:24; 1 Esd 5:1; Neh 7:70–71), by Aristotle (*Nicomachean Ethics* 8.12.4) to denote a "family founder," and Josephus (*Against Apion* 1.130) of Noah's status as the "founding father" of the Jewish people.

he speaks of the Son in the third person: "I will be *his* Father, and *he* will be my Son." The Son's response, dramatically enacted in 2:12–13, follows the same pattern: "I will proclaim your name to my brothers and sisters, in the midst of the congregation I will praise you . . . I will put my trust in *him* . . . I am with the children whom *God* has given me."[31] In both passages, the shift from second to third person in the speeches of the *dramatis personae* infers the community's presence in the drama as divinely addressed participants. Their presence is further indicated by Jesus's declarations that he is "in the midst of the congregation" (2:12) and "Behold! I am with the children whom God has given me" (2:13). The author's later emphasis on the community's confession, in 4:14 and 10:23, responds to the divine family confessions and actualises the community's adoption. In "saying the same things" (ὁμο–λογία) that God (1:5) and the Son (2:12–13) have said, the community will find their true and enduring identity, an identity capable of successfully persevering through despair, doubts, and sufferings.

In the remainder of Heb 2, two disparate Christologies, *Christus Victor* and High Priest, are deliberately shaped to address theodical concerns and questions. Both passages, 2:14–15 and 2:16–18, emphasise Jesus's full immersion in the human condition and his powerful past, present, and future actions. Like his "siblings," Jesus "partook in flesh and blood," and as humanity's representative *Christus Victor* triumphed. His victory, however, was paradoxically preceded by defeat, as it was "through death" that he "destroyed the one who has the power of death – that is, the devil" (2:14). In 2:15 the theodical goal of the *Christus Victor* portrayal is forcefully pronounced: Jesus's defeat of death and the devil has "freed those who all their lives have been enslaved by their fear of death." The emphasis on the fragility and frustration of human existence in 2:5–9, 14–18 reaches its nadir in this visceral characterisation of the darkest terror haunting human existence. Though the emotional impact of this assertion is somewhat muted to modern ears, who know nothing of ancient mortality rates, it would have resonated deeply with the addressed community, reminding them of one of the most powerfully transformative effects that the Christ event has had on their lives. The author's description in 2:15 is entirely focused on the experiential effect of this liberation, so we can assume it coheres closely with the community's own experience. Something this profound and life-changing would not be poetically exaggerated, nor shrouded in a misty cloud of "soteriological metaphor." Rather, the content of this liberation, which ensured the community of eternal salvation (7:25), surely was encountered in sharply defined, transformative experiences, and probably

---

31. On Jesus's role as the older brother of the community, see Patrick Gray, "Brotherly Love and the High Priest Christology of Hebrews," in *The Letter to the Hebrews: Critical Readings*, 93–107.

included charismatic experiences of the Holy Spirit and the "powers of the age to come" (2:4; 6:4–5), the conclusive forgiveness and cleansing of sins (2:17; 9:26–28), and the experience of acceptance in God's forever family (2:12–13).

An even more significant portrayal of Christ's past, present, and future commitment to his people concludes the chapter in 2:16–18. Yet again Jesus is said to have "become like his brothers and sisters in every way," though in this instance the purpose of his identification is to equip him as the "merciful and faithful high priest" who makes "atonement for the sins of the people" (2:17). In addition to severing the guilt-inducing link between sin and suffering, this text adapts one of the more popular theodicies, the divine test (cf. Gen 22:1; Job 1–2). Thus, Jesus's sufferings tested his obedience and perseverance. Having passed that test, he now "is able to help those who are being tested" (2:18).

The wealth of Christologies in Heb 2 all issue in one common end: the Son's full identification with humanity and the human condition. In the short span of just fourteen verses, 2:5–18, no less than seven Christologies appear: (1) Adamic (2:6–11); (2) "pioneer of salvation" (2:10); (3) Son of God (2:11–13); (4) *Christus Victor* (2:14–16); (5) Isaianic Sin-bearer (2:9, 17); (6) High Priest (2:17–18); and (7) elder "brother" (2:11–13). In each successive christological portrait, the Son's human experience is chiefly characterised by the suffering he endured (2:9, 10, 14, 18), and in almost every case his suffering is said to have issued in some distinct form of divine vindication. Thus, the last Adam is "crowned with glory and honor" (2:9), the pioneer has been made perfect (2:10), the victor has conquered the devil and freed captive humanity (2:14–15), and the Son has been appointed as the heavenly High Priest (2:17). With Christ as the exemplar of the life of faith, the author establishes a hortatory pattern of "suffering/vindication" that would surely diminish the theodicy concerns of the suffering community.

COMPARING AND CONTRASTING
ROMANS 8 AND HEBREWS 2

As we have begun to see, the theodical strategies of Heb 2 and Rom 8 pursue similar goals and find expression in a variety of shared themes and topics. These similarities in strategies and themes become even more pronounced when the two texts are compared and contrasted side by side. To communities mired in despair and feeling forsaken by God, both authors provide perspective and impart significance by plotting them within the pre-creational plans of God, which are presently unfolding and leading them into their heavenly destiny. Before they came into existence, they were "foreknown" by God and "predestined to be conformed to the image of his Son" (Rom 8:29). And though destined for heavenly glory (8:18, 21, 30; Heb 2:10), their present painful experience of a state and status "a little lower than the angels" (2:7) is integral to God's eternal plan. Nevertheless, having experienced God's sure "testimony" (συμμαρτυρέω, Rom 8:16; συνεπιμαρτυρέω, Heb 2:4), they can be confident that he is carefully coordinating "all things to work together for their good" (Rom 8:28).

The most important indication of God's control of human history and good intentions towards humanity is evidenced in the Christ event, which both authors attribute to divine initiative and love. God "sent his own Son . . . as a sin offering, to condemn sin in the flesh" (Rom 8:3) and he "did not spare his own Son, but gave him up for us all" (8:32). Assertions of God's initiative also are repeatedly indicated in Heb 2: Jesus "was made a little lower than the angels, and because of the suffering of death is now crowned with glory and honor, so that by the grace of God he might taste death for all" (2:9); "it was fitting" that God "would make the pioneer of their salvation perfect through sufferings" (2:10); Jesus "was obligated to become like his siblings" so that he might offer a priestly "atonement for sins" (2:17); and, having been divinely "tested" through sufferings, Jesus can help his siblings who are being tested by the same sufferings (2:18). Additionally, the praise that Jesus offers "in the midst of the congregation" may be celebrating his Father's initiative and planning, their successful outcome leading Jesus to "put his trust in him" (2:12–13). Both authors also believe that divine love and compassion have largely motivated these actions (Rom 8:15–16, 28, 35, 39; Heb 2:11–13, 17).

The addressed communities are securely woven into this tapestry of divine planning and action through the Son's identification with humanity, which both texts forcefully assert and invest with the utmost significance. Immersing himself fully in the Adamic age of sin and death, Jesus appeared in the "likeness [ὁμοίωμα] of sinful flesh," and by becoming a "sin offering" he "condemned sin in the flesh" (Rom 8:3). Hebrews is more emphatic: Jesus was "obligated to become like [ὁμοιόω] humans in every respect," so he could "make an atonement for the sins of the people" (2:17); he "shared" in the "flesh and blood" of "the children," so that through his death and resurrection he could rescue them from their "lifelong fear of death" (2:14–15). Moreover, he representatively fulfilled God's creation intent for humanity, which involved first being "made lower than the angels," then, after "suffering" and "tasting death for all," he fulfilled the promise of Ps 8:4–6, being "crowned with glory and honor" and assuming a status superior to the angels (2:9).

As evidenced in Rom 8 and Heb 2, both Paul and Hebrews would heartily endorse the Reformed maxim, "we know him by his benefits." Both authors also would undoubtedly consider the greatest benefit attending the Christ event to be membership in the divine family, since this experience is unsurpassed in its ability to provide assurance of God's love and acceptance, while at the same time relativising earthly sufferings. Though the addressed communities might feel "condemned" (Rom 8:1, 34) and perhaps even "ashamed" of their family identity (Heb 2:11), the one who could condemn and should feel ashamed, Jesus, does neither! Instead, he welcomes them into the family of God with open arms and proudly proclaims their shared family identity as siblings (2:12–13; cf. 2:17; Rom 8:29). The Spirit effects the family welcome in the communities at Rome, and in response the Roman Christians have effusively and ecstatically proclaimed the fatherhood of God, "crying out, 'Abba, Father!'" (8:15–16). Both authors also propose another important family activity: being "led" (ἄγω) by God on the path through sufferings into heavenly glory (Rom 8:14; Heb 2:10).

Great emphasis also is placed on forgiveness of sin (Rom 8:2–3; Heb 2:11, 17) and divine assistance, which finds expression in a variety of ways. In Rom 8 the Spirit is largely instrumental, setting the Roman Christians "free from the law of sin and death" (8:2), imparting resurrection power (8:11), and helping them to "put to death" the "deeds of the body" (8:13). The Spirit also provides assistance in their prayers, "helping" (συναντιλαμβάνομαι) and interceding for them (8:26). In Heb 2 assistance is offered by Jesus, who "did not come to help [ἐπιλαμβάνω] angels, but to help [ἐπιλαμβάνω] the seed of Abraham" (2:16). Since he has passed the divine test of suffering, "he is able to help" (βοηθέω) those who are being similarly "tested" by their sufferings (2:18). In Rom 8:34, an important act of assistance, intercession, is rendered by Jesus in his priestly capacity, while in Heb 2:11, 17 the author briefly introduces what will become his main topic in Heb 7–10: Jesus's high priestly ministry. Jesus "sanctifies" his siblings (2:11) and as "a merciful and faithful high priest" he "makes atonement" for them (2:17).

A final benefit attending the Christ event involves being "set free" from the fearful grip of death. In both Rom 8 and Heb 2 personal experience confirms this divine act of liberation. Proof that the Roman Christians truly have been "set free [ἐλευθερόω] from the law of sin and death" (8:2) is provided by the same "life-giving" "Spirit of life" that "raised Jesus from the dead" and which is "indwelling within" them (8:11).[32] Ironically, this resurrection power will help them "put to death the deeds of the body" (8:13). Equally important is the Spirit's role in transforming their relationship to God, exchanging the "spirit of slavery" (δουλεία) that produces "fear" (φόβος) for a "spirit of adoption" that

---

32. For emphasis, in 8:11 Paul repeats three times that the Romans are indwelt by the Spirit: τὸ πνεῦμα . . . οἰκεῖ ἐν ὑμῖν . . . τοῦ ἐνοικοῦντος . . . πνεύματος ἐν ὑμῖν.

confirms "sonship" (Rom 8:15–16). The same imagery is used in Heb 2:15 to describe Christians being "set free" (ἀπαλλάσσω) from the "lifelong slavery [δουλεία] to the fear [φόβος] of death," and both occurrences should be considered no mere rhetorical flourish, since many early Christians were personally familiar with the ignominies and horrors of slavery.[33]

An eschatological "now, but not yet" tension is decisive in both texts, and Hebrews even uses the ambiguous "now, but not yet" (νῦν δὲ οὔπω) phrase in relation to Jesus's exaltation (2:8). Though in their earthly circumstances the addressed community presently is unable to "see" the effects of Jesus's representative exaltation to lordship (2:8), if they look into the eschaton they can "now see Jesus crowned with glory and honor" (2:8–9). Such a vision would provide experiential clarity to the "now, but not yet" tension in which they presently exist and substantiate by sight their imminent vindication. The same tension creates metaphysical fissures across the entirety of Rom 8, situating the Roman Christians at an eschatological crossroads where they must choose either the Adamic age of sin and death or the eschatological age of life and peace (8:2–13). Furthermore, their rich experience of the Spirit represents only the "first fruits" (ἀπαρχή, 8:23), while their membership in the family of God, though experienced "now" (8:15–16), is "not yet" fully effected (8:23).

The entire created realm also is implicated in this tension, since it is symbiotically fused with human destiny. The unfulfilled promise of creation's "subjection" (ὑποτάσσω) to humanity in Heb 2:8, which implies its present subjection to a hostile power, is comparable to Paul's claim that creation has been "subjected" (ὑποτάσσω) to "futility" (Rom 8:20). And imparting cosmic significance to the early church's sufferings is Paul's portrayal of personified creation sympathetically "groaning" (στενάζω, 8:22–23) with them, as both "eagerly await" (ἀπεκδέχομαι, 8:19, 23; cf. Heb 9:28) the restoration of God's intent for creation (Rom 8:19–25): an eschatological "revealing of the children of God" (8:18, 21) and the "subjection" of creation to Jesus's lordship (Heb 2:8–9).[34] Under Jesus's lordship, redeemed humanity will no longer "subject" creation to misguided attempts at gaining mastery over it, nor abuse it as a commodity.

---

33. Though difficult to estimate, since "hardly any genuine statistics are available," the slave population in the Roman era typically is thought to have represented 15–30% of the total population (Walter Scheidel, "The Roman Slave Supply," in *The Cambridge World History of Slavery. Volume 1: The Ancient Mediterranean World*, ed. Keith Bradley and Paul Cartledge [Cambridge: CUP, 2011], 287–310, here 287). Given the "colossal scale of human suffering" caused by the Roman slave system, Scheidel ("Roman Slave Supply," 309) characterises it as "one of the darkest chapters of human history."

34. An illuminative study of such "personalistic nature texts" and the interconnection of humans and the world has recently been offered by Mari Joerstad, *The Hebrew Bible and Environmental Ethics: Humans, Nonhumans, and the Living Landscape* (Cambridge: CUP, 2019).

There are two notable differences between Rom 8 and Heb 2. First, the almost complete lack of a human agential response in Heb 2 sharply contrasts with Paul's recurring emphasis on mutual agency (Rom 8:4–6, 16–17, 23, 26, 28–29, 37).[35] The passivity in Heb 2, however, is soon replaced by vigorous exhortations to persevere, which begin in 3:6 and persist throughout the remainder of the "word of exhortation." Much more consequential are their differing depictions of the immanent agent performing divine action. In Rom 8 the indwelling Spirit is almost entirely responsible (8:2, 4–6, 9–11, 13–16, 23, 26–27), while Heb 2 repeatedly stresses Jesus's immanence and intimate acquaintance with the community's travails: he presently is "sanctifying" (ἁγιάζων) "those who are being sanctified" (ἁγιαζόμενοι; 2:11) and, standing "in the midst" of their gathering, he welcomes them with open arms (2:12–13). Furthermore, Jesus presently is "taking hold" of them (2:16)[36] and "helping" them pass their divine test (2:18).[37]

CONCLUSION

Perhaps as a result of our comfortable and long lives, we often fail to hear the cries of suffering that rise from the pages of the NT. Not surprisingly, then, we also fail to adequately appreciate the NT's theodical responses to those cries, even in much-beloved and oft-read texts like Rom 8 and Heb 2. In those texts, the despair, doubts, and sufferings of the early church meet their match in impassioned defenses of God's goodness, power, and love. At the centre of those defenses stands God's most powerful act of love, the giving of his Son, and the essential proof of this divine action is located by both authors in the early church's experience of God's fatherly love. Only such an experience can explain

---

35. On Paul's soteriological agency, see John M. G. Barclay, "'By the Grace of God I Am What I Am': Grace and Agency in Philo and Paul," in *Divine and Human Agency in Paul and His Cultural Environment*, ed. John M. G. Barclay and Simon J. Gathercole, LNTS 335 (London: T&T Clark, 2006), 140–57.

36. So Cockerill, *The Epistle to the Hebrews*, 149: Jesus "does not superintend their journey from a distance, but he 'takes hold' of them and guides them by the hand."

37. Though cf. Frank J. Matera, "Moral Exhortation: The Relation between Moral Exhortation and Doctrinal Exposition in the Letter to the Hebrews," *Toronto Journal of Theology* 10 (1994): 169–82, here 182: Hebrews's portrayal of the immanent Jesus is "only a shadow of Paul's doctrine of the Spirit by which the Christian is empowered to do God's will"; and Jared Compton, *Psalm 110 and the Logic of Hebrews*, LNTS 537 (London: T&T Clark, 2015), 171: Jesus's "absence" from the community was a major factor motivating the writing of Hebrews, and the author only offers "one or two hints… about Jesus' present ministry (see, e.g., 2.18; 7.25)." Markus Bockmuehl, "The Dynamic Absence of Jesus in Hebrews," *JTS* 70, no. 1 (2019): 141–62, is more willing than Matera or Compton to recognise indications of Jesus's presence in Hebrews, yet he still contends that Hebrews primarily portrays Jesus as absent.

Paul's remarkable claim that "the present sufferings are not worthy to be compared with the glory that is about to be revealed in us" (Rom 8:18).

SELECT BIBLIOGRAPHY

Attridge, Harold W. *A Commentary on the Epistle to the Hebrews*. Hermeneia. Philadelphia: Fortress, 1989.

Barclay, John M. G. "'By the Grace of God I Am What I Am': Grace and Agency in Philo and Paul." In *Divine and Human Agency in Paul and His Cultural Environment*, edited by John M. G. Barclay and Simon J. Gathercole, 140–157. LNTS 335. London: T&T Clark, 2006.

———. *Paul and the Gift*. Grand Rapids: Eerdmans, 2015.

Bockmuehl, Markus. "The Dynamic Absence of Jesus in Hebrews." *JTS* 70, no. 1 (2019): 141–162.

Cockerill, Gareth Lee. *The Epistle to the Hebrews*. NICNT. Grand Rapids: Eerdmans, 2012.

Cohick, Lynn H. "Poverty and Its Causes in the Early Church." In *Poverty in the Early Church and Today: A Conversation*, edited by Steve Walton and Hannah Swithinbank, 16–27. London: T&T Clark, 2019.

Compton, Jared. *Psalm 110 and the Logic of Hebrews*. LNTS 537. London: T&T Clark, 2015.

Crenshaw, James L. *Defending God: Biblical Responses to the Problem of Evil*. Oxford: OUP, 2005.

———. "The Shift from Theodicy to Anthropodicy." In *Theodicy in the Old Testament*, edited by James L. Crenshaw, 1–16. Philadelphia: Fortress, 1983.

Dunn, James D. G. *The Theology of Paul the Apostle*. Grand Rapids: Eerdmans, 1998.

Eisenbaum, Pamela. "Redescribing the Religion of Hebrews." In *"The One Who Sows Bountifully": Essays in Honor of Stanley K. Stowers*, edited by Caroline Johnson Hodge, Saul M. Olyan, Daniel Ullucci, and Emma Wasserman, 283–293. BJS 356. Providence: Brown Judaic Studies, 2013.

Ellingworth, Paul. *The Epistle to the Hebrews: A Commentary on the Greek Text*. NIGTC. Grand Rapids: Eerdmans, 1993.

Erdkamp, Paul. "Famine and Hunger in the Roman World." In *The Routledge Handbook of Diet and Nutrition in the Roman World*, edited by Paul Erdkamp and Claire Holleran, 296–307. London: Routledge, 2019.

Eskola, Timo. *Theodicy and Predestination in Pauline Soteriology*. WUNT 2/100. Tübingen: Mohr Siebeck, 1998.

Ferreira, Johan. "Reconsidering the Poor: A Fresh Translation of Matthew 5:3." In

Fountains of Wisdom: In Conversation with James H. Charlesworth, edited by Gerbern S. Oegema, Henry W. Morisada Rietz, and Loren T. Stuckenbruck, 107–126. London: T&T Clark, 2022.

Frey, Jörg. "Paul's View of the Spirit in the Light of Qumran." In *The Dead Sea Scrolls and Pauline Literature*, edited by Jean-Sébastien Rey, 237–260. STDJ 102. Leiden: Brill, 2014.

Gray, Patrick. "Brotherly Love and the High Priest Christology of Hebrews." In *The Letter to the Hebrews: Critical Readings*, edited by Scott D. Mackie, 93–107. T&T Clark Critical Readings in Biblical Studies. London: Bloomsbury, 2018.

Guthrie, George H. "Hebrews' Use of the Old Testament: Recent Trends in Research." In *The Letter to the Hebrews: Critical Readings*, edited by Scott D. Mackie, 355–375. T&T Clark Critical Readings in Biblical Studies. London: Bloomsbury, 2018.

Holmén, Tom. *Theodicy and the Cross of Christ: A New Testament Inquiry*. LNTS 567. London: T&T Clark, 2019.

Hübner, Sabine R., and David M. Ratzan, "Fatherless Antiquity? Perspectives on 'Fatherlessness' in the Ancient Mediterranean." In *Growing Up Fatherless in Antiquity*, edited by Sabine R. Hübner and David M. Ratzan, 3–28. Cambridge: CUP, 2009.

Huebner, Sabine R. *The Family in Roman Egypt*. Cambridge: CUP, 2013.

Jewett, Robert. *Romans: A Commentary*. Hermeneia. Minneapolis: Fortress, 2006.

Joerstad, Mari. *The Hebrew Bible and Environmental Ethics: Humans, Nonhumans, and the Living Landscape*. Cambridge: CUP, 2019.

Koester, Craig R. *Hebrews: A New Translation with Introduction and Commentary*. AB 36. New York: Doubleday, 2001.

Laato, Antti, and Johannes C. de Moor. "Introduction." In *Theodicy in the World of the Bible*, edited by Antti Laato and Johannes C. de Moor, vii–liv. Leiden: Brill, 2003.

Laes, Christian. *Children in the Roman Empire: Outsiders Within*. Cambridge: CUP, 2011.

Lane, William L. *Hebrews 1–8*. WBC 47A. Dallas: Word, 1991.

———. *Hebrews 9–13*. WBC 47B. Dallas: Word, 1991.

Mackie, Scott D. "'Behold! I Am with the Children God Has Given Me': Ekphrasis and Epiphany in Hebrews 1–2." In *Son, Sacrifice, and Great Shepherd: Studies on the Epistle to the Hebrews*, edited by Eric F. Mason and David M. Moffitt, 43–77. WUNT 2/510. Tübingen: Mohr Siebeck, 2020.

Matera, Frank J. "Moral Exhortation: The Relation between Moral Exhortation and Doctrinal Exposition in the Letter to the Hebrews." *Toronto Journal of Theology* 10 (1994): 169–182.

Newsom, Carol A. *The Spirit within Me: Self and Agency in Ancient Israel and Second Temple Judaism*. AYBRL. New Haven: Yale University Press, 2021.

Scheidel, Walter. "Demography." In *The Cambridge Economic History of the Greco-Roman World*, edited by Walter Scheidel, Ian Morris, and Richard Saller, 38–86. Cambridge: CUP, 2007.

———. "The Roman Slave Supply." In *The Cambridge World History of Slavery*. Vol. 1: *The Ancient Mediterranean World*, edited by Keith Bradley and Paul Cartledge, 287–310. Cambridge: CUP, 2011.

Shantz, Colleen. *Paul in Ecstasy: The Neurobiology of the Apostle's Life and Thought*. Cambridge: CUP, 2009.

Stone, Michael E. *A Commentary on the Book of Fourth Ezra*. Hermeneia. Minneapolis: Fortress, 1990.

Wreford, Mark. "Diagnosing Religious Experience in Romans 8." *TynBul* 68, no. 2 (2017): 203–222.

PART III

Divine Action in Hebrews

CHAPTER 7

Divine Action in the Jewish Scriptures according to Hebrews

George H. Guthrie

INTRODUCTION

In Hebrews God functions as the great presupposition and primary reference point of the discourse, its most important actor[1] and speaker, the one who sets "the agenda for what he does,"[2] as noted by Fellipe do Vale in this volume's introductory essay. Often in Hebrews both God's acts and his voice are communicated in the words of the Jewish Scriptures.

Accordingly, this essay offers a reflection on divine action in Hebrews as it relates to those Scriptures. The chapter develops in three movements. First, we consider "Divine Action and the Scriptures," that is, especially, God's act of speaking Scripture but also phenomena surrounding the appropriation of Scripture in Hebrews, especially the theological axioms undergirding the author's patterns of appropriation. Second, as we probe the incorporation of

---

1. It seems odd that for the majority of approaches to the theology of the book of Hebrews, "God" does not factor as a main "motif" for discussion. Thus Nils Dahl's lament for NT theology generally, offered a generation ago (Nils A. Dahl, "The Neglected Factor in New Testament Theology," *Reflections* 73, no. 1 [1975], 5–8), still is largely true for the book of Hebrews, in spite of progress being made in some quarters, for example, Paul Ellingworth, *The Epistle to the Hebrews: A Commentary on the Greek Text* (Grand Rapids: Eerdmans, 1993) and Mathias Rissi, *Die Theologie des Hebräerbriefs: Ihre Verankerung in der Situation des Verfassers und seiner Leser* (Tübingen: J. C. B. Mohr [Paul Siebeck], 1987).

2. Fellipe do Vale, "Divine Action, Theological Method, and Scripture's Narrative," in the present volume, 6.

Scripture in Hebrews we begin to encounter various references to those speaking Scripture in the book, which evokes an assessment of "Divine Action and Divine Referents in Hebrews," particularly God's interaction within the Trinity, manifested as scripturally expressed communication. Finally, we assess "Other Divine Actions as Reflected in the Scriptures," that is, the ways that our author reflects on the various scripturally expressed actions of the divine, apart from specific references to persons of the Trinity.

DIVINE ACTION AND THE SCRIPTURES

Hebrews embodies a theology grounded in the word of God (1:1–2), a theology that radiates outward from the book's Christology in the introduction (1:1–4) and first christological movement (1:5–14).[3] No characteristic of Hebrews reflects this orientation to God's voice more overtly than the introductory formulae with which the author introduces scriptural quotations, for time and again the author of Hebrews presents the Scriptures as falling from the lips of God, shaped most often with variations of the verb λέγω.[4] Thus, in Hebrews God articulates himself and[5] speaks of himself and to himself, as well as to people in the world.[6] God's speaking and his actions must be conceived of as interrelated, the former a "fundamental dimension" of the latter.[7]

Accordingly, the Scriptures shape the very framework and fabric of Hebrews's discourse on God's ongoing work of redemption in the world. The author integrates quotations, allusions, echoes, and references to topics, events, persons, or institutions of the older testament into a hermeneutically complex, highly crafted, Christocentric theology of new covenant life for God's people. In one reckoning of data in the book, across forty-eight passages we find thirty-seven quotations, forty overt allusions, and a number of "echoes," to use Richard Hays's terminology.[8]

In recent decades, work on the appropriation of the Jewish Scriptures

3. Udo Schnelle, *Theology of the New Testament* (Grand Rapids: Baker Academic, 2009), 635.
4. The verb is used as an IF twenty-five times in the book, twenty-two of these with God the Father, Christ, and the Spirit as the speakers: for example, 1:5–7, 13; 2:12; 3:7, etc. Human beings other than Christ are presented as speaking Scripture at 2:6, 9:20, and 12:21, on which see later in this chapter.
5. Hans Hübner, *Biblische Theologie des Neuen Testaments Band 3: Hebräerbrief, Evangelien und Offenbarung: Epilegomena* (Göttingen: Vandenhoeck & Ruprecht, 1995), 19.
6. Joachim Ringleben, *Wort und Geschichte: Kleine Theologie des Hebräerbriefs* (Göttingen: Vandenhoeck & Ruprecht, 2019), 13.
7. Schnelle, *Theology of the New Testament*, 632–33.
8. See, for example, George H. Guthrie, "Hebrews," in *Commentary on the New Testament Use of the Old Testament*, ed. G. K. Beale and D. A. Carson (Grand Rapids: Baker Academic, 2007), 919–95.

in Hebrews forms an expanding subdiscipline in Hebrews studies, scholars addressing issues such as the form of the scriptural texts used by the author of Hebrews, rabbinic techniques of appropriation, and hermeneutical approaches evinced in the book.[9] Yet, for the purposes of the present essay, two developments in recent research demand special attention: the theological axioms that undergird Hebrews and the divine, personal interactions evoked in the integration of the Scriptures in the book. I address these in turn.

Scholars such as Daniel Patte and Susan Docherty have placed an emphasis on the theological axioms that lay behind the handling of Scripture in Second Temple Judaism. Concerning Hebrews specifically, Docherty argues that discernible theological axioms lay behind the appropriation of Scripture in the book. For example, for many Jews of the period God's word stands as authoritative, particular, coherent, and historically synthetic.[10]

First, Hebrews reads Scripture, as the words of God, as having an inherent and unassailable authority.[11] We might say that the words of God are authoritative "speech acts" according to Hebrews. Consequently, not only are God's words perceived to be true but they demand a response of obedience, as with, "Today, if you hear his voice, do not harden your hearts . . ." (Heb 3:7–8),[12] applying Ps 95:7–11 to the author's original audience (Heb 3:12–19).[13]

Second, as was the case with other Jewish interpreters of the period, for Hebrews the details of the scriptural text are significant, providing insight into God's actions.[14] God shapes Scripture particularly, imbuing every part of a text with significance. For example, at Heb 8:8, 13 the author plucks the word καινός ("new") from the quotation of Jer 31:31, highlighting its importance for an understanding of the history of redemption. The word speaks to the unfolding of narrative accounts of God's working in the world. If God initiates a "new" covenant, it must mean that the first covenant, in some sense, was doomed to obsolescence (8:13).

---

9. See an introduction on the topic, for example: Susan E. Docherty, *The Use of the Old Testament in Hebrews: A Case Study in Early Jewish Bible Interpretation* (Tübingen: Mohr Siebeck, 2009); G. H. Guthrie, "Hebrews' Use of the Old Testament: Recent Trends in Research," *Currents in Biblical Research* 1, no. 2 (2003): 271–94; Guthrie, "Hebrews," 919–23; Dana M. Harris, "The Use of the Old Testament in the Epistle of Hebrews," *Southwestern Journal of Theology* 64, no. 1 (2021): 91–106.

10. See Daniel Patte, *Early Jewish Hermeneutic in Palestine* (Missoula, MT: Scholars Press, 1975), 65–74, in which he points to theological axioms behind the targums; Docherty, *The Use of the Old Testament in Hebrews*, 179–81; 196–98. Patte specifically emphasises the idea that Scripture is seen as historically synthetic.

11. Docherty, *Old Testament in Hebrews*, 180–81, 197.

12. Scripture quotations are from the NIV unless otherwise noted.

13. Docherty, *Old Testament in Hebrews*, 197–98.

14. Docherty, *Old Testament in Hebrews*, 180.

However, not only may specific words in a passage be seized upon and read as resonant with significance, but even word order within a passage may be heard as evoking a particular interpretation of reality,[15] as seen in the quotation of Ps 40:6–8 at Heb 10:5–10. Commenting on this quotation, the author notes that the coming of Christ to do God's will has led to the abrogation of the old covenant sacrifices (10:8–9). In verse 9 he notes, "He sets aside the first [part of the passage having to do with sacrifices] to establish the second [part of the passage having to do with Jesus Christ's obedience]," the setting aside and establishing constituting sequential actions on the part of God; this sequence stands reflected in the very shape of the text.

A third theological axiom behind Hebrews's appropriation of biblical material concerns the coherence, or integrated nature, of Scripture.[16] For our author, God's words as embodied in Scripture constitute an interconnected whole. For instance, the author makes extensive use of "verbal analogy," often bringing passages together and interpreting one in light of the other, based on shared wording.[17] The axiom underlying this hermeneutical move has to do with the coherence of the Scriptures as a whole, God perceived as speaking (and thus acting) consistently and coherently.[18] Since all the words of Scripture are perceived to be God's words and God speaks truly, never contradicting himself, insight into particular actions of God as reflected in the Scriptures can be gained by reading Scripture in light of Scripture.

In the introduction to this volume, Fellipe do Vale notes that Christians have a narrative to which they are committed, "namely, an arrangement of divine action whose distinct components come together to weave a history. . . ."[19] This insight relates directly to a fourth and final axiom underlying our author's engagement of the Scriptures: that God's communication undergirds what might be called a synthetic view of history. As lord of history, one who speaks throughout history with a consistent voice and for his consistent purposes, God shapes all of history to a desired end.[20] Thus, all of history may be perceived as a synthetic whole based on the presence of God in history and his active work in the context of history.

---

15. Docherty, *Old Testament in Hebrews*, 180.

16. Docherty, *Old Testament in Hebrews*, 197.

17. Verbal analogy is the rabbinic tool of appropriation used most extensively in the book. For example, the three pairs of passages in the catena of texts in 1:5–13 each are brought together on the basis of common terminology.

18. Docherty, *Old Testament in Hebrews*, 194–95; Guthrie, "Hebrews," 928.

19. do Vale, "Divine Action, Theological Method, and Scripture's Narrative," 12.

20. Patte, *Early Jewish Hermeneutic in Palestine*, 66–68.

In Hebrews, for example, the revelation in and through the Son builds upon and flows from the prior revelation through the prophets (Heb 1:1–2; 12:25–27).[21] The worship practices under the old covenant and those of the new may be read in light of each other.[22] Since all of history is God's history, the eras of revelation are both distinct and profoundly interrelated. Moreover, God's acts as reflected in the Scriptures have ongoing relevance, for the living God lives through all the ages of the world and works in an ongoing way to bring about his desired ends in the world,[23] leading the people of God to anticipate the end of history when Christ returns (Heb 1:13; 2:5–9; 9:28).

DIVINE ACTION AND DIVINE REFERENTS IN HEBREWS

THREE DIVINE REFERENTS IN HEBREWS

But to whom do we refer when we speak of the divine in Hebrews? Who is this God who speaks and acts in human history and in and through the Scriptures? This question brings us to another productive body of recent research that relates directly to the actions carried out by divine agents as they speak the Scriptures in Hebrews.[24] For example, two scholars have probed the interpersonal communication of Father, Son, and Spirit in Hebrews. In his work entitled, "God Has Spoken: The Renegotiation of Scripture in Hebrews,"[25] Matthew Malcolm notes that Father, Son, and Spirit speak in an identifiable pattern in the first two of three main movements in the book.[26] The Father speaks to the Son in the chain quotation of 1:5–13, the Son speaks the words of Ps 22:22 to the Father at 2:12, and the Spirit speaks to the people of God through Ps 95:7–11 at 3:7–11.[27] In the second major movement of Hebrews, God the Father speaks the words of proclamation to the Son through Ps 2:7 and 110:4 (5:5–6, and then continues to speak in the following chapters), the Son speaks

---

21. E.g., Scott D. Mackie, "Early Christian Eschatological Experience in the Warnings and Exhortations of the Epistle to the Hebrews," *TynBul* 63 (2012): 93–114.
22. Richard Joseph Ounsworth, *Joshua Typology in the New Testament* (Tübingen: Mohr Siebeck, 2012); Benjamin J. Ribbens, *Levitical Sacrifice and Heavenly Cult in Hebrews* (Berlin: de Gruyter, 2016); Gareth Lee Cockerill, *The Epistle to the Hebrews* (Grand Rapids: Eerdmans, 2012), 56.
23. Docherty, *Old Testament in Hebrews*, 177.
24. As noted in do Vale, "Divine Action, Theological Method, and Scripture's Narrative," 15.
25. Matthew R. Malcolm, "God Has Spoken: The Renegotiation of Scripture in Hebrews," in *All That The Prophets Have Declared: The Appropriation of Scripture in the Emergence of Christianity*, ed. Matthew R. Malcolm (West Ryde, Australia: Paternoster, 2015), 174–81.
26. He reads those movements as 1:1–4:16, 4:14–10:25, and 10:19–13:25.
27. Malcolm, "God Has Spoken," 179.

the words of Ps 40:6–8 to the Father (10:5–10), and the Holy Spirit speaks of the new covenant at Jer 31:31–34 (38:31–34 LXX; Heb 10:15–17). Malcolm finds the order of divine interaction significant for Hebrews, stating that

> This rhythm – of God speaking Scripture to the son; Jesus speaking Scripture to God; and the Holy Spirit speaking Scripture to the children – illustrates the pervasive influence of the renegotiated conceptualizations at the core of the emerging Christian movement. They have the capacity to articulate and structure formational Christian discourse.[28]

Similarly, in her 2020 monograph, *Divine Discourse in the Epistle to the Hebrews: The Recontextualization of Spoken Quotations of Scripture*, Madison Pierce utilises prosopological exegesis, which "interprets texts by assigning 'faces' (πρόσωπα), or characters, to ambiguous or unspecified personal (or personified) entities represented in the text in question."[29] In order to clarify dynamics in the text, the interpreter identifies participants who speak, or are addressed, or are referred to, in or through the text. Pierce explains:

> Simply by assigning a text a new "face," a dialogical relationship is established where the text assumes previous knowledge of the character, and the character is thus illuminated further by the text. Thus, when the author of Hebrews presents the Father saying to Jesus, "You are my Son; today, I have begotten you" (1:5), he is both illuminating scripture and teaching his audience about Jesus – the Son of God.[30]

Pierce notes that although the technique is used elsewhere in the NT, Hebrews, especially in the first two great movements of the discourse,[31] develops discussion around the interpersonal speaking of Father, Son, and Spirit. She describes the author's use of prosopological exegesis as "ubiquitous and methodical and exceptional," and concludes that it is "central to the author's portrayal of God because God confirms the author's characterization himself."[32]

---

28. Malcolm, "God Has Spoken," 181.

29. Madison N. Pierce, *Divine Discourse in the Epistle to the Hebrews: The Recontextualization of Spoken Quotations of Scripture* (Cambridge: CUP, 2020), 4.

30. Pierce, *Divine Discourse*, 5.

31. Pierce follows Cynthia Westfall in identifying the movements as 1:1–4:16, 4:11–10:25, and 10:19–13:25. See Pierce, *Divine Discourse*, 176–77; Cynthia Long Westfall, *A Discourse Analysis of the Letter to the Hebrews: The Relationship between Form and Meaning* (London; New York: T&T Clark, 2005), 136–37.

32. Pierce, *Divine Discourse*, 201.

Our topic demands at least a brief interaction with this approach, for early and often in Hebrews the reader comes upon language, formulas, theological descriptions, and even warnings that evoke a theology of the One God as tripersonal.[33] As Wesley Hill, quoting Robert Jenson, notes in his *Paul and the Trinity*, for Paul "God the Father and Christ and the Spirit all demand dramatically coordinating mention."[34] The same can be said of Hebrews.

THE ACTIONS OF YAHWEH: FATHER, SON, AND SPIRIT

Due to our space constraints, the question must be addressed with just one prime example that involves the three persons of the Trinity and how Scripture is perceived as speaking of them and their interrelated actions.[35] The illustrative detail I wish to note attends to the way that Father, Son, and Spirit all are referred to as "Lord" or presented as the Lord in relation to OT Yahweh passages. For Hebrews, the one Lord, described in three persons, acts in and in relation to the Scriptures.[36]

The author of Hebrews refers to the Father as "Lord" in relation to at least two quotations in the book (and perhaps several others that are more ambiguous). First, consider the quotation of Ps 110:4 (109:4 LXX) at 7:21:

---

33. A binatarian view of Hebrews, with emphasis on Father and Son but not the Spirit, simply will not do on closer examination. For Hebrews as proto-Trinitarian, see, for instance, Stephen Motyer, "The Spirit in Hebrews: No Longer Forgotten?," in *Spirit and Christ in the New Testament and Christian Theology: Essays in Honor of Max Turner*, ed. I. Howard Marshall, Volker Rabens, and Cornelis Bennema (Grand Rapids: Eerdmans, 2012), 213–27; Hübner, *Biblische Theologie des Neuen Testaments*, 19; R. B. Jamieson, *The Paradox of Sonship: Christology in the Epistle to the Hebrews* (Downers Grove: IVP Press, 2021), 71–75.

34. As seen in Wesley Hill, *Paul and the Trinity: Persons, Relations, and the Pauline Letters* (Grand Rapids: Eerdmans, 2015), 135; Robert W. Jenson, *Systematic Theology* (New York; Oxford: OUP, 1997), 1:92.

35. While it is true that Hebrews also depicts human voices as speaking Scripture, the role that those voices play in the "quadralogue" of Hebrews is not my primary concern at this point, since my essay's focus is on the divine. Nevertheless, the introductory formulae in Hebrews by which the Scriptures are presented as spoken by human beings needs further exploration. This quadralogue – between Father, Son, Spirit, and human beings – provides an important framework from which to read the book's theology. Let me say at this point that the primary implication is that for Hebrews God's voice is the dominant voice of Scripture; however, the exceptions bear witness to God's interaction with human beings in the production of what we have come to know as the Scriptures, and this is no surprise. Scripture, though the voice of God, speaks in human voices and through human agents (e.g., 1:1–2). Yet, what is truly unique about Hebrews is the framework in which the human voice speaks, for here that voice joins the voices of Father, Son, and Spirit in a quadralogue, even paralleling the pattern of the Son who speaks to the Father.

36. On the use of "Lord" as a title for God in both the OT and the NT, see David B. Capes, *Old Testament Yahweh Texts in Paul's Christology* (Tübingen: J. C. B. Mohr, 1992), 34–37; Larry Hurtado, "Lord," in *Dictionary of Paul and His Letters*, ed. Gerald F. Hawthorne, Ralph P. Martin, and Daniel G. Reid (Downers Grove: IVP Press, 2020), 560–69.

But he became a priest with an oath when God[37] said to him:

> "The Lord has sworn
>   and will not change his mind:
>   'You are a priest forever.'"

The translators of the Septuagint render the divine name for "Yahweh" (יהוה) with the term κύριος. That our author reads the "Lord" of Ps 110:4 as a reference to God the Father is clear from his interaction with Ps 110 thus far in Hebrews (e.g., 1:3, 13 with reference to Ps 110:1). At 5:5–6, in an introduction on the ordination of the Son as High Priest, the "Father" speaks the words of Ps 2:7 (5:5; read in light of the quotation of the psalm in 1:5) and also speaks Ps 110:4 (5:6). Thus, the Lord, who is the Father, acts with the words of Ps 110:4, ordaining the Son to be "high priest in the order of Melchizedek" (5:10).[38]

Second, the author of Hebrews refers to the Son as Yahweh. At Heb 1:8–9, in the voice of God the Father and via the words of Ps 45:6–7, the Son is proclaimed as "God." It is likely that this psalm was employed by the author of Hebrews for its explicit address of Christ as God, reflecting his unique person and position.[39] In parallel fashion,[40] expressed in a psalm focused on Yahweh (Ps 102:25–27/LXX 101:26–28),[41] the author of Hebrews celebrates the Son as

---

37. The term "God" in the NIV translation is implied but not overtly expressed in the Greek text, which reads, ὁ δὲ μετὰ ὁρκωμοσίας διὰ τοῦ λέγοντος πρὸς αὐτόν, straightforwardly, "but he with an oath through the one saying to him . . ."

38. The quotation of Prov 3:11–12 at Heb 12:5–6 presents a second clear example of God the Father being referred to as "Lord" in association with Scripture. Earlier in Hebrews the author writes of the Son leading the "sons" of God to glory (2:10), the fatherhood of God strongly implied in the passage (so Amy L. B. Peeler, *You Are My Son: The Family of God in the Epistle to the Hebrews*, LNTS 486, [London: Bloomsbury T&T Clark, 2014], 80–82). Later in the book, the "Lord" (κύριος; translating יהוה) who disciplines in Prov 3:11–12 is none other than God the Father, which is made clear almost immediately following the quotation: "God is treating you as his children. For what children are not disciplined by their father?" (12:7). He is the "Father of spirits" who disciplines his children for their good (12:9–10). Thus, God the Father is the "Lord" of whom the proverb speaks.

39. So, for example, August Strobel, *Der Brief an die Hebräer* (Göttingen: Vandenhoeck & Ruprecht, 1991), 23–24. Here God the Father addresses the Son as "God" with a vocative form: "Your throne, O God, will last for ever and ever." On which see, for example, William R. G. Loader, *Sohn und Hoherpriester: eine traditionsgeschichtliche Untersuchung zur Christologie des Hebräerbriefes* (Neukirchen-Vluyn: Neukirchener Verlag, 1981), 25; Otto Michel, *Der Brief an die Hebräer* (Göttingen: Vandenhoeck & Ruprecht, 1966), 118; Ringleben, *Wort und Geschichte: Kleine Theologie des Hebräerbriefs*, 34; Ceslas Spicq, *L'Épître aux Hébreux* (Paris: Gabalda, 1952), 2:19.

40. Michel, *Der Brief an die Hebräer*, 118.

41. "The Lord" (*yahweh*) is referred to 8 times in the Hebrew version of the psalm (Ps 102:1–2, 13, 16–17, 20, 22–23) and is also addressed as "God" (102:24). The term for "Lord" does not appear in verse 26 of the Hebrew version of the psalm (102:26 LXX; 102:25 ET), but the context is clear that the Lord is being addressed.

"Lord" (1:10–12). Speaking of the use of "Lord" in tandem with "God," James Swetnam says of 1:8, 10, "This is of crucial significance. The two principal Old Testament designations for the divinity are here applied to the Son without qualification."[42] In Hebrews's contextualisation of the psalm, God the Father speaks this Scripture to the Son, and so the Father himself, who is Lord, addresses the Son as "Lord," that is, "Yahweh."[43] Accordingly, the author of Hebrews reflects a fuller understanding of Yahweh's multi-personal identity as revealed through the Christ event.

Third, the author of Hebrews considers the Holy Spirit to be Yahweh. Our author presents two passages from the Jewish Scriptures as spoken by the Holy Spirit: Ps 95:7–11/94:7–11 LXX (3:7–11) and Jer 31:31–34/38:31–34 LXX (8:8–12). In the second of these, Jer 31:31–34 is presented in full at Heb 8:8–12 and in part at 10:15–17.[44] At the end of his treatment of Jesus's superior new covenant offering, the author drives home the decisiveness and eternal effectiveness of that offering with,

The Holy Spirit also testifies to us about this. First he says:

> "This is the covenant I will make with them
>> after that time, says the Lord.
> I will put my laws in their hearts,
>> and I will write them on their minds." (10:15–16)

---

42. J. Swetnam, "Hebrews 1, 5–14: A New Look," *Melita Theologica* 51, no. 1 (2000): 61.

43. Pierce, *Divine Discourse*, 57–58. For further discussion on context of this psalm, its uses in Second Temple Judaism, and the forms of the text in the MT, LXX, and Hebrews, see Guthrie, "Hebrews," 939–42.

44. In her prosopological exegesis of this quotation in Hebrews 8, Madison Pierce suggests that the Father is the speaker of the Jeremiah text. She admits that the Father, Son, and Spirit are all viable candidates but depends on proximity in the discourse as the deciding factor. Her logical move is as follows. In the first part of chapter 8 the Father is the active agent; he appoints the Son as high priest (8:3), and he probably should be understood as the one who sought for a new covenant (8:7). She reasons, "if the Father is the one acting, then he is also likely the one who seeks a place for a second covenant (8:7) . . . " (Pierce, *Divine Discourse*, 85–86). Yet it should be pointed out that the Father is not mentioned overtly in the first verses of Hebrews 8.

Pierce's argument from proximity fails to take into account why the author repeats the portion of Jer 31:31–34 found at Heb 10:15–17. With the repetition the author crafts an *inclusio* that frames the section of the book that expounds the Son's superior new covenant offering. Thus, the truncated portion at 10:15–18 intentionally reminds the reader of where the discussion on that new covenant offering started: with the quotation of the whole at 8:7–12. With the closing of the inclusio, the topic of the Son's superior offering draws to a close. From a discourse standpoint, the two quotations from Jeremiah 31 are made functionally proximate by their shared task in marking the beginning and ending of the climactic movement in the book's Christology. What is beyond dispute is that the author of Hebrews overtly identifies the Holy Spirit as the "Lord" who speaks the quotation found at 10:15–18, and it is reasonable to assume that the Spirit also speaks the fuller quotation at 8:7–13. The Holy Spirit is "the Lord" who speaks this passage from Jeremiah.

Note the parallel between "after he says" (μετὰ γὰρ τὸ εἰρηκέναι) in the introductory formula and "after those days the Lord says" (μετὰ τὰς ἡμέρας ἐκείνας, λέγει κύριος) in the quotation; note also that the passage spoken by the Spirit is in first person and that the Holy Spirit who testifies (Μαρτυρεῖ) is identified as "the Lord" (κύριος; rendering יהוה) who speaks throughout the passage.[45] In this word of prophecy, the Spirit is the "I" who makes the covenant, puts laws on hearts and writes them on minds, and treats sins as decisively dealt with by the sacrifice of Christ. In the face of ambiguity concerning the speaker of Jer 31:31–34 (38:31–34 LXX) at 8:8–12, it seems preferable to follow the author's own prosopological exegesis of the quotation found at 10:15–18, identifying the Holy Spirit with Yahweh.

INTERPERSONAL ACTIONS OF THE DIVINE IN HEBREWS

For Hebrews, then, God is Yahweh, the Lord, who speaks, and his communication is tri-personal – Father, Son, and Spirit each acting as Yahweh in relation to scriptural passages. Yet, as we probe further, particularly in the act of speaking the scriptural passages, each member of the Trinity seems to direct his words primarily towards distinct parties. The Father speaks words to the Son. The Son speaks words to the Father. The Spirit primarily speaks words to human beings.

First, as we consider the actions of the Father as he speaks the Scriptures, he primarily addresses or acts concerning the Son but also speaks of the angelic beings.[46] In the string of passages in 1:5–14, the Father is said to have spoken to or of the Son the words of Ps 2:7; 2 Sam 7:14/1 Chron 17:13 (1:5); Deut 32:43 (or Ps 97:7; 1:6);[47] Ps 45:6–7 (1:8–9); Ps 102:25–27 (1:10–12); and Ps 110:1 (1:13). Of the angelic beings the Father has spoken Ps 104:4, creating the angelic beings as "spirits, and his servants flames of fire" (1:7); ultimately, the angels serve as a foil for reflections centred on the Son, whom they worship.

In 1:5–14 the Father has acted by enthroning the Son as Messiah (1:5, 13), commanding the angels to worship him (1:6), declaring the eternality of the Son's reign and anointing him (1:8–9), and creating the universe through him (1:10–12 read in light of 1:2). Furthermore, on the basis of its verbal analogy with Ps 110:1, the author introduces Ps 8:4–6 in Heb 2:5–9.[48] In light of

---

45. As an example of the Spirit being identified with the "Lord" of an OT passage, see Paul's statement "The Lord is the Spirit" at 2 Cor 3:17. He means that the "Lord" of which Exod 34:34 speaks. See George H. Guthrie, *2 Corinthians*, Baker Exegetical Commentary on the New Testament (Grand Rapids: Baker Academic, 2015), 225–26.

46. For a detailed assessment, see Pierce, *Divine Discourse*, 35–90.

47. On which see Guthrie, "Hebrews," 930–33.

48. This is done in part to make a transition to the incarnation and in part to dispel confusion between the seemingly contradictory time frames of Ps 110:1 ("until I make your enemies a footstool for your feet") and Ps 8:6 ("you put everything under his feet"), on which see Guthrie, "Hebrews," 946–47.

Ps 8:4–6 we read that the Father cares for and remembers human beings, including the Son (2:6); he made the Son incarnate and then "crowned [him] with
glory and honor," putting everything in subjection to him (2:7–9). In light of the
Christ event, read with reference to Isa 8:18, the author declares that "God" ("the
Father" as per the familial language in context) has "given" children to the Son
as siblings (ἃ παιδία ἅ μοι ἔδωκεν ὁ θεός), and, with reference to Prov 3:11–12,
comments that as a good father he disciplines these sons and daughters (12:5–
6). Furthermore, as noted earlier, in the exaltation the Father has appointed the
Son as a High Priest according to the order of Melchizedek (5:6, 10) and in the
process changed the law of priestly appointment (7:11–14).

Second, whereas the Father primarily acts with reference to the Son, when
the Son speaks the Scriptures he primarily carries out reciprocal acts in relation
to the Father.[49] We have already noted that the Son acts as the Father's agent
in creating the universe (1:2, 10–12). Moreover, he has sat down at the Father's
right hand and waits until his enemies will be put under his feet (1:13). In the
words of Ps 22:22, while singing hymns the incarnate Son proclaims the Father's
name to his brothers and sisters (2:12), and, according to Isa 8:18, he trusts the
Father (2:13). Furthermore, in coming into the world the Son speaks the words
of Ps 40:6–8 (10:5–7), determining to do God's will. At the end of the age the
Son, "he who is coming," will come to bring salvation to those who await him
(9:28; 10:37–38; Isa 26:20/Hab 2:3–4 LXX).

Finally, the Spirit speaks the words of the Scriptures in relation to humanity.[50]
The Spirit exhorts, both rebuking people and giving them strong encouragement
through promises (3:7–11; Ps 95:7–11). He swears that the wilderness wanderers
will not enter his rest (Ps 95:11; Heb 3:11). Yet, in the very structure of the old
covenant tabernacle, the Holy Spirit "makes clear" (δηλοῦντος τοῦ πνεύματος
τοῦ ἁγίου) that, during Jeremiah's time, the way into the Holy Place had yet to
be disclosed (9:8–10). But, as noted earlier in this essay, the Spirit is also the one
who makes the new covenant, putting laws on people's hearts and minds and
forgiving them decisively (10:16–17; Jer 31:33–34). Moreover, he testifies about
the efficacy of Christ's sacrifice (10:15).

---

49. Pierce, *Divine Discourse*, 91–134.
50. Pierce, *Divine Discourse*, 135–74. On the Spirit in Hebrews, see, for example, Martin Emmrich,
"Pneuma in Hebrews: Prophet and Interpreter," *Westminster Theological Journal* 64, no. 1 (2002): 55–71;
idem, "Hebrews 6:6–4 – Again! (A Pneumatological Inquiry)," *Westminster Theological Journal* 65, no. 1
(2003): 83–95; John R. Levison, "A Theology of the Spirit in the Letter to the Hebrews," *CBQ* 78, no. 1
(2016): 90–110; Stephen Motyer, "The Spirit in Hebrews: No Longer Forgotten?," in *Spirit and Christ in
the New Testament and Christian Theology: Essays in Honor of Max Turner*, ed. I. Howard Marshall, Volker
Rabens, and Cornelis Bennema (Grand Rapids: Eerdmans, 2012), 213–27.

OTHER ACTIONS OF GOD IN THE SCRIPTURES

We have seen already that in Hebrews God acts by speaking Scripture, that he speaks in the voice of Father, Son, and Spirit, and that the actions of each person of the Trinity seem to be directed primarily towards distinct parties. However, there are a few points in Hebrews at which God speaks and the particular person of the Trinity is not specified as the actor. At some points the specific person can be identified from the broader context, as with the earlier cases concerning Ps 110:4 at Heb 7:21 (the Father) and Jer 31:31–34 at Heb 8:7–13/10:15–17 (the Spirit). However, there are a number of places where θεός is used without reference to one of the persons of the Trinity. Consequently, in this final movement of the essay I note the other divine actions in the book that are expressed in the Scriptures but not identified with a specific member of the Trinity. These actions primarily reflect on the actions of God as expressed in the narrative accounts of Scripture.

An exception to this general pattern concerns the character of God, reflected on by our author in light of Prov 3:11–12 – God helps his people and will never leave or abandon them (12:5–6). Yet the abundance of evidence for this assurance may be found in scriptural narratives, for Hebrews sees the Scriptures as embodying "a coherent narrative about what God is doing to create, redeem, sustain, and perfect creatures" in the world.[51] The author of Hebrews evokes the acts of God through the *exempla* of Hebrews 11 and in the cultic acts related to the establishment of the new covenant.

For example, God created the universe by his word (11:3), which from the book's broader context we understand to have been carried out by the Son as the agent of the Father (1:2, 10–12). God approved of Abel's gifts (11:4), and he commended Enoch, taking Enoch away (11:5). He warned Noah (11:7) and made a promise to Abraham, swearing by himself (6:13–14; 11:17–18). He has built the eternal city to which his people look forward (11:10, 16). God gave power to Sarah and Abraham to bear a child who would become a multitude (11:11–12). Yet in relation to this child, Isaac, God tested Abraham, who trusted that God could raise the dead if necessary (11:19).

During the time of the exodus God drowned the Egyptians attempting to follow the Israelites through the Red Sea (11:29), and took down the walls of Jericho as the Israelites entered Canaan (11:30). As the author moves to a conclusion of the *exempla*, it is implied that God carried out many acts of deliverance in response to the faithful but especially approved of the active faith

---

51. do Vale, "Divine Action, Theological Method, and Scripture's Narrative," 4.

posture of his people (11:32–40). God also vindicates/judges his people (10:30–31), and thus warns them in light of the end of the age when he will shake heaven and earth (12:20, 26; Hag 2:6).

CONCLUSION

To what end do the scriptural actions of the divine tend in Hebrews? Ultimately, for our author, God has taken the initiative and acted in the world, providing "something better" (κρεῖττόν τι) for his new covenant people, by which the people of Scripture's narrative accounts would be perfected alongside the recipients of the new covenant (11:40). God had ordained the first covenant (9:20), but "something better," the new covenant work that God effected through the Messiah, has come. As we have seen, that new covenant work is carried out in various ways by Yahweh as "actor" – God the Father, Son, and Spirit – communicating his authoritative words to himself and to humans in the world. He thus carries out a conversation with himself to specific redemptive ends. We might say that the *ad intra* conversation within the Trinity (and Trinitarian theology) has been made *ad extra* by its inscripturation.[52] Thus, in expressing the various divine actions in the book, as those actions are reflected on in relation to the words of God, our author has a sophisticated, "proto-Trinitarian" theology that frames his approach to drawing the people of God into new covenant conversation with God.[53]

SELECT BIBLIOGRAPHY

Capes, David B. *Old Testament Yahweh Texts In Paul's Christology*. WUNT 2/47. Tübingen: J. C. B. Mohr, 1992.

Cockerill, Gareth Lee. *The Epistle to the Hebrews*. NICNT. Grand Rapids: Eerdmans, 2012.

Dahl, Nils A. "The Neglected Factor in New Testament Theology." *Reflections* 73 (1975): 5–8.

---

52. Thus, the statement in do Vale, "Divine Action, Theological Method, and Scripture's Narrative," 9, that "the doctrine of the Trinity is not obviously about divine action" should be considered further in light of the Trinitarian presentation of Scripture in Hebrews.

53. Echoing the words of William Abraham in do Vale, "Divine Action, Theological Method, and Scripture's Narrative," 4. See William J. Abraham, *Divine Agency and Divine Action*, vol. 1, *Exploring and Evaluating the Debate* (Oxford: OUP, 2017), 175.

Docherty, Susan E. *The Use of the Old Testament in Hebrews: A Case Study in Early Jewish Bible Interpretation.* WUNT 2/260. Tübingen: Mohr Siebeck, 2009.

Ellingworth, Paul. *The Epistle to the Hebrews: A Commentary on the Greek Text.* NIGTC. Grand Rapids: Eerdmans, 1993.

Emmrich, Martin. "Hebrews 6:6–4 – Again! (A Pneumatological Inquiry)." *WTJ* 65, no. 1 (2003): 83–95.

———. "Pneuma in Hebrews: Prophet and Interpreter." *WTJ* 64, no. 1 (2002): 55–71.

Guthrie, G. H. "Hebrews' Use of the Old Testament: Recent Trends in Research." *Currents in Biblical Research* 1 (2003): 271–94.

Guthrie, George H. *2 Corinthians.* Baker Exegetical Commentary on the New Testament. Grand Rapids: Baker Academic, 2015.

———. "Hebrews." In *Commentary on the New Testament Use of the Old Testament*, edited by G. K. Beale and D. A. Carson, 919–95. Grand Rapids: Baker Academic, 2007.

Harris, Dana M. "The Use of the Old Testament in the Epistle of Hebrews." *SwJT* 64 (2021): 91–106.

Hill, Wesley. *Paul and the Trinity: Persons, Relations, and the Pauline Letters.* Grand Rapids: Eerdmans, 2015.

Hübner, Hans. *Biblische Theologie des Neuen Testaments Band 3: Hebräerbrief, Evangelien und Offenbarung: Epilegomena.* 3. Göttingen: Vandenhoeck & Ruprecht, 1995.

Hurtado, Larry. "Lord." In *Dictionary of Paul and His Letters*, edited by Gerald F. Hawthorne, Ralph P. Martin, and Daniel G. Reid, 560–69. Downers Grove: IVP Press, 2020.

Jamieson, R. B. *The Paradox of Sonship: Christology in the Epistle to the Hebrews.* Foreword by Simon J. Gathercole. Studies in Christian Doctrine and Scripture. Downers Grove: IVP Press, 2021.

Jenson, Robert W. *Systematic Theology.* 2 vols. New York; Oxford: OUP, 1997.

Lane, William L. *Hebrews 1–8.* WBC 47A. Dallas: Word Books, 1991.

Levison, John R. "A Theology of the Spirit in the Letter to the Hebrews." *CBQ* 78, no. 1 (2016): 90–110.

Loader, William R. G. *Sohn und Hoherpriester: eine traditionsgeschichtliche Untersuchung zur Christologie des Hebräerbriefes.* Wissenschaftliche Monographien zum Alten und Neuen Testament 53. Neukirchen-Vluyn: Neukirchener Verlag, 1981.

Mackie, Scott D. "Early Christian Eschatological Experience in the Warnings and Exhortations of the Epistle to the Hebrews." *TynBul* 63 (2012): 93–114.

Malcolm, Matthew R. "God Has Spoken: The Renegotiation of Scripture in Hebrews." In *All That the Prophets Have Declared: The Appropriation of Scripture in the Emergence of Christianity*, edited by Matthew R. Malcolm, 174–81. West Ryde, Australia: Paternoster, 2015.

Michel, Otto. *Der Brief an die Hebräer*. KEK. Göttingen: Vandenhoeck & Ruprecht, 1966.

Motyer, Stephen. "The Spirit in Hebrews: No Longer Forgotten?" In *Spirit and Christ in the New Testament and Christian Theology: Essays in Honor of Max Turner*, edited by I. H. Marshall, Volker Rabens, and Cornelis Bennema, 213–27. Grand Rapids: Eerdmans, 2012.

Ounsworth, Richard Joseph. *Joshua Typology in the New Testament*. WUNT 2/328. Tübingen: Mohr Siebeck, 2012.

Patte, Daniel. *Early Jewish Hermeneutic in Palestine*. Missoula, MT: Scholars Press, 1975.

Pierce, Madison N. *Divine Discourse in the Epistle to the Hebrews: The Recontextualization of Spoken Quotations of Scripture*. SNTSMS 178. Cambridge: CUP, 2020.

Ribbens, Benjamin J. *Levitical Sacrifice and Heavenly Cult in Hebrews*. BZNW 222. Berlin: de Gruyter, 2016.

Ringleben, Joachim. *Wort und Geschichte: Kleine Theologie des Hebräerbriefs*. Göttingen: Vandenhoeck & Ruprecht, 2019.

Rissi, Mathias. *Die Theologie des Hebräerbriefs: Ihre Verankerung in der Situation des Verfassers und seiner Leser*. WUNT 41. Tübingen: J. C. B. Mohr (Paul Siebeck), 1987.

Schnelle, Udo. *Theology of the New Testament*. Grand Rapids: Baker Academic, 2009.

Spicq, Ceslas. *L'Épître aux Hébreux*. Études Bibliques 2. Paris: Gabalda, 1952.

Strobel, August. *Der Brief an die Hebräer*. Das Neue Testament Deutsch. Göttingen: Vandenhoeck & Ruprecht, 1991.

Swetnam, J. "Hebrews 1, 5–14: A New Look." *Melita Theologica* 51 (2000): 51–68.

Weiss, Hans-Friedrich. *Der Brief an die Hebräer: Übersetzt und Erklärt*. KEK. Göttingen: Vandenhoeck & Ruprecht, 1991.

Westfall, Cynthia Long. *A Discourse Analysis of the Letter to the Hebrews: The Relationship Between Form and Meaning*. LNTS. London; New York: T&T Clark, 2005.

CHAPTER 8

Creation, Divine Action, and Hebrews

Craig G. Bartholomew[1]

INTRODUCTION

One thing I did while writing this chapter was to read through Hebrews noting every example of divine action. It is no understatement to say that Hebrews is simply awash with divine action from beginning to end. For instance, chapter 3, verse 12 refers to God as "the living God," and throughout Hebrews we see God acting as such. He speaks, in both literal and metaphorical senses; he appoints; he anoints; he creates; he transforms; he adds to testimony; he gives; he subjects; he builds; he rests; he sees; he judges; he promises; he makes covenants; he raises from the dead; he makes complete, etc. Hebrews is also overtly Trinitarian, describing copious acts by the Son and the Spirit.[2]

THE CHALLENGES

In the light of the abundance of evidence for divine action, I must regretfully note that for some time now this theme has not fared well in biblical studies and theology. The challenge has come from two directions, namely, *history and science.*

As a philosopher, Alvin Plantinga has addressed both challenges. Historical

---

1. NRSV is used throughout for biblical quotations. I am grateful to Gary Cockerill for his insightful comments on the first draft of this chapter.
2. On the Spirit in Hebrews, see the chapter by Mary Healy.

criticism/s (history) has been around for well over 100 years now, and we are all familiar with forms of historical criticism that bracket out the possibility of divine action as part of the method or lens through which they analyse the Bible.[3]

Under the label of Historical Biblical Criticism (HBC) – as opposed to Traditional Biblical Commentary (TBC) – Plantinga distinguishes between Troeltschian HBC, which excludes direct action by God in the world, and Duhemian HBC, which resists any theological or metaphysical assumption that is not held by everyone – for our purposes – in the guild of biblical studies.[4] The latter, unlike the former, does not assume that God takes no action in the world but resists taking such action into account in biblical studies until there is more evidence and consensus in the guild. Plantinga analyses both approaches and concludes, "Either way, therefore, the traditional Christian can rest easy with the claims of HBC; she need feel no obligation, intellectual or otherwise, to modify her belief in the light of its claims and alleged results."[5]

More recently the challenge has come from science, especially in relation to Special Divine Action (SDA), which is clearly front and centre in Hebrews. Science appears to have become something of a new magisterium in relation to theology, and a large number of projects and publications have emerged exploring this interface. In the process, SDA has emerged as the major stumbling block for science. Again, Plantinga has repeatedly attended to this issue, most recently and lucidly in his *Where the Conflict Really Lies*.[6] He concludes that there is no conflict between science and special divine action.

It is important to note that Plantinga's forays into biblical studies and theology emerge out of his exhaustive and creative work on warrant and epistemology.[7] This relates to the earlier book edited by Plantinga and Nicholas Wolterstorff, *Faith and Rationality*.[8] As they surveyed the dominant epistemologies at work in

---

3. See William J. Abraham, *Divine Revelation and the Limits of Historical Criticism* (Oxford: OUP, 1982).

4. Alvin Plantinga, *Knowledge and Christian Belief* (Grand Rapids: Eerdmans, 2015), chapter 8. For Plantinga's more detailed attention to this question, see his *Warranted Christian Belief* (New York: OUP, 2000), chapter 12. For a creative dialogue with Plantinga, see the essays by Alvin Plantinga, Robert Gordon, and Craig Bartholomew in *"Behind" the Text: History and Biblical Interpretation*, SAH Series 4, ed. Craig G. Bartholomew, C. Stephen Evans, Mary Healy, and Murray Rae (Grand Rapids: Zondervan Academic, 2003).

5. Plantinga, *Knowledge*, 106.

6. Alvin Plantinga, *Where the Conflict Really Lies: Science, Religion, and Naturalism* (New York: OUP, 2011).

7. See Plantinga's trilogy, *Warrant: The Current Debate* (New York: OUP, 1993); *Warrant and Proper Function* (New York: OUP, 1993); and *Warranted Christian Belief*.

8. Alvin Plantinga and Nicholas Wolterstorff, eds., *Faith and Rationality: Reason and Belief in God* (Notre Dame, IN: University of Notre Dame Press, 1984).

academia, they discovered that *classical foundationalism* wielded great influence but the evidence for it was decidedly weak.[9] Plantinga and Wolterstorff went on to argue, in different ways, that belief in God is properly basic, as are related beliefs like the authority of the Bible and the trustworthiness of its message.

There are two important caveats to this view. First, Plantinga is not arguing that there are not good reasons for believing in God – there are! – but he is arguing that the Christian scholar does not need to wait until the evidence is secure and achieves consensus before putting this belief to work in one's scholarship. Belief in God is a *properly basic belief,* and the Christian scholar is warranted in assuming it and putting it to play in one's work apart from the evidence for or against it. Second, Plantinga is not arguing that there is not a great deal to be learnt from HBC and contemporary science. On the contrary, he asserts that there is much to be learnt from both enterprises. For example, he encourages us to think of HBC as an Enlightenment *project* and says, "HBC is a *project* rather than a *method.* Someone who does traditional biblical commentary may use the same methods as someone who practices HBC; the difference comes out in what they assume or take for granted in carrying out their projects."[10] Like Abraham,[11] Plantinga is particularly attentive to the philosophical presuppositions at work in historical criticism and in theology of science today.

Plantinga, Wolterstorff, and many other Christian philosophers have played a seminal role in removing obstacles to taking divine action in all its forms seriously. However, until recently, we have lacked a robust, comprehensive, contemporary theology of divine action. In my view, William Abraham with his four volumes, which merit close attention, has gone a long way towards filling this gap. Readers will find an excellent introduction to Abraham's recent work in Fellipe do Vale's introductory chapter to this volume. As we noted in the preface, Abraham eagerly desired to contribute to this book before his untimely death, and we thought it fitting to dedicate this volume to him. It is sufficient here to provide a taste of what Abraham offers:

> In the end claims about divine action are first and foremost theological claims. For far too long theologians have been intimidated by faulty philo-sophical assumptions about agency and action; they have acted as if they had

---

9. On classical foundationalism, see the discussions in Craig G. Bartholomew and Michael W. Goheen, *Christian Philosophy: A Narrative and Systematic Introduction* (Grand Rapids: Baker Academic, 2013).

10. Plantinga, *Knowledge,* 99.

11. Abraham, *Divine Revelation,* 1–7. See also Craig G. Bartholomew, *God Who Acts in History: The Significance of Sinai* (Grand Rapids: Eerdmans, 2020); *The Old Testament and God*, Old Testament Origins and the Question of God 1 (London: SPCK; Grand Rapids: Baker Academic, 2022).

been secretly given a contraceptive pill by philosophers which has prevented a robust account of divine agency and divine action from coming to birth. They need to come off the pill, recover their nerve, have fresh intercourse with their own rich traditions of reflection on divine action, and bear fresh witness to the wonders God has performed in creation and redemption.[12]

Abraham's feisty, constructive approach resonates deeply with the ethos of the KLC's Scripture Collective.[13]

DIVINE ACTION AND CREATION

Philosophically and theologically we are, thus, in an excellent position to reengage with divine action in Hebrews, with one important caveat. Historically, all orthodox Christians have affirmed the doctrine of creation, which was never the subject of controversial councils as were other doctrines.[14] However, it is a fundamental doctrine – alas, it is so pervasive that it is easily overlooked with fatal consequences. Creation is a central part of that nexus of beliefs within which divine action makes sense, and it informs the content of divine action, not least in relation to eschatology. Let me explain.

Divine action never makes sense by itself but only in the context of a nexus or web of beliefs. One reason why many critical biblical scholars struggle with it is because they are attempting to find a place for it – if at all – within an alien nexus. Utterly fundamental and central to divine action is the Trinitarian God, the subject of divine action, and the second most fundamental aspect is the doctrine of creation. It is hard to overstate just how fundamental and comprehensive is the doctrine of creation as the first act of the great drama of Scripture. John 1:3 provides us with a marvellous lens in this respect: "All things came into being through him, and without him not one thing came into being." To capture this insight, it is helpful to work through Gen 1:1–2:3 and list every single thing that comes into existence as a result of God's creation: light and darkness; the two great places of heaven (the abode of God) and the earth; the three great places in "the earth" of earth, sky, and sea; the creatures and plants that fill these

---

12. William J. Abraham, *Divine Agency and Divine Action*, vol. 1, *Exploring and Evaluating the Debate* (Oxford: OUP, 2017), 15.

13. See Craig G. Bartholomew, David J. H. Beldman, Amber L. Bowen, and William Olhausen, eds., *The Scripture and Hermeneutics Seminar: Retrospect and Prospect*, Scripture Collective 1 (Grand Rapids: Zondervan Academic, 2022).

14. See Bruce R. Ashford and Craig G. Bartholomew, *The Doctrine of Creation: A Constructive Kuyperian Approach* (Downers Grove: IVP Academic, 2020).

places; night and day; time and history; humankind, etc. Such a list enables us to see just how comprehensive and foundational is the doctrine of creation. When it comes to divine action, the act of creation is *sui generis*; all other divine action – from our perspective – takes place in and in relation to the creation. Hebrews (1:2) also knows of "all things," and if you work through Hebrews noting all the things that are referred to – for example, angels, human beings, earth, heaven, the incarnate Son, Abraham, Moses, fertile ground, death, covenant, marriage, history, etc. – they are all part of the goods, as it were, of creation. Apart from creation they would not exist or be possible.

Not surprisingly, therefore, Hebrews articulates a strong, biblical doctrine of creation. The Son is the one through whom God created the world (1:2, 10), and we grasp the doctrine of creation by faith (11:3). Providence or *creatio continua* is inseparably related to creation, and the Son sustains the universe in existence by his word (1:3): "The Son sustains the world by the same word through which it was created (compare 11:3)."[15] He sits down after completing his work of purification at the right hand of God and thus rules over the creation (1:3), accompanying it to its destination which is he himself ("heir of all things," 1:2).

The themes of rest and resurrection are also important creation motifs in Hebrews. "Rest" (3:7–4:13) links intertextually back into Gen 2:1–3, the goal of creation. Sarana evocatively notes of the seventh day in Gen 2:1–3:

> The ascending order of Creation, and the "six-plus-one" literary pattern that determines the presentation of the narrative, dictates that the seventh day be the momentous climax. Man is indeed the pinnacle of Creation, but central to the cosmogonic drama is the work of God, the solo performer. . . . The seventh day is the Lord's Day, through which all the creativity of the preceding days achieves fulfillment. . . . Its blessed and sacred character is a cosmic reality entirely independent of human effort.[16]

In an important article, Gareth Cockerill relates rest to "a kingdom that cannot be shaken" in 12:28 and rightly observes, "There are features of Hebrews that suggest that this 'Unshakeable Kingdom' is the fulfilment rather than the replacement of creation."[17] Resurrection is, at least on the surface, more of a minor theme in Hebrews. Nevertheless, as Cockerill demonstrates, it is present

---

15. Gareth L. Cockerill, *The Epistle to the Hebrews*, NICNT (Grand Rapids: Eerdmans, 2012), 95.

16. Nahum Sarna, *Genesis*, JPS Torah Commentary (Jerusalem: Jewish Publication Society, 1989).

17. Gareth L. Cockerill, "From Deuteronomy to Hebrews: The Promised Land and the Unity of Scripture," *SBJT* Spring 24, no. 1 (2020): 83–100, 90.

and central to chapter 11.[18] And, of course, at the heart of the great benediction of 13:20–21 is the resurrection of Jesus. Few have set out as clearly the connection between Christ's resurrection and creation as Oliver O'Donovan. He notes of the resurrection of Jesus, "The work of the Creator who made Adam, who brought into being an order of things in which humanity has a place, is affirmed once and for all by this conclusion."[19] Also, "The sign that God has stood by his created order implies that this order, with mankind in its proper place within it, is to be totally restored at the last."[20]

Thus, clearly Hebrews espouses a strong, rich doctrine of creation.[21] This excludes a Platonic background or worldview to Hebrews,[22] since in line with the rest of the Bible creation is affirmed as fundamentally good. There is nothing in Hebrews to support the view of the soul trapped in matter and needing to be rescued from it. Also excluded is Käsemann's proposal that Hebrews's background is found in pre-Christian Gnosticism.[23] At the heart of Gnosticism in its many types is the view that the material universe is not good and that souls need to be rescued from evil matter and taken to heaven. It will be clear from the preceding that Hebrews does not espouse such a view. Of course, a Gnostic or Platonic worldview does not preclude divine action, unlike what Troeltschian HBC avers, but it situates divine action within a very different nexus of beliefs, leading to a divergent view of the divine and of divine action.

I just footnoted Ceslas Spicq. His two-volume commentary was the culmination of the mid-twentieth-century view that the author of Hebrews was a converted Philonist. However, the years following Spicq's commentary tempered this approach, and he himself came to modify it.[24] Ronald Williamson's

---

18. Gareth L. Cockerill, "The Better Resurrection (Heb 11:35): A Key to the Structure and Rhetorical Purpose of Hebrews 11," *TynBul* 51, no. 2 (2000): 215–33.

19. Oliver O'Donovan, *Resurrection and Moral Order: An Outline for Evangelical Ethics* (Grand Rapids: Eerdmans, 1986), 14.

20. O'Donovan, *Resurrection*, 15.

21. Edward Adams, "The Cosmology of Hebrews," in *The Epistle to the Hebrews and Christian Theology*, ed. Richard Bauckham, Daniel R. Driver, Trevor A. Hart, and Nathan MacDonald (Grand Rapids: Eerdmans, 2009), 112–39, 129, asserts that, "The author of Hebrews appears to interpret Gen 1:2a LXX as implying that the ordered world was created out of pre-existent, invisible matter." I do not find his argument on this convincing.

22. Ceslas Spicq, *L'Épître aux Hébreux*, 2nd ed., 2 vols., Étude biblique (Paris: Gabalda, 1953), finds the background in Philo and Platonism. Adams, "Cosmology," is an important corrective in this area. Inter alia he stresses Plato's positive attitude towards the word in his *Timaeus*, but in his corpus as a whole Plato is ambivalent to the world. One thinks, for example, of Plato's parable of the cave in his *Republic*. One needs to remember as well, that biblically heaven – cf. Plato's eternal realm of Ideas – is created as well as the earth.

23. Ernst Käsemann, *The Wandering People of God: An Investigation of the Letter to the Hebrews* (Minneapolis: Augsburg, 1984).

24. See Ceslas Spicq, "L' Épître aux Hébreux, Apollos, Jean-Baptiste, les Hellénistes et Qumrân," *Revue de Qumran*, 1/3 Feb (1959): 365–90. Spicq came to discern more of a Qumranic background to Hebrews.

study demonstrated that most proposed parallels between Hebrews and Philo are unconvincing.[25] Indeed, "We will not find any parallel between Hebrews and Philo that demands a connection between the two."[26] Nevertheless, connections with Platonism continue to be made. In his very useful commentary, James Thompson, for example, argues:

> Like Clement of Alexandria, Origen, and other early Christian writers, [the author of Hebrews] affirmed Christian convictions that could not be reconciled with Platonism while employing Platonic categories to interpret Christian existence. Thus while the author is not a consistent Platonist, he employs categories that were probably known to educated people throughout the ancient world. The Platonic distinction between the transcendent/eternal and the earthly/mortal could be easily incorporated into the biblical faith to provide the vocabulary for instructing believers that they should place their trust not in visible realities but in that which is beyond their perception.[27]

This sounds innocuous enough, but we see problems; for example, Thompson comments on Hebrews 1:12 that "This contrast between the material creation and the abiding reality reflects the author's indebtedness to the Platonic tradition, according to which the transcendent world is eternal, while the material creation is subject to change."[28] In his commentary words like "better" and "remain" are read through the lens of Platonism, more precisely of a Platonic ontology. We will come to 1:12 later.

Gnosticism remains a perennial temptation for the Christian church, despite it having been resoundingly rejected by church fathers like Irenaeus. Indeed, Gnosticism is never far away whenever a robust and comprehensive doctrine of creation is lost sight of, a temptation that modern Christianity has often succumbed to. Spykman notes of evangelical Christianity, for example,

25. Ronald Williamson, *Philo and the Epistle to the Hebrews* (Leiden: Brill, 1970).

26. Kenneth Schenck, *A Brief Guide to Philo* (Louisville, KY: Westminster John Knox Press, 2005), 81. However, see the whole of Schenck's *Brief Guide to Philo*, chapter 5.

27. James W. Thompson, *Hebrews*, Paideia (Grand Rapids: Baker Academic, 2008), 24. See also James W. Thompson, *The Beginnings of Christian Philosophy: The Epistle to the Hebrews*, CBQMS 13 (Washington, D.C.: The Catholic Biblical Association of America, 1982).

28. Thompson, *Hebrews*, 51. For a fascinating critique of Thompson's approach, see Edward Adams, "Cosmology." Adams, "Cosmology," 137, as we will see later, does argue for the dissolution of creation in Hebrews, but notes that "some interpreters deduce that the writer expects the created order with its materiality to be obliterated from existence and salvation to be consummated in a non-material, heavenly realm. If so, the author's eschatology would come very close to Valentinian eschatology and the end-time scenarios of the Nag Hammadi tractates, *Origin of the World* and *Concept of Our Great Power*. However, there is good reason to think that a re-creation of the cosmos after its dissolution is anticipated, even though there is no overt reference to it."

that "a heavy emphasis on second-article theology tends to crowd out serious reflection on the first article. In its passionate concern to proclaim Jesus Christ as Saviour, it sidelines a fundamental concern with the work of God the Father in creation. It gives the impression of bypassing creation in a hasty move to take a shortcut to the cross."[29] This is problematic, because without the backdrop of creation evangelicals end up with a *reductionistic* view of the cross, the work of Christ, the church, the world, etc. In other words, a truncated view of creation skews our understanding of the content of divine action. Unhelpful dualisms such as sacred/secular, church/world, soul/body, being/becoming, etc., soon follow, with disastrous consequences for the witness of the church. Such a failure to think through how the doctrine of creation frames and bleeds into all other doctrines is not confined to evangelicals. It is astonishing how common it is for scholars to address topics like the doctrine of the Spirit, the work of Christ, the church and eschatology, mission, etc., without attending closely to the role of creation in such doctrines. This spells trouble theologically, and as Gunton, for example, has pointed out, once we realise that the basic distinction is not between spirit and matter or time and eternity but between *the uncreated God and the creation*, then we are able to see that God's action in relation to his creation is precisely what we would expect.[30] God speaking, for example, which is utterly central to Hebrews, is not surprising but just what we would expect from the relational God who has *created* the world and humans in his image.

John Calvin understood the centrality of the doctrine of creation when he described the world as the theatre of God's glory.[31] It is brought into existence by God, and as such is very good (Gen 1:31). It bears the marks of his handiwork and thus reflects his glory (Rom 1:20). It is this witness of the creation that sinners suppress, a reminder that sin mars and scars the witness of the creation to God's glory. According to Paul in Romans 8, the creation itself groans as it keenly anticipates being released from bondage and corruption into freedom. This alerts us to the relationship between creation and eschatology. In line with Paul, Ola Tjørhom notes, "The Father is the creator, the Son is the ultimate liberator of creation, and the Holy Spirit conveys life to all created beings.

---

29. Gordon J. Spykman, *Reformational Theology: A New Paradigm for Doing Dogmatics* (Grand Rapids: Eerdmans, 1992), 176.

30. Colin E. Gunton, *Act and Being: Towards a Theology of the Divine Attributes* (Grand Rapids: Eerdmans, 2002).

31. On 1:10–12, John Calvin, *Commentary on the Epistle of Paul to the Hebrews* (Bellingham, WA: Bible Software, 2010), 48, comments, "What David says about the heavens perishing, some explain by adding, 'Were such a thing to happen,' as though nothing was affirmed. But what need is there of such a strained explanation, since we know that all creatures are subjected to vanity? for to what purpose is that renovation promised, which even the heavens wait for with the strong desire as of those in travail, except that they are now verging towards destruction?"

Surely, a misplaced confusion of creation and redemption must be avoided."[32] He asserts, "Actually, without creation there is nothing to save – creation is the 'stuff' of salvation,"[33] and observes, "When the first Christians – being a tiny and insignificant minority in society – were able to maintain the immense cosmic scope of the drama of salvation in Christ, it becomes odd when we today are so bent on retracting into cramped, personalised, or private positions."[34]

Whereas few would deny the robust doctrine of creation in Hebrews, when it comes to Hebrews's eschatology very different views are held. According to L. D. Hurst, "the Epistle to the Hebrews continues to be a storm-center of debate in NT study,"[35] and this is certainly true of Hebrews's eschatology. As I have noted elsewhere, Romans *and* Hebrews are the two great unpackings of the gospel in the NT. Romans is widely acknowledged as such, but, in my view, Hebrews is as important. Thompson observes, "As the book with the longest sustained argument in the NT, Hebrews is one of the earliest examples of Christian theology as faith seeking understanding."[36] Both letters unpack the Christ event in depth, but intriguingly they use very different vocabularies to do so. Romans's vocabulary is more legal whereas Hebrews's is primarily cultic. According to Thompson, "Only the author of Hebrews describes the work of Jesus in high priestly and sacrificial terms."[37] Knowing what we do about contextualisation, this is not a surprise or a problem but a testimony to the richness of the gospel. However, it becomes a problem if these two great epistles present radically different eschatologies. There are many authors we could turn to at this point, but we will focus on Gabriel Josipovici's intriguing literary reading of Hebrews.[38]

CREATION AND ESCHATOLOGY IN HEBREWS: JOSIPOVICI

Lest the reader think we have strayed from divine action, I remind you that creation and the inauguration of the eschaton are two great, related divine acts.

---

32. Ola Tjørhom, *Embodied Faith: Reflections on a Materialist Spirituality* (Grand Rapids: Eerdmans, 2009), 33.

33. Tjørhom, *Embodied Faith*, 36.

34. Tjørhom, *Embodied Faith*, 37.

35. L. D. Hurst, *The Epistle to the Hebrews: Its Background of Thought* (Cambridge: CUP, 1990), 2.

36. Thompson, *Hebrews*, 3.

37. Thompson, *Hebrews*, 3–4.

38. Gabriel Josipovici, *The Book of God: A Response to the Bible* (New Haven: Yale University Press, 1988), chapter XIII.

Josipovici's discussion of Hebrews is fascinating. He is attentive to hermeneutics – how we read – and begins with a discussion of Philip and the Ethiopian eunuch (Acts 8:27–38) and the Emmaus road narrative (Luke 24:13–35). He says of the latter that it could be "a parable of interpretation"[39] and notes insightfully, "In one sense the remaining portions of the NT only develop and repeat this climactic scene of Luke's Gospel."[40] However, for Josipovici Hebrews most fully articulates this approach to the OT. He quotes Graham Hughes with approval: "The writer of Hebrews is the theologian who, more diligently and successfully than any other of the NT writers, has worked at what we now describe as hermeneutics."[41]

Like all the authors of the NT, the author of Hebrews is concerned to show that the OT is fulfilled in Jesus. But how to open the eyes of one's hearers to see this? Paul, according to Josipovici, asks people to look inward,[42] whereas Hebrews asks its readers to look at Scripture. Intriguingly, Josipovici thinks that the order of Hebrews is related to the author working through the OT. Angels are attended to before Abraham because of Gen 6:1–4. Having examined the ways in which Hebrews reads the OT, Josipovici concludes, "It is in Hebrews, however, that we find the most powerful and inclusive attempt to read the Hebrew scriptures from its particular point of view. No one, reading that epistle, is ever likely to be able to read what comes before it in the Bible, in quite the same way again."[43] Josipovic is, however, less optimistic than Hughes about Hebrews's reading of the OT. Referring back to the Emmaus road narrative, Josipovici comments, "The reader of the Bible who has not broken bread with Jesus must, I think, remain unpersuaded."[44]

Josipovici focuses on Jer 31 with its promise of a new covenant in the last days and its use in Heb 8:1–13 to make his point. Hebrews quotes Jer 31:31–34, which Josipovici examines in its broader context. He notes of Jer 31 and the new covenant:

> Restoration here is not abstract, it is not a description of the inner workings of the self; it involves rather such things as vineyards, animals, towers and gates. The law may be inscribed in the hearts of men, but here a real Jerusalem and real fields and farms are being referred to. It is not simply that the author of

39. Josipovici, *The Book of God*, 258.
40. Josipovici, *The Book of God*, 260.
41. Graham Hughes, *Hebrews and Hermeneutics: The Epistle to the Hebrews as a New Testament Example of Biblical Interpretation*, SNTSMS 36 (Cambridge: CUP, 1979), 3.
42. This comment seems to me clearly incorrect.
43. Josipovici, *The Book of God*, 264.
44. Josipovici, *The Book of God*, 265.

Hebrews has given the passage a meaning which the original did not have, but that by so doing he has *obscured the meaning it did have*. The concreteness of God's dealings with Israel, his concern not with an abstract entity but with animals and trees and buildings, has completely vanished from Hebrews. It is not that an old meaning has been subsumed into a new one but that a new meaning has blotted out the old.[45]

Josipovici also finds the reading of the OT in the list of heroes of faith in 11:1–40 wanting. This passage does not chime with our memories of the characters referred to from the OT itself. Drawing on anthropological terms, rather than Hebrews providing us with a *thick* reading of the OT, it is *thin*: "if the author of Hebrews does see Jesus in terms of the OT past, his sense of that past is remarkably thin."[46]

I argued earlier that in Romans Paul anticipates the redemption of the creation. Josipovici, however, contends that his reading of Hebrews is true of the NT as a whole. He acknowledges the shift from Israel in the OT to Christianity; the latter is a religion of individuals and not of a people, and it is not confined to one place but for all places and times. For Josipovici, "It was natural therefore that despite its attempt to retain much of the vocabulary of the Hebrew culture from which it sprang, it would be forced to drain that vocabulary of its original meaning."[47] Similarly, he finds in the Gospels' emphasis on the kingdom of God being not of this world a similar draining of meaning and shift in the way in which we think about culture and humans.

We might call what Josipovici identifies in Hebrews a *spiritualising tendency* that detracts from the rich, visceral texture of the creation we find so clearly in the OT. As G. R. Lilburne notes, "The problem appears to be that while the Hebrew Scriptures speak centrally of the land, its preservation and proper use, this concern is entirely lost in the New Testament. By universalizing the scope of God's reign, the New Testament appears to trivialize the concern with place and locality and to move its spirituality beyond issues of land."[48] Similarly, W. D. Davies says of the land in the NT: "In sum, for the holiness of place, Christianity has fundamentally, though not consistently, substituted the holiness of the Person; it has Christified holy space."[49]

---

45. Josipovici, *The Book of God*, 266–67. Emphasis original.

46. Josipovici, *The Book of God*, 270.

47. Josipovici, *The Book of God*, 274.

48. G. R. Lilburne, *A Sense of Place: A Christian Theology of the Land* (Nashville: Abingdon, 1989), 10.

49. W. D. Davies, *The Gospel and the Land: Early Christianity and Jewish Territorial Doctrine* (Berkeley: University of California Press, 1974), 36. Of course, considerable further work has been done on land in the NT since Davies.

Related to this are two texts in Hebrews that appear on the surface to teach the dissolution of the creation at the end of history. In Heb 1:10–12 the author quotes the LXX of Ps 102:26–27:

¹⁰And,

> "In the beginning, Lord, you founded the earth,
>   and the heavens are the work of your hands;
> ¹¹they will perish, but you remain;
>   they will all wear out like clothing;
> ¹²like a cloak you will roll them up,
>   and like clothing they will be changed.
> But you are the same,
>   and your years will never end."

These verses teach that the heavens and the earth, i.e., the creation, will perish, wear out, be rolled up and changed. Among others, Edward Adams argues that "The statements of vv. 11a–12b express, as much as they do in their original psalmic context, the destructibility of the natural world."[50]

12:26–27 is the other passage in Hebrews:

²⁶At that time his voice shook the earth, but now he has promised, "Yet once more I will shake not only the earth but also the heaven." ²⁷This phrase, "Yet once more," indicates the removal of what is shaken – that is, created things – so that what cannot be shaken may remain.

Adams argues that "the author of Hebrews thus envisions in this passage a cosmic catastrophe that results in the dissolution of the cosmos,"[51] which he takes to refer to the heaven and earth's pre-creation condition.

JOSIPOVICI: EVALUATION

Taking all this together, it is easy to see how Davies reads 12:18–24 to mean that "Christians . . . have no permanent home on earth but are seekers for a city

---

50. Edward Adams, *The Stars Will Fall from Heaven: "Cosmic Catastrophe" in the New Testament and Its World*, LNTS 247 (London: T&T Clark, 2007), 184–85.

51. Adams, *Stars Will Fall*, 190–91.

to come . . . a city that cannot be touched, eternal in the heavens."[52] Read thus, it would appear that the eschatology of Hebrews is very different from that of Paul and makes the goal of history heaven rather than the new heavens and new earth of Revelation, where heaven comes down to earth (Rev 21:1–8). Josipovici, of course, thinks that Paul and the rest of the NT line up with Hebrews. However, for a number of reasons, this reading of Hebrews's eschatology is, in my view, incorrect.

First, the eschatology in the prologue of Heb 1:1–4 is the same as that in Paul and the rest of the NT, albeit expressed in terms of the author's favourite metaphor, namely, speech. The author affirms the authority of the OT ("God spoke"), but now this same God has spoken in the eschaton ("in these last days" ἐπ᾽ ἐσχάτου τῶν ἡμερῶν τούτων) by a Son. The Son has been appointed heir of all things, and he is the one through whom God created the world. Paul Ellingworth and Eugene Nida helpfully sum up v. 2b as follows: "By God's command and appointment, his Son is shortly to take possession of the entire universe. But in any case, the universe belongs by right to the Son, since it was through him that God made it and everything it contains."[53] Now it is very hard to see how the Son will inherit all things if they, i.e., the creation, are annihilated. As Adams notes, "In Heb. 1:2, the Son is said to be "heir of all things" (κληρονόμον πάντων), which implies that at the eschaton there will be a cosmos (πάντα) for him to inherit."[54] It is precisely all the things of the creation that he inherits, and this means we must revisit 1:10–12 and 12:26–27 to see if those interpreting them to mean the dissolution of creation are correct. Adams, it should be noted, argues that after the dissolution the world is recreated. He says of Hebrews, "However, there is good reason to think that a re-creation of the cosmos after its dissolution is anticipated, even though there is no overt reference to it."[55]

Second, it is not true that Hebrews has no interest in the concrete realities of created life such as land, agriculture, and crops. In 6:1–8, one of the several strong warnings in Hebrews, the author reaches for an illustration which indicates otherwise. In 6:7–8 he writes:

> [7]Ground that drinks up the rain falling on it repeatedly and that produces a crop useful to those for whom it is cultivated receives a blessing from God.

---

52. Davies, *Gospel and the Land*, 162.

53. Paul Ellingworth and Eugene A. Nida, *A Handbook on the Letter to the Hebrews*, UBS Handbook Series (New York: United Bible Societies, 1994), 8.

54. Adams, "Cosmology," 137.

55. Adams, "Cosmology," 137.

⁸But if it produces thorns and thistles, it is worthless and on the verge of being cursed; its end is to be burned over.

It could be argued that the author simply reaches for an illustration here and that its theology is of little import. However, as we discover in sermons, illustrations are often profoundly revealing of the theology or worldview at work. One cannot but hear echoes in these verses of the very material blessings of the OT. Several commentators have noticed intertextual links with Deut 11:26–28 in these verses,⁵⁶ and the broader context of Deut 11 (see especially 11:13–17) evokes the sort of blessing the author of Hebrews uses as an illustration.

Third, while it is certainly true that the NT casts a universal vision relevant to all times and places, it is difficult to see why this necessarily drains its language of the rich materiality of creation. In the OT the election of Israel always has its eye on the recovery of God's reign over the whole creation. The covenant with Abram is aimed at blessing for all the nations (Gen 12:1–3). And at Sinai, even as YHWH promises the assembled Israelites that they will be his treasured possession, a holy nation and a royal priesthood, he reminds them that "the whole earth is mine" (Exod 19:5). It is precisely this extension of blessing to all nations and the whole *creation* that the NT, and Hebrews, has in mind so that the universal vision of the NT does not subvert the materiality of the OT but exalts it. Far from draining the OT of its rich, material content, the NT enhances it. Rather than the eschatology of the NT, including Hebrews, being thin, it is exceptionally thick.

Fourth, the phrase "kingdom of God/heaven" does not occur in Hebrews, although the image of Christ as king is central. The word "kingdom" (βασιλεία) occurs three times in 1:8; 11:33; and 12:8. In 1:8 and 12:8 it does indeed have the meaning of "kingdom of God," but clearly this is not common vocabulary for the author as in the synoptic Gospels. However, this does not mean that the same eschatological conceptuality is not present – as we have seen with the prologue, it certainly is. This is also true of other NT authors. In John's gospel the expression "kingdom of God" only occurs twice (3:3, 5), but John has his own language for the same reality: vocabulary such as "eternal life," which is not life in heaven but the life of the age to come. Similarly, as many have noted, the expression "kingdom of God/heaven" alerts us to the fact that the king is God, who dwells in heaven, but extends his reign over his creation.⁵⁷ Roman citizens living far from Rome would have understood that when Paul said that our

---

56. Cockerill, *The Epistle to the Hebrews*, 278–79.
57. See, for example, N. T. Wright, *Jesus and the Victory of God*, Christian Origins and the Question of God (London: SPCK, 1996).

citizenship is in heaven (Phil 3:20), he was not asserting that heaven is our final destination but that when we are in need help would come from heaven to where we are in the creation. Thus, correctly understood, the kingdom of God evokes the reverse of what Josipovici asserts.

Fifth, what of Heb 1:10–12 and 12:26–27? I have attended to these verses in some detail elsewhere and readers are referred to those discussions.[58] Cockerill points out that Ps 102:26–27 is quoted in these verses to "affirm his [the Son's] sovereign deity and role as final judge of all."[59] Certainly judgement and the culmination of history are in view, but what does this entail for the creation? What does the author mean when he says of the heavens and the earth that "they will perish, but you will remain" (αὐτοὶ ἀπολοῦνται, σὺ δὲ διαμένεις)? ἀπόλλυμαι can mean "be destroyed" or "cease to exist," but it need not be limited to these senses.[60] For example, B. F. Westcott argues, "The idea, as it is afterwards developed (xii. 26ff.), is of change, transfiguration, and not of annihilation."[61] Similarly, Hugh Montefiore comments that "the Psalmist looks forward to a new heaven and a new earth.... It will be as though God were to give them a new suit of clothes."[62] Ellingworth notes that important background to the imagery here is found in passages like Isa 34:4; 51:6; Rev 6:12–17, and the same verb (ἀπώλετο) is used of the judgement of the flood in 2 Pet 3:6. Now, certainly the flood "destroyed" the earth, but it did not annihilate the creation. What we have here, I suggest, is typical, biblical language of *judgement*, but without implying the dissolution of the creation. Cockerill's chiastic analysis of these verses makes it clear that clothing is a central metaphor,[63] and Montefiore's interpretation seems to me closer to the thought of the author of Hebrews.

---

58. Craig G. Bartholomew, *Where Mortals Dwell: A Christian View of Place for Today* (Grand Rapids: Baker Academic, 2011), chapter 8; Craig G. Bartholomew, *Introducing Biblical Hermeneutics: A Comprehensive Framework for Hearing God in Scripture* (Grand Rapids: Baker Academic, 2015), chapter 14.

59. Cockerill, *The Epistle to the Hebrews*, 112.

60. The implications of reading it as destroyed are significant, encouraging a focus on the things of heaven rather than those on earth. For example, Thompson, *Hebrews*, 269, comments that, "The author emphasizes that the kingdom is 'unshakable' and therefore belongs to the stable, heavenly world. When all the material things that they touch have been removed, the 'unshakable kingdom' will remain." Gareth L. Cockerill, *Hebrews: A Bible Commentary in the Wesleyan Tradition* (Indianapolis, IN: Wesleyan Publishing House, 1998). 44, similarly comments that, "Someday this visible universe will become threadbare. It will be changed, removed. The Son is permanent, but the universe is not." Such readings, I suspect, confirm the sort of critique we find in Josipovici. The word for "perish" in the Hebrew of Ps 102:27(26) is the verb אָבַד. Notably, it is often used for judgment in the OT, as opposed to annihilation. It should also be noted that v. 29(28) follows vv. 26(25)–27(26), with the children of YHWH's servants living securely in God's presence, presumable in the land.

61. B. F. Westcott, *The Epistle to the Hebrews* (London: Macmillan, 1889), 28.

62. Hugh W. Montefiore, *The Epistle to the Hebrews*, Black's New Testament Commentaries (London: A&C Black, 1964), 48.

63. Cockerill, *The Epistle to the Hebrews*, 112–13.

Exegetically, I am not persuaded that ἀπολοῦνται is best translated as "will perish," especially if "perish" is understood as dissolution and/or annihilation. But what intrigues me is the failure of commentators to explore the logical, theological, and philosophical implications of taking Heb 1:10 to mean the end of the creation. Take logic, firstly. I quoted Nida and Ellingworth approvingly earlier about the Son shortly taking possession of the universe. However, when it comes to v. 11 they comment without any sense of contradiction, "They will disappear [perish] may be rendered as 'They will no longer be seen,' or 'They will no longer exist,' or 'There will be a time when they will no longer be.'"[64] Assuming that the universe of which Christ is soon to take possession is the heavens and earth of 1:10, then if it is to no longer exist or be, then what precisely is Christ to take possession of? Logically, this does not make sense. Nor does it make sense theologically. For example, when Christ becomes incarnate he assumes human flesh, and he carries this back with him into heaven. As Cockerill asserts of 2:9, "The Pastor is affirming the continued humanity of the exalted and eternal Son as the representative of the people of God."[65] As part of the creation – if you will excuse the blasphemy – is his flesh, his humanity, also destroyed? And what of humans? We are unimaginable apart from the creation of which we are a part. Are we also destroyed with the perishing of the heavens and the earth? And what of angels? Are they destroyed, too? Finally, philosophically such a reading does not make sense. The problem with the creation is not its transitoriness but the disfiguring of it by sin. The change the creation needs is not annihilation but purification from sin through judgement. There is certainly a contrast in 1:10–11 between the unchanging God and the changing creation, but the language is typical biblical language of judgement leading to purification and renewal and not of the dissolution of the creation.

Finally, what of the language of heaven found so strongly in Hebrews and especially in 12:18–24? Does not this language identify heaven as our ultimate destination, so that the readers should fix their hopes and aspirations on the eternal realm above to which they really belong? In one sense, of course, we should be attentive to heaven because it is the dwelling place of God. Indeed, the distinction between the two major places of heaven and earth is fundamental to the entire Bible, and doubtless Hebrews focuses unique attention on heaven. However, Hebrews's realised eschatology that we have already come to the heavenly Zion is by no means unique to this author, even if the vocabulary is. In Ephesians, Paul, with his eschatology of all things – things in heaven and things

64. Ellingworth and Nida, *Handbook*, 21.
65. Cockerill, *The Epistle to the Hebrews*, 133.

on earth – being gathered up in Christ (1:10), asserts that we have already been raised up and sit with Christ in the heavenly places (2:6). What are we to make of such language in Paul and in Hebrews? It is surely related to the eschatology of the NT, according to which the kingdom has already come but remains to be finally consummated. In Christ we *already* partake of eternal life, but we also long for the day when we shall do so fully.

A crucial question is: what happens to our view of earth when we focus on heaven? Are we to see the earth as secondary and heaven as our true home? Such a view is not uncommon, but it is damaging to the witness of the church. Far from a focus on our king in heaven making the things of the earth becoming strangely dim, as the chorus has it, earthly things come into proper focus as God's good creation. The world is not God – and nor, for that matter, is heaven – but it is his creation, and as such it bears witness to his glory. Heaven is his throne and earth his footstool, and thus in terms of priority the throne by far comes first. However, in terms of human beings, speaking of "the earth" as secondary is unhelpful. We only exist as part of the creation, of "the earth," and we live on the earth for God and seek to enhance his reputation. As such, we pray for the day when his kingdom will come *on earth*, just as it is in heaven.

For all these reasons, we should reject the sort of reading of Hebrews proposed by Gabriel Josipovici. Creation and eschatology are integrally related in Hebrews, in Paul, and in the rest of the NT. Hebrews does not give with one hand in the prologue and take away with the other in the rest of the book. The Son will indeed inherit all things.

CONCLUSION

We have every reason to approach divine action in Hebrews with confidence, excavating its exceptionally rich theology and its implications for us today. However, what I have tried to show in this chapter is that in order to do so we need a robust doctrine of creation. From a human perspective, divine action and creation are inseparable. The creation is the context in which we experience God's work, even as he sustains us and the cosmos in existence. Without such a doctrine firmly in place, our view of divine action will, I suspect, become reductionistic and we will fail to see how it relates to all of life.

Take the ongoing priesthood of Jesus, for example. As the one who rules over all and will soon inherit all things, he intercedes *for us*. But who are we? The author of Hebrews turns to Ps 8 in Heb 2:5–9. Ps 8 provides a marvellous perspective on the glory of being human and being called to be royal stewards over

God's creation. Scholars disagree as to whether Heb 2:8 refers to humankind or to Jesus.[66] What is clear is that our identity is tied up with that of the incarnate one. He is the representative person who will subject all things beneath his rule. Having been and being human, he knows, as Hebrews stresses, the challenge of living up to this vocation of royal stewardship. Thus, quite wonderfully, we can rightly expect that Jesus's intercession will relate to *all* aspects of our lives as humans. This has significant practical implications. It encourages us to bring every aspect of life to him, whether it be the war in Ukraine or our most personal struggles with prayer, knowing that he has a vested interest in all things.

There remains much more work to be done on divine action and creation in Hebrews. Because creation is so foundational, it seeps into every aspect of divine action covered in this book. I briefly indicated how creation relates to God speaking, but this and so many more areas of God's action remain to be unpacked in detail in relation to creation. My proposal is that as we do this, we will be amazed at the breadth and scope of God's action and will be encouraged to accompany the Spirit in the work he is busy with in our lives and in his creation.

SELECT BIBLIOGRAPHY

Abraham, William J. *Divine Agency and Divine Action.* Vol. 1, *Exploring and Evaluating the Debate.* Oxford: OUP, 2017.

———. *Divine Revelation and the Limits of Historical Criticism.* Oxford: OUP, 1982.

Adams, Edward. "The Cosmology of Hebrews." In *The Epistle to the Hebrews and Christian Theology,* edited by Richard Bauckham, Daniel R. Driver, Trevor A. Hart, and Nathan MacDonald, 112–39. Grand Rapids: Eerdmans, 2009.

———. *The Stars Will Fall from Heaven: "Cosmic Catastrophe" in the New Testament and Its World.* LNTS 247. London: T&T Clark, 2007.

Ashford, Bruce R., and Craig G. Bartholomew. *The Doctrine of Creation: A Constructive Kuyperian Approach.* Downers Grove: IVP Academic, 2020.

Bartholomew, Craig G. *God Who Acts in History: The Significance of Sinai.* Grand Rapids: Eerdmans, 2020.

———. *Introducing Biblical Hermeneutics: A Comprehensive Framework for Hearing God in Scripture.* Grand Rapids: Baker Academic, 2015.

---

66. See Ellingworth and Nida, *Handbook,* and Cockerill, *The Epistle to the Hebrews,* on this passage and verse.

———. *The Old Testament and God.* Old Testament Origins and the Question of God 1. London: SPCK; Grand Rapids: Baker Academic, 2022.

———. *Where Mortals Dwell: A Christian View of Place for Today.* Grand Rapids: Baker Academic, 2011.

Bartholomew, Craig G., David J. H. Beldman, Amber L. Bowen, and William Olhausen, eds. *The Scripture and Hermeneutics Seminar: Retrospect and Prospect.* Scripture Collective 1. Grand Rapids: Zondervan Academic, 2022.

Bartholomew, Craig G., and Michael W. Goheen. *Christian Philosophy: A Narrative and Systematic Introduction.* Grand Rapids: Baker Academic, 2015.

Bartholomew, Craig G., Stephen Evans, Mary Healy, and Murray Rae, eds., *"Behind" the Text: History and Biblical Interpretation.* SAH Series 4. Grand Rapids: Zondervan Academic, 2003.

Bauckham, Richard, Daniel R. Driver, Trevor A. Hart, and Nathan MacDonald, eds., *The Epistle to the Hebrews and Christian Theology.* Grand Rapids: Eerdmans, 2009.

Calvin, John. *Commentary on the Epistle of Paul to the Hebrews.* Bellingham, WA: Bible Software, 2010.

Cockerill, Gareth Lee. "The Better Resurrection (Heb 11:35): A Key to the Structure and Rhetorical Purpose of Hebrews 11." *TynBul* 51, no. 2 (2000): 215–33.

———. *The Epistle to the Hebrews.* NICNT. Grand Rapids: Eerdmans, 2012.

———. "From Deuteronomy to Hebrews: The Promised Land and the Unity of Scripture." *SBJT* 24, no. 1 (2020): 83–100.

———. *Hebrews: A Bible Commentary in the Wesleyan Tradition.* Indianapolis: Wesleyan Publishing House, 1998.

Davies, W. D. *The Gospel and the Land: Early Christianity and Jewish Territorial Doctrine.* Berkeley: University of California Press, 1974.

Ellingworth, Paul, and Eugene Albert Nida. *A Handbook on the Letter to the Hebrews.* UBS Handbook Series. New York: United Bible Societies, 1994.

Gunton, Colin E. *Act and Being: Towards a Theology of the Divine Attributes.* Grand Rapids: Eerdmans, 2002.

Hughes, Graham. *Hebrews and Hermeneutics: The Epistle to the Hebrews as a New Testament Example of Biblical Interpretation.* SNTSMS 36. Cambridge: CUP, 1979.

Hurst, L. D. *The Epistle to the Hebrews: Its Background of Thought.* SNTSMS 65. Cambridge: CUP, 1990.

Josipovici, Gabriel. *The Book of God: A Response to the Bible.* New Haven: Yale University Press, 1988.

Käsemann, Ernst. *The Wandering People of God: An Investigation of the Letter to the Hebrews.* Minneapolis: Augsburg, 1984.

Lilburne, G. R. *A Sense of Place: A Christian Theology of the Land.* Nashville: Abingdon, 1989.

Montefiore, Hugh W. *The Epistle to the Hebrews*. Black's New Testament Commentaries. London: A&C Black, 1964.

O'Donovan, Oliver. *Resurrection and Moral Order: An Outline for Evangelical Ethics*. Grand Rapids: Eerdmans, 1986.

Plantinga, Alvin. *Knowledge and Christian Belief*. Grand Rapids: Eerdmans, 2015.

———. *Warrant and Proper Function*. New York: OUP, 1993.

———. *Warrant: The Current Debate*. New York: OUP, 1993.

———. *Warranted Christian Belief*. New York: OUP, 2000.

———. *Where the Conflict Really Lies: Science, Religion, and Naturalism*. New York: OUP, 2011.

Plantinga, Alvin, and Nicholas Wolterstorff, eds. *Faith and Rationality: Reason and Belief in God*. Notre Dame, IN: University of Notre Dame Press, 1984.

Schenck, Kenneth. *A Brief Guide to Philo*. Louisville, KY: Westminster John Knox Press, 2005.

Spicq, Ceslas. *L'Épître aux Hébreux*. 2nd ed. 2 vols. Étude biblique. Paris: Gabalda, 1953.

———. "L' Épître aux Hébreux, Apollos, Jean-Baptiste, les Hellénistes et Qumrân." *Revue de Qumran*, 1/3 Feb (1959): 365–90.

Spykman, Gordon J. *Reformational Theology: A New Paradigm for Doing Dogmatics*. Grand Rapids: Eerdmans, 1992.

Thompson, James W. *The Beginnings of Christian Philosophy: The Epistle to the Hebrews*. CBQMS 13. Washington, D.C.: The Catholic Biblical Association of America, 1982.

———. *Hebrews*. Paideia. Grand Rapids: Baker Academic, 2008.

Tjørhom, Ola. *Embodied Faith: Reflections on a Materialist Spirituality*. Grand Rapids: Eerdmans, 2009.

Westcott, B. F. *The Epistle to the Hebrews*. London: Macmillan, 1889.

Williamson, Ronald. *Philo and the Epistle to the Hebrews*. Leiden: Brill, 1970.

Wright, N. T. *Jesus and the Victory of God*. Christian Origins and the Question of God. London: SPCK, 1996.

CHAPTER 9

"A Fearful Thing to Fall into the Hands of a Living God"

Divine Action in Human Salvation

Amy Peeler[1]

INTRODUCTION

"We sincerely trust and earnestly pray that it may please our God to strike terror into the souls of many who read this article, that their false peace may be disturbed."[2] So writes a commentator on the epistle to the Hebrews, and it is possible this sentiment might have been echoed by the author of the letter itself. Hebrews is a beautiful sermon, brimming with stirring affirmations of confidence, but there is no denying that it is also a text of terror. Those who read Hebrews, especially the warning passages, know that eternity hangs in the balance.[3] The pathos of this letter indicates that the author had grave concerns for the audience to whom he is writing. Even though he is convinced that they have faith and salvation (6:9; 10:39), on multiple occasions he employs intense language to compel them to hold fast to it.

---

1. The Scripture translations in this chapter are my own.
2. Arthur W. Pink, *Exposition of Hebrews* (Grand Rapids: Baker, 1954), 299.
3. Interpreters have debated the number and scope of the warning passages in Hebrews. See Herbert W. Bateman IV, "Introducing the Warning Passages in Hebrews: A Contextual Orientation," in *Four Views on the Warning Passages in Hebrews*, ed. Herbert W. Bateman IV (Grand Rapids: Kregel Academic & Professional, 2007, 27). I will focus on 2:1–4; 3:7–4:13; 6:4–8; 10:26–31; 12:12–29.

The call to maintain their confession – a plea for human action – is only possible, however, within the author's unfathomably rich and distinct portrayal of God's divine action. The communicative and revelatory God is now speaking in the person of the Son (Heb 1:1–2), who has carried out the divine plan for salvation with his perfect self-offering (for example, Heb 9:14; 10:10). Hebrews is an early, insightful, and influential example of, in John Webster's words, "Christian theology" because it talks, first and foremost, of "God and God's actions."[4] As a biblical scholar trained by those unapologetic of their epistemological faith commitments, I am grateful to have always been taught to notice the simple yet inexhaustibly powerful affirmation of the text. It tells us, in William Abraham's words, "who God is, what God has done, and why God has acted and acts as he does."[5] While I deeply appreciate the rigor that arises in philosophical and theological discussions, I believe the most benefit arises from those philosophers and theologians who never stray too far from the textual anchor in Scripture. A child could read the Bible and affirm that God acts, and in God's economy revealed by Jesus (Matt 18:3/Mark 10:14/Luke 18:17) this trusting affirmation is the way of God and the way of life. Although it takes no complex thought but only trust and dependence to see divine action, at the same time God's living word (Heb 4:12) grows with us, inviting us at each stage of intellectual and spiritual development into deeper contemplation of our affirmations of God's work.

In this essay, I hope to contribute contemplation to the theme of divine action for human salvation as communicated by the author of the epistle to the Hebrews. I am choosing to trace the theme of salvation through the author's fearful rhetoric of warning. I do so for two reasons. First, for many readers this is an aspect of the sermon that grabs attention and demands explanation. Some have difficulty hearing the rest of Hebrews if pressing questions about these warning passages linger. Second, and more fundamental to the focus of this volume, these are the passages where readers might be tempted to emphasise the necessity of human action and thus miss the fact that any such action can only take place within the economy, as Fellipe do Vale argues in the introduction, that is "established by God."[6] Although the warnings in Hebrews will be my focus, they certainly do not stand alone. The author artfully weaves them together with incredible encouragements that extol the magnitude of God's

4. John Webster, "Theological Theology," in *Confessing God: Essays in Christian Dogmatics II* (London: Bloomsbury T&T Clark, 2005), 25.

5. William J. Abraham, *Divine Agency and Divine Action*, vol. 1, *Exploring and Evaluating the Debate* (Oxford: OUP, 2017), 163.

6. Fellipe do Vale, "Divine Action, Theological Method, and Scripture's Narrative," 9.

gracious salvation. In fact, the warnings in this sermon increase in intensity because the author also presents the magnitude of his listeners' salvation with growing clarity.

This chapter follows the rhetoric of the author through his sermon, pausing at five sections where he garners the attention of his listeners with a warning. Initially, I will attend to what each text affirms about God's action, including both what God has done and what he could do if the warning is not heeded. Through this theological attention, it will become clear that not all the warnings are the same. Although they are all grounded in the salvific work of God in Christ's priestly vocation, they become increasingly intense as the author describes more of the specifics of Christ's work and its effects.

By attending to the action of God and the rhetorical prowess of the author, only then can readers aptly decide how humans should respond to the progressively intense calls of the text. In each section, I will be attentive to what the author is asking them to fear and what sin leads to this fearful result. In order to avoid this sin and this result, he asks them to respond in particular ways. These are human responses, the author will make clear, that are only possible within the gracious action of God. Throughout the sermon, the author holds together the theme of divine salvific action with the human response of fear. He is asking them to live in healthy fear of the God who has acted and is acting to perfect their salvation.

HEBREWS 2:1–4

The opening of Hebrews's second chapter comes only fourteen verses after the book's beginning, but in those fourteen verses the author has contributed some of the most influential theology in all the NT. He has extolled the excellency of the Son by describing his relationship with God (1:1–5), a relationship that places the Son decidedly above the angels (1:4–14). The vast majority of the first chapter depicts God's action for and through the work of the Son. The author describes the Son as acting with God in creating (1:2, 10), sustaining (1:3), and reigning over all things (1:2, 8, 13) eternally (1:10–11), so that he fittingly bears the name of God as God's Son (1:5, 8, 10). The author begins to describe the human salvation achieved by the divine work of God the Father and Son by stating that the Son has made purification for sins (1:3), that enemies are being put under his feet (1:13), and, most explicitly, that the angels are sent out to minister to those who are about to inherit *salvation* (1:14).

Hebrews 2:1 follows directly on this depiction of divinely wrought salvation and builds upon it: "because of this" (2:1). Because of the salvation the Son has guaranteed, the author recommends a particular response from his community. The first warning encompasses verses 1–4, but is built upon four key phrases: "attend carefully" (v. 1), "lest we drift away" (v. 1), "just punishment" (v. 2), and "how will we escape?" (v. 3). As the author seeks to enliven their focus, he does so by calling them to attend to the action of God.

In this section, the author asks his listeners to pay attention to "what they have heard" (v. 1), but the fact is obvious that they have only heard anything because God has decided to speak, both in the prophets and preeminently in the Son (1:1–2). Because God has communicated, they have something to which they can listen. Here in 2:1–4, as was true in his opening statements, the author reminds his listeners that God has always been a God who chose to communicate. The "word spoken through the angels" (2:2), as the author's readers would likely know, refers to the law God delivered to the people of Israel from Sinai.[7] When that law was transgressed, God meted out punishment, a process that occurred almost right away when the people created and worshipped the golden calf while Moses was still on the mountain (Exod 32:1–8). The punishments for the transgressions of the divinely given law, all the way from the drinking of the pulverised calf (Exod 32:20) to the exile, show that the God who gave the law was both real and took the promises of the covenant seriously. A constructed idol could not punish, and a distant uninterested God would not care enough to do so. If this was true for the people of Israel, how much more, the author of Hebrews wonders, will just punishment be a reality for him and his listeners if they ignore "so great a salvation" (2:3). This short phrase summarises what he has already claimed about God's action through the Son and also previews all that he will say about this salvation throughout the sermon. God has given full and final salvation in the Son of God, the Messiah. This salvation, however, is not just something about which the author's listeners have studied, but it is also a reality they have experienced.

The punishment for this audience would certainly be just, because God has not only been at work in the past but also in the present in their very midst. The Son of the speaking God, fittingly, was communicative as well. He spoke about the salvation he was bringing (2:3), so that others could share it with this community. This indicates that the author believes that divine action can be worked through the bodies – in this instance, the voices – of humans. In addition to this, God has given this community direct divine witness through signs

---

7. Paul and Luke also refer to the law as angelically delivered (Gal 3:19; see also Acts 7:30, 38, 53), as does Jubilees 1.27, 29; 2.1; 5.1–2, 6, 13; 6.22; 30.12, 21; 50.1–2, 6, 13). See helpful background discussion in Harold W. Attridge, *The Epistle to the Hebrews*, Hermeneia (Philadelphia: Fortress Press, 1989), 65, n. 28.

and wonders, various powers, and distributions of the Holy Spirit (2:4). Present readers might long to know more specifics, but the list of powerful gifts confirms that God has been at work in an undeniable way. The warning concludes with this statement: all this has happened among the community because God has willed it. The divine work here is staggering. God has accomplished salvation and then communicated it through the law, through humans, and through supernatural manifestations. If the audience turns away from this revelation, God will punish it. This is a God to fear because this God is serious about the salvation only he has the power to produce. The author asks his listeners to fear drifting away from the good and powerful God described in chapter 1 and falling into the punishment reserved for those who do not attend to and obey the message of salvation this God is bringing.

As the first warning, the text falls short of the intensity of those warnings that follow in part due to its brevity. As I stated, the focus on the action of God is incredibly robust, and even within this warning the author increases the intentionality of the human response. First, in 2:1 he wants them to avoid "drifting away," a passive verb that conveys being caught up by swirling water (παραρρέω). This word is built upon the verb ῥέω (which means "to flow"). The image is striking, but it is one in which humans have less agency. By 2:3, however, the author warns his listeners against ignoring (ἀμελέω) the great salvation that has been revealed. It is clear he is speaking to those who have already heard the good news and chosen to disregard it. Each warning focuses on a different aspect of "apostasy" – turning away from God. In 2:1–4, that turning away is the sin of ignoring God's message of salvation. The consequence if this happens is even more certain than the "just punishment" the disobedient Israelites received, and for some Israelites transgression of the law meant mortal death (Exod 32:28). In sum, the author seeks to get the attention of his listeners with this paragraph by naming the certainty of punishment but waiting to disclose the details until he paints the great salvation with more color.

The audience will avoid this certain punishment by "attending carefully" to God's communication. This human action of attention is only possible, as stated, because God has chosen to reveal the salvation achieved by the Son. Moreover, attention is also possible because of the gift God has given to this community. God has given them power and the very Spirit of God, the Holy Spirit (2:4). Because this author will posit the Holy Spirit as a communicator of God's revelation (3:7; 10:15), to have the Holy Spirit within the community means that they can receive the message God sends to them from heaven by communicating through the Son. In other words, God has given everything needed for them to listen.

172

Analysis of the first warning confirms the overwhelming emphasis on divine action in salvation, communication, and empowerment. To allow oneself to be pulled away from God's work so that eventually one chooses to ignore it would certainly be worthy of punishment, and so the author is right to stir within his listeners the fear of responding to the salvation of God in this dismissive way.

HEBREWS 3:7–4:13

The first warning comes after the author's treatment of the Son's relationship with God (1:1–13), and the second follows the author's treatment of the Son's relationship with humanity as described in 2:5–18. Right after the warning in 2:1–4, the author puts forth Ps 8, a hymn that praises God for blessing human-ity, as a narrative of the human life of the Son (2:5–9).[8] From there he proclaims the full incarnate human experience of the Son from his taking on flesh and blood to his death (2:14). This allows the author to name explicitly for the first time the Son's high priesthood (2:17). Throughout 2:5–18, the author describes "the great salvation" as the shared yet distinct movements of God the Father and God the Son. For example, the Son tastes death for all, but does so by God's grace (2:10). Because of the Son's actions, God gives children to him (2:13). The drama of the salvific work appears when the author asserts that the Son, through his death, rescued those who were enslaved to the fear of death, whose overlord is the devil (2:14–15). In this rescue, the Son has dealt with the sins of the people (2:17). The Son, whom the author has shown is rightfully addressed as God (1:8), has enacted what is necessary to free humanity from the related shackles of sin and death in line with the gracious activity of his Father.[9]

With the majesty of Christ's sonship in view, eternal and incarnate, then, the depiction of salvation in 2:5–18 prepares the way for what follows where the author again urges his community to attention. Consider, he says, the one whom God sent and appointed as High Priest, even Jesus (3:1). After extolling the supremacy of Jesus in comparison with Moses (3:2–6), the author encourages

---

8. Scholars debate if the psalm should be interpreted anthropologically or christologically, but I find the both/and approach as articulated by David Moffitt the best interpretation (*Atonement and the Logic of Resurrection*, NovTSup 141 [Leiden: Brill, 2011], 128).

9. The relationship between sin and death is a complex issue in Hebrews. The warnings have already disclosed that transgression can result in death (2:2/Exod 32:28) and will elaborate on the consequences for the wilderness generation in 3:7–4:13, whose bodies fell in the wilderness (4:17). Hence the Son's atone-ment for sins is what allows them to be free from the power of death. See Karen H. Jobes, *Letters to the Church: A Survey of Hebrews and the General Epistles* (Grand Rapids: Zondervan, 2011), 117–23; Gareth Lee Cockerill, *The Epistle to the Hebrews*, NICNT (Grand Rapids: Eerdmans, 2012), 146–47.

them to hold fast to their hope in him (3:6). His charge to remain a part of the household over which Christ reigns leads into the most extensive warning section of the sermon.

This warning is built upon the account of the Israelites whom God had redeemed from slavery but who then failed to trust that God could take them into the land of promise. Consequently, God made their fears a reality, and they were not able to enter the land. This was not because God was incapable of bringing them in, but because they chose not to trust in his integrity and capability. They did not believe that God was able to take them into the land, and hence they doubted his promise to do so. The author communicates this narrative through citations of portions of Ps 95:7–11 (LXX). He does not want his community to follow Israel's example of unfaithfulness.

Throughout this first section of the warning (3:7–18), God's action is on display. The author recalls God's redemption (their fathers were in the wilderness, 3:8, because God had brought them out of Egypt, 3:16), God's works (3:9), and God's enacting of consequences (3:11, 17, 18). With all this divine activity of redemption and revelation, it is striking that what God is inviting them into is not divine activity but divine *rest* (3:11). Although God is inviting them into rest, as was true in the warning in 2:1–4, divine activity is not a thing of the past. A vital aspect of divine activity in the present is God's speech. With the frequent citations of the psalm, the author reminds his community that God is still speaking. They too can hear God's voice (3:7, 15).

The rhetoric of warning by this point in the sermon has increased in intensity. In this second warning, the author names the punishment that came to those who transgressed and disobeyed the word God gave to them through the angels (2:2). The author has assured his listeners of their relationship with Christ, but also reminded them of the necessity of holding fast to it (3:6, 14). Since they know that Christ is exalted (1:1–14) and know that he has humbled himself to enter and transform the human condition (2:5–18), the author can name the dire consequences of failing to trust in that revelation. The wilderness generation, as described in 3:7–4:11, violated God's angelically delivered word given at Sinai. He now names explicitly some of the punishments that come for transgressing those commands, namely, exclusion from God's space (3:11), which resulted in mortal death (3:17).

The author asks his audience to pay attention (βλέπετε), lest their hearts like those of the wilderness generation entertain distrust. If they succumb to the evil of not trusting who God is and what God has said, they will take the fateful step of turning away from God (3:12). To avoid turning away from the source of life, the living God (3:12), who is the creator and sustainer of life

(1:2–3), they must encourage one another each day (3:13). Communal honesty and support among the family of God (3:6) is the way to avoid sin's deceit (3:13). The author charges them to hold fast to their participation in Christ and among Christ's siblings (3:14).

In the second section of the warning (4:1–11), God's invitation into rest continues (4:1, 3–5). Again, the author shows that if God has been resting since the seventh day (4:4), and in that time both sustaining and redeeming creation, then his rest is a very active one (4:10). By inviting the community into rest that is still available (4:9), the promise of God is also communicated to them (4:1). Both generations have been gospeled (εὐηγγελισμένοι) by God's word (4:2, 6). This was not the "gospel" of the death and resurrection of the Son for the wilderness generation, but it was the good news from God inviting redeemed humans into the place of God's presence.[10]

He asks them (and himself!) explicitly to fear lest some of them fail to reach God's rest, as happened to the generation who had to wander in the wilderness (4:1). Their story demonstrates that although they heard God's word, they did not respond faithfully by joining themselves with those who heard and responded in faith, namely, Joshua and Caleb (4:2; see Num 13:30–14:38; 26:65; 32:12). Instead, they were apathetic to God's word. Because they did not trust in it, they did not act on it (4:6). This is the grievous sin the author highlights in this section: namely, to fail to trust in God's promises and then act on them.

If the author and his readers want to be those who go into God's "rest," they must be people who trust God's power to keep the divine promises (4:3). The situation is so urgent as to demand haste (σποθδάσωμεν) in the movement towards God's rest. They need to advance so that they do not drift away (2:1). If they are moving forward by trusting in God, they will not fall like those who neither trusted what God had said nor obeyed it (4:11). Although they are not moving into the land of Canaan, they too are following God's lead (2:10), and so need to trust that God can bring them into his "rest." Rest for the community of this sermon is not only a portion of land on earth in which they can cease fighting against their enemies, although they do look forward to stewarding the unshakable elements of creation (Heb 2:5–10; 12:26–28), but rest is ultimately to dwell with God forever. This is the hope of the true country and heavenly city the author discusses in 11:10, 14–15; 12:22–24. It is "God's own ultimate rest,

---

10. Mary Healy suggests, "they were 'evangelized' in that they experienced the foreshadowing of the gospel, God's mighty work of redemption through their deliverance from Egypt," *Hebrews*, CCSS (Grand Rapids: Baker Academic, 2016), 87.

the goal of creation, the intended destiny of God's people."[11] Falling short of this rest is highly worthy of fear. That trust that God will lead his people to this rest will result in obedience along the way, no matter what hardship they face.

At its close, this warning section culminates in the oft-quoted statements about God's word. God's living word is so powerful that the author can compare it to a sword that penetrates the human person deeper than any natural instrument (4:12–13). The author closes this section with a chilling image of everything naked and exposed before the eyes of God's word.[12] He has been warning his listeners not to harden their hearts, but even if they tried to perform this hardening, the speaking God could cut through any barrier. Throughout this section, then, the actions of God evoke fear – certainly, fear of the punishment of being excluded from God's blessed rest and fear of God's word, which leaves no recourse for pretense. The resting God is not a slumbering giant, but, with the repose of his work done, fearfully acts to bring humanity to join in the divine rest.

Although several phrases of Hebrews 4:12 are quoted so often as to become familiar and unthreatening, a double-edged blade that can cleave not only body but also soul hanging over one's nakedness and to which one must give an account is not an image that cajoles. It is an image that strikes fear into us. This is not, however, a fear that drives one to cower away from God – for how could one hide from such an all-seeing word? This is, rather, a fear that drives people to honesty and exposes the spaces of distrust to a God who already knows them.

It is no surprise, then, that such an image leads immediately to the assurances of the High Priest (4:14–16). One who knows his people from the outside as Creator and from the inside as a fellow human is the only one who can offer the transformative grace they need when they see themselves for what they really are. It makes sense that from the beginning of chapter 3 the author has been urging his listeners to hold fast to their High Priest. He is the one who has already entered God's rest since he has sat down next to God after completing his work (1:3, 13). Only as they stay tethered to him can he sympathetically expose and forgive their sin along with their tendencies to lack trust and therefore disobey, so that they can reach God's rest with him.

---

11. Cockerill, *Hebrews*, 212.

12. I recognise that this has been variously interpreted, including as a form of judgement administered towards the wilderness generation (James Swetnam, "Jesus as Logos in Heb 4:12–13," *Biblica* 62.2 (1981): 214–24) or in resonance with the Genesis creation/fall narrative (Angela Costley, "A New Look at Hebrews 4:12–13," *PIBA* 40 (2019): 23–42). I find the sacrificial imagery appropriate to the context (see Attridge, *Hebrews*, 136) and disagree that the slaughter has to assume destruction (Paul Ellingworth, *The Epistle to the Hebrews: A Commentary on the Greek Text*, NIGTC [Grand Rapids: Eerdmans, 1993], 265) but emphasises the full exposure that is necessary preparation for service to God. By portraying a blade poised at their exposed neck as a lamb prepared for the slaughter, a sacrificial image leads well into the presentation of the empathetic High Priest.

HEBREWS 6:4–8

In 4:14–5:10 the author introduces the subject of priesthood, which he will develop in 7:1–10:18, before chiding his audience for their lack of maturity (5:11–14). Pledging to move on to more complicated themes (6:1–3), he launches into one of the most debated sections of the letter. Attention to divine action cannot solve all debates about this passage, but it can yield affirmations concerning God on which many different theological traditions can agree.

Although the focus in 6:4–6 is upon what a human might do, the action of God courses beneath the surface. It is God who has enlightened the people the author is describing by speaking through the radiant Son (1:3). It is God who gave them the heavenly gift, the Holy Spirit, and the powers of the coming age (2:4). It is God who gives the word. There is plausible reason to interpret the first statement of the warning to mean that it is God who cannot renew again unto repentance once one has fallen away from these gifts. This impossibility is not due to divine impotence, but to the fact that the incarnate Son, who by his willing death defeated death, cannot die again for those who have rejected his provision.[13] Divine action is also the focus of the nature parable in 6:7–8. God sends rain and causes vegetation. It is God who blesses nature, and by virtue of echoes with the creation narrative and other biblical texts (Dan 7:11; 2 Peter 3:10–12), it is also God who administers the curse which ends in burning. In sum, the Son of God has, once and for all, achieved salvation. God the Father (as well as the Holy Spirit) has communicated this salvation to humans. If it makes sense to purge useless produce, then God would be within reason to administer judgement against those who reject the salvation that has been offered.

Notice how the author creates the intensity of this warning. He uses four phrases to describe people who commit this deed of rejection (those who have once been enlightened, those who have tasted of the heavenly gift, those who have become sharers of the Holy Spirit, and those who have tasted of the good word of God and the powers of the age to come, 6:4–5), which connect with other descriptions of the community (1:2; 2:3; 3:1, 14; 10:32). The author describes this "falling away" as repeated crucifixion and public shaming of

---

13. Ellingworth lays out the options for God or humans as the subject of ἀδύνατος (Ellingworth, *Hebrews*, 319). Johnson seems to embrace an anthropological interpretation highlighting human experience, "it is impossible to 'renew to repentance' people who have proven capable of turning away from their own most powerful and transforming experience" (Luke Timothy Johnson, *Hebrews: A Commentary*, NTL [Louisville, KY: Westminster John Knox Press, 2006], 163). Allowing the full force of the warning, Cockerill concludes, "Thus the primary explanation for the impossibility of the apostates' restoration is not to be found merely in the hardening of their hearts but in the magnitude of the salvation they have rejected and the finality of their rejection" (Cockerill, *Hebrews*, 275).

the Son. In addition to the consequences described by curses and burning, the author begins this warning in 6:4–8 with the word, Ἀδύνατον, "impossible," fronting the closed door to repentance for those who would effectively ask that Christ be crucified again since they are rejecting his previous work. With this language he presents for his audience the fear of falling away from the incredible goods of being a Christ confessor and falling into God's judgement of fruitless things. If the warning in 3:7–4:13 propelled them to the throne of their gracious High Priest (4:14–16), this one compels them to stay there so that they might not be guilty of such an egregious sin of rejecting Christ's work of forgiveness for sins and defeat of death. As the author is asking them to hold fast to Christ, it is not surprising that he will next turn to the divine promises that ground Christ's enduring priesthood (7:1–8:13).

It is important to notice that the author does not address his listeners directly in this passage. Instead, he describes a certain group of people who share a similar beginning with the audience but – as the following verses (6:9–10) will show – are not to be identified with them. Hence, although the descriptions are intense, the author allows his listeners to contemplate the gravity of the situation by putting it at a remove from them. If they had already turned away, he would not need to warn them. He may not speak directly to them in this passage, but he certainly speaks directly to them with it. They need not fear the curse of conflagration if they remain open to the reception of the ample gifts of salvation God gives in Jesus Christ.

HEBREWS 10:26–31

In the extensive section between the warnings in 6:4–8 and 10:26–31, the author attends to God's promises and finds them steadfast. The promise to the Son of priesthood (Ps 110:4; Heb 7:1–28) is bound up with the promise to the people of a new covenant (Jer 31:31–34; Heb 8:1–10:18). The former makes the latter possible. Because of what Christ has done, the new covenant is inaugurated. God's faithfulness to divine promises is why this community can hold fast to their confession of hope (10:23). That theological proclamation that "the One who promised is faithful" would make a rousing end to 6:12–10:23, but the author proceeds to add an exhortation about the importance of community (10:24–25). These two verses provide important context for understanding the warning that follows. Without them, sinning willfully could seem to include anything, but with them readers can better understand what the author is arguing for in response to the salvific action of God.

In this warning section, the author depicts God's work in a multitude of ways. As the One who is true and has created a true message, God also granted this community knowledge of it. The true message is that the Son of God has already made a sacrifice for sins (10:26). He has shed his blood, which brings about the sanctifying new covenant (10:29), and sent out the Spirit of grace (10:30). If someone sins willfully after reorienting his or her entire life around this true divine communication, that person should fear God's fiery consuming judgement. The author of Hebrews believes that God disclosed the divine promise for judgement in the law, and so he cites God's speech from Deuteronomy. God will give back what the people give (Heb 10:30/Deut 32:35). In other words, if they follow idols God will allow them to see how inert those idols really are. They should fear rejecting the sacrifice given for sins and being left to those idols that could never save. If they fail to pay attention to the revelation of God through Christ (2:1–4), they will miss out on dwelling in God's presence forever (3:7–4:13); fail to experience God's blessings now and be open to judgement in the end (6:4–6); and, although they were God's people, find themselves in association with the enemies of God who are justly judged (10:26–31). The Lord has promised to judge his people (Heb 10:30/Deut 32:26), and to fall into the judgement justly exercised at the hand of God is worthy of fear.

Much is at stake here for the readers' conception of God's action. The entirety of Hebrews does not give an image of a God who delights in punishment, but of a God who has taken a stand against the havoc of sin and death. If someone dissociates from the remedy to sin and death offered by God through Christ, then the person is exposed to the just wrath of God against those enemy forces.

Rhetorically, the author prepares for this scriptural citation from Deut 32:25–26 by directly addressing his community in this warning. He is not describing a hypothetical group, as was true in 6:4–8, but it is about those to whom he is speaking: "If *we* sin" (10:26). Hence, the intensity has increased because he is speaking explicitly about a possibility in community (as he did in 2:1–4, but this time with more chilling detail). He describes the willful sin as equal to trampling the Son of God, counting his blood as common, and insulting the gracious Spirit (10:29). The person who sins in this way rejects all that is true of Christ: that he is the eternal and sovereign Son (1:1–13); that he has fully and finally dealt with the problem of sin (8:1–10:18); and that, because of his work, the Spirit has invited humanity into its effects (2:4; 6:4). Such people reject what they have been taught and what they have experienced personally. Verses 24 and 25 illuminate the tragic reality that such actions against active trust in Christ are joined with a departure from those who gather in his name. This sin of disrespectful rejection places a person among God's enemies (10:27). As was true in 3:7–19 and 6:4–8, the result is God's fiery judgement and the possibility of death.

The admonition in this warning is clear: remain trusting in God within the community of Christ confessors. If they fail to keep up the habit of gathering for the sharing of love and encouragement, the deceitfulness of sin and the specter of disbelief will have more opportunity to grow in their individual and disconnected hearts. There is a price to pay by being part of this community, as the author will describe in 10:32–34. Nevertheless, the cost is counterbalanced by blessing, the encouragement they receive from one another *because* they go together into the holy place of God before the throne to receive grace (4:14–16/10:19–22). To respond to the warning, they must continue in their worship of the One God who has communicated in the Son, gathering with others under the confession of God's work in Christ. This is the way to ensure that each of their individual hearts can stay free of deception and be steadfast in its trust in God. Consequently, the author calls his listeners to endurance (10:36) and expresses hope that they will endure unto salvation (10:39).

HEBREWS 12:12–29

The call to endurance propels the author to recount those from their family of faith who have endured in their trust in God, resulting in the catalogue of the faithful throughout Heb 11. The pinnacle of faithfulness is Jesus himself, who endured the cross (12:1–3). The author then transitions from the stories of others back to the community and their need to endure difficulties. These struggles are not signs that God has abandoned them, but, quite to the contrary, they are evidence that God is allowing them to grow in maturity (12:4–11). One of the major themes throughout 11:1–12:13 is endurance. This theme shapes how readers hear the warnings that follow.

In the first set of warnings (12:12–17), the possibility of not seeing the Lord (12:14), falling short of the grace of God (12:15), being defiled and causing defilement (12:15), and failing to obtain the blessing of inheritance like Esau (12:15–17), the work of God is understated, explicitly present only in the reference to God's grace.

The warning rhetoric becomes quite intense in this section of the chapter, especially with the example of Esau. The author describes him as immoral and profane (πόρνος ἤ βέβηλος) – likely a way of emphasising Esau's flippant treatment of his placement in the covenant family.[14] The way the author tells the story could sound like God's rejection even of heartfelt repentance. Instead, it is best read in alignment with the previous warnings. The author elides Esau's selling of the birthright/eating of the meal with his inability to inherit the blessing, showing that Esau's tears did not effect change with regard to the blessing because he had given up his birthright.[15] It would be as if someone would ask for God's blessing after having cut off his or her relationship with Jesus, but God does not grant salvation if one is not a part of the family under Jesus the Son. As inheritance can only come from birthright, so too God's blessing can only come through the Christ confession. It is not that God is unmoved by contrition, but God is unmoved if the sadness concerns the absence of blessing rather than grief over the person's rejection of Christ. In this way, though the intensity has increased, the discussion of Esau aligns with the previous warnings. If a person wants a different salvific option other than the work of Christ, God's blessing of salvation is impossible. The story of Esau evokes the fear of being outside the salvific family of God as one rejects association with the Son and his work on the cross.

Consequently, in light of this warning in these verses (12:12–17), the author admonishes the congregation to endure hard things, which builds upon the discussion of God's discipline (12:1–13). The author does ask them to be attentive to and even pursue the virtues of peace, holiness, and grace (12:14–15), but these are virtues that God has already provided in Christ (Heb. 2:9, 11; 4:16; 9:13; 10:10, 14, 29; 12:11). The complement to this is that he asks them to avoid bitterness, defilement, and flippancy towards the gracious inheritance they have from God. The positive instructions and the negative instructions are different ways of stating the same thing. The congregation must continue to trust so that they can continue to receive what God is giving them. They do not need to obtain the virtues but endure in maintaining and maturing in them.

Most strikingly, the author says that his readers cannot give up Christ as Esau gave up his birthright. They should not choose pleasure over family as Esau did (12:14–17). The ridiculousness of Esau's trade powerfully emphasises the author's point. Because of hunger, Esau gave up his precious birthright.

---

14. Johnson notes the correspondence to the marriage metaphor in Israel's Scriptures (Johnson, *Hebrews*, 324).

15. I am arguing that the antecedent of αὐτήν be εὐλογίαν and not μετανοίας. Ellingworth argues for the opposite in part due to the prominence of repentance in Hebrews (Ellingworth, *Hebrews*, 668). The grammatical agreement of the feminine as well as the logic I have just articulated spurs me to read that Esau was seeking for the blessing (See also Cockerill, *Hebrews*, 641).

Although the congregation's difficulties are heavier than his, namely persecution, they would be giving up something so much more valuable if they walked away from their confession of Christ. Consequently, the comparison shows them that no matter how hard things are, it is never worth it to give up on one's confession of Christ.

Although the next paragraph (12:18–24) is a source of great comfort to the congregation because the author proclaims that they have approached the mountain of God,[16] it also includes a powerful sense of warning. The action of God is dominant here as the author clearly evokes the Sinai narrative (Exod 19:16–19), where God is the cause of all the fearful sights and sounds. Most strikingly, God has given the punishment for inappropriately transgressing the line over to where God's holiness dwells – namely, death (Heb 12:20/ Exod 19:12). God has not changed. He remains "judge of all" (Heb 12:23), so if the congregation tries to approach God without the forgiveness and sanctification Christ has procured, the same judgement of death will come upon them.

The chapter then transitions to the final and climactic warning. In this section (12:25–29), divine activity is at the centre. God, as was emphasised at the very beginning of the sermon (1:1–2), is the God who speaks (12:25), and the kind of speech God issues is warning about future events. Through the citation of Haggai 2:6, the author shows how God's voice dismantles, shaking all things in heaven and on earth so that only the unshakable remains. The final statement of the chapter, "God is a consuming fire," fits into this theme as well. God burns away everything that is not in faithful response to him (Deut 4:24), including the enemies opposed to God's will (Deut 9:3). These statements about the warning voice of God align with the section on the Word of God in 4:12–13 where divine speech exposes, purges, and judges. In this instance, however, the prophet has in view a final event ("and yet *once* more") in which God shakes all things so that only the eternal remains.

The transformation of created things juxtaposed with that which remains creates a connection with the statements about creation in the opening catena (Heb 1:10–12). The speaking God is the enduring person who both brought creation into being and will shape the state of the created kingdom over which he will reign forever. Only as this congregation stays attentive and obedient to him can they hope to endure this great shaking.

---

16. I read this in line with the author's statement that they can approach the throne of grace (4:16) and go into the holy place (10:19). Johnson also sees this as an "entry into God's life" (Johnson, *Hebrews*, 330).

If the congregation is not attentive to all the ways God is warning them (12:25) through the prophets, through the Son, and through the sermon from this pastor, and depart (ἀποστρέφω) from the God who is graciously communicating to them, their punishment will be as assured as the generation who heard God speaking from the mountain and disobeyed. However, because they have heard of God's salvation with utmost clarity and power through the person of the Son, their punishment would be greater. They will face the consuming fire (Heb 12:29) of God's final judgement as those who have rejected the great and only salvation God has provided. It is right to see this as resonate with the fire that is about to devour adversaries (10:27).[17] If the hearers of Hebrews, by virtue of not listening and not trusting, put themselves outside of the reign of the Son, they will be among the shaken things that do not remain, the things that are consumed by God's fire.

The encouragement embedded in this warning is that the congregation is already receiving this unshakable kingdom (12:28). In addition to persevering in their attentive listening so that they can remain turned towards God rather than turning away from him, they are encouraged by God to respond with gratefulness (12:28). With an attitude of thanksgiving, they can serve God in a pleasing way which includes having reverence – this is the attitude with which Jesus approached his Father in the face of death (5:7) – *and* fear. In this final climactic warning about the end of the world as his hearers know it, the author shows that fear is not in antithesis to maintaining a healthy relationship with God but is a necessity.

CONCLUSION

In Hebrews God is a mighty actor. God creates and sustains all things. Through the work of the Son to take on flesh, suffer, die, and defeat death, internal cleansing and eternal salvation are now available. Even more, God is active in communicating this great salvation to humanity, and in this sermon that communication comes to this congregation. In light of all that God has done and is continuing to do, this author uses these warning sections to move the weary congregation to fear so that they will not turn away from their sovereign and gracious God.

---

17. Ellingworth, *Hebrews*, 691.

SELECT BIBLIOGRAPHY

Abraham, William J. *Exploring and Evaluating the Debate.* Vol. 1, *Divine Agency and Divine Action.* Oxford: OUP, 2017.

Attridge, Harold W. *The Epistle to the Hebrews: A Commentary on the Epistle to the Hebrews.* Hermeneia. Philadelphia: Fortress Press, 1989.

Bateman, Herbert W., IV. "Introducing the Warning Passages in Hebrews: A Contextual Orientation." In *Four Views on the Warning Passages in Hebrews*, edited by Herbert W. Bateman IV, 23–85. Grand Rapids: Kregel Academic & Professional, 2007.

Cockerill, Gareth Lee. *The Epistle to the Hebrews.* NICNT. Grand Rapids: Eerdmans, 2012.

Costley, Angela. "A New Look at Hebrews 4:12–13." *Proceedings of the Irish Biblical Association* 40 (2019): 23–42.

Ellingworth, Paul. *The Epistle to the Hebrews: A Commentary on the Greek Text.* NIGTC. Grand Rapids: Eerdmans, 1993.

Healy, Mary. *Hebrews.* CCSS. Grand Rapids: Baker Academic, 2016.

Jobes, Karen H. *Letters to the Church: A Survey of Hebrews and the General Epistles.* Grand Rapids: Zondervan, 2011.

Johnson, Luke Timothy. *Hebrews: A Commentary.* NTL. Louisville, KY: Westminster John Knox Press, 2006.

Moffitt, David M. *Atonement and the Logic of Resurrection in the Epistle to the Hebrews.* NovTSup 141. Boston/Leiden: Brill, 2011.

Pink, Arthur W. *Exposition of Hebrews.* Grand Rapids: Baker, 1954.

Swetnam, James. "Jesus as Logos in Heb 4:12–13." *Bib* 62.2 (1981): 214–24.

Webster, John. *Confessing God: Essays in Christian Dogmatics II.* London: Bloomsbury T&T Clark, 2005.

CHAPTER 10

Hebrews's Eschatology and
the Action of God

Steve Motyer[1]

INTRODUCTION

The days are long gone when Hebrews was regarded as Platonic, with an interest only in a world "up there" as distinct from a world "yet to be."[2] It is now widely accepted that Hebrews, like the rest of the NT, is full of a lively expectation of a "world to come" (Heb 2:5). Indeed, this reality is underlined in the magnificent catena of quotations with which the letter begins. Here the unending life and rule of the Son of God ("your throne, O God, will last for ever and ever . . . you remain the same, and your years will never end," 1:8, 12) is contrasted with the *impermanence* of the present earth and heavens ("they will perish . . . they will all wear out like a garment," 1:11). This opening contrast is picked up and balanced at the end of the letter by the glorious passage on which we will focus, also involving a key OT quotation (Hag 2:6):

> Now he has promised, "Once more I will shake not only the earth but also the heavens." The words "once more" indicate the removing of what can be shaken – that is, created things – so that what cannot be shaken may remain. (Heb 12:26–27)

---

1. Biblical quotations are from the NIV unless otherwise indicated.
2. See L. D. Hurst, *The Epistle to the Hebrews: Its Background of Thought*, SNTSMS 65 (Cambridge: CUP, 1990).

So Hebrews's message is set against a cosmic background involving both loss and renewal, and this shapes everything that falls between these opening and closing quotations. "Faith" in Hebrews – such a key theme – is always forward-looking and involves acting now in the light of what will be, because like Moses we are "looking ahead to [our] reward." Thus, we too "persevere" because by faith we can "[see] him who is invisible" (11:26–27). The one who is invisible, and whom we see (2:9), is of course the risen Christ, who is now seated "at my right hand until I make your enemies a footstool for your feet." This quotation of Ps 110:1, with which the opening catena reaches a climax (1:13–14), introduces an "until" which frames the forward-looking dynamic of Hebrews's theology. The story of salvation – indeed, the story of the risen Christ – is not yet complete. But one day it will be – the day when "he will appear a second time, not to bear sin, but to bring salvation to those who are waiting for him" (9:28).

In the light of the interest of this volume in divine action, our task in this essay is twofold:

1. To gain an overview of Hebrews's eschatology, in particular asking how God is active in what we discover; and then
2. in the light of 1., to discuss how we may understand God's action theologically as we live now in the interim between the great acts of creation and final re-creation.

HEBREWS'S ESCHATOLOGY: AN OVERVIEW

We will divide this section into two, first considering eschatology proper (i.e., those elements which are definitely "not yet") and then the ways in which Hebrews's eschatology could be called "inaugurated" – i.e., looking at elements of the age to come which are brought into our present experience. Obviously it is in connection with this second focus that the issue of present divine action is particularly raised.

ESCHATOLOGY "PROPER"

The expectation of final judgement is the absolute horizon of Hebrews's worldview. The author fears that his readers may not "escape" if they persist in their present course of action (2:3), which is to turn their backs on the confession of Jesus as Son of God and Messiah. Unless they "hold [their] original conviction firmly to the very end" (3:14), there is a danger that they will face the same fate as the Exodus generation "whose bodies perished in the wilderness" (3:17) and who failed to "enter [God's] rest . . . because of their unbelief" (3:18–19). Because God's "rest" is interpreted not as political settlement but as God's own eternal life opened up to his people (4:6–11), the stakes are enormously high for the readers of Hebrews. They may "fall into the hands of the living God" (10:31), who is a "consuming fire" (12:29), and thus end up being "burned" like the weeds produced by worthless ground (6:8). "The judgment," which follows immediately upon death according to 9:27, is the theological scaffold for this author, within which everything is constructed.

But the author has confidence that the readers will not suffer this fate. "We do not belong to those who shrink back and are destroyed, but to those who have faith and are saved," he declares (10:39; cf. 6:9–10). It is more than possible now, because of Jesus, to enter God's rest: "we who have believed enter that rest" (4:3).

The final destruction which the author and his readers will avoid, because of Jesus, has a fascinating cosmological component. In order to explore this, we turn to the powerful passage with which the main argument of the letter reaches its climax, 12:25–29, already quoted in part:

> See to it that you do not refuse him who speaks. If they did not escape when they refused him who warned them on earth, how much less will we, if we turn away from him who warns us from heaven? At that time his voice shook the earth, but now he has promised, "Once more I will shake not only the earth but also the heavens." The words "once more" indicate the removing of what can be shaken – that is, created things – so that what cannot be shaken may remain.

At the heart of the created world, it appears, there is an unshakeable core which will "remain" when God "shakes" and removes everything else. This unshakeable core is immediately revealed –

> Therefore, since we are receiving a kingdom that cannot be shaken, let us be thankful, and so worship God acceptably with reverence and awe, for our "God is a consuming fire."[3] (12:28–29)

This is the basis of the elements of "inaugurated" eschatology, which we will explore shortly: the "unshakeable" kingdom of God is already present within the created world and its reception is a continuous process which "we" experience.

---

3. The quotation is of Deut 4:24.

187

But first it is important to notice – with many others[4] – how this passage looks back to the opening use of Psalm 102 in 1:10–12, thus forming a kind of *inclusio* around the letter:

> In the beginning, Lord, you laid the foundations of the earth,
>> and the heavens are the work of your hands.
> They will perish, but you remain;
>> they will all wear out like a garment;
> You will roll them up like a robe;
>> like a garment they will be changed.
> But you remain the same,
>> and your years will never end. (1:10–12; Ps 102:25–27
>> [LXX 101:26–28])

The "Lord" here (in the author's reading of the psalm) is the Son through whom God "made the ages" (1:2, my translation: ἐποίησεν τοὺς αἰῶνας), and the connection with that basic statement of creation in 1:2 gives us some insight into the meaning of the important word αἰών in Hebrews. NIV renders it "the universe" in 1:2,[5] but the word never loses the sense of an "epoch" or "time span" because – as we can see from the quotation of Psalm 102 – "the earth" and "the heavens" are never considered just as physical entities. They are created with a built-in timeline, progressing inevitably towards dissolution, "wearing out" and needing to be "changed." Their "perishing" – amazingly – is implicit in their founding. The plural "ages" is sometimes just a rhetorical emphasis (e.g., 13:21), but it can also express something of the complexity of the created earth and heavens, which progress through successive "ages" on their way to dissolution (cf. 11:3). Most often, αἰών in the singular means "the age to come," as we see both in the crucial quotation of Psalm 110:4 (Jesus will be "priest εἰς τὸν αἰῶνα according to the order of Melchizedek"[6]) and in the introductory quotation from Psalm 45, "your throne, O God, is εἰς τὸν αἰῶνα τοῦ αἰῶνος."[7]

Implicitly, the coming αἰών is a world that lasts beyond the present failing creation which *as created* is going to be shaken out of existence – "removed" (12:27). This passing away of the "earth and the heavens" (1:10–11, 12:26) gives a special flavour to the "salvation" which is announced so emphatically at the end of chapter 1 and then unpacked throughout the letter: how can humans

---

4. E.g., Gareth Lee Cockerill, *The Epistle to the Hebrews*, NICNT (Grand Rapids: Eerdmans, 2012), 665.
5. Cf. NRSV "the worlds."
6. 5:6; also 6:20; 7:17, 21, 24, 28.
7. 1:8, quoting Ps 45:6 (LXX 44:7).

survive in a world which passes away? There is no basis for survival here. Yet there are those "who will inherit salvation" (1:14) because *the Lord* "remains." The one who made the earth and the heaven outlives them: "They will perish, but you remain" (1:11a).

This verb "remain" (διαμένειν) expresses this "outliving," the lastingness both of Jesus the Creator and therefore of those who are connected to him. They need not fear the "shaking" of the earth and the heaven, provided, of course, that they do not neglect the salvation they enjoy in connection to him (2:1–3a). Following 1:11, the verb μένειν (also drawn from Ps 110:4) expresses both Christ's lastingness[8] and the consequent lastingness of what he creates beyond the present heaven and earth – the lasting "city" (13:14; cf. 11:16); the lasting "possessions" which are so much "better" than our possessions here (10:34); and, supremely, the lastingness of the coming world (12:27): what cannot be shaken will "remain"! (ἵνα μείνῃ τὰ μὴ σαλευόμενα).[9]

This framing of salvation as *deliverance from the built-in impermanence of the created order* has extraordinary contemporary resonance. The fragility of our ecosystem, the sense that the planet is groaning under our presence, the way in which climate change is making our environment hostile to us, and above all the ever-present threat of our own death (the earth, despite its incredible longevity, cannot give us more than a few years of life) – all these underline our impermanence in the world. Hebrews underlines that impermanence: it is written into the very stuff of creation! But at the same time, Hebrews offers us a "lasting" Saviour.

The basis of this lasting salvation is the "purification for sins" which the Son has "made" (1:3; NIV "provided"). The double use of the verb ποιεῖν in the preface (1:1–4) – the Son who "made" the αἰῶνες (1:2) has now "made" purification for sins (1:3) – introduces the work of salvation as a subsequent and parallel act of creation. Divine action is thus written all over Hebrews, because God acts not just in creation and in final judgement and re-creation, but in the work of salvation, "bring[ing] his firstborn into the world" (1:6)[10] so that the Son may

---

8. Cf. "he remains a priest for ever" (7:3), "because Jesus remains [*NIV: lives*] for ever, he has a permanent priesthood" (7:24).

9. I am grateful for Craig Bartholomew's emphasis (in his essay in this volume, 160–64, especially 162–63) on the *re-making* of creation rather than its destruction in Hebrews's eschatology. The coming αἰών, he argues, is an age of *this* world, not of some other. The Kingdom that lasts is part of *this* creation, which is destined to be "inherited" by the Son through whom it was made (1:2): and therefore we above all people should value the present creation because of its ongoing relationship to him.

10. It is true that many (e.g., Cockerill, *Hebrews*, 104–108; William L. Lane, *Hebrews 1-8* [WBC 47A, Dallas: Word, 1991], 26–28) do not find a reference to the incarnation in 1:6, but refer it rather to Christ's exaltation in "the world to come" (2:5). I remain convinced, however, that God's action in "bringing" the Son into the world most naturally (at this point in the letter) leads our minds to the incarnation.

become a merciful and faithful High Priest and lead many sons and daughters to glory (2:10, 17). The author's use of the Day of Atonement as an explanatory metaphor for this work of salvation reaches a climax in 9:27–28 with the only reference to the second coming of Christ in Hebrews:[11]

> Just as people are destined to die once, and after that to face judgment, so
> Christ was sacrificed once to take away the sins of many; and he will appear
> a second time, not to bear sin, but to bring salvation to those who are waiting
> for him.

This is a unique "take" on the second coming in the NT, using the image of the high priest emerging triumphantly from the Most Holy Place, the work of atonement complete, to be greeted by the worshippers waiting for him outside the sanctuary. The reappearance of the high priest was the high point of the Day of Atonement ritual, leading to a blessing in which the divine name was actually used for the only time in the year, and giving assurance that Israel's sin had truly been dealt with.[12]

So the work of salvation is all part of God's creatorial action, calling into being a kingdom which cannot be shaken at the heart of this present failing universe. Another "present continuous" tense underlines the way in which this work is going on currently:

> When this priest had offered for all time one sacrifice for sins, he sat down at
> the right hand of God, and since that time he waits for his enemies to be made
> his footstool. For by one sacrifice he has made perfect forever those who are
> being made holy. (10:12–14)

There is a double paradox here which the author finds in Psalm 110:1, to which he alludes. On the one hand the work is complete, signalled by Christ's victorious "sitting" at God's right hand, but on the other, he is still "waiting" for final victory. Similarly, the objects of his work (us) are already "made perfect," but at the same time are undergoing a process of "being made holy." This is the stuff of "inaugurated eschatology," to which we now turn. As we do so, we are particularly interested in noticing any ways in which Hebrews conceives of God *acting directly within the present world*, in anticipation of the world to come:

---

11. – and, indeed, the only place in the NT where it is called the "second" coming.

12. A vivid passage in Sirach 50:5–21 depicts the dramatic appearance of Simon son of Onias (high priest c. 220–195 BCE) from the Most Holy Place, underlining the glory of the occasion and the joy of the worshippers.

what exactly is the experience of "being made holy," and in what ways do we directly experience God's action within this process?

"INAUGURATED" ESCHATOLOGY

The author's concern for his readers is a good starting-place, for he is worried that they are turning their backs on tangible experiences of God's power. The powerful warning passage in 6:4–6 lists the key experiences which, if denied, will stop the readers from ever being "brought back to repentance" (6:6). The list is successively epexegetic (I think), so that each item progressively unpacks the preceding one:

- Enlightened
- Tasted the heavenly gift
- Shared in the Holy Spirit
- Tasted God's good word
- Tasted the powers of the coming age

The last item, in particular, underlines the anticipatory eschatological quality of these experiences. Each of them was undoubtedly clear and identifiable within the readers' history. These experiences have brought them together as a worshipping group – something which some of them are already moving away from (10:25). We can suitably imagine "charismatic" occasions of glossolalia, prophecy, and healings within a worship setting, experiences about which the author – and presumably the readers, when they first had them – entertain no doubt: these were real "tastings" of God's power, divine actions in the world.[13]

For the author, such actions are an essential element of the experience of the unshakeable kingdom. He has already listed them in 2:4, when he referred to the "signs, wonders and various miracles, and . . . gifts of the Holy Spirit distributed according to his will" by which "God also testified" (συνεπιμαρτυροῦντος τοῦ θεοῦ) alongside the witnesses to the salvation "which was first announced by the Lord" (2:3). Here the use of the double prefixed preposition συνεπι- vividly expresses God's action supporting and expanding the testimony of the human witnesses. As they recognise these actions of God and embrace the salvation to which these signs and the accompanying message testify, the readers become

---

13. See Steve Motyer, "The Spirit in Hebrews: No Longer Forgotten?," in *The Spirit in the New Testament and Christian Theology. Essays in Honor of Max Turner*, ed. I. Howard Marshall, Volker Rabens, and Cornelis Bennema (Grand Rapids: Eerdmans, 2012), 213–27, where I seek to argue that the target recipients of Hebrews were a Jewish-Christian charismatic group still worshipping within the synagogue – but now tempted to give up their "extra" messianic faith and revert to being "just Jews."

part of the family of the Messiah, being "made holy" like the "pioneer of their salvation" to whom they now belong (2:10–11).

In 2:9 the author summarises the heart of this experience with the claim "we see Jesus." To enter into this experience of salvation gives a new visionary grasp on Jesus – which is not just a new cognitive understanding of him, I think we must say, but also a personal encountering which can be described as a "seeing." This use of visionary language is important in Hebrews, and is especially prominent in ch. 11 where the roll call of OT saints highlights the "seeing" which lay behind the extraordinary actions by which their "faith" was expressed. Abraham was "looking forward to the city with foundations, whose architect and builder is God" (11:10). The earliest patriarchs (including Sarah) "saw [the things promised] and welcomed them from a distance . . . longing for a better country – a heavenly one" (11:13, 16). Moses was "looking ahead to his reward" and "persevered because he saw him who is invisible" (11:26–27). All these OT "seeings by faith" are encouragements to the readers to do the same, to "fix our eyes on Jesus, the pioneer and perfecter of faith, [who] for the joy set before him endured the cross, scorning its shame, and sat down at the right hand of the throne of God" (12:2).

The faith of these OT forerunners was sustained by, and evoked, divine actions by which God vindicated their trust in him. Gary Cockerill points out to me how Heb 11 is framed around faith in God's ability to perform wonders within the world – the translation of Enoch (11:5), the flood (11:7), the birth and "resurrection" of Isaac (11:11–12, 17–19), the Passover and the exodus (11:28–29), "up to and including 'women receiving their dead back to life'" (11:35).[14]

So we realise that the application of Ps 110:1 to Jesus in 1:13 and 10:12–13 is an instance of this "seeing": a new reading of the psalm in the light of the "seeing" of Jesus which has been conveyed through the preaching of the gospel and the charismatic experiences by which it has been "confirmed" (2:3) to the faith of the readers. We see him, seated at the right hand of God. This "seeing" is clearly in play, also, in the magnificent "two mountains" passage with which the author underlines to the readers the glorious destination towards which their new worship is taking them:

> You have come to Mount Zion, to the city of the living God, the heavenly Jerusalem. You have come to thousands upon thousands of angels in joyful assembly, to the church of the firstborn, whose names are written in heaven. You have come to God, the Judge of all, to the spirits of the righteous made

---

14. Personal communication, September 2, 2022.

perfect, to Jesus the mediator of a new covenant, and to the sprinkled blood
that speaks a better word than the blood of Abel. (Heb 12:22–24)

This is highly visual, inspiring writing, building on an equally evocative
description of the terrifying Mount Sinai which is *not* the readers' destination
(12:18–21). They do not "approach" a terrifying God who shouts unbearable
commands at them, but they "approach" Mount Zion, on the summit of which
the Party to end all parties is taking place. The NIV's repeated "you have come"
is misleading, because it implies arrival. The picture (as with Mount Sinai) is of
reaching the foothills and "drawing near" (προσέρχεσθαι) to the final, age-to-
come festivities on the mountain. That is the readers' present position – unless
they choose to throw it all away. It is absolutely imperative that they listen to the
voice speaking to them now from heaven (12:25) – speaking, we understand,
precisely through this writing, the author's letter. It is reminding them of the
truths they are in danger of rejecting: not least the truth of final judgement and
the awfulness of "fall[ing] into the hands of the living God" (10:31). If that
should be their fate, their "approach" will be in vain and they will never reach
that festal gathering in the unshakeable kingdom.

The author thus uses a string of biblical images and ideas to capture and
illumine the present experience of the readers as they join this new worship –
worship of God marked by the "powers of the coming age" (6:5) and offered
through Jesus Christ the High Priest of the new covenant. "Entering the rest"
is another image which, like the approach to Mount Zion, holds both "coming
age" and "present inaugurated" elements. It is possible to "enter the rest" now
through faith, in the "today" which is our present experience (3:13; 4:3). But the
exhortation is to *strive* to enter the (eschatological) rest, which we may fail to
enter if we fall into disobedience (4:11).

God's action is thus written all over our present experience, according to
Hebrews: not just in the direct, shared charismatic experiences of prophecy,
healing, and glossolalia but also in the inner conviction which can be described
as a "seeing" of Jesus and in the prophetic rereadings of Scripture which help us
to know what exactly we are "seeing" about him.

THEOLOGICAL REFLECTION ON GOD'S ACTION

The interest of this volume is to move beyond the Bible to theology and to offer
some reflections in the light of Hebrews on understanding God's action in the
world today. Hebrews gives no grounds for denying the reality of divine action

in the world – quite the opposite. But what might we say, as we try to make sense of Hebrews's perspectives for today – especially in view of the fact that God's action is by no means self-evident to the world at large? In spite of passionate desires to be able to *demonstrate* divine activity in the world, especially through well-publicised healing campaigns, Christians seem to find it impossible to "cut through" with convincing evidence. On what grounds, therefore, may we with integrity claim that "God acts" today? How might Hebrews help us?

The nub issue is whether the *faith* by which we "see" Jesus and discern God's action in our lives is open to public scrutiny, or whether it stands beyond the normal bounds of public discourse. Do we recuse ourselves from public debate and retreat into private language when we state our faith that "the universe in time and space was formed by God's word" (Heb 11:3), that God's Son "upholds all things by his powerful word" (Heb 1:3), and that ultimately one day "[Christ] will appear for a second time to those who are waiting for him to bring salvation" (Heb 9:28)?[15]

There is much that can be said to argue that such faith is reasonable and does not require a sacrifice of the intellect. In seeking to persuade his readers not to abandon this faith, the author of Hebrews appeals to the evidence ("signs, wonders and various miracles") by which the word was "confirmed" to them when they first heard it (Heb 2:3–4). However – and here's the problem – the whole faith package is not contained within the "message" of the miracles. Even if it could be acknowledged as certain by all, the greatest miracle still does not contain within it the message summarised by these three faith statements. Miracles "confirm" or "strengthen" faith; they do not communicate it. As illustrated by the remarkable example of Pinchas Lapide, even the resurrection of Jesus can be accepted by someone who does not therefore buy into the Christian message.[16]

As we just saw, the sequence of faith experiences which culminates with "tast[ing] . . . the powers of the coming age" *starts* simply with being "enlightened." This word matches the simple "seeing" of Jesus which is at the heart of all faith and gives all our experiences an interpretative framework. Faith begins with having "the eyes of [the] heart . . . enlightened," as Paul puts it (Eph 1:18), although he uses this expression to underline that this enlightenment can grow and deepen – indeed, it can and must be "confirmed" as it takes the kind of active steps illustrated by the faith heroes of the OT in Hebrews 11.

A long biblical and theological tradition affirms that this experience of "enlightenment" at the heart of faith is a gift of God, a creative act by which

---

15. All three translations mine.

16. See Pinchas Lapide, *The Resurrection of Jesus. A Jewish Perspective* (Eugene, OR: Wipf & Stock, 2002).

he brings faith to birth in us. Often the self-perception of believers will accord with this – a sense that their faith was born out of being "touched" by God's love impacting them from 'outside and making Jesus real to them. In most cases, however, the experience is already interpreted even as it occurs, because it is a response to the communication of the message of the gospel. Sadly the undeniable truth of such experiences cannot in itself constitute an argument for the reality of God's action through Christ, for experiences like this are evidenced outside Christian contexts as well.[17]

It is worth considering a British theological tradition around God's action associated with the names of Austin Farrer and Rowan Williams, and bringing this into dialogue with Hebrews. Farrer suggested that "infinite" action cannot occur within a "finite" world, because by definition (as finite creatures) we cannot perceive the infinite. When God acts, therefore, his action cannot in itself carry any indication that it is "infinite" in origin. Farrer proposed that God's action will always therefore appear to us as an action of processes within the world, particularly of people within the world. Thus, *faith* will discern some actions as "dual" actions both of God and of human or physical processes. The fact of "creation" means that *within* finite created life the infinite will of God is operating, in and through human wills and physical processes.[18]

Even miraculous happenings involve shifts in the arrangement of matter, which *faith* may call a divine act but which is also open to sceptical or naturalistic explanations. Believers give thanks to God for answered prayer. Sceptical doctors scratch their heads and don't know why the cancer vanished.

Recently Rowan Williams has developed Farrer's explanation of divine action as the key idea in his magnificent survey of historical Christology, *Christ the Heart of Creation*.[19] Williams argues that a theology emphasising direct divine intervention, seeing it as a distinct act creating effects in the world, produces a Christology which was decisively *rejected* in the early church and in subsequent developments. The struggle within Christology has always been to find a way of understanding Christ's divine and human natures not

---

17. See William Miller and Janet C'de Baca, *Quantum Change: When Epiphanies and Sudden Insights Transform Ordinary Lives* (New York: Guilford Press, 2001). For dramatic healings which likewise can occur in many settings, not just in response to Christian prayer, see Deepak Chopra, *Quantum Healing: Exploring the Frontiers of Mind/Body Medicine* (New York: Bantam, 2015).

18. See Robert MacSwain (ed), *Scripture, Metaphysics and Poetry: Austin Farrer's* The Glass of Vision *with Critical Commentary* (Farnham: Ashgate, 2013): this includes the text of Farrer's 1948 Bampton Lectures in which he elaborated this approach to divine action. See also the essay collection by Brian Hebblethwaite and Edward Henderson, eds., *Divine Action: Studies Inspired by the Philosophical Theology of Austin Farrer* (Edinburgh: T&T Clark, 1990).

19. Rowan Williams, *Christ the Heart of Creation* (London: Bloomsbury Continuum, 2018). The book was published to commemorate the 50th anniversary of Farrer's death in 1968.

as rivals competing for space within the one person, and each diminishing the other in the process, but rather to conceive of Christ as *fully* human and *fully* divine, so that all of his actions were simultaneously actions both of God and of a man within a single undivided person. This kind of Christology, Williams suggests, *requires* something like Farrer's "dual action" view, and then *entails* a corresponding understanding of God's action within the world – starting, as he shows, with an understanding of the church (as the "body" of Christ) experiencing and expressing the life of the Holy Spirit in the same way. The Spirit lives within us not by bypassing our humanity, but by filling our humanity with new life and by speaking and acting through our hands and voices. We *aspire* to Farrer's "dual action" when we embrace a call to live in the Spirit!

Coming back to Hebrews, we must note the very striking way in which God's action within the world is signalled at the start by the extraordinary statement in 1:3 that the eternal Son, having made the αἰῶνες, now "sustain[s] all things by his powerful word." The metaphor of "the word" carries Hebrews's sense of how God's infinite action, through the Son, sustains the world and leads it towards his destiny for it. Looking at the letter as a whole, can we gain a sense of what this "word" looks like, at least in part?

I want to connect with what Fellipe do Vale writes earlier in this volume about developing the notion of *narrative* in connection with doing theological work on God's action: theology, he says, must seek to articulate a "coherent narrative ecosystem" embracing the whole range of God's actions from creation to final perfection.[20] We can apply this fruitfully to Hebrews. I find it helpful to use the paired terms "drama" and "metadrama" to unpack Hebrews's "narrative ecosystem" of "the word."[21] The *drama* of Hebrews is the underlying storyline of the Son, the Creator of the αἰῶνες, telling how he has become High Priest for us through incarnation, suffering, and death, and now has entered the heavenly sanctuary on our behalf. There he presents his sacrifice before God and intercedes for us so that we, too, may (in due course) enter that sanctuary – climb to the heights of Mount Zion and join the "festal gathering" there in order finally to experience God's unshakable kingdom beyond this temporary and fragile world.

Woven into this drama is Hebrews's *metadrama*, which is all about *the readers* and the author's attempt to persuade them to stay committed to their place in the drama – i.e., to stay true to the word they have heard. This is the word which summarises the drama, telling the story of "the salvation" first spoken by

---

20. Fellipe do Vale, "Divine Action, Theological Method, and Scripture's Narrative," 11.

21. See Kevin J. Vanhoozer, *The Drama of Doctrine: A Canonical-Linguistic Approach to Christian Theology* (Louisville, KY: Westminster John Knox Press, 2005).

the Lord then "confirmed to us by those who heard him" (2:3). To this story "we must pay the most careful attention . . . so that we do not drift away" (2:1).[22] The "word" moves away from the events themselves (summarised in the drama of creation, redemption, and re-creation) into a successive *testimony*, passed on in order to evoke the *faith* that will bring the readers into their participation in the drama and confirm them in it. The battle for faith is the *metadrama* into which we, like the first readers, are summoned by this word.

This message, passed on, becomes "the good word of God" (6:5, literal translation of καλὸν θεοῦ ῥῆμα) which gripped and drew the first readers into their commitment to Jesus as the Christ. Hebrews's chosen metaphor for this being gripped is "tasting," which does not imply a kind of dilettante "try it and see" engagement but a full participatory involvement, like Jesus himself "tast[ing] death for everyone" (2:9). So, to "taste the heavenly gift" (further defined as a "taste" of God's good word, of the Holy Spirit, and of "the powers of the coming age," 6:4–5) is to receive these things fully into ourselves, to become intimately connected to them. It is still sadly possible to reject this connection, because it is a *relational* connection which calls for two-sided commitment: hence the passion of the letter and the loving concern that motivates it.

The letter itself participates in this "journey of the word." It is a "word of exhortation" (λόγος παρακλήσεως) which the author urges his readers to "bear with" (13:22). Here, "bear with" (NIV, NRSVue) is not a good translation since it implies a kind of apology – as though the author regrets writing at such length and asks for their indulgence. "Pay attention" would be better,[23] echoing the encouragement to "remember your leaders, who spoke the word of God to you. Consider the outcome of their way of life and imitate their faith" (13:7). The "word of God" is spoken from within a life of faith and has to be received in the same way. This is exactly what the author has done, speaking the word from within faith in order to encourage faith – and in the process giving numerous examples of the way in which faith shapes lifestyle and enables a "seeing of the unseen."

Thus, within the metadrama – the battle for this response of faith – God's word has six forms:

- God's new speaking in the Son (1:2). His speaking summarises the Son's whole ministry – all that he has done for us – so this speaking is also a foundational element of the "drama."

---

22. Vanhoozer uses the notion of "performance," paired with "drama," to develop this movement of "the word" into the life of the church: see Vanhoozer, *Drama of Doctrine*, especially Part 4 (363–444).

23. So, e.g., CEV ("pay close attention"); Cockerill, *Hebrews*, 719.

- The message of salvation, which began with Christ and is passed on by those who heard him, confirmed by signs and wonders (2:3–4). Interestingly, this does not seem to include records of Christ's earthly teaching.
- The preaching of God's word in the church (13:7), perhaps including prophetic utterances.
- What James calls "the implanted word" (Jas 1:21 NRSVue): i.e., the "tasting" of the word of God as an inner experience of being "gripped" – perhaps accompanied by experiences of prophecy or glossolalia or other "powers" (6:4–5).
- God's word through the prophets (1:1): i.e., OT Scripture, which now needs to be reread in the light of the new "speaking" of God through the Son. Authoritative teachers (like the author of Hebrews) need to communicate how the new relates to the old. Here, too, prophecy may play a role.
- God's word written in new communications like this "word of exhortation" (13:22), which may, of course, exemplify the rereading of Scripture and lead to renewed experiences of being gripped and a stronger faith in appropriating the message of salvation.

All these forms of "the word" are aspects of the way in which the Son "sustain[s] all things by his powerful word." And all six fit well with a "dual action" conception of God's action in the world. In each case, in different ways, human words are coterminous with the speech of God. But, of course, "the powerful word" by which the Son "sustain[s] all things" (1:3) is much bigger. It forms the cosmic background to this playing out of God's words in the metadrama involving the readers. There is a play within a play here – the metadrama set within the big picture of God's dramatic action through the Son in the world and beyond it. What gives the metadrama its huge power is the expectation of God's *final* action shaking the earth and the heaven and bringing a judgement for which we *must* be prepared. The thought that his readers might fall away and not enter life is what motivates the author to write the letter!

There is a rich theological background to this interplay between the two "plays," namely, the two sides of *wisdom*: as practical human action in the world which is informed by, and built upon, the grand wisdom of God by which the world was made and upon which it runs. This dialectic between cosmic and local "wisdom" matches these two aspects of "the word of God" in Hebrews.[24]

Hebrews's eschatology thus enables us to focus some general insights into

---

24. On this dialectic within wisdom, see the summary of Wisdom's "pilgrimage" in B. Witherington III, *Jesus the Sage: The Pilgrimage of Wisdom* (Edinburgh: T&T Clark, 1994), 114–15.

the theology of the letter and also some general reflections on divine action in the world. Writing, editing, and publishing books like this one may in themselves also be activities of the Christ who "sustain[s] all things by his powerful word" – we hope so!

SELECT BIBLIOGRAPHY

Chopra, Deepak. *Quantum Healing. Exploring the Frontiers of Mind/Body Medicine*. New York: Bantam, 2015.

Cockerill, Gareth Lee. *The Epistle to the Hebrews*. NICNT. Grand Rapids: Eerdmans, 2012.

Hebblethwaite, Brian, and Edward Henderson, ed. *Divine Action: Studies Inspired by the Philosophical Theology of Austin Farrer*. Edinburgh: T&T Clark, 1990.

Hurst, L. D. *The Epistle to the Hebrews: Its Background of Thought*. SNTSMS 65. Cambridge: CUP, 1990.

Lane, William L. *Hebrews*. Word Biblical Commentary 47. Dallas: Word, 1991.

Lapide, Pinchas. *The Resurrection of Jesus: A Jewish Perspective*. Eugene, OR: Wipf & Stock, 2002.

MacSwain, Robert, ed. *Scripture, Metaphysics and Poetry: Austin Farrer's* The Glass of Vision *with Critical Commentary*. Farnham, UK: Ashgate, 2013.

Miller, William, and Janet C'de Baca. *Quantum Change: When Epiphanies and Sudden Insights Transform Ordinary Lives*. New York: Guilford Press, 2001.

Motyer, Steve. "The Spirit in Hebrews: No Longer Forgotten?" In *The Spirit in the New Testament and Christian Theology: Essays in Honor of Max Turner*, edited by I. Howard Marshall, Volker Rabens, and Cornelis Bennema, 213–27. Grand Rapids: Eerdmans, 2012.

Vanhoozer, Kevin J. *The Drama of Doctrine: A Canonical-Linguistic Approach to Christian Theology*. Louisville, KY: Westminster John Knox Press, 2005.

Williams, Rowan. *Christ the Heart of Creation*. London: Bloomsbury Continuum, 2018.

Witherington, Ben, III. *Jesus the Sage: The Pilgrimage of Wisdom*. Edinburgh: T&T Clark, 1994.

PART IV

The Ongoing Priesthood of Jesus

CHAPTER 11

The Present Priesthood
of the Son of God

". . . he sat down . . ."
(An Alternate to David M. Moffitt)

Gareth Lee Cockerill

INTRODUCTION

The pastor who wrote Hebrews focuses our attention on the incarnate, eternal Son of God *now* seated at God's right hand and on this divine Son's action as the all-sufficient High Priest, Guarantor of the new covenant, and fully adequate Saviour, perennially available for the people of God in the "today" of their pilgrimage.[1] The present reality of this High Priest and the actions that made possible and now comprise his ongoing ministry constitute the "main point" of Hebrews's theological exposition (8:1–2), the only sufficient means for perseverance (10:19–25; 12:1–3), and the source of both the encouragement and warning (10:19–31) that sustain God's people in continuing faithfulness. Thus, the writer of Hebrews focuses our attention on the person and actions of "the Apostle and High Priest whom we confess" (3:1), the "Great High Priest" (4:14)

---

1. The author of Hebrews has thought deeply about the work of Christ, meditated long and fruitfully on the OT, and carefully fashioned Hebrews to meet the needs of his hearers because of his deep concern for them. Thus, it is appropriate to call him "the pastor."

"over the house of God" (10:21) "who has sat down on the right hand of the throne of the Majesty in the heavens" (8:1).[2]

The purpose of this paper is to present the nature, magnitude, and effectiveness of this Son's present ongoing action as "a Great High Priest" "over the house of God." In order to achieve this purpose, I will first lay a foundation for our discussion by demonstrating the divine character of the present actions of our High Priest, by which he makes "eternal salvation" available, and those past actions by which he became the "Source" (5:9) of that salvation. I will also show that these actions and the benefits they provide are a present reality, readily available in the eternal, incarnate Son now seated at God's right hand.

Then I will build on that foundation by reviewing in greater detail what Hebrews says about the past and present actions that constitute the Son's ongoing priesthood and the benefits that he, through these actions, provides. The pastor keeps his hearers engaged by gradually revealing the Son's actions, their significance, and related benefits. This account occurs primarily in Heb 1:1–2:18 and 4:14–10:25. A conversation between the Father and the Son at the occasion of the Son's exaltation/session unifies these two major sections.[3] Hebrews 3:1–6 provides a bridge between them. Thus, after laying the aforementioned foundation, I will examine in order Heb 1:1–2:18; Heb 3:1–6; and Heb 4:14–10:25. By following this contextual approach, we join the first hearers in discovering both the benefits now available through the perennially ongoing actions of our "Great High Priest" and the intimately related and ever-relevant actions by which the eternal Son became this "Source of eternal salvation."

FOUNDATIONAL PREMISES:
THE DIVINE CHARACTER AND EVER-PRESENT REALITY OF OUR HIGH PRIEST AND HIS ACTIONS

THE DIVINE CHARACTER OF OUR HIGH PRIEST AND HIS ACTIONS

The pastor who wrote Hebrews firmly believes that through the Son's incarnation, obedience, faithful endurance of suffering and death, exaltation,

---

2. On the contemporary, perennial present of the exalted Son/High Priest, see Gareth Lee Cockerill, "The Truthfulness and Perennial Relevance of God's Word in the Letter to the Hebrews," *Bib Sac* 172, no. 686 (June 2015): 190–202. Translations of Hebrews throughout this chapter are my own unless otherwise indicated.

3. See George H. Guthrie's chapter in this volume, "Divine Action in the Jewish Scriptures according to Hebrews," 137–43, and the extensive analysis of this Father-Son dialogue in Madison N. Pierce, *Divine Discourse in the Epistle to the Hebrews: The Recontextualization of Spoken Quotations of Scripture*, SNTSM 178 (Cambridge: CUP, 2020). See also Cockerill, "Perennial Relevance," 190–202, and the references there cited.

session, and continuing priestly ministry God intervenes in the normal course of world events for the world's redemption.[4] The divine character of these actions is substantiated by the way in which Hebrews speaks of the eternality of the Son of God who carries out these actions, whose deity is confirmed by his role in the creation and final judgement of the world (1:10–12). It is further attested by the involvement of the Father and the Spirit in the Son's actions.[5]

First, then, the divine character of the Son's actions is confirmed by the way Hebrews grounds these actions in his eternal deity. What the Son has become and the ministry he has now obtained through the actions of his incarnate obedience and subsequent exaltation are the fulfillment of what he has always been as the eternal Son of God.[6] The pastor *never isolates* the incarnation or exaltation/ session of the Son from his eternal deity. It is the eternal Son whose exaltation he proclaims (1:1–14; 7:1–28). It is the eternal Son who becomes incarnate in order to take his place at God's right hand (2:5–18; 8:1–10:18). Furthermore, the effectiveness of the "eternal salvation" of which the Son has become "the Source" (5:9) is dependent upon the eternal deity that empowered his incarnate obedience and subsequent session.[7] No wonder the pastor keeps his hearers' eyes on this all-sufficient High Priest who is able to sustain their perseverance in obedience.

Second, the Son's role in both creation and final judgement (1:1–4, 10–12) confirms his deity and thus the divine character of his actions. The author of Hebrews would never reduce God's actions to the processes immanent in creation. On the contrary, belief in creation by the word of God is the foundation for his conviction that the God who created the world intervenes in the order of creation for its redemption and in the lives of his people for their perseverance (11:2).[8] The saving actions of the Son who created the universe are, then, necessarily divine action.

---

4. While the Son may have been subject to crucifixion because of his humanity, he "endured a cross, despising the shame" (12:2) and overcame death through divine power. See Gareth Lee Cockerill, *The Epistle to the Hebrews*, NICNT (Grand Rapids: Eerdmans, 2012), 322–24.

5. Hebrews was an important source for the church fathers' conviction that "the one God has three internal relations which define both his creative and his redemptive activity" (Gerald Bray, "The Church Fathers and Biblical Theology," in *Out of Egypt: Biblical Theology and Biblical Interpretation*, SAH Series 5, ed. Craig Bartholomew, Mary Healy, Karl Möller, and Robin Parry [Grand Rapids: Zondervan, 2004], 37). On the Trinity in Hebrews, see Pierce, *Divine Discourse*, mentioned earlier; R. B. Jamieson, *The Paradox of Sonship: Christology in the Epistle to the Hebrews*, Studies in Christian Doctrine and Scripture (Downers Grove: IVP Academic, 2021); and also Nick Brennan, *Divine Christology in the Epistle to the Hebrews: The Son as God*, LNTS 656 (London; New York: T&T Clark, 2022).

6. See Cockerill, *The Epistle to the Hebrews*, 91–93.

7. Nick Brennan, in his published doctoral dissertation, *Divine Christology*, just cited, shows clearly and definitively the comprehensive way in which the Son's eternal deity is fundamental to Hebrews's description of what the Son does and the salvation he provides.

8. Cockerill, *The Epistle to the Hebrews*, 523–25. See Craig Bartholomew's chapter in this volume, "Creation, Divine Action, and Hebrews," 148–67.

Third, the involvement of the Father and the Spirit in the actions by which the eternal Son became "the Source of eternal salvation" also underscores the divine character of these actions. The Father proclaims the Son's deity and effectually invites him to take the seat at his right hand as all-sufficient High Priest (1:1–14; 7:1–28). It is by this action that the Son becomes "the Source of eternal salvation" and, thus, fulfills his role as the ultimate revelation of the Father. Furthermore, since the Son offers himself "through the eternal Spirit" (Heb 9:14), it should be no surprise that the ultimate rejection of the Son's self-offering is described as insulting "the Spirit of grace" (Heb 10:29).[9]

THE EVER-PRESENT REALITY OF OUR HIGH PRIEST AND HIS ACTIONS

The past divine actions by which our High Priest took his seat at God's right hand are ever-present in the present divine actions by which he exercises his perpetual priestly ministry. Although Heb 7:25 calls the present activity of our High Priest "intercession," the pastor never pictures the One seated at God's right hand as pleading with the Father. He describes the present priestly actions of the Son by enumerating the benefits the Son now provides as the "Source of eternal salvation" (5:9) and eternal "High Priest according to the order of Melchizedek" (5:10). Our High Priest now bestows on those who draw near to God through him cleansing from sin and access to God's presence. Through him they find the "mercy" of cleansing and the "grace" for perseverance in faithful living (4:14–16) that frees them from the fear of death (2:14–16) as they anticipate his return with "salvation for those awaiting him" (9:28).[10] His effective priesthood guarantees the new covenant that provides heart transformation and intimacy with God (10:14–18). The past actions of incarnate obedience and exaltation cannot be separated from this present ministry because the Son "has been perfected" by them (7:28) as all-sufficient Saviour. These actions cannot be relegated merely to the past because he is *now* the eternal, *incarnate*, *exalted* Son of God *seated* at God's right hand as all-sufficient High Priest who administers the benefits of "such a great salvation" (2:3).

---

9. For a discussion of "by the eternal Spirit," see Cockerill, *The Epistle to the Hebrews*, 397–401, and for "insulted the Spirit of Grace," see pp. 487–91.

10. This present priestly ministry will, of course, reach its climax at this time when the Son returns with "salvation" (9:28) at the judgment (12:25–29). That, however, is the subject of Steve Motyer's chapter entitled "Hebrews Eschatology and the Action of God." On the present reality of the Father's invitation and the Son's answer, see n. 2 on p. 204.

HEBREWS 1:1–2:18: "SIT AT MY RIGHT HAND" (1·13)

It is time to review in greater detail what Hebrews says about the past and present actions that constitute the Son's ongoing priesthood and the benefits that
he, through these actions, provides. Heb 1:1–2:18 affirms the Son's deity and
describes his incarnation, suffering, exaltation/session, and continuing ministry
as the divine actions that provide salvation.[11] His deity and the significance of
these events underscores the magnitude of the salvation he has provided. These
two chapters set the stage for the way in which Heb 4:14–10:25 reveals the full
significance of the Son's deity and divine actions, showing how they fulfill the
Sinai covenant by providing the salvation that it only foreshadowed.[12]

Heb 1:1–2:18 consists of four subdivisions: 1:1–4; 1:5–14; 2:1–4; and 2:5–
18. Hebrews 1:1–4 sets the stage for the Father-Son conversation that follows.[13]

---

11. The limited scope of this essay prevents the interaction with Michael Wade Martin and Jason A.
Whitlark, *Inventing Hebrews: Design and Purpose in Ancient Rhetoric*, SNTSM 171 (Cambridge: CUP,
2018) that it deserves. Their structural analysis of Hebrews as an example of ancient deliberative rhetoric is
insightful but runs beyond the evidence. In particular, it fails to account for the fact that Hebrews is biblical
interpretation. Martin and Whitlark recognise the uniqueness of the prologue (1:1–4, which they label
exordium) and the essential unity of these first two chapters of Hebrews (designating 1:5–14 as *narratio*
followed by its appropriate *argumentatio* in 2:1–18; see 106–17, *passim*), but I find their denial of the structural significance of 4:14–16 and 10:19–25 and their attempt to sunder 5:1–6:20 from 7:1–10:18 (120–27)
unconvincing.

12. There is an extensive discussion of Hebrews 1–2 in David M. Moffitt, *Atonement and the Logic
of Resurrection in the Epistle to the Hebrews*, NovTSup (Leiden: Brill, 2013), 1–144. (I am using the 2013
paperback of Moffitt's work rather than the 2011 hardback.) Moffitt is, in my judgment, correct in arguing
that the place of the Son's exaltation, called the οἰκουμένη in 1:6, is the heavenly world to be identified with
the heavenly homeland that the people of God will receive in fulfillment of God's promise to Abraham. He
is also correct in arguing that the relationship between this heavenly homeland and the present world is not
to be understood in terms of "spiritual" versus "material." The heavenly world is, if anything, more "real" or
"concrete" than the present world. He is, finally, correct in asserting the importance of the Son's humanity
for his becoming superior to the angels and is to be commended for his defense of the Son's continuing
humanity. However, he tends to overemphasis the role of the Son's humanity and to skew its significance
by isolating it from the Son's eternal deity and from other factors (obedience, sacrificial death, exaltation)
that are just as important to the Son's superiority (on p. 141, for instance, he affirms that the Son's being
human is *the* "crucial" factor). As noted earlier, Hebrews never refers simply to the humanity of the Son, but
always to the incarnation, to the eternal Son *who has assumed* the humanity of the people of God. Moffitt,
on the other hand, minimises the clear description of the Son's eternal deity in 1:1–3, 10–12, and speaks of
Jesus being human almost as something separate from his eternal sonship. To put it simply, when the Son's
humanity is in view in Hebrews, it is always the incarnate humanity of the eternal Son of God. Furthermore,
it is the eternal, *incarnate* Son who is the Son seated at God's right hand.

The Son's eternal sonship, assumption of humanity, perfect obedience in the face of suffering, and his
self-offering in death are all crucial for his becoming superior to the angels by "making purification for sin"
and taking his seat at God's right hand. It is in his being perfected as the fully sufficient High Priest and
"Source of eternal salvation" (5:9) that he becomes superior to the angels who cannot provide salvation but
are merely "sent out to serve those who are about to inherit salvation" (1:14).

13. Heb 1:1–4 is justly called the prologue, for it introduces the entire book. However, it is also closely
related to and provides specific introduction for 1:5–2:18.

The Father addresses the Son in 1:5–14, and the Son answers in 2:5–18 (especially 2:10–13). Between this address and answer, the pastor warns his hearers lest they neglect the "such a great salvation" that has been provided by no one less than the eternal, incarnate, exalted Son of God (2:1–4).

HEBREWS 1:1–4: "ONE WHO IS SON"

Heb 1:1–4 sets the stage for this Father-Son conversation by substantiating the finality of God's Son-mediated revelation. The divine, eternal character of God's agent makes this revelation ultimate. We are given a panorama of the Son's divine actions. He is the "Son," who at his exaltation became universal heir, who is the agent of creation, who governs the universe by the "word of his power," and who thus radiates and perfectly expresses the reality of God. By speaking in the Son, God is revealing himself through himself.

This opening description concludes by focusing attention on the culmination of God's self-revelation in the eternal Son who "by making purification for sins sat down at the right hand of the Majesty in the highest." "Purification for sins" is both the first hint of the Son's incarnation and the initial description of the benefits provided by the incarnate, exalted Son. The following divine conversation elucidates the implications of the Son's deity and the divine actions of making purification and exaltation through which the Son entered into his ongoing ministry as all-sufficient Saviour and God's ultimate self-revelation.[14]

HEBREWS 1:5–14: "SIT AT MY RIGHT HAND"

These verses illuminate the close relationship between the Son's eternal deity and the exaltation/session by which, according to 1:1–4, he entered into his ongoing ministry. They elicit two questions in the minds of the pastor's congregation: What is the salvation that the eternal Son seated at God's right hand provides? By what means has he taken his seat at God's right hand in order to provide this salvation?

Let us summarise the content of these foundational verses before turning to the relationship that they elucidate and the questions they suggest: God speaks 2 Sam 7:14; Ps 2:7; Ps 45:6–7; Ps 102:25–27; and Ps 110:1 to the Son on the occasion of his exaltation/session announced in Heb 1:4. The Father addresses the Son as "Son," "God," and "Lord"; confirms the Son's eternal deity as creator, sovereign over, and judge of the universe; and effects the Son's session by inviting him to sit at God's right hand.[15]

---

14. Cockerill, *The Epistle to the Hebrews*, 93–97.

15. The eternal, exalted Son stands in sharp contrast to the creaturely, servant angels (1:14). Contrary to Moffitt, Hebrews is not contrasting the angels as "spirits" in 1:14 with the Son as a human being (Moffitt,

Let us turn first to the relationship between eternal sonship and exaltation/ session that is so fundamental to the Son's ongoing ministry. The divine action of the Father (speech) brings the divine action of the Son (exaltation/session) to fruition and thus ushers the Son into the full exercise of his filial inheritance as the "Source of eternal salvation" (5:9) and the ultimate revelation of God. This relationship between eternal sonship and exaltation has already been implied by the way in which "Son" is immediately described as the One "whom he made heir of all things" in 1:2. First, it is of the nature of sons to be heirs.[16] So this eternal Son entered into the full privileges of his sonship when he had made purification for sins and "sat down at the right hand of the Majesty in the highest" as the "heir of all things."[17] By inviting him to take this exalted position, the Father brings him into his inheritance (Heb 1:13; Ps 110:1) and declares openly, "you are my Son, today have I begotten you" (Heb 1:5; Ps 2:7). The Son publicly inherits the name that had been his from eternity – "Son."[18] Because he is the eternal Son who has entered into the full exercise of his sonship at God's right hand, he is the ultimate revelation of God and the "Source" of the "such a great salvation" introduced in Heb 2:3.[19]

Atonement and the Logic of Resurrection, 50–53). Rather, we have the eternal nature of the Son (1:10–12) followed by his position/function at God's right hand (1:13), contrasted with the nature of the angels as "ministering spirits" (1:14a) and their position/function as "sent out" (not enthroned in heaven) to serve those "about to inherit salvation" (1:14b). In fact, Moffitt tends to sideline the clear affirmation of the Son's eternal deity as creator and sovereign of the universe in 1:10–12. For instance, on p. 73 he almost reduces the term "Son" to a mere designation for the Davidic messiah. In line with this, he often speaks of the Son as "being" human to the neglect of his "becoming human." In one sense, the eternal Son of 1:10–12 has always been superior to the ministering, created (1:7) angels. In the sense that is important for the pastor and for the perseverance of the community that he is addressing, however, the eternal, incarnate, obedient, now exalted Son has, through his saving work, become "superior" to them as "the Source of eternal salvation" (5:9).

16. Mary Healy, *Hebrews*, CCSS (Grand Rapids: Baker, 2016), 36.

17. These two clauses, "whom he made heir of all things" and "he sat down at the right hand..." are chiastically parallel, demonstrating that they refer to the same event. See Daniel J. Ebert IV, "The Chiastic Structure of the Prologue of Hebrews," *TJ* 13 NS (Fall 1992): 163–79, and John P. Meier, "Structure and Theology in Heb 1,1–14," *Bib* 66 (1985): 168–89.

18. There is, then, no conflict between the statements that assume the eternal deity of the Son in 1:1–14 (such as "through whom he created the worlds" in verse 2 and the entirety of verses 10–12) and God's announcement at the exaltation, "today have I begotten you" (v. 5). See Cockerill, *The Epistle to the Hebrews*, 91–98, 103–4.

19. Brennan, *Divine Christology*, 71. Thus, there is no need to posit a twofold sonship in Hebrews according to which the eternal Son of God becomes the Davidic Son of God at the exaltation. Pace Stephen J. Wellum, "Jesus as Lord and Son: Two Complementary Truths of Biblical Christology," *CTR* 13, no. 1 (Fall 2015): 40–45, and especially Jamieson, *The Paradox of Sonship*. Jamieson betrays the weakness of his case when he admits that Hebrews uses "Son" in the Davidic sense *only once* – in 1:5 (pp. 119–20). The pastor who wrote Hebrews was probably not ignorant that the original referent of Pss 2:7, 45:6–8, 110:1, and 2 Sam 7:14 was the descendant of David. However, their fulfillment has so utterly transcended that referent that it has transformed their significance. God no longer addresses these words to a "king" (the word doesn't occur in Hebrews) who is metaphorically called God's "son" on a few occasions, but to God's eternal Son

HEBREWS 2:1–4: "SUCH A GREAT SALVATION"

The pastor's hearers want an answer to the first question mentioned earlier: "What is this salvation made available through the Son's ongoing ministry?" In the warning of 2:1–4 the pastor describes what the Son has provided as "such a great salvation" (2:3). From 1:1–14 we know that it is so "great" because it has been provided by the eternal Son seated at God's right hand. In 2:5–18 that greatness will be magnified by the incarnation through which the Son took his seat at God's right hand as the provider of that salvation. So far, we know that it involves "purification for sins" (1:3). Heb 1:14 suggests that the faithful will "inherit" it through the eternal, exalted Son who has become "heir of all things."

This emphasis on the saving sufficiency of the eternal and exalted Son forces the hearers to ask the second question mentioned earlier: "What did the eternal Son do in order to make 'purification for sins' and accept the invitation to God's right hand as the exalted Son?" Thus far, the pastor has only hinted at the incarnate obedience (e.g., "you loved righteousness but hated lawlessness," 1:9) by which the Son has taken his seat at God's right hand as the "Source of eternal salvation" (5:9). The pastor will begin to explain the significance of this incarnate obedience, which is no less a divine action than the exaltation, in 2:5–18.

HEBREWS 2:5–18: "SO THAT . . . HE MIGHT TASTE DEATH"

Heb 2:5–10 uses Ps 8:4–6 to introduce the eternal Son's incarnation and obedient suffering as the means by which he made "purification for sins" and took his seat on high. Heb 2:9 makes the Son's death *on behalf of all humanity* the central purpose of his assuming human nature and the obvious means of his providing "purification for sin" (1:3). This assertion casts grave doubt from the outset on David Moffitt's identification of Christ's sacrifice with his glorified body presented in heaven rather than with his obedience and death.[20] It is by his "suffering," culminating in his death, that he is "perfected" as the Saviour who is able to bring "many sons and daughters into glory" (2:10).

In 2:11–13 the eternal Son answers the Father's invitation to take his seat at the right hand by affirming and thus effecting his incarnation. He responds to the Father's declaration of sonship (1:5) by identifying with his "brothers and

---

who has assumed the sovereign rule of the universe at God's right hand. It is not that the Son had to fulfill God's adoption of David as his "son," but God made such a proclamation to David in anticipation of what the Son already was and would do. The Son reestablishes the divine rule in a way David could never have done because the Son is God! Pierce, *Divine Discourse*, 45, may overstate the case when she says, on the basis of prosopological exegesis, that "arguments that cite the previous attribution of these texts to the human Davidic monarch are not applicable," but she sees clearly that Hebrews never alludes to Davidic rule and that kingship has been absorbed and taken up entirely into the title and person of the divine Son.

20. Moffitt, *Atonement and the Logic of Resurrection*, 255, 299.

sisters" (Heb 1:12, quoting Ps 22:22), answers the Father's proclamation of his sovereignty (1:10–12) by affirming his incarnate faithfulness (Heb 2:13a, quoting 2 Sam 22:3/Isa 8:17), and accepts the Father's invitation to his right hand for himself and his "children" (Heb 2:13b, quoting Isa 8:18).[21] Thus, the performative divine speech of Father and Son finds fulfillment in the entire course of divine actions – both incarnation and exaltation – by which the Son has become the present "Source of eternal salvation" (5:9).

Heb 2:14–18 expands our knowledge of "such a great salvation" (2:3) and the benefits that accrue from the eternal Son's present divine actions by announcing the priestly character of the incarnate suffering by which he became "a merciful and faithful High Priest." By fully identifying with the humanity of the people of God and "tasting death" for everyone, the Son has made purification for sins as High Priest and has thus delivered the people of God from the judgement that made death so terrifying and from the consequent lifelong bondage to the devil (2:14–18) through fear of death.[22] Furthermore, we now know that the suffering by which the Son was tested and perfected as our Saviour (2:10) enables him to effectively help us, his people, when we are tempted to fall away due to suffering. The term "merciful and faithful High Priest" is pregnant with meaning that will become clear when the pastor returns to the Son's priesthood in 4:14–16. It is only the eternal Son of God who can live an obedient human life and overcome death on behalf of the people of God.

HEBREWS 3:1–6: "A WITNESS OF THE THINGS YET TO BE SPOKEN" (3:5)

As noted earlier, 3:1–6 is a bridge between 1:1–2:18 and 4:14–10:25. It spans a gap so that the pastor can show how the Sinai covenant reveals the full

---

21. Cockerill, *The Epistle to the Hebrews*, 142.

22. When discussing 2:5–18, Moffitt, *Atonement and the Logic of Resurrection*, 118–44, fails to see that the relationship between the "Son" and the "sons" precedes the incarnation and, indeed, is the motivation for it. While the Son's universal concern is indicated by the fact that he "tasted death" for everyone, it is also clear that he became a human being assuming "blood and flesh" because the "children" ("whom God had given him") were "blood and flesh." The plight of the faithful is presented as motivation for the incarnation. This approach is in accord with Hebrews's pastoral concern for encouraging the perseverance of the people of God. Furthermore, contrary to Moffitt's claim (*Atonement and the Logic of Resurrection*, 119–20), Hebrews denies the authority of angels even in the present age. They are, even now, "ministering spirits sent forth to serve" (1:14), temporal beings (1:7).

Finally, Moffitt's contention (pp. 133–41) that Adam speculations similar to those found in *L.A.E.* and *The Cave of Treasures* underlie Hebrews 2:8–10 is unconvincing. The sources are too late and, upon examination, the points of connection prove superficial.

significance of the eternal Son's incarnation, session, and ongoing ministry introduced in 1:1–2:18. That covenant with its priesthood was a divinely intended type, without which God's people would have been unable to adequately understand the eternal, incarnate Son seated at God's right hand or the benefits he provides. According to 4:14–10:25, the Son's divine salvific actions fulfill all that was anticipated, but not provided, by the OT priesthood and the Sinai covenant. This bridge spans the distance between the first mention of the Son's priesthood in 2:16–18 and its fuller exposition beginning in 4:14–16.

Moses and Christ are the two pylons of this bridge. Each of them has a distinct function in relation to the one "house" or people of God stretching throughout time. By witnessing "of the things yet to be spoken" [by God], Moses was *faithful* as a *steward* "in God's house." Moses *established* the Sinai covenant with its priesthood and sacrificial system as a witness to Christ.

Correspondingly, Christ was *faithful* as the eternal *Son* "over God's house" by the incarnate obedience through which he *fulfilled* the Sinai covenant and thus took his seat at God's right hand as "High Priest forever" (5:10) and "Guarantor" (7:22) of the new covenant. Thus, by providing the "great salvation" that fulfilled Moses's witness he became the ultimate revelation of God.[23]

HEBREWS 4:14–10:25: "WE HAVE SUCH A PRIEST WHO HAS SAT DOWN" (8:1)

Heb 4:14–6:20, the first half of Hebrews's second major division (4:14–10:25), prepares the hearers for the resumption of the Father-Son dialogue in the second half (7:1–10:18).[24] I will pay particular attention to the theological exposition in 4:14–16 and 5:1–10 rather than to the exhortation in 5:11–6:20. The divine conversation proper consists of the Father's address (7:1–28; cf. 1:5–14) and the Son's answer (8:1–10:18; cf. 2:5–18). Heb 10:19–25 concludes this section with a grand summary and pastoral application of the benefits perpetually available from the actions of our "Great Priest." Thus, I will discuss these sections (4:14–16; 5:1–10; 7:1–28; 8:1–10:18; 10:19–25), with special emphasis on 9:23–10:18 (the climax of 8:1–10:18) and 10:19–25.

HEBREWS 4:14–16: "A GREAT HIGH PRIEST"

This passage resumes the high priest theme and provides a twofold whetting of the hearers' appetite for the full development of the priestly significance

---

23. See Brennan, *Divine Christology*, 112–13.
24. Cockerill, *The Epistle to the Hebrews*, 70–76, 218–20.

of the eternal Son's actions. First, it stimulates their hunger with a cameo picture of everything necessary for the Son's full sufficiency as "the Source of eternal salvation" (5:9) – eternal sonship ("the Son of God"), the divine actions of exaltation ("passed through the heavens"), incarnation (he is "Jesus"), and ongoing priesthood ("Great High Priest"). All of these themes will be developed in what follows.

The passage then awakens the hearers' desire with a description of the benefits provided by this "Great High Priest" and the actions of his ongoing ministry that anticipate and will be explained by 7:1–10:18. This High Priest is able to help us overcome the "weakness" that leaves humanity prone to sin because he has lived a human life in which he overcame every temptation. As will become clear from what follows, through this High Priest we can come into the presence of God in order to find the "mercy" of forgiveness and the "grace" necessary for faithful living until final entrance into the destiny that God, through him, has prepared for the faithful (see 12:22–24).

HEBREWS 5:1–10: THE SON'S PRIESTHOOD COMPARED WITH AARON'S PRIESTHOOD

This bold claim that God's Son is the "Great High Priest" calls into question the Aaronic priesthood established by the Sinai covenant. How do we know that the Son has replaced the Aaronic priesthood? If so, how do the two priesthoods relate to each other? In 5:1–10 the pastor outlines the answers to these questions that will be expanded in 7:1–10:18.

A comparison of the two priesthoods demonstrates that Aaron typified the essential characteristics and actions of priesthood, which the Son has now fulfilled. Every priest had to identify with humanity, offer sacrifice, exercise a priestly ministry, and be called by God (5:1, 4). Aaron's need to sacrifice for himself (5:3) demonstrated the sinfulness of his humanity (5:2b) and thus the limitation of his ministry. He could not remove the sin that barred access to God (5:2a), despite the fact that he had been called by God (5:4). On the other hand, the Son's sacrifice (5:7) was the incarnate (human) obedience (5:8) by which he obtained an effective ministry as "the Source of eternal salvation" (5:9) through which the faithful access the divine presence. Furthermore, God may have called Aaron (5:4), but he established the eternal Son as Priest by the divine oath found in Ps 110:4 (5:5–6).[25]

In 7:1–28 the pastor will contrast the eternal Son's priestly call by divine

---

25. For this explanation of 5:1–10, see Cockerill, *The Epistle to the Hebrews*, 229–51. It has been followed most recently by David G. Peterson, *Hebrews: An Introduction and Commentary*, TNTC 15 (Downers Grove: IVP Academic, 2020), 138, n. 11.

oath with "the law of fleshly ordinance" (7:16) that established the mortal and thus temporary Aaronic priesthood. In 8:1–10:18 he will show how the Son's human obedience was the effective sacrifice that did away with sin. The Aaronic priesthood's ineffectiveness as a means of approaching God was essential to its intended typological function.[26]

HEBREWS 7:1–28: AN ETERNAL PRIEST ESTABLISHED BY THE OATH OF GOD

In 7:1–28 the Father resumes the conversation begun in 1:1–14 by confirming the priesthood and the eternity of the exalted Son with the oath of Ps 110:4: "You are a priest forever according to the order of Melchizedek." Heb 7:28c summarises this chapter: "The word of the *oath*, which came after the law, appoints a Son [as High Priest] . . . *forever*" (emphasis added).[27] This new "forever" Priest's effectiveness is guaranteed by the eternity of his person ("without beginning of days or end of life," 7:3; "by the power of an indestructible life," 7:16, cf. 7:15–16, 24–25)[28] and the certainty of the divine oath by which he is confirmed (7:20–22). His *eternal* deity and appointment by *divine oath* enable him to succeed

---

26. Thus, although the OT instituted the Aaronic sacrifices "for sins" (10:18), its prophesy of a new priesthood (Ps 110:4; Heb 7:11–14) and covenant (Jer 31:31–34; Heb 8:6–13) betrayed the inadequacy of those sacrifices. Benjamin J. Ribbens, *Levitical Sacrifice and Heavenly Cult in Hebrews*, BZNW 222 (Berlin/Boston: Walter de Gruyter, 2016), 236–40, argues that the pastor who wrote Hebrews believed that the old sacrifices were "sacramental types" through which those who lived before Christ participated in his sacrifice. The pastor, however, is interested in the perseverance of his hearers, and is unconcerned with such speculation about those who lived before Christ.

27. For the way in which 7:28 summarises 7:1–28 and introduces 8:1–10:18, see Cockerill, *The Epistle to the Hebrews*, 343–45.

28. In his discussion of 7:1–28 Moffitt, *Atonement and the Logic of Resurrection*, 194–205, continues to sideline the significance of eternal preexistence for the sufficiency of Christ's priesthood. Instead he argues that Jesus assumed a new kind of life, an "indestructible life," at the time of his resurrection as part of his preparation for entering heaven (i.e., his "perfection"). In order to do this, Moffitt minimises the affirmations of the Son's eternity in 1:1–14 and summarily dismisses the evidence gathered by Neyrey demonstrating that the language of 7:3 was language used to describe deity (J. H. Neyrey, "'Without Beginning of Days or End of Life' [Hebrews 7:3]: Topos for a True Deity," *CBQ* 53 [1991]: 439–55). He has to work around the fact that the Son is foreshadowed by one "without beginning of days or end of life" (7:3), of whom it is witnessed that "he lives" (7:8). The Son "remains" (7:24) and is "always living" (7:25). He is priest "by the power of an indestructible life" (7:16). There is not a word about the Son assuming a new kind of eternal life. Moffitt admits the preexistence of the Son as a "heavenly being" in Hebrews chapter one, though this preexistence plays little or no role in Moffitt's understanding of Hebrews. Moffitt moves the point of importance from the assumption of humanity by the eternal Son of God (affirmed repeatedly by Hebrews) to the assumption of a special "resurrection life" (never affirmed by Hebrews). I agree with Moffitt that Hebrews believes in the resurrection, but it nowhere affirms or even hints that Jesus assumed a new kind of "resurrection life" that he did not have before. There is no point in saying that the Son could not have had "indestructible" life before he died. The paradox is already there in Christian theology, in the rest of the NT, and in Hebrews. Hebrews has already emphatically asserted that the *eternal* Son (1:1–4, 7–12) assumed humanity and "tasted death" (2:9). The writer deliberately uses the word "indestructible" because the eternal life of the Son could not be destroyed by his human death. Though he assumed our dying humanity, he was not limited by mortality as were the Aaronic priests (7:23). See Brennan, *Divine Christology*, 142–44.

where the *mortal* Aaronic priests established only by a " *fleshly ordinance*" failed. God appoints the eternal Son as Guarantor of the "better" new covenant because only he can overcome the sinful mortality of the old priests and thus "remain" a High Priest forever, able to save the faithful "completely" until they reach their destiny (7:24–25). In the eternal Son, God himself guarantees the forgiveness, access to God, and empowerment for persevering obedience that are available under this covenant.[29] Thus, no one can doubt the divine character of the saving actions described in the next section.

HEBREWS 8:1–10:18: EFFECTIVE SACRIFICE, ETERNAL HEAVENLY HIGH PRIEST, MEDIATOR OF THE NEW COVENANT

Heb 7:28 continues by affirming that the Son, appointed priest by divine oath, "is perfected forever."[30] That perfecting is the story of 8:1–10:18, the story of how the Son becomes the sufficient High Priest and new covenant Guarantor by offering the ultimate sacrifice for sin. At the heart of this section (10:5–10), the Son responds to the Father's oath with the ultimate affirmation of his incarnate obedience (Ps 40:6–8).

Heb 8:1–10:18 can best be understood as a symphony in three movements – 8:1–13; 9:1–22; and 9:23–10:18 (see Figure 1 at the end of this chapter).[31] Each movement progresses through the themes of *sanctuary, sacrifice,* and *covenant.* The crucial nature of the central sacrifice theme is shown by the greater attention it receives in each successive movement: because the Son has made an adequate sacrifice for sin (theme two), he has entered God's presence as High Priest of the heavenly sanctuary (theme one) and become the Mediator/ Guarantor of the new covenant (theme three).[32] Thus, these three themes correspond to the threefold understanding of Christ's self-offering as atonement for

---

29. Brennan, *Divine Christology,* 169–70.

30. I have argued elsewhere that in Hebrews the eternal Son is "perfected" as "the source of eternal salvation" (5:9) through his incarnate obedience. Thus, by this "being perfected" he is consecrated High Priest and enters the heavenly sanctuary on behalf of the people of God. His "perfecting" of believers is an appropriate corollary. By cleansing them from sin he enables them to enter God's presence. See the comments on 5:9–10; 7:25, 28; and 10:14 in my commentary (Cockerill, *The Epistle to the Hebrews,* 248–51, 334–37, 343–45, 450–53).

31. See Gareth Lee Cockerill, "Structure and Interpretation in Hebrews 8:1–10:18: A Symphony in Three Movements," *BBR* 11 (2001): 179–201, as well as Cockerill, *The Epistle to the Hebrews,* 335–460.

32. Moffitt, *Atonement and the Logic of Resurrection,* 289–95, admits that the death of Jesus establishes the New Covenant, though he argues that the sacrifice which atones for sin is the presentation of his resurrected body in heaven. By thus separating Christ's death from his sacrifice, Moffitt fails to see that it is in fact by offering a *sufficient sacrifice for sin* that Christ has taken the curse of the old covenant upon himself and inaugurated the new covenant. Thus, as just mentioned, he fractures Hebrews's vision which sees Christ's sufficient sacrifice for sin as the sacrifice of priestly consecration that enabled Christ to enter heaven as all-sufficient High Priest on our behalf and the sacrifice by which Christ became Guarantor of the new covenant (7:22).

sin (*sacrifice*) and therefore as priestly consecration (*sanctuary*) and new covenant inauguration (*covenant*). They reveal the priestly significance of the Son's divine saving actions – exaltation/session (*sanctuary*), incarnate obedience (*sacrifice*), and ongoing priestly ministry (*covenant*). My emphasis will be on Heb 9:23–10:18, the third climactic movement of this symphony.

Movement One, Heb 8:1–13. The first movement modestly claims that Christ's *sacrifice* (8:3–5, theme two) must be "something" of a different quality from the Aaronic sacrifices because it qualifies him for high-priestly ministry in a heavenly *Sanctuary* (8:1–2; cf. Ps 110:1, theme one),[33] and inaugurates the better *Covenant* of Jer 31:31–34 (8:6–13, theme three).

Movement Two, Heb 9:1–22. The second movement begins with a Pentateuchal description of the two-part earthly *sanctuary* (9:1–10, theme one) and concludes with a like description of the *old covenant's* inauguration (9:16–22, theme three). The blood sacrifices that inaugurated the old covenant show that its curse continues over the covenant-breaking people of God.[34] The old sanctuary shows that its animal-blood sacrifices could neither cleanse from sin nor give access to God's presence.[35] Thus, from the viewpoint of the old, God's people are (1) *cursed* due to covenant violation, (2) *polluted* by sin, and thus (3) *excluded* from God's presence.

The central *sacrifice* part of this second movement, found in 9:11–15, tells us that the "something" (8:3) Christ offered is "himself through the eternal spirit blameless to God" (9:14; cf. 7:25). This is the once-for-all Day of Atonement sacrifice that meets these needs by atoning for sin:[36] (1) Christ's "blood," that

---

33. In my judgment, Hebrews identifies heaven, the dwelling place of God, as the "Most Holy Place" rather than conceiving of heaven as either being or containing a two-part sanctuary with a "Holy Place" and a "Most Holy Place." First of all, 9:23–24 identifies τὰ ἅγια, "the sanctuary," as heaven itself. Second, there is no function for an outer sanctuary or "Holy Place" in heaven. In the description of the earthly tabernacle in 9:1–10 the outer sanctuary only emphasises lack of access to God. It is best to follow Westcott, who argues that both ἅγια ("sanctuary," 8:2; 9:23–24) and σκηνή ("tent," 8:2; 9:11) have the same referent but provide different perspectives on that referent. See B. F. Westcott, *The Epistle to the Hebrews: The Greek Text with Notes and Essays* (1892; repr., Grand Rapids: Eerdmans, 1951), 214. For further discussion, see Cockerill, *The Epistle to the Hebrews*, 351–57, and literature there cited.

34. Following Scott Hahn's truly groundbreaking work on 9:15–22. See S. W. Hahn, "A Broken Covenant and the Curse of Death: A Study of Hebrews 9:15–22," *CBQ* 66 (2004): 416–36, and Scott W. Hahn, "Covenant, Cult, and the Curse-of-Death: Διαθήκη in Heb 9:15–22," in *Hebrews: Contemporary Methods – New Insights*, ed. Gabriella Gelardini, Biblical Interpretation Series 75 (Atlanta: Society of Biblical Literature, 2005), 65–88.

35. As described in 9:1–10, the two-part nature of the tabernacle, limitation of access to the high priest alone once a year, and its earthly nature underscore the lack of access into God's presence under the old order.

36. Moffitt, *Atonement and the Logic of Resurrection*, 229, wrongly claims that Hebrews says Jesus offers "body, blood, and self." The primary description is "himself" (7:27; 9:14). Since Christ's obedience culminates in his death, his "blood" is closely associated with his sacrifice. It is the "means" by which he enters the heavenly sanctuary (9:11). Since the crucified and risen Christ is in the heavenly sanctuary, the pastor can

is, his obedient pouring out of his life in death, is the means by which he enters God's heavenly presence as our High Priest.[37] (2) Christ's blood is also the agent that removes the pollution that prevented our entrance by cleansing "our conscience from dead works to serve the living God."[38] (3) Finally, by his death

---

refer to his "blood" being there and crying out for mercy (12:24). But Hebrews *never* says that Jesus offers his blood. On the offering of Jesus's "body" in 10:10 see n. 49.

37. Moffitt, *Atonement and the Logic of Resurrection*, 221–78, etc., argues first, that sacrificial "blood" represents the life of the sacrifice offered in the Most Holy Place rather than its death on the altar. He contends that this is the way the OT understood the Day of Atonement ritual. It was not the slaughter of the victim, but the application of the blood/life in the Most Holy Place that constituted the sacrifice proper. Indeed, 9:7 speaks of the Aaronic high priest entering once a year and offering the blood of the sacrifice. Second, Moffitt argues that in Hebrews Christ's blood represents his appearing in a glorified body endued with resurrection life in heaven as the true locus of his sacrifice (developed extensively throughout his book but summarised on p. 255).

There are serious problems with both of these assertions. (1) Moffitt, *Atonement and the Logic of Resurrection*, 289–95, admits that "blood" does represent sacrificial death in the description of old covenant inauguration in 9:15–22 that immediately follows and is closely related to the description of Christ's sacrifice by analogy with the Day of Atonement in 9:11–14. (2) Moffitt, *Atonement and the Logic of Resurrection*, 279, admits the presence of other OT sacrificial rituals in Hebrews, even in 9:11–14, yet he depends too heavily on the Day of Atonement ritual. However, since Christ's sacrifice adequately deals with sin, it is also a sacrifice of high priestly consecration and a new covenant inaugurating sacrifice. Furthermore, as I will show when commenting on 10:5–10, Christ's incarnate obedience takes the place of *all* Old Testament sacrifices. (3) The centrality of Christ's death as the purpose of his incarnation, so clearly affirmed in 2:9, makes it very unlikely that Hebrews would remove that death from being central to his sacrifice. (4) When commenting on 9:11–14, Moffitt does not argue that the Son carried his blood into the Most Holy Place, which seems a bit strange if that blood actually represented the eternal life of his resurrected body offered within the sanctuary. He does, however, claim that 9:11–14 locates Christ's sacrifice inside the heavenly sanctuary. However, the only statement in this passage that might do so is "through his own blood he entered once for all *having obtained an eternal redemption*." The italicised words represent a perfect participle phrase, which could refer to subsequent action and thus could be translated something like "in order to obtain an eternal redemption" (in heaven). Moffitt, *Atonement and the Logic of Resurrection*, 223, n. 13, cites Porter that subsequent perfect participles often indicate subsequent action. The perfect, however, can be taken in contrast with the aorist of "he entered once for all" as emphasising the continual validity of this redemption. Indeed, even if the perfect is taken as subsequent, it does not clearly locate Christ's sacrifice in the heavenly Most Holy Place. (5) To most people schooled in biblical categories, "shed blood" is a very strange and counterintuitive metaphor for a resurrection body brought into God's presence, especially since Hebrews nowhere comes anywhere near making this identification explicit. Finally, one must remember that even the blood the high priest took into the earthly Most Holy Place was *shed* blood – it was life poured out in death. Thus, it seems very problematic to separate this blood from the death of the victim. It is like trying to argue that all quarters are only "tails" and not "heads."

38. Since 9:7 has just described the Aaronic high priest's offering blood in the earthly Most Holy Place, 9:12 would have been the natural place for the pastor to describe the Son as carrying his blood into the heavenly Most Holy Place if that had been his intention. Despite several English translations (NRSV, NAB) and various commentators (most recently John W. Kleinig, *Hebrews*, Concordia Commentary [St. Louis: Concordia Publishing Company, 2017], 412, 427, and Healy, *Hebrews*, 173), 9:12 does *not say* that the Son entered "with" his own blood but "by means of his own blood" (διά followed by the genitive). This seems to be an odd way of speaking if the pastor intended to imply that the Son followed the pattern of the Aaronic high priest (9:7) by carrying his blood into the heavenly sanctuary (pace Ribbens, *Levitical Sacrifice*, 113–19, 131). The pastor is preparing for 10:12. The eternal Son of God, in contrast to the Aaronic high priest, did *not* smear his blood on the "mercy seat"; he "*sat down*" on it "at the right hand of God" (10:12, emphasis added). Unfortunately, in his insightful book, *Face to Face with God: A Biblical Theology of Christ*

Christ has taken the old covenant curse upon himself, establishing the new covenant with its privileges of forgiveness and empowered obedience (9:15; cf. 10:15–18).[39] Thus, it is only by these divine actions that the Son has obtained "an eternal redemption" – a term broad enough to include all of the benefits just enumerated.

Movement Three, Heb 9:23–10:18. In the second movement the writer has shown that the incarnate, exalted Son of God is able to provide what the old order anticipated but could not produce. The third movement, 9:23–10:18, reveals the full extent of these benefits that accrue from the Son's continuing divine actions as High Priest and clarifies the reason for the effectiveness of the Son's sacrifice. The brief opening *sanctuary* (9:23–24) and concluding *covenant* (10:15–18) sections give way to an extensive central *sacrifice* section that divides neatly into three parts: 9:25–10:4; 10:5–10; and 10:11-14. In the second of these three parts, the heart of this section, the Son responds to the Father's declaration of his priesthood announced in 5:5–6 and explained in 7:1–28.

The opening two-verse *sanctuary* section, 9:23–24, announces clearly that by means of his effective sacrifice the Son has removed the sin barrier and entered once for all into heaven itself to appear before God as High Priest "on our behalf."[40] The *covenant* section (10:15–18) brings this third movement to a climax by affirming the benefits this exalted Son of God provides for the people of God as the new covenant Guarantor (7:22) – cleansing from sin and hearts empowered for obedience. According to the first (9:25–10:4) and third (10:11-14) parts of this sacrifice section, the "once for all" character of this sacrifice and the Son's subsequent session confirm this sacrifice's definitive nature.[41]

However, 10:5–10, the heart of this final sacrifice section, clarifies the *reason why* Christ's sacrifice is effective and is thus a key to understanding the benefits provided by the continuing actions of our "Great Priest" (10:21). The incarnate Son answers the Father's oath of priesthood with Ps 40:6–8: "A body

---

as Priest and Mediator, Evangelical Studies in Biblical Theology (Downers Grove: IVP Academic, 2022), T. Desmond Alexander fails to see this crucial contrast and its significance for the sacrifices of the old and new high priests.

39. The first covenant section, 8:7–13, quotes both Jeremiah's description of the failure of the old covenant because it had been broken by the people's sin (8:7–9; Jer 31:31–32) and God's promise of a new covenant that would overcome their disobedience (8:10–13; Jer 31:33–34). The second covenant section, 9:16–22, describes how the Son took the curse of the old covenant's disobedience upon himself and thus inaugurated the promised new covenant with its benefits. Thus, the third covenant section brings this entire symphony to its conclusion by describing the Son seated at God's right hand as the administrator of the benefits of the "better" covenant promised in Jer 31:33–34.

40. Cockerill, *The Epistle to the Hebrews*, 415–17.

41. On the threefold division of this final sacrifice section, see Cockerill, *The Epistle to the Hebrews*, 411–14 and the exposition of 9:24–10:14 that follows.

you have prepared for me . . . Behold, I have come . . . *to do your will*, O God"
(emphasis added).[42] The eternal Son guarantees the new covenant through his
incarnate obedience.

Christ's sacrifice was effective *because it consisted of the eternal Son of God
living an incarnate life of complete obedience to the will of God climaxing in the
obedient offering of himself on the cross*, thus making "purification for sins" so that
by it "we have been sanctified."[43] During his earthly life he "loved righteousness
and hated lawlessness" (1:9), as demonstrated by the fact that he was "tempted in
every way" like we are yet "without sin" (4:15). In this way Christ learnt what it
was like to live a life of completed obedience in the face of suffering and death
(5:8). Thus, "through the eternal Spirit" he "offered himself *blameless* to God"
(9:14, emphasis added). The Son was able to live this obedient human life and
overcome death on behalf of the people of God *only* because he is the eternal Son
who offers himself "through the *eternal* Spirit" (9:14, emphasis added). Thus,
the Son's incarnate obedience is the *divine action* at the heart of his becoming the
"Source" (5:9) of "such a great salvation" (2:3). His sacrifice is confirmed by the
resurrection, for the eternal Son at God's right hand is still the human "Jesus."[44]

---

42. It is unclear to me why Pierce, *Divine Discourse*, 115, seems to suggest that the Son quotes Ps 40:6–8
(Heb 10:5–10) in response to Jer 31:31–34 rather than Ps 110:4, since Jer 31:31–34 is not addressed to the
Son. Harold Attridge accurately describes the relationship between Ps 110:4, Ps 40:6–8, and Jer 31:31–34:
"This exposition [Heb 8–10] culminates in a quotation of the Son's words [Ps 40:6–8], which ultimately
constitute the response to his appointment by God as high priest [Ps 110:4]. These words also show how
God fulfills the promise recorded in the citation of Jeremiah at 8:8–12 [Jer 31:31–34], how, that is, God
makes a new covenant by inscribing laws onto human hearts" (Harold W. Attridge, "Giving Voice to Jesus:
Use of the Psalms in the New Testament," in *Essays on John and Hebrews*, ed. Harold W. Attridge [Grand
Rapids: Baker Academic, 2010], 327).

43. Thus, Michael Kibbe, *Godly Fear or Ungodly Failure? Hebrews 12 and the Sinai Theophanies*,
BZNW (Berlin/Boston: De Gruyter, 2016), 163, n. 91 is incorrect when he says, "It is outside the bound-
aries of Hebrews's cultic perspective to say that Christ offered himself on earth but not in the earthly
sanctuary." Hebrews teaches that Christ's earthly obedience culminating in the cross *was* the sacrifice by
which he entered the heavenly sanctuary as High Priest and Mediator of the new covenant.

44. The writer reserves the name "Jesus" for the incarnate Son of God, introducing it in 2:8 when he
turns to the incarnation. Thus, it is clear that the body through which Jesus offered his obedience has
risen, since the exalted Son at God's right hand is still "Jesus." Moffitt has argued, in my judgment rightly,
that not only 13:20–21 but also 5:7 implies Jesus's resurrection. He is also correct when he argues that the
advanced teaching on the high priesthood of the Son of God does not negate the basic belief in the resurrection affirmed in 6:1–2 (Moffitt, *Atonement and the Logic of Resurrection*, 181–94). My own article, Gareth
Lee Cockerill, "The Better Resurrection (Heb. 11:35): A Key to the Structure and Rhetorical Purpose of
Hebrews 11," *TynBul* 51 (2000): 214–34, greatly strengthens Moffitt's arguments for the resurrection in
Hebrews 11. He is certainly correct that, if the faithful of Hebrews 11 anticipated a resurrection to eternal
life, it would be strange if the one who culminates that list in 12:1–3, Jesus, did not experience the same (see
the Moffitt reference just cited). As "the Pioneer and Perfecter of the way of faith," this Jesus is the one who
opens the way for those who went before, as well as those who will come after, to enter the heavenly promised
land. For these arguments, see Cockerill, "The Better Resurrection (Heb. 11:35)," 214–34. The resurrection
confirms the incarnate offering of the Son but, pace Moffitt, it is not the resurrected body endowed with a
newly received "indestructible life" presented in heaven that is the Son's sacrifice.

The nature of this sacrifice as divine action is demonstrated by the way it makes the sacrifices of the old covenant obsolete, establishes the Son as all-sufficient Saviour, and makes possible the benefits now available through his actions as High Priest and Mediator.

First, the incarnate obedience of the Son of God, described here in 10:5–10, did what the "blood of bulls and goats" (10:4) could never do by replacing not only the Day of Atonement sacrifice but *all* of the old covenant sacrifices ("sacrifice and offerings, whole burnt offerings and sacrifices for sin") collectively understood as "sacrifices for sin."[45] The Son's incarnate obedience is the comprehensive remedy for all that those sacrifices were unable to accomplish – forgiveness, cleansing, and access to God.[46]

Second, it was by persistence in faithful obedience despite the suffering that climaxed in the cross that the eternal Son was "perfected" as our Saviour (2:10).[47] Thus, it is misleading to separate the Son's life of obedience from the cross as Schreiner does when he says that 10:5–10 refers "to Jesus' death, *not* his entire life" (emphasis added).[48] Heb 10:5–10 makes no explicit mention of Jesus's death, but quotes the Son as saying that God prepared a "body" as the vehicle for his incarnate obedience.[49] We know that his obedience began with the incarnation because he lived a sinless life (4:15). Furthermore, his life of human obedience was not complete until the obedience of the cross, at which time it

---

45. Second Temple Judaism tended to see the entire sacrificial system as remedy for sin (Ribbens, *Levitical Sacrifice*, 49–51).

46. Thus, the ἄφεσις in 10:18 should be understood as a comprehensive "release" from sin. Cockerill, *The Epistle to the Hebrews*, 458–60. See also the "removal" (ἀθέτησιν) of sin in 9:26 (Kevin B. McCruden, "The Eloquent Blood of Jesus: The Neglected Theme of the Fidelity of Jesus in Hebrews," *CBQ* 75 [2013]: 505). Ribbens fails to see that both the rhetorical location of this passage and the fact that it is the Son's answer to the Father's oath identify it as the key, climactic description of the Son's sacrifice. Thus, Ribbens attempts to identify Christ's sacrifice as his blood carried into heaven on the basis of dubious implications from various passages (*Levitical Sacrifice*, 99–142) and then conforms his understanding of this passage to that conclusion (*Levitical Sacrifice*, 143–48). This passage, however, clearly identifies the Son's *earthly obedience* as taking away the sin that all of the OT sacrifice "for sins," the "blood of bulls and goats" (10:4), could not take away.

47. See n. 30 earlier. David G. Peterson, *Hebrews and Perfection: An Examination of the Concept of Perfection in the Epistle to the Hebrews*, SNTSMS 47 (Cambridge: CUP, 1982), 73, argues that the whole series of events from incarnation to exaltation constituted the perfection of Christ as Saviour. It is better, however, to say that it is the exalted Son who has been "perfected," since Hebrews attributes the Son's perfection directly to his suffering and obedience (2:10; 5:8–9).

48. Thomas R. Schreiner, *Commentary on Hebrews*, Biblical Theology for Christian Proclamation (Nashville: Holman Reference, 2015), 300, n. 484, citing Philip Edgcumbe Hughes, *A Commentary on the Epistle to the Hebrews* (Grand Rapids: Eerdmans, 1977), 399, and Peterson, *Perfection*, 148.

49. Heb 7:25 and 9:14 affirm that the Son offered "himself" while 10:10 speaks of the "offering of the body" that God prepared for him as the vehicle for obedience. This is no contradiction, for the eternal Son is fully present in the body of his incarnate obedience and that body represents the totality of his now-incarnate person.

was offered in its entirety to God – "Once for all."[50] The cross is, then, the climax of the Son's obedience and the culmination of his sacrifice. His offering was not merely a "death" that removed the curse of disobedience (9:16–22), but a life of obedience unto death that empowers God's people for persevering obedience (9:14).

Furthermore, since this sacrifice effectively atoned for sin, it also became a sacrifice of priestly consecration and covenant inauguration. Thus, it established the Son as both High Priest seated at God's right hand (9:23–24) and Guarantor of the new covenant (10:15–18).[51] We can summarise the three closely interrelated benefits available through the Son's present, continuing divine actions as cleansing from sin, free access to God, and a new way of life characterised by forgiveness and empowerment for persevering obedience.[52] The first is closely associated with his atoning sacrifice (10:5–10); the second, with his session as High Priest at the Father's right hand (9:23–24; 10:11–14); and the third, with the new covenant that he mediates and guarantees (10:15–18). This third movement climaxes with the Son, who has provided cleansing from sin through offering his life of obedience on the cross (10:5–10) and is seated at God's right hand as the High Priest through whom we draw near to God (10:11–14), administering the benefits of cleansing and transformation promised in the new covenant (Heb 10:15–18).

---

50. This is what 5:8 means by "he learned obedience." It does not mean that he learnt to be obedient, but that he "learned" or experienced what it meant to be obedient consistently until the end of his life. Strictly speaking, the Son did not have a life of perfect human obedience to offer until the successful conclusion of that life of obedience on the cross. Thus, though every act of obedience was offered to God, the final offering of that obedient life coincides with its conclusion on the cross. See Harold W. Attridge, *The Epistle to the Hebrews*, Hermeneia (Philadelphia: Fortress Press, 1989), 276.

51. Moffitt, *Atonement and the Logic of Resurrection*, repeatedly asserts that Hebrews consistently locates Christ's sacrifice in heaven (e.g., p. 274). On p. 275 he identifies 7:26, 8:1–2, 9:11, 9:23–25, and 10:12 as the places that affirm this location. However, *none* of these passages actually affirm that Christ offered his sacrifice in heaven. The place that comes closest is 8:1–4. Here the pastor says that (1) the Son serves as priest in the heavenly sanctuary. (2) Every priest must offer sacrifice. (3) Thus, he must have "something" to offer. (4) If he were on earth, he would not be a priest because there are already priests performing the offerings required by the OT law in the earthly tabernacle. The "something" of 8:3 becomes "himself through the eternal Spirit" (9:14) and then "the body of Jesus Christ once for all" (10:10). Now, this "something" is clearly there to evoke the hearers' curiosity and to emphasise that the Son's sacrifice must be different from the earthly sacrifices and appropriate for entrance into the heavenly sanctuary. But, especially in light of the clear statements of 10:5–10, it need not mean that his sacrifice was actually offered inside the heavenly sanctuary. On 8:1–4 see Alexander, *Face to Face with God*, 88–90, quoting Geerhardus Vos.

52. The Son has provided a definitive "sanctification" or cleansing from sin by which the faithful have been "perfected" in the sense of being made fit to enter God's presence. They continue in that sanctification by drawing near through their High Priest to receive forgiveness and grace for perseverance in obedience. See Cockerill, *The Epistle to the Hebrews*, 450–53 on 10:10, 14.

HEBREWS 10:19–25: "A GREAT PRIEST OVER THE HOUSE OF GOD"

It is appropriate to conclude our study by examining the way in which the pastor describes the benefits of the Son's continuing actions in order to apply them to his hearers' need for perseverance in faithful obedience. He highlights the amazing fact that "we have authorization for entrance into the Most Holy Place" – intimate access to God. The pastor has brought to fruition what he anticipated when he returned to the subject of priesthood in 6:20 – the Son is our "Forerunner" who, unlike the old high priests (9:1–10), has entered God's presence in such a manner that he has opened the way for us to follow. This "way" is "new," that is, ever fresh, and "living" or ever effective because it has been established by the divine actions of the eternal Son of God – by the "indestructible life" (7:16) of the eternal Son who offered himself "by the eternal Spirit" (9:14) and who ever lives to intercede for his own (7:25). Thus, it is administered by the one truly "Great Priest" for the benefit of the faithful who are members of his "House."[53]

The pastor paints this beautiful picture of access to God in all of its attractiveness as motivation for his hearers to draw near through their "Great Priest" in order that they might persevere in obedience by holding onto their "hope" of ultimate entrance (9:28; 12:22–24, 25–29). He has not forgotten, however, that the "veil" once separating us from God has been removed by atonement for sin through the "blood of Jesus." "Drawing near" both requires and is the means of cleansing from sin that involves forgiveness and grace for holy living. Those who draw near must do so with sincere faith, allowing Jesus to provide the inward and outward cleansing described as a "sprinkled" conscience and a "washed" body. Having called his hearers to persevere by drawing near, the pastor turns their attention to concern for the people of God. Perseverance is a matter for the entire "House" over which the Son is "Great Priest."

CONCLUSION

It is time to summarise this discussion of the divine actions pertinent to the Son's on-going ministry. Heb 1:1–2:18 describes the incarnation, death, exaltation, and session of the eternal Son of God as the divine actions by which he fulfilled his sonship and became the "Pioneer" of his people's "salvation," administering its benefits through the divine actions of his on-going ministry. Ps 110:1, the Father's invitation for the Son to take the seat at the right hand "of

---

53. For a detailed interpretation of 10:19–25, see Cockerill, *The Epistle to the Hebrews*, 464–81; for the identification of the "veil" and its relation to "his flesh," see pp. 468–71.

the Majesty on High" (1:3, 13), was the Father's divine action that joined with the Son's divine actions to bring him into the fulfillment of his sonship. This section ends with the announcement that through these divine actions the Son has become a High Priest who delivers the people of God from the sin and fear of death by which they have always been plagued (2:14–18).

Heb 4:14–10:25 takes up this theme, expounding the significance of the Son's deity and the divine actions outlined in 1:1–2:18 as the fulfillment of the OT priesthood and the Sinai covenant that was both the basis for and dependent upon that priesthood. The Son's incarnate obedience climaxing in the cross was the all-sufficient sacrifice that atoned for sin, making the practice of all OT sacrifices obsolete. Based on this atoning sacrifice, the Son assumed his seat at God's right hand as the all-sufficient High Priest. By this sacrifice he also took upon himself the old covenant curse on disobedience, thereby becoming Mediator of the new covenant. According to Ps 110:1, the Father invited the Son to sit at his right hand. According to Ps 110:4, the Father proclaims the One at his side High Priest. As the High Priest at God's right hand, the Son exercises the present divine actions of cleansing from sin, access into God's presence, and grace for persevering faithfulness until God's people enter God's eternal "rest." As Mediator of the new covenant, the Son provides ongoing forgiveness, heart transformation, and intimacy with God. His high priesthood and covenant mediatorship reinforce and supplement each other. By becoming High Priest and Mediator, the Son fulfills his role as the ultimate revelation of God, which is also a "divine action" – he is "the radiance of God's glory and the exact representation of God's very being" (1:3).

In conclusion, it is important to recall that Hebrews never describes the ongoing divine actions of this all-sufficient High Priest as petition, but as administration of the benefits available through him. Only 7:25 (cf. 9:25) uses the term "intercession" for his ministry, despite the priestly connotations of that term. The pastor's conviction that the Son's completed saving work has been accepted by the Father and the fundamental role played by Ps 110:1 in Hebrews (1:3, 13; 4:14–16; 8:1–2; 12:1–3) make the pastor's hesitancy to use intercession language understandable. Contrary to some of the most beautiful hymnody, the Son does not "stand" before God's throne. The Father *himself* has invited the Son to take his seat next to him on his throne as evidence that the Son's saving work *is complete* (10:11–14). The Son has no need to petition the Father. His "intercession" consists in his authority as the "Source of eternal salvation" (5:9) to administer its benefits to all who "draw near to God through him."[54]

---

54. Alexander, *Face to Face with God*, 75–80, fails to note the significance of the Son's session for his intercession.

His ability to "sympathise" (4:14–16) does not equip him to petition the Father but to administer the grace necessary for faithful perseverance.[55] This understanding of the continuing work of Jesus as High Priest is in full accord with the author's pastoral goal and rhetorical purpose that his hearers persevere as the faithful people of God. We can now draw near to receive the "mercy" of forgiveness and the "grace" for persevering obedience until our final entrance into the "rest" that is the inheritance of the people of God.[56]

Figure 1: A Symphony in Three Movements: Heb 8:1–10:18[57]

(A Son Perfected Forever, Heb 7:28)

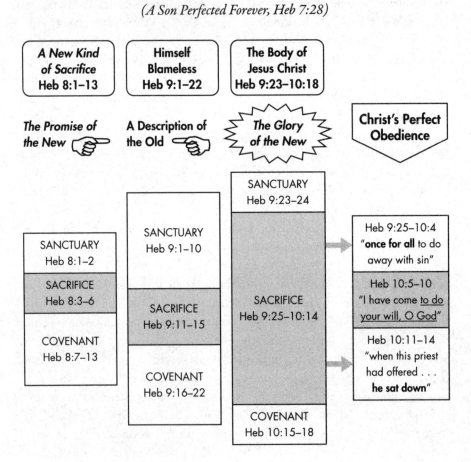

55. Cockerill, *The Epistle to the Hebrews*, 225–27.

56. Cockerill, *The Epistle to the Hebrews*, 227–28.

57. Cockerill, "Structure and Interpretation in Hebrews 8:1–10:18," 179–201; Cockerill, *The Epistle to the Hebrews*, 335–460.

SELECT BIBLIOGRAPHY

Alexander, T. Desmond. *Face to Face with God: A Biblical Theology of Christ as Priest and Mediator.* Evangelical Studies in Biblical Theology. Downers Grove: IVP Academic, 2022.

Attridge, Harold W. *The Epistle to the Hebrews.* Hermeneia. Philadelphia: Fortress Press, 1989.

———. "Giving Voice to Jesus: Use of the Psalms in the New Testament." In *Essays on John and Hebrews*, edited by Harold W. Attridge, 320–30. Grand Rapids: Baker Academic, 2010.

———. "God in Hebrews: Urging Children to Heavenly Glory." In *Essays on John and Hebrews*, edited by Harold W. Attridge, 308–19. Grand Rapids: Baker Academic, 2010.

Brennan, Nick. *Divine Christology in the Epistle to the Hebrews: The Son as God.* LNTS 656. London, New York: T&T Clark, 2022.

Cockerill, Gareth Lee. "The Better Resurrection (Heb. 11:35): A Key to the Structure and Rhetorical Purpose of Hebrews 11." *TynBul* 51 (2000): 214–34.

———. *The Epistle to the Hebrews.* NICNT. Grand Rapids: Eerdmans, 2012.

———. "Structure and Interpretation in Hebrews 8:1–10:18: A Symphony in Three Movements." *BBR* 11 (2001): 179–201.

———. "The Truthfulness and Perennial Relevance of God's Word in the Letter to the Hebrews." *BSac* 172, no. 686 (2015): 190–202.

Ebert, Daniel J. IV. "The Chiastic Structure of the Prologue of Hebrews." *TJ* 13NS (1992): 163–79.

Ellingworth, Paul. *The Epistle to the Hebrews: A Commentary on the Greek Text.* NIGTC. Grand Rapids: Eerdmans, 1993.

Hahn, S. W. "A Broken Covenant and the Curse of Death: A Study of Hebrews 9:15–22." *CBQ* 66 (2004): 416–36.

———. "Covenant, Cult, and the Curse-of-Death: Διαθήκη in Heb 9:15–22." In *Hebrews: Contemporary Methods – New Insights*, edited by Gabriella Gelardini, 65–88. Biblical Interpretation Series 75. Atlanta: Society of Biblical Literature, 2005.

Healy, Mary. *Hebrews.* CCSS. Grand Rapids: Baker, 2016.

Hughes, Philip Edgcumbe. *A Commentary on the Epistle to the Hebrews.* Grand Rapids: Eerdmans, 1977.

Jamieson, R. B. *The Paradox of Sonship: Christology in the Epistle to the Hebrews.* Foreword by Simon J. Gathercole. Studies in Christian Doctrine and Scripture. Downers Grove: IVP Academic, 2021.

Kibbe, Michael. *Godly Fear or Ungodly Failure? Hebrews 12 and the Sinai Theophanies.* BZNW 216. Berlin/Boston: De Gruyter, 2016.

Kleinig, John W. *Hebrews*. Concordia Commentary. St. Louis: Concordia Publishing Company, 2017.

Martin, Michael Wade, and Jason A. Whitlark, *Inventing Hebrews: Design and Purpose in Ancient Rhetoric*. SNTSMS 171. Cambridge: CUP, 2018.

McCruden, Kevin B. "The Eloquent Blood of Jesus: The Neglected Theme of the Fidelity of Jesus in Hebrews." *CBQ* 75 (2013): 504–20.

Meier, John P. "Structure and Theology in Heb 1,1–14." *Bib* 66 (1985): 168–89.

Moffitt, David M. *Atonement and the Logic of Resurrection in the Epistle to the Hebrews*. NovTSup 141. Leiden/Boston: Brill, 2013.

Neyrey, J. H. "'Without Beginning of Days or End of Life' (Hebrews 7:3): Topos for a True Deity." *CBQ* 53 (1991): 439–55.

Peterson, David G. *Hebrews and Perfection: An Examination of the Concept of Perfection in the Epistle to the Hebrews*. SNTSMS 47. Cambridge: CUP, 1982.

———. *Hebrews: An Introduction and Commentary*. TNTC 15. Downers Grove: IVP Academic, 2020.

Pierce, Madison N. *Divine Discourse in the Epistle to the Hebrews: The Recontextualization of Spoken Quotations of Scripture*. SNTSMS 178. Cambridge: CUP, 2020.

Ribbens, Benjamin J. *Levitical Sacrifice and Heavenly Cult in Hebrews*. BZNW 222. Berlin/Boston: Walter de Gruyter, 2016.

Schreiner, Thomas R. *Commentary on Hebrews*. Biblical Theology for Christian Proclamation. Nashville: Holman Reference, 2015.

Wellum, Stephen J. "Jesus as Lord and Son: Two Complementary Truths of Biblical Christology." *CTR* 13, no. 1 (2015):23–45.

Westcott, B. F. *The Epistle to the Hebrews: The Greek Text with Notes and Essays*. Reprint, Grand Rapids: Eerdmans, 1951.

CHAPTER 12

The Holy Spirit and Christ's
Ongoing Priesthood in Hebrews

Mary Healy

INTRODUCTION

At the heart of the theology of the letter to the Hebrews is the author's ground-breaking insight: Jesus Christ is High Priest in a way that fulfills and infinitely surpasses the Levitical priesthood of the old covenant.[1] The defining moment of his priesthood is his death on the cross, in which he offered himself as the once-for-all sacrifice in atonement for sin (2:17; 7:27; 9:26; 10:10). Yet his priesthood did not end with his sacrificial death. It continues forever, since the risen Christ "always lives to make intercession" for "those who draw near to God through him" (7:25); he is the "minister [*leitourgos*] in the sanctuary and the true tent" (8:2) and "the mediator of a new covenant" (9:15) who does not cease to represent God to humanity and humanity to God.[2]

---

1. The fact that Christ is nowhere else in the NT referred to as a priest (*hiereus*) is unsurprising, given the fact that in first-century Judaism "priest" had a very specific meaning: it denoted a descendant of Aaron who offered animal sacrifices in the Jerusalem temple according to the prescriptions of the Mosaic law – none of which applies to Christ, as our author readily acknowledges (7:14–16; 8:4–5; 13:11–13). Hebrews is, nevertheless, developing a theme that is implicit in the Gospels and Paul. See Brant Pitre, "Jesus, the New Temple, and the New Priesthood," *Letter & Spirit* 4 (2008): 47–83; Crispin H. T. Fletcher-Louis, "Jesus as the High Priestly Messiah" (Parts 1 and 2), *JSHJ* 4, no. 2 (2006): 155–75 and *JSHJ* 5, no. 1 (2007): 57–79; and Albert Vanhoye, *Old Testament Priests and the New Priest*, trans. J. Bernard Orchard (Petersham, MA: St Bede's, 1986), 267–69.

2. Author's translation here and throughout (unless otherwise noted). See Alan J. Torrance, "Reclaiming the Continuing Priesthood of Christ," in Oliver D. Crisp and Fred Sanders, eds., *Christology, Ancient and*

In this letter dominated by the portrayal of Christ the "great High Priest" after the order of Melchizedek, there seems to be little place for reflection on the Holy Spirit. The letter contains a mere seven direct references to the Spirit, who can seem "a bit-part player, the weak link in the divine triumvirate (or 'bi-umvirate') of God and faithful Son."[3] It is not surprising that for the past century, the scholarly consensus has been that the Holy Spirit plays no role in the argument of the letter and that Hebrews essentially has no pneumatology.[4] Recent scholarship has, however, begun to challenge that assessment.[5] Jack Levison has cogently argued that Hebrews does indeed have a coherent pneumatology in that its references to the Spirit are integral to the letter's argument, consistent with one another, rooted in Israelite literature, and clearly related to other NT conceptions of the Spirit.[6] The present essay seeks to build on Levison's insights by showing how Hebrews envisions the Holy Spirit as a divine agent whose activity in the believing community is an intrinsic dimension of Christ's ongoing priestly mediation.[7] I will first examine what the letter says about the Spirit's role in Christ's sacrifice itself (9:13–14), and then show how a fuller appreciation of the author's thought here sheds light on his remaining six references to the Spirit.

Modern: Explorations in Constructive Dogmatics (Grand Rapids: Zondervan, 2013), 184–204, and Gerald O'Collins, SJ, and Michael Keenan Jones, *Jesus Our Priest: A Christian Approach to the Priesthood of Christ* (Oxford: OUP, 2010), 55.

3. David M. Allen, "'The Forgotten Spirit': A Pentecostal Reading of the Letter to the Hebrews?" in *Journal of Pentecostal Theology* 18 (2009): 53.

4. See, e.g., H. B. Swete, *The Holy Spirit in the New Testament* (1909; repr., Eugene, OR: Wipf & Stock, 1998), 248–49; Barnabas Lindars, *The Theology of the Letter to the Hebrews*, NTT (Cambridge: CUP, 1991), 56; and Paul Ellingworth, *The Epistle to the Hebrews: A Commentary on the Greek Text*, NIGTC (Grand Rapids: Eerdmans, 1993), 66, 143.

5. Jack Levison, "A Theology of the Spirit in the Letter to the Hebrews," *CBQ* 78 (2016): 90–110; Steve Motyer, "The Spirit in Hebrews: No Longer Forgotten?" in *The Spirit and Christ in the New Testament and Christian Theology: Essays in Honor of Max Turner*, ed. I. Howard Marshall, Volker Rabens, and Cornelis Bennema (Grand Rapids: Eerdmans, 2012) 213–28; Allen, "Forgotten Spirit"; Martin Emmrich, *Pneumatological Concepts in the Epistle to the Hebrews: Amtscharisma, Prophet & Guide of the Eschatological Exodus* (Lanham, MD: University Press of America, 2003).

6. Levison, "A Theology of the Spirit," 92.

7. This article will not directly address those currents of biblical interpretation that exclude *a priori* the possibility of divine action (for arguments against such claims, see Mary Healy, "Behind, in Front of... or Through the Text? The Christological Analogy and the Lost Realm of Biblical Truth" and other essays in *"Behind" the Text: History and Biblical Interpretation*, SAH Series 4, ed. Craig G. Bartholomew, C. Stephen Evans, Mary Healy, and Murray Rae [Carlisle, UK: Paternoster / Grand Rapids: Zondervan, 2003]). Our purpose here, rather, is to show that for Hebrews the divine agency of the Holy Spirit is so fundamental that to deny it from the outset is to preclude the possibility of understanding the letter on its own terms.

THE SPIRIT IN CHRIST'S ATONING SACRIFICE

Only one passage in Hebrews, and indeed in the entire NT, directly links the Spirit with Christ's atonement. In this key text, 9:13–14, Hebrews ascribes to the Spirit an essential role in Christ's once-for-all sacrifice offered on the cross.

> For if the blood of goats and bulls and the sprinkled ashes of a heifer sanctifies those who are defiled for the purification of the flesh, how much more will the blood of Christ, who through an eternal Spirit [*pneuma aiōnion*][8] offered himself without blemish to God, purify our conscience from dead works to serve the living God. (9:13–14)

Given the fact that all other references in Hebrews to *pneuma* in the singular (except 4:12) refer unambiguously to the Holy Spirit (2:4; 3:7; 6:4; 9:8; 10:15, 29), it is unlikely that the enigmatic phrase "eternal spirit" refers simply to Jesus's inner disposition, as some argue.[9] Rather, as F. F. Bruce notes, in the background of this description of Christ's redemptive self-offering (9:13–15) seems to be the Isaian Servant of the Lord, who "makes himself a guilt offering" and bears the sin of many (Isa 53:10, 12), thereby procuring their salvation.[10] The servant is introduced with the Lord's declaration: "I have put my Spirit upon him, he will bring forth justice to the nations" (Isa 42:1; cf. 11:2; 61:1). "It is in the power of the Divine Spirit, accordingly, that the Servant accomplishes every phase of his ministry, including the crowning phase in which he accepts death for the transgression of the people, filling the twofold role of priest and victim, as Christ does in this epistle."[11] For Hebrews, as for the NT in general, Jesus is that Servant, empowered by the Spirit of God to stand as a representative of the people, offering to God a life free from blemish in perfect fulfillment of God's will (cf. Isa 53:8–11).

But the writer seems to intend yet more with the phrase "eternal Spirit," a *hapax legomenon* in the Bible. Albert Vanhoye, drawing from St. John Chrysostom, argues that this phrase alludes to the fire on the altar of sacrifice in

---

8. The absence of the definite article in this phrase tells us little if anything about its proper interpretation, since there are over 50 instances of anarthrous *pneuma hagion* in the NT, most of them referring unambiguously to the Holy Spirit. See Philip Edgcumbe Hughes, *A Commentary on the Epistle to the Hebrews* (Grand Rapids: Eerdmans, 1977), 359 n. 7.

9. See Harold W. Attridge, *The Epistle to the Hebrews: A Commentary on the Epistle to the Hebrews* (Hermeneia; Philadelphia: Fortress, 1989) 114, and Luke Timothy Johnson, *Hebrews: A Commentary* (NTL; Louisville, KY: Westminster John Knox Press, 2006), 238.

10. F. F. Bruce, *The Epistle to the Hebrews*, rev. ed., NICNT (Grand Rapids: Eerdmans, 2012), 217.

11. Bruce, *The Epistle to the Hebrews*, 217.

the old covenant.[12] The fire on the altar was what transformed the slain animal into smoke rising up to God. It was no ordinary fire, for it had been miraculously ignited by God when the altar was first dedicated (Lev 9:24; cf. 2 Chron 7:1). Since only fire that came from God was capable of making the sacrifices holy and acceptable to him, the priests had to take care never to let the fire go out (Lev 6:12–13; cf. 2 Macc 1:18–36; *1 Esdras* 6:23). It was therefore called the "perpetual fire" (*'esh tamid*, Lev 6:6[13]). Hebrews suggests, then, that the "perpetual fire" of the old covenant foreshadowed the eternal divine fire that engulfs Christ's sacrifice – namely, the Holy Spirit.[14] It was the Spirit who set the incarnate Son ablaze in the furnace of his passion, moving him to offer up to God the most perfect act of obedient love that could ever come from a human heart (cf. 5:8–9; 10:5–7), thus atoning for all sins for all time.

> Other passages in the sermon show that the force of the Spirit carried out the sacrificial transformation by inspiring Jesus with two closely connected spiritual attitudes: perfect docility towards God (Heb 5:8) and complete solidarity with us (4:15). The human nature of Christ was thus raised up to God, that is to say it passed from the plane of flesh and blood, where it was by reason of the incarnation (Heb 2:14), to the plane of perfect and definitive union with God in heavenly glory (9:24).[15]

Through the Spirit the incarnate Son, who was "made like his brethren in every respect" (2:17) and was therefore "beset with weakness" (5:2), was perfected in holiness and made capable of a divine glory in which all his brethren could share (cf. 2:9–11).[16] As St. Athanasius put it, Christ took what is ours that we might have what is his.[17] Calling the Spirit "eternal" (*aiōnion*) links this phrase with the other uses of "eternal" in the letter, referring to that which is of the divine realm in contrast to what is earthly and temporal. Only one who is animated from within by the "eternal Spirit" (*pneuma aiōnion*) is able to accomplish an "eternal redemption" (*aiōnia lutrōsis*, 9:12) and "eternal salvation" (*sōtēria aiōnia*, 5:9), thereby winning an "eternal inheritance" (*aiōnia klēronomia*, 9:15)

---

12. Albert Vanhoye, *A Different Priest: The Letter to the Hebrews*, trans. Leo Arnold, Series Rhetorica Semitica (Miami: Convivium, 2011), 283–84.

13. Lev 6:13 in most English editions.

14. The Holy Spirit is also associated with fire in Matt 3:11, Luke 3:16, and Acts 2:3–4.

15. Vanhoye, *A Different Priest*, 284–85.

16. See Rom 15:16, 1 Cor 6:11, and 1 Pet 1:2 for other NT references to the sanctifying role of the Holy Spirit.

17. Athanasius, Letter 59, *To Epictetus*.

for those who are called. It is the Spirit who transforms Jesus's passion from a mere execution into an infinitely efficacious saving sacrifice.

Pope John Paul II, in his encyclical on the Holy Spirit, reflected on this mystery:

> The Old Testament on several occasions speaks of "fire from heaven" which burnt the oblations presented by men (cf. Lev 9:24; 1 Kgs 18:38; 2 Chr 7:1). By analogy one can say that the Holy Spirit is the *"fire from heaven" which works in the depth of the mystery of the Cross*. . . . The Holy Spirit as Love and Gift *comes down, in a certain sense, into the very heart of the sacrifice* which is offered on the Cross. Referring here to the biblical tradition, we can say: *He consumes this sacrifice with the fire of the love* which unites the Son with the Father in the Trinitarian communion. And since the sacrifice of the Cross is an act proper to Christ, also in this sacrifice he *"receives" the Holy Spirit.* He receives the Holy Spirit in such a way that afterwards – and he alone with God the Father – can *"give him" to the Apostles, to the Church, to humanity.* He alone "sends" the Spirit from the Father. (cf. John 15:26)[18]

Hebrews makes clear that Christ's sacrifice does not merely accomplish the one-time negative result of cleansing human beings of the defilement of sin. Rather, its ultimate purpose is to establish the "new covenant" (9:15) that enables believers to enter into God's presence and "worship the living God" (9:14) – that is, to share in Christ's own communion of love with the Father. Even more, it qualifies them to live a priestly life (12:28), in which they offer a continuous "sacrifice of praise" and present all their good works and sufferings as "sacrifices pleasing to God" (13:15–16). Christ thus continues in office as the High Priest who presides over the unceasing liturgy in the true, heavenly sanctuary, in which all his brethren participate.

The remaining six references to the Spirit in Hebrews enable us to sketch how the "eternal Spirit" who empowered Christ in his once-for-all sacrifice on the cross relates to his ongoing priestly mediation. They can be broadly divided into two categories: the Spirit as God's active power, giving grace to his people (2:3–4; 6:4–6; 10:28–29), and the Spirit as the one who speaks through Scripture (3:7–8; 9:8–9; 10:14–17).[19] Significantly, all but two of these (9:8–9;

---

18. John Paul II, *Dominum et vivificantem* [*Lord and Giver of Life*], encyclical letter, Vatican website, May 18, 1986, https://www.vatican.va/content/john-paul-ii/en/encyclicals/documents/hf_jp-ii_enc_1805 1986_dominum-et-vivificantem.html. Italics in the original.

19. Lindars, *Theology of the Letter to the Hebrews*, 56–58.

10:14–17) belong to the "warning passages" in Hebrews (2:1–4; 3:7–4:13; 5:11–6:12; 10:19–39; 12:14–29). I will consider each in turn.

THE SPIRIT AS GOD'S ACTIVE POWER

THE SPIRIT AS GOD'S WITNESS TO SALVATION (HEBREWS 2:3–4)

In the letter's first warning passage (2:1–4), the writer solemnly declares the credentials of the gospel that his audience has come to believe.

> . . . how shall we escape if we neglect so great a salvation? It was declared at first by the Lord, and it was confirmed for us by those who heard him, while God also bore witness by signs and wonders and various miracles and by distributions of the Holy Spirit [*pneumatos hagiou merismois*] according to his will. (2:3–4)

The gospel was not only announced by human preachers, but it was authenticated by God himself through signs, wonders, miracles, and "distributions of the Holy Spirit" (cf. Mark 16:20). The latter phrase, reminiscent of Paul's description of charisms distributed (*diairoun*) by the Spirit (1 Cor 12:11), may refer to supernatural gifts of the Spirit or it may refer, as Allen contends, to the experienced outpouring of the Spirit himself, "repeated Pentecosts for the communities who have received the message of salvation."[20] Either way, the author takes for granted that his audience had, like the Pauline churches (cf. Rom 15:19; 1 Cor 1:5–7; 2:4; 12:7–11; Gal 3:5), directly experienced the Spirit in his supernatural manifestations, powerfully confirming that the gospel is true. As Levison points out, this passage is evocative of the Pentecost event in Acts. The "distributions of the Spirit" recall the "tongues as of fire, distributed [*diamerizomenoi*] and resting on each one of them" (Acts 2:3). The trio of signs, wonders, and miracles is the same trio used (in different order) in Peter's Pentecost speech in reference to Jesus (Acts 2:22). In both cases, the Spirit's gifts testify to a "salvation" (Acts 2:21; 4:12) that is "great" (cf. Acts 2:11). Since the outpouring of the Spirit, as depicted in Acts, was not a one-time event but something continually renewed in the church (Acts 4:30–31; 8:6–17; 10:44–46; 19:6), there are likewise no grounds for assuming that Hebrews is referring only to a past experience when the community first heard the gospel. Rather, it is their *continued* experience of the Spirit's manifestations that ought to convince believers of the greatness of the salvation won by Christ, and the folly of abandoning it (2:1–2).

---

20. Allen, "Forgotten Spirit," 56.

Signs, wonders, and miracles done in the power of the Holy Spirit (cf. Matt 12:28; Luke 4:18; Acts 10:38) were Jesus's own messianic credentials, revealing him to be "the one who is to come" (Luke 7:20–23; Acts 2:22). That the Spirit of God could manifest such power in and through the believers addressed in Hebrews demonstrates that the same Spirit who anointed Jesus is now at work in them. Jesus the High Priest presides over a community of believers who are not only passive recipients of his redemption but "share in" (cf. 3:14) his Spirit-empowered, risen, divine life.

PARTAKERS OF THE HOLY SPIRIT (HEBREWS 6:4–6)

The next reference to the Spirit comes in a warning that catalogs the privileges of the Christian life, in chiastic form.

> For it is impossible to restore again to repentance those
>> who have once been enlightened,
>>> who have tasted the heavenly gift,
>>>> and have become partakers [*metochous*] of the Holy Spirit,
>>> and have tasted the good word of God
>> and the powers [*dynameis*] of the age to come,
> if they fall away, since they crucify the Son of God on their own account
> and hold him up to contempt. (6:4–6)

This description is remarkable for its experiential emphasis: Christian faith is not merely a set of doctrines but a vivid experience of new things. The list of five elements is structured so as to highlight the Holy Spirit at the centre.[21] The readers have become "partakers [*metochoi*] of the Holy Spirit," just as Hebrews said earlier that they are "partakers [*metochoi*] of Christ" (3:14). Through the Holy Spirit they have been "enlightened" – that is, their minds have been illumined by faith to understand the mystery of salvation in Christ.[22] They have "tasted" the inexpressibly good gifts of God and the powers of "the age to come," the eschaton.[23] These gifts "on the one hand proclaim that the messianic age has begun (Acts 2:11ff) and on the other give a real foretaste, an actual beginning of the age to come (Matt 12:32)."[24] Here, too, there are unmistakable allusions to

---

21. Motyer, "The Spirit in Hebrews," 220.

22. Cf. similar "enlightenment" language in 2 Cor 4:6, Eph 5:14, and 1 Pet 2:9.

23. The experiential language of "tasting the heavenly gift" may allude to the Eucharist and, further back, to the manna in the desert (Exod 16; cf. Ps 34:9; 1 Pet 2:3); "tasting the good word of God" alludes to Ps 19:10–11.

24. George Montague, *The Holy Spirit: Growth of a Biblical Tradition* (1976; repr., Eugene, OR: Wipf & Stock, 2006), 320.

the Pentecost event, where the infant church tasted the "new wine" of divine life (Acts 2:13) and experienced the signs and wonders that signal "the last days" (cf. Acts 2:17–19).[25] The word for "powers" (*dynameis*) in Hebrews 6:5 (elsewhere often translated "miracles") probably refers both to power for sanctification (cf. 10:14; 12:10, 14; 13:12) and to the healings, exorcisms, and other mighty deeds that are visible evidence of the Spirit's activity in Christians. As in 2:4, the writer is describing the new life into which Christ's sacrifice has introduced believers as one of perceptibly experiencing his own divine life through the Spirit, as a foretaste of the glory to come.

> The author of Hebrews, then, might be said to view the Christian and the Christian community as living already now penetrated to the heart by a shaft of light from heaven, a light that is sweetness and joy as much as it is power. So permanent is this gift, so keen its foretaste of glory and so assured is it by the Spirit even amid persecution and temptation, that it would be unthinkable to turn from "so great a salvation" (2:3) and from such a "spirit of grace" (10:29).[26]

THE SPIRIT OF GRACE (HEBREWS 10:28–29)

Hebrews again invokes the Spirit in another stern warning against apostasy, using a classic lesser-to-greater argument:

> One who has violated the law of Moses dies without pity at the testimony of two or three witnesses. How much worse punishment do you think will be deserved by one who has trampled on the Son of God, and profaned the blood of the covenant by which he was sanctified, and outraged the Spirit of grace? (10:28–29)

"The Spirit of grace" (*to pneuma tēs charitos*) is a NT *hapax legomenon*, which elsewhere appears only in Zechariah 12:10:

> I will pour out on the house of David and the inhabitants of Jerusalem a spirit of grace (LXX: *pneuma charitos*) and supplication, so that, when they look on me, on him whom they have pierced, they shall mourn for him, as one mourns for an only son, and weep bitterly over him, as one weeps over a firstborn.

---

25. Levison, "A Theology of the Spirit," 103–104, lists four allusions to Pentecost: the "heavenly" gift (Heb 6:4), alluding to the wind "from heaven" (Acts 2:2); the call to repentance (Heb 6:4; Acts 2:38); the Spirit as "gift" (Heb 6:4; Acts 2:38); and the "powers" or "miracles" of the age to come (Heb 6:5; Acts 2:17, 19).

26. Montague, *Holy Spirit*, 320.

In Zechariah, the "spirit of grace" signifies a divine gift of compunction by which God's people become acutely aware of their own sinfulness and respond with heartfelt contrition. For the early church, this passage could not be seen as anything other than a prophecy of Christ, the true "firstborn" and "only son" who was "pierced" on the cross. The Holy Spirit, then, is the "spirit of grace" who unveils the truth of Christ's atoning passion in the heart of the believer and arouses consequent repentance and conversion. That the writer to the Hebrews can speak of the Spirit as having been "outraged" or "insulted" (*enubrizō*) is evidence that he recognises the Spirit's personhood, though without the developed Trinitarian theology of a later era.[27] The term "grace" (*charis*), close in meaning to "gift" (*dorea*) in Heb 6:4, underscores God's magnanimity in bestowing his heavenly treasures through the Spirit. To turn away from Christ after receiving such gifts is to "outrage" the Spirit of grace. It is "to refuse the Holy Spirit's inner summons to conversion, willfully rejecting the mercy and grace that are available from 'the throne of grace' (4:16)."[28]

In all three of these passages, Hebrews draws an inseparable connection between the Holy Spirit and Christ's redemption. As High Priest, Christ is mediator of the salvation that *consists in* partaking of the Spirit and his heavenly gifts. Those who "draw near to God through him" (7:25) perceptibly experience the divine life and power in which they have come to share. The negative corollary underscored by Hebrews is that those who apostatise after partaking of the Holy Spirit and his gifts "crucify the Son of God on their own account" (6:6), which is at the same time to affront "the very Spirit whose evidential gracious gifting is the hallmark of new covenant inauguration."[29] But those who "hold fast the confession of our hope without wavering" (10:23) will receive "a great reward" (10:35).

THE SPIRIT AS SPEAKING THROUGH SCRIPTURE

In three places Hebrews refers to the Holy Spirit as speaking through Scripture (3:7–8; 9:8–9; 10:14–17).[30] The writer takes for granted the early Christian

---

27. Cf. Isa 63:10, where God's "holy Spirit" is grieved by the rebellion of the exodus generation.

28. Mary Healy, *Hebrews*, CCSS (Grand Rapids: Baker Academic, 2016), 219.

29. Allen, "Forgotten Spirit," 58.

30. In 20 of the 35 direct biblical quotations in Hebrews, God is the grammatical subject in the context. Four quotations are attributed to the Son (2:12, 13a, 13b; 10:5–7), and five to the Holy Spirit (3:7b–11; presumably 4:3, 5, 7; 10:16–17). See William L. Lane, *Hebrews 1–8*, WBC 49A (Dallas: Word, 1991), cxvii. Significantly, in those biblical texts that Hebrews attributes to the Spirit, God is the speaker; in those it attributes to Christ, a human interlocutor (the psalmist or the prophet) is the speaker.

conviction that the Holy Spirit is the inspirer of the sacred writings.[31] As Motyer and Levison note, however, scholarship has given insufficient attention to the significance of the present tense in these three instances – the Spirit *says*, the Spirit *shows*, the Spirit *bears witness* – and the seamless movement from biblical citation to present-day application.[32] The Spirit is not only the divine author who inspired the biblical author to write a text in the remote past, but the divine interpreter who makes the Scriptures a "living and active" word by which God addresses his people in the present (cf. 4:12). "When the Spirit speaks the reader hears the divine *viva vox* that confronts head on in the here and now."[33] In each of these passages (and, by extension, in the other biblical texts that are actualised in Hebrews), the Holy Spirit reveals to believers how Scripture is fulfilled in Christ and in their present life in him.

THE HOLY SPIRIT SAYS (HEBREWS 3:7–8)

In Hebrews 3:7–8 the Spirit speaks the words of Psalm 95 (Ps 94 LXX):

> Therefore, as the Holy Spirit says, "Today, if you hear his voice, do not harden your hearts as in the rebellion, on the day of testing in the wilderness...." (Heb 3:7–8; cf. 4:7)

The quotation moves seamlessly into a lengthy midrash on the psalm (3:7–4:16). Three times the author quotes the same line, "Today, if you hear his voice, do not harden your hearts," insisting that the Holy Spirit is speaking through the psalm *today*, exhorting the Christian community to hold fast their faith in Christ (3:14). The "voice" that believers are to "hear" is that of God speaking through the Holy Spirit, who makes the words of the psalm a living reality in the present generation by urging believers to respond to the grace of Christ with steadfast faith. As Motyer points out, the present tense suggests a "charismatic" use of the biblical text: "The Holy Spirit has 'given' this text and this reading of it to the author, so that he can deliver it to the 'Hebrews' as a *new* word from God – a word made present by new insight and application."[34] But the Holy Spirit's speaking through the psalm is not merely a contemporary application or midrash on the text. Rather, it is a bringing to light of what is already latent in the biblical word. It shows that the psalm's ultimate reference point is not the

---

31. Cf. Mark 12:36; Acts 1:16; 2 Tim 3:16; 2 Pet 1:21.

32. Levison, "A Theology of the Spirit," 96–100; cf. Motyer, "The Spirit in Hebrews," 222–26. Both are drawing from Emmrich, *Pneumatological Concepts*.

33. Emmrich, *Pneumatological Concepts*, 34.

34. Motyer, "The Spirit in Hebrews," 223.

rebellion of ancient Israel at Massah and Meribah (Exod 17) or at Kadesh (Num 14), but the present-day Christian community who face the same crisis of faith as they stand on the threshold of their heavenly inheritance. The Holy Spirit unveils the present, eschatological realities that the ancient types foreshadowed.

THE HOLY SPIRIT DISCLOSES (HEBREWS 9:8–9)

The Spirit's speech in Hebrews 9:8–9a involves a more original and daring interpretation of Scripture. After recalling the floor plan of the wilderness tabernacle with its first and second "tent," i.e., the Holy Place and the Holy of Holies, the author writes,

> By this the Holy Spirit shows [*dēlountos*] that the way into the sanctuary is not yet manifested as long as the first tent is still standing, which is symbolic for the present age. (Heb 9:8–9a)

Here the Holy Spirit is again revealing hidden truths about God's plan that could not have been known before Christ.[35] Motyer, followed by Levison, claims that "the interpretation is so radical that it amounts virtually to a *reversal* of the original meaning": whereas in the OT the tabernacle, or tent of meeting, was a place of meeting between God and his people, Hebrews views it as a barrier between God and his people.[36] But this is to misunderstand the author's claim. He is emphasising the inaccessibility of the Holy of Holies, signaled by the restrictions noted in 9:7: "into the second *only* the high priest goes, and he *but once* a year" (emphasis added). The Mosaic legislation already emphasised the unapproachability of God's dwelling by its strict prohibitions: no lay Israelite may draw near to the tabernacle, on pain of death; only Levites may enter the courtyard surrounding it; only priests may enter the Holy Place; and only the high priest may enter the Holy of Holies, and he but once a year. "Hebrews draws on the Jewish tradition that the divisions in the tabernacle or temple mirror the division between earth and heaven, the inaccessibility of the holy of holies representing the separateness from earth of God's holy presence in heaven."[37] As Hebrews has shown, the whole system ultimately failed to bring about the true intimacy with God in his heavenly dwelling that was its ultimate goal.

---

35. The verb *dēloō* is often rendered here simply as "indicates" or "shows," but it can have the stronger meaning "disclose, reveal, manifest, exhibit."

36. Motyer, "The Spirit in Hebrews," 226; Levison, "A Theology of the Spirit," 99.

37. Andrew Lincoln, "Hebrews and Biblical Theology," in *Out of Egypt: Biblical Theology and Biblical Interpretation*, SAH Series 5, ed. Craig G. Bartholomew, Mary Healy, Karl Möller, and Robin Parry (Grand Rapids: Zondervan, 2004), 325.

Now the Holy Spirit reveals that this inaccessibility was a temporary phase, to endure only as long as "the first tent is still standing," i.e., while the old covenant dispensation was still in place.[38] The Spirit reveals that the earthly tabernacle, with its zones of restricted access, was only a sign pointing to God's true sanctuary in heaven, which was formerly inaccessible to God's people but now has been opened to all who are purified in the blood of Christ (9:14).

Thus, for Hebrews the Spirit is not playing fast and loose with Scripture, arbitrarily reversing the meaning, but rather is revealing the christological depths hidden within the institutions and rites of the old covenant. Nor can the Spirit properly be said to make "use" of Scripture, which suggests an instrumentalizing of biblical texts in the service of a different agenda. Rather, for Hebrews, the Spirit's work is a matter of *illuminating* Scripture by revealing the "good things that have come" (9:11), to which Scripture points in a hidden way.[39] This is no mere intellectual exercise. Hebrews interweaves the tabernacle symbolism with affirmations of the saving work that Christ the High Priest does for believers *now*: he "perfects the conscience of the worshiper" (9:9), "secures an eternal redemption" (9:12), and "purifies your conscience from dead works" (9:14). The Holy Spirit, by unveiling the meaning of Scripture, enables the believer both to *understand* and to *participate in* these "good things that have come" (9:11).

THE HOLY SPIRIT TESTIFIES (HEBREWS 10:14–17)

Finally, the Spirit is heard again in a reprise of a quotation from Jeremiah concerning the "new covenant" (quoted in full in Hebrews 8, and repeated in part in Hebrews 10):

> For by a single offering he has perfected for all time those who are being sanctified. And the Holy Spirit also testifies to us; for after saying, "This is the covenant that I will make with them after those days," the Lord says, "I will put my laws on their hearts, and write them on their minds," and "I will remember their sins and their misdeeds no more." (10:14–17)[40]

---

38. As Vanhoye observes (*A Different Priest*, 255), for Hebrews "the age to come" was inaugurated by Christ's resurrection and Christians already participate in it through faith and baptism (cf. 6:5), even while the present defective age endures. Hebrews recognises the former dispensation as nearing its end (8:13; 9:26).

39. As Lincoln notes ("Hebrews and Biblical Theology," 318), "what God has done in Christ is the decisive and determinative speech-act. According to Hebrews, this means . . . that it should be impossible to drift back to an earlier stage of revelation or to hold a view of God's inspired oracles in Scripture in which these simply sit alongside and are left undisturbed by the new word God has spoken in the Son."

40. I have translated this sentence in accord with what some commentators hold is the solution to its grammatical problem. The clause that begins "for after saying. . ." appears at first to be a subordinate clause that is missing a main verb. Translators usually supply a phrase like "then he adds" at 10:17a. However, "says

What precisely does the Spirit testify to? Not the Jeremiah text itself, but the statement that immediately precedes it, in verse 14: "For by a single offering [Christ] has perfected for all time those who are sanctified." The Holy Spirit bears witness to believers regarding the all-sufficiency of Christ's sacrifice for their sanctification, and he does so precisely by *giving* them what Jeremiah prophesied: "the real, inner experience of the 'law in the heart' accompanied by a deep consciousness of the forgiveness of sins."[41] That which Christ the High Priest has accomplished for their salvation becomes a concrete, existential experience through the witness of the Spirit. Thus, the Holy Spirit does not merely reveal the new covenant established by Christ; he enacts it in the heart and mind of the believer, empowering the believer to live as Christ lived – in perfect obedience to the Father.

> The Spirit of Christ not only brings us face to face with evangelical truth, he also applies the saving work of Christ to our hearts and lives. Through the blessing of the Holy Spirit which Christ has poured out from heaven we are enabled to experience the regenerating power of God. The benefits of the Savior's atoning death are made a vital and transforming reality.[42]

CONCLUSION

Hebrews's seven references to the Holy Spirit, taken together, present a coherent picture of the believing community's present experience of the Spirit, who simultaneously reveals and imparts to them "the good things that have come" – that is, the realities of the new covenant that Christ has inaugurated by his sacrificial death. The same Spirit who inflamed Christ with the burning divine love that made his self-offering on the cross an efficacious sacrifice (9:13–14) is now at work in the believers. The Spirit bestows supernatural charisms that bear witness to the greatness of salvation (2:3–4); the Spirit enables believers to "taste" the gifts and powers of the age to come (6:4–6); the Spirit arouses an awareness of sin and heartfelt repentance (10:28–29); and the Spirit speaks, discloses, and testifies to the fulfillment of the old covenant types in Christ and the present life of the Christian community (3:7–8; 9:8–9; 10:14–17). Moreover, as Christ was "made perfect" through his obedient suffering (2:10; 5:9; 7:28),

---

the Lord" (*legei kyrios*) in the middle of the quotation (10:16b) can be understood as the main verb, especially considering that the letter was designed for oral proclamation. See Motyer, "The Spirit in Hebrews," 224.

41. Motyer, "The Spirit in Hebrews," 225.
42. Hughes, *Hebrews*, 351.

so those called by him are also "made perfect" (10:14) and qualified as priests of the new covenant who enter into the true Holy of Holies.[43] This implies that the "eternal Spirit" who inspired Jesus's self-offering on the cross is active in believers as well. As Jesus offered the Father his once-for-all sacrifice through the Spirit, who made it holy and acceptable to God, so believers today offer the Father pleasing worship in Christ through the Spirit. Thus the author exhorts, "let us offer to God acceptable worship, with reverence and awe" (Heb 12:28–29), and then details in what that worship consists: praise and intercession (13:15, 18) along with acts of generosity and loving service to others (13:16). In short, by the action of the Holy Spirit the whole life of Christians is now qualified to be a priestly life, in which all one's words and deeds can be offered in union with Christ as "a sacrifice of praise" that is pleasing to God.

SELECT BIBLIOGRAPHY

Allen, David M. "'The Forgotten Spirit': A Pentecostal Reading of the Letter to the Hebrews?" *Journal of Pentecostal Theology* 18 (2009): 51–66.

Attridge, Harold W. *The Epistle to the Hebrews: A Commentary on the Epistle to the Hebrews*. Hermeneia. Philadelphia: Fortress, 1989.

Bruce, F. F. *The Epistle to the Hebrews*. Rev. ed. NICNT. Grand Rapids: Eerdmans, 2012.

Ellingworth, Paul. *The Epistle to the Hebrews: A Commentary on the Greek Text*. NIGTC. Grand Rapids: Eerdmans, 1993.

Emmrich, Martin. *Pneumatological Concepts in the Epistle to the Hebrews: Amtscharisma, Prophet & Guide of the Eschatological Exodus*. Lanham, MD: University Press of America, 2003.

Fletcher-Louis, Crispin H. T. "Jesus as the High Priestly Messiah" (Parts 1 and 2), *JSHJ* 4, no. 2 (2006): 155–75 and *JSHJ* 5, no. 1 (2007): 57–79.

Healy, Mary. "Behind, in Front of . . . or Through the Text? The Christological Analogy and the Lost Realm of Biblical Truth." In *'Behind' the Text: History and Biblical Interpretation*, edited by Craig Bartholomew, C. Stephen Evans, Mary Healy, and Murray Rae, 181–95. SAH Series 4. Carlisle, UK: Paternoster; Grand Rapids: Zondervan, 2003.

———. *Hebrews*. CCSS. Grand Rapids: Baker Academic, 2016.

---

43. As many commentators point out, Hebrews's use of "make perfect" (*teleioō*) alludes to the use of the same verb in the Septuagint to translate the biblical expression meaning to "ordain" a priest (*teleioō tas cheiras*, i.e., "fill the hands," LXX Exod 29:9; Lev 8:33; Num 3:3; etc.).

Hughes, Philip Edgcumbe. *A Commentary on the Epistle to the Hebrews*. Grand Rapids: Eerdmans, 1977.

John Paul II. *Dominum et vivificantem* [*Lord and Giver of Life*], encyclical letter, Vatican website, May 18, 1986, https://www.vatican.va/content/john-paul-ii/en/encyclicals/documents/hf_jp-ii_enc_18051986_dominum-et-vivificantem.html.

Johnson, Luke Timothy. *Hebrews: A Commentary*. NTL. Louisville, KY: Westminster John Knox Press, 2006.

Lane, William L. *Hebrews 1–8*. WBC. Dallas: Word Books, 1991.

Levison, Jack. "A Theology of the Spirit in the Letter to the Hebrews." *CBQ* 78 (2016): 90–110.

Lincoln, Andrew. "Hebrews and Biblical Theology." In *Out of Egypt: Biblical Theology and Biblical Interpretation*, edited by Craig Bartholomew, Mary Healy, Karl Möller, and Robin Parry, 313–38. SAH Series 5. Grand Rapids: Zondervan, 2004.

Lindars, Barnabas. *The Theology of the Letter to the Hebrews*. NTT. Cambridge: CUP, 1991.

Montague, George. *The Holy Spirit: Growth of a Biblical Tradition*. Reprint, Eugene, OR: Wipf & Stock, 1976.

Motyer, Steve. "The Spirit in Hebrews: No Longer Forgotten?" In *The Spirit and Christ in the New Testament and Christian Theology: Essays in Honor of Max Turner*, edited by I. Howard Marshall, Volker Rabens, and Cornelis Bennema, 212–28. Grand Rapids: Eerdmans, 2012.

O'Collins, Gerald, SJ, and Michael Keenan Jones. *Jesus Our Priest: A Christian Approach to the Priesthood of Christ*. Oxford: OUP, 2010.

Pitre, Brant. "Jesus, the New Temple, and the New Priesthood." *Letter & Spirit* 4 (2008): 47–83.

Swete, H. B. *The Holy Spirit in the New Testament*. 1909. Reprint, Eugene, OR: Wipf & Stock, 1998.

Torrance, Alan J. "Reclaiming the Continuing Priesthood of Christ." In *Christology, Ancient and Modern: Explorations in Constructive Dogmatics*, edited by Oliver D. Crisp and Fred Sanders, 184–204. Grand Rapids: Zondervan, 2013.

Vanhoye, Albert. *A Different Priest: The Letter to the Hebrews*. Translated by Leo Arnold. Series Rhetorica Semitica. Miami: Convivium, 2011.

———. *Old Testament Priests and the New Priest*. Translated by J. Bernard Orchard. Petersham, MA: St Bede's, 1986.

CHAPTER 13

New Covenant, High Priesthood, and Sacrifice[1]

Is the Eucharist in Hebrews?

Scott W. Hahn

INTRODUCTION

Over a half century ago, F. F. Bruce pronounced the letter to the Hebrews to be "among the more difficult books of the New Testament." In search of a unifying principle he settled on what he called "inwardness of true religion." According to Bruce, true religion, as presented in Hebrews, is not only nonliturgical but anti-liturgical: "True religion or the worship of God is not tied to externalities of any kind."[2] In 1975, R. Williamson took up Bruce's assertion and made of it an argument.[3] In the end, Williamson also rejected any eucharistic allusions

---

1. All Scripture quotations, unless otherwise indicated, are from the RSV.

2. F. F. Bruce, *The Epistle to the Hebrews*, rev. ed. (Grand Rapids: Eerdmans, 1990), xi–xii. Also see R. Williamson, "The Eucharist and the Epistle to the Hebrews," *NTS* 21 (1975): 300–12: "To the Christian reader who comes to such a passage as this [Heb. 10:19–20] from within a strong tradition of eucharistic faith and practice such an association of words and ideas is almost irrepressible. But there seems to be no good ground for thinking that such an association was present in the mind of the author of Hebrews" (307). For Williamson, Hebrews has "rendered obsolete every . . . material means of communion between God and the worshipper" (310); all such "outward ordinances" have come to an end, for the gospel "can never be anticipated materially in a sacramental cultus" (312).

3. Williamson, "The Eucharist and the Epistle to the Hebrews": "To the Christian reader who comes to such a passage as this [Heb. 10:19–20] from within a strong tradition of eucharistic faith and practice such

whatsoever in Hebrews – and, like Bruce, concluded that Hebrews has "rendered obsolete every . . . material means of communion between God and the worshipper." All "outward ordinances" have come to an end, since the gospel of the new covenant "can never be anticipated materially in a sacramental cultus."[4] Their strongest support is that there is no explicit mention in Hebrews of the eucharistic rite.

LITURGICAL CONTEXT, EUCHARISTIC HOMILY

I would propose, however, that the Eucharist is implicit throughout the text. As Stephen Fahrig argues in a recent dissertation, "The Context of the Text," Hebrews is best read as a "Eucharistic Homily," originally proclaimed to an assembly of new covenant believers.[5] This is a likely *Sitz im Leben* for Hebrews, which provides the context that would make the text intelligible to its earliest readers. It is also the context that makes the text more comprehensible for readers today. I wish to show how the Eucharist is an important – though implicit – theme in Hebrews.

In his monumental work *The New Testament and the People of God*, N. T. Wright notes how widespread and central was the Eucharist (and baptism) in the early church:

> It is clear, remarkably, that these two basic forms of Christian praxis were equally taken for granted as early as the 50s of the first century. Paul can write of baptism as a given, from which theological conclusions can be drawn (Romans 6.3–11). He can describe, or allude to, the Eucharist in similar fashion (1 Corinthians 10.15–22), taking it (as read) that the Corinthian church regularly meets to partake of the Lord's Meal together, and moving on to argue on this basis about what is and is not appropriate . . .[6]

Or, in the language of Hebrews, they undergo the "enlightenment" of Christian ablutions and they "taste the heavenly gift" (6:4).

These, Wright goes on to say, "were not strange actions which some

---

an association of words and ideas is almost irrepressible. But there seems to be no good ground for thinking that such an association was present in the mind of the author of Hebrews" (307).

4. Williamson, "The Eucharist and the Epistle to the Hebrews," 310, 312.

5. S. Fahrig, "The Context of the Text: Reading Hebrews as a Eucharistic Homily" (unpublished Ph.D. Dissertation, Boston College, 2014). Also see J. Swetnam, *Hebrews: An Interpretation* (Rome: Gregorian Biblical Press, 2016).

6. N. T. Wright, *The New Testament and the People of God* (Minneapolis: Fortress, 1992), 362.

Christians might on odd occasions perform, but ritual acts which were taken for granted, part of that praxis which constituted the early Christian worldview."[7] The worldview Wright evokes is the only worldview that makes Hebrews intelligible. The text presents a consistent and comprehensive vision of a new and eternal covenant *that is essentially cultic.* Yet Wright observes a rather glaring omission in this cultic worldview: "Among the striking features of early Christian praxis must be reckoned one thing that early Christians did *not* do. Unlike every other religion known in the world up to that point, the Christians offered no animal sacrifices."[8] Such a novel cultic worldview is precisely what one discovers with a eucharistic reading of the new covenant in Hebrews, then and now.

Yet the word "Eucharist" does not appear in Hebrews, nor do analogous terms such as "breaking of the bread." But there is a preponderance of imagery normally associated with early Christian liturgy. First, the assembly is made up of those who have "been enlightened . . . and *tasted the heavenly gift*" (6:4). Second, we read that the congregation is "sanctified through the offering of the body of Jesus Christ once for all" (10:10). Third, the assembly has come to experience the "blood that speaks more graciously than the blood of Abel" (12:24). Fourth, the author confidently asserts that the Christian assembly has "an altar from which those who serve the tent have no right to eat" (13:10). Furthermore, the assembly's festival is shared not only among Christians on earth, but also with "innumerable angels in festal gathering" (12:22) and the "spirits of just men made perfect" (12:23) . . . "the great . . . cloud of witnesses" in heaven (12:1). The text describes realised eschatology in a cultic setting – and for primitive Christianity, this meant the Eucharist. Hebrews also relies on the eucharistic typology that would become commonplace in early Christian commentaries, art, and liturgical poetry. The author invokes Abel's offering, Melchizedek's priestly blessing, and God's oath of blessing to Abraham after he offered Isaac. These factors point to the Eucharist as an interpretive key for reading the homily known as Hebrews.

PROTO-EUCHARISTIC ELEMENTS IN HEBREWS: NEW COVENANT, BODY, BLOOD

Nevertheless, Bruce and Williamson could argue that the eucharistic meaning of each of these details is contestable. What remains uncontested, however, is the overarching *theme* of the book of Hebrews. What is invoked most frequently

---

7. Wright, *The New Testament and the People of God*, 363.
8. Wright, *The New Testament and the People of God*, 363.

and forcefully in the text is the *covenant* – and, specifically, the *new covenant*. Yet this, in itself, may be evidence supporting a eucharistic reading of Hebrews. The author presents Jesus as the mediator of a new covenant, a "better covenant" established by the ritual sprinkling of blood just like the former covenant. As High Priest of *this* covenant, Jesus offers his *body and blood* as a once-for-all sacrifice on our behalf, a perpetual self-offering. Its effect is nothing less than "eternal salvation" (5:9) and "eternal redemption" (9:12) by "the blood of the eternal covenant" (13:20).

What I propose is that the Eucharist may be a prominent yet *implicit* theme of Hebrews, despite the term's absence. Contrariwise, explicit references to the *Eucharist* are only found in *later* first-century sources (Didache, Ignatius); whereas in the first generation, NT authors prefer to denote (what was later called) the Eucharist in terms drawn from the words that are attributed to Jesus in the earliest gospel traditions: *the new covenant* (Luke 22:20; 1 Cor 11:25) or the *blood of the covenant* (Matt 26:28; Mark 14:24). This may prove to be relevant to our thesis, especially since these key words/phrases are at the heart of the argument of Hebrews – where they occur in a strikingly disproportionate and probative manner. To wit, just over half of the NT occurrences of the word for "covenant" (*diatheke*) are found in Hebrews (17/33). Likewise, just over half of the NT references to *new covenant* are found in Hebrews (4/7: 8:8, 13; 9:15; 12:24).[9]

Notably, the term *new covenant* appears in the collection of books Christians later came to know as the old covenant, but it occurs only once: "Behold, the days are coming, says the LORD, when I will make a *new covenant* with the house of Israel and the house of Judah" (Jer 31:31, emphasis added). Jeremiah speaks of a *berith chadasha*, which is rendered in the Septuagint as *diathēkē kainē* – a new covenant.

The notion of a *new covenant* is introduced by the author of Hebrews *for the first time* in Heb 8:8–12, with an extensive quotation from this oracle (Jer 31:31–34), which also happens to be the single longest OT quotation anywhere in the NT. Scholars agree that Jer 31:31 is certainly the primary source for all the other (half-dozen) occurrences of the phrase in the NT. Scholars also agree the

---

9. For the seven occurrences of *new covenant, kainē diathēkē* occurs in Luke 22:20; 1 Cor 11:25; 2 Cor 3:6; and Heb 8:8, 13, 9:15, while a similar phrase, *diathēkē nea,* occurs in Heb 12:24, also rendered as "new covenant," where the risen Christ is a priestly mediator whose "sprinkled blood ... speaks more graciously than the blood of Abel." See Scott W. Hahn, *Consuming the Word: The Eucharist and the New Testament in the Early Church* (New York: Doubleday, 2013), 23: "Dense with sacrificial imagery, the line may well be a reference to the Church's Eucharistic liturgy, the 'assembly [*ekklesia*, church] of the first-born' who have gathered at 'Mount Zion' (a probable allusion to the traditional site of Jesus' Last Supper) 'in the city of the living God, the heavenly Jerusalem' with 'innumerable angels in festal gathering.'" For arguments demonstrating *diathēkē* as *covenant* (vs. *testament*) in Gal 3:15 and Heb 9:16, see Scott W. Hahn, *Kinship by Covenant*, Anchor Bible Reference Library (New Haven: Yale University Press, 2009), 256–64; 317–24.

new covenant is the centrepiece and principal theme of the entire epistle, along with Jesus's *high priesthood* – a notion not explicitly found anywhere else in the NT. Generally, Hebrews is also unique among NT writings in its focus on the cultic/liturgical aspects of the covenant, both old and new.

COVENANT, CULT, AND PRIESTLY MEDIATION: OLD AND NEW

In ancient Israel, the ratification of covenants and their renewal consisted essentially of a *liturgy*: ritual words and sacrificial actions done in God's presence. This liturgical dimension of covenant making appears frequently in the OT, where the priests mediate the covenant on God's behalf (Num 6:22–27). Reflecting on the OT traditions of "covenant," the author of Hebrews, while not forgetting the legal dimension, places the liturgical (or cultic) in the foreground. The mediation of both covenants is primarily priestly and cultic, the sacred realm of liturgy, which is precisely what remains in the foreground of the argument of Hebrews. In both the OT and the NT, the cultic mediation of the covenant is (high) priestly.

This focus explains the author's emphasis on the superiority of Christ's high priesthood, in general, and his new covenant sacrifice, in particular, both of which are primarily developed in Hebrews 8–9.[10] Here the author contrasts two covenant orders: the old (8:3–9:10) and the new (9:11–28). Both covenants have a cultus which includes a high priest (*archiereus* 8:1, 3; 9:7, 11, 25) or "celebrant" (*leitourgos*, 8:2, 8:6) who performs ministry (*latreias*, 8:5; 9:1, 6) in a tent sanctuary (*skēnēs*, 8:2, 5; 9:2–3, 6, 8, 11, 21), entering into a holy place (*hagia*, 8:2; 9:2–3, 12, 24) to offer (*prospherein*, 8:3; 9:7, 14, 28) the blood (*haima*, 9:7, 12, 14, 18–23, 25) of sacrifices (*thysias*, 8:3–4, 9:9, 23, 26) which effects purification (*hagiazein*, 9:13; *katharizō*, 9:14, 22–23) and redemption (*lytrōsis*, 9:12, 15) of worshippers (*laos*, 8:10, 9:7, 19; *latreuontoi*, 9:9, 14) who have transgressed cultic law (*nomos*, 8:4; 9:19).

As William Lane notes: "The essence of the two covenants is found in their cultic aspects; the total argument is developed in terms of cultus.... The interpreter must remain open to the internal logic of the argument from the cultus."[11] Similarly, Albert Vanhoye observes:

---

10. On the cultic background of Heb 9, see J. Swetnam, "A Suggested Interpretation of Hebrews 9,15–18," *CBQ* 27 (1965): 375; J. Behm, "Diatheke," *TDNT*, 2:131–32; and Albert Vanhoye, *Old Testament Priests and the New Priest* (Petersham, MA: St. Bede's, 1986), 176–77.

11. William L. Lane, *Hebrews 9–13*, WBC 47B (Dallas: Word, 1991), 235.

Our author rightly sees very close ties between cult and covenant. The value of a covenant depends directly on the act of worship which establishes it. A defective liturgy cannot bring about a valid covenant.... The reason for this is easily understood. The establishment of a covenant between two parties who are distant from each other can only be accomplished by an act of mediation and, when it is a question of mankind and God, the mediation has of necessity to be conducted through the cult.[12]

As the High Priest, Christ is the mediator of a new and better covenant (8:6; 9:15) founded on his more perfect sacrifice (10:14), which alone expiates transgressions committed under the law of the old covenant (9:15, 19, 26). Thus, Jesus alone provides believers with entrance and access to the true tabernacle and heavenly sanctuary (8:2; 10:19), the real Holy of Holies (6:19–20).

Outside of Hebrews the word "covenant" is, as I said, seldom referenced (just 16x in 26 books) – and "new covenant" even less (3x). In all of Jesus's sayings, we find just one instance when he uses the word (and phrase) to describe a specific liturgical act. In 1 Corinthians, Paul provides the earliest historical record of the event: "In the same way [Jesus] also [took] the cup, after supper, saying, 'This cup is the *new covenant* in my blood. Do this, as often as you drink it, in remembrance of me'" (1 Cor 11:25; cf. Luke 22:20, emphasis added). For Paul (and Luke), Jesus explicitly ratifies what he calls the *new covenant* by instituting (what others will later call) the *Eucharist*; he also commands the apostles to "do this in remembrance of me." Closely related, but slightly different, Matthew and Mark show Jesus using sacrificial language in their institution narratives: "This is my blood of the covenant, which is poured out for many for the forgiveness of sins" (Matt 26:28). With these cultic terms, Jesus initiated the sacrificial offering that he would consummate on Calvary and then, after his resurrection and ascension, offer continuously – as "a priest forever" (Heb 6:20; 7:3, 17, 21–24; 8:3).

FROM ROMAN EXECUTION TO NEW COVENANT SACRIFICE

Jesus's death was clearly an essential aspect of his once-for-all sacrifice, the singular unrepeatable sacrifice of the new covenant. All Christians in every age agree on this point. But it may be useful for us to ask: how did this consensus come about? What made Jesus's crucifixion a sacrifice? To those formed by millennia

---

12. Vanhoye, *Old Testament Priests and the New Priest*, 181–82.

of Christian tradition, the idea seems self-evident, but to a first-century Jew it would have seemed unthinkable. Sacrifice was permitted in only one place: the holy city of Jerusalem, inside the holy temple, upon the sacrificial altar. Yet Jesus was crucified outside the city walls, a good distance from the temple, with no altar in sight. To even the most careful observer, Jesus's suffering and death would have appeared to be a profane event, just another brutal Roman execution. Jesus's devout followers might have judged his death to be an act of martyrdom (like the deaths of the seven brothers recounted in 2 Maccabees 7), but not a sacrifice. As Vanhoye observes:

> It must be acknowledged that the person and activity of Jesus in no way corresponded to what would have been expected of a priest at that time . . . From the point of view of the Old Testament cult, the death of Jesus in no way appeared as a priestly offering; it was in fact the very opposite of a sacrifice. Indeed, sacrifices did not consist in the putting to death of a living person, still less in his sufferings, but in rites performed by the priest in the holy place. . . . Now Jesus' death had taken place outside the Holy City. It had not been accompanied by liturgical rites. It was viewed as a legal penalty, the execution of a man condemned to death.[13]

In other words, the sacrificial nature of Christ's death as a priestly offering could not have been recognised by Jewish witnesses at Golgotha – even by his devout followers – strictly on the basis of OT cultic norms and Jewish sacrificial rites in the first century. What other grounds, then, did the first Jewish Christians (like the author of Hebrews) have for reconceptualizing the death of Christ in terms of a covenant sacrifice?

Vanhoye suggests that the answer may only be found by a close and careful analysis of the early gospel traditions, particularly the eucharistic institution narratives:

> Another Gospel tradition . . . suggests a connection between Jesus' death and a sacrificial rite. It occurs in the account of the Last Supper, what has been transmitted both by St. Paul and by the three Synoptics. In themselves, Jesus' actions – rendering thanks to God for the bread and the wine, breaking the bread and passing the cup – do not constitute a ritual sacrifice. . . . Among the words spoken by Jesus, however, there is an expression that possesses an

---

13. Vanhoye, *Old Testament Priests and the New Priest*, 50; also see A. N. Chester, "The Final Sacrifice," in *Sacrifice and Redemption*, ed. S. Sykes (Cambridge: CUP, 1991), 57–72.

undeniably sacrificial connotation, for it unites the word "blood" with the word "covenant." These words have an obvious connection with the words pronounced by Moses at the sacrifice accomplished on Sinai as a way of sealing the covenant between the People of Israel and Yahweh . . .[14]

Interpreters find the likely source for the theological convergence of precisely those themes that the author of Hebrews uses to argue his case, especially the closely related notions of "blood" and "new covenant." Moreover, the synoptic traditions of the eucharistic institution narratives also seem to be the most likely primary source for the author's understanding of Christ's death as a priestly sacrifice.[15]

CULTIC FORM AND EUCHARISTIC ALLUSIONS

It turns out that this is really not such a bold hypothesis after all, as many scholars have recognised the formative influence of the eucharistic background in the argument of Hebrews, notwithstanding the lack of explicit references.[16] The various subtle allusions to the Eucharist throughout the epistle, especially in Hebrews 9,[17] are not plain or direct, but fit well with the author's allusive style,

---

14. Vanhoye, *Old Testament Priests and the New Priest*, 53–54. See A. Nairne, *The Epistle of Priesthood* (Edinburgh: T&T Clark, 1915), 18, who links "covenant" in 9:16–17 with the Last Supper where the new covenant was ratified by "a sacramental representation of death on the part of him who transacts the covenant."

15. See B. Pitre, *Jesus and the Last Supper* (Grand Rapids: Eerdmans, 2015), 117–20; 137–45; 417–21; J. Bergma, *Jesus and the Old Testament Roots of the Priesthood* (Steubenville, OH: Emmaus Road, 2021). Also J. Hughes, "Hebrews IX 15ff. and Galatians III 15ff.," *NovT* 21 (1976–77): 51: "What was the source of the author's concept of Christ's death as both consummating the old and ratifying the new covenant? . . . Those who heard the Lord would have told their hearers about . . . the Last Supper and the meaning and significance of Christ's death. . . . If it may be assumed that the recipients were Jews . . . then those who heard the Lord would surely have correlated . . . Jesus' *covenantal* interpretation of his forthcoming death (the words of the Last Supper) with that event itself."

16. E. Mascall, *Corpus Christi* (London: Longmans, 1955), 109, who notes that: "If from one point of view we are bound to say there is nothing about the Eucharist in the Epistle to the Hebrews, from another point of view we might almost say that the Epistle is about nothing else." J. Swetnam, "Christology and the Eucharist in the Epistle to the Hebrews," *Bib* 70 (1989): 74–95: "The hypothesis of the importance of the eucharist gives a coherence, relevance, and depth to the letter which is otherwise lacking" (75). J. Field, *The Apostolic Liturgy and the Epistle to the Hebrews* (London: Rivingtons, 1882), offers a 600-page analysis of "an unbroken thread of allusion" to the Eucharist "woven into the whole fabric of the apostle's argument" (9). Nairne, *Hebrews*, 359: "References [to the Eucharist] . . . are hardly ambiguous, and here too it would seem that this sacramental system of the Church was taken for granted."

17. The eucharistic background is particularly important in Hebrews 9, where we find one of the most significant and frequently-cited examples of eucharistic allusion (vv. 19–20): "For when every commandment of the law had been declared by Moses to all the people, he took the blood . . . saying, "*This is the blood of the covenant which God commanded you.*" The wording breaks from the LXX reading of Exod 24:8,

especially if – as some scholars argue – the author's style reflects a form of the *disciplina arcana*, the ancient Christian practice of avoiding explicit references to the Christian mysteries in public contexts.[18]

Indeed, it is noteworthy that, apart from the Synoptic institution narrative traditions (Matt 26; Mark 14; Luke 22), the only NT writer to explicitly refer to the eucharistic praxis of the church is Paul, and he does so only once as he addresses the serious abuses of the Eucharist in the Corinthian church (1 Cor 10:16–11:34). Indeed, what scholars generally recognise to be the central rite and constant fixture in the first generation of Christian worship is nowhere (else) treated explicitly in the NT.

Therefore, what made Jesus's death at Calvary a sacrifice was the Eucharist he established in the upper room – in explicitly sacrificial terms – precisely by ratifying the new covenant and instituting the Eucharist with his disciples. There he made an offering of his "body" and "blood." He declared it to be his "memorial," a term (Gk *anamnesis*; Heb *zikkaron*) associated with the temple's sacrificial liturgy.[19] And he performs his action in terms of both cultic sacrifice (Exod 24:3–11) and prophetic categories, that is, the *new covenant* of Jeremiah's oracle (Jer 31:31).[20]

If we think of the Last Supper as only a meal, then Calvary is simply an execution. But if, in fact, Jesus instituted the Eucharist as the sacrificial memorial of the new covenant, then we can see how the sacrifice that he initiated in the

---

but precisely matches the Synoptic tradition of Jesus's words in the cup-saying at the Last Supper (cf. Mark 14:24; Matt 26:28). See also J. Dunnill, *Covenant and Sacrifice in the Letter to the Hebrews* (Cambridge: CUP, 1993), 246–47, and J. Coppens, "The Church, the New Covenant of God with His People," in *The Birth of the Church: A Biblical Study* (Staten Island, NY: Alba House, 1968), 19: "[The] eucharistic setting is bound up so intimately with the notion of covenant that in Hebrews 9:20 the terms of the Old Covenant's conclusion (Ex. 24:8) are conveyed in words that seem to have been influenced by the eucharistic words of the Church."

18. See Field, *Apostolic Liturgy and Hebrews*, 8–9: "His allusions to [the Eucharist] are rarely evident upon the surface of his words.... It cannot be without design that they are thus veiled over. We must infer that the system of concealing the Eucharistic mystery from unbelievers was already practised in the Apostolic age.... He alludes to it in such a way that only the fully instructed Christian can recognise it." On first century Jewish-Christian cultic customs of the *disciplina arcana*, see J. Jeremias, *The Eucharistic Words of Jesus* (New York: Scribner's, 1966): "The whole environment of primitive Christianity knows the element of the esoteric.... Although it has been generally recognized that this is true of the Hellenistic world . . . we also find an arcane discipline in Palestine.... The newly discovered Essene texts have disposed of the last doubt concerning this" (125–26). "The intention is that non-Christians should not understand the references.... [for example] the conspicuous absence of any reference to the Eucharist in Hebrews" (134).

19. On *remembrance/memorial* as cultic-sacrificial terminology, see F. Chenderlin, *"Do This as My Memorial,"* Analecta Biblica (Rome: Pontifical Biblical Institute, 1982) and Pitre, *Jesus and the Last Supper*, 417–21.

20. Both strands of new exodus typology (cultic/prophetic) converge in the dual Eucharistic traditions; see Pitre, *Jesus and the Last Supper*, 93–120: "blood of the covenant" (Exod 24:8; cf. Matt 26:28, Mark 14:24) and "new covenant" (Jer 31:31; cf. Luke 22:20).

upper room was consummated at Calvary. At the same time, if what Jesus did in the upper room turns his crucifixion into a sacrifice, then we can see how, for the author of Hebrews, Jesus's resurrection and ascension are what transform that same sacrifice into a heavenly liturgy – and an earthly sacrament.[21]

EUCHARIST AS DIVINE ACTION OF THE SPIRIT

From now on, Jesus's body is not only glorified in heaven but also *communicable* on earth, which is exactly the *divine action* of the Holy Spirit (Heb 9:14).[22] For the author of Hebrews, what the OT "gifts and sacrifices," "the food and drink," could never do, that is, "perfect the conscience of the worshipper" (9:9–10), is what our High Priest now does – for us on earth – by means of the "gifts and sacrifices" he offers in heaven (8:3). Indeed, this is the new covenant "food and drink" we share in the Eucharist: "How much more shall the blood of Christ . . . through the eternal Spirit . . . purify your conscience . . . to serve the living God" (9:14). It should be noted, perhaps, that Jesus does this only for those whose consciences still need to be purified (us), not for "spirits of just men [already] made perfect" (12:23).

---

21. On the significance of the resurrection in Hebrews, see David M. Moffitt, *Atonement and the Logic of Resurrection in the Epistle to the Hebrews* (Leiden: Brill, 2011). On the ascension as the commencement of Jesus's royal enthronement and high priestly ministry, see W. Milligan, *The Ascension and Heavenly Priesthood of Our Lord* (London, Macmillan, 1901).

22. On the history of exegesis of this crucial passage, see J. J. McGrath, *"Through the Eternal Spirit": An Historical Study of the Exegesis of Hebrews 9:13–14* (Rome: Pontifical Gregorian University, 1961), 231–47. On the notion of *divine action*, I am indebted to the monumental project of W. J. Abraham, *Divine Agency and Divine Action*, 4 vols. (New York: OUP, 2017–2021); see especially IV, 81: "In the west the gold standard for work on divine action in the Eucharist is that of Thomas Aquinas." Not surprisingly, I demur from Abraham's rejection of Aquinas's "untenable metaphysical theory" (83). Abraham favorably cites (91–92) the analytic theology of J. Arcadi, *An Incarnational Model of the Eucharist* (New York: CUP, 2018), whose application of speech-act theory to the Eucharist is profound; Arcadi sees the words of consecration effecting a "eucharistic theophany" (ch. 2, 62–110). Abraham's more sympathetic treatment of Aquinas on the Holy Spirit's "divine action" in the mystery of the Eucharist is found in ch. 8 of *Divine Agency and Divine Action*, vol. 2, *Soundings in the Christian Tradition*: "The form is constituted by the original words of institution given by Christ," as a "performative act," in which "the principal agent at work in the sacrament is Christ" (as heavenly high priest); yet "Aquinas can just as readily speak of the Holy Spirit as the agent . . ." (141). Abraham praises "the depth and sophistication of Aquinas' account of the Eucharist," where he finds "a raft of divine actions carried out through the human acts of consecration; the multiple effects drive one to speak of a unique form of causality, aptly named sacramental causality. This thick description of divine causality in turn underwrites . . . the central act of worship in the church" (147). He also notes: "Aquinas is first and foremost a theologian seeking to explain what is involved in a complex causal account of divine action in the Eucharist. . . . He is governed by a vision of divine power to act that would never have entered the head of Aristotle. He has a much richer ontology of divine agency" (152). For Aquinas's treatment of Eucharistic allusions in Hebrews, in contrast to the merely symbolic sacraments of the Old Law, see Thomas Aquinas, *Commentary on the Epistle to the Hebrews* (South Bend, IN: St. Augustine's Press, 2006), 187–219.

What, then, is Hebrews telling us? Christ's sacrifice does not consist *simply* of his suffering and death on the cross, but in his perfect act of self-offering to God *through* suffering and death. His suffering and death are terminated, to be sure, but *not* his high priesthood and self-offering, which continue forever in heaven: his divinised human flesh/body that was crucified, resurrected, and ascended, who is now enthroned in heaven. As royal High Priest, he enacts his own everlasting high priestly ministry. And he does this through the once-for-all (i.e., perpetuated) sacrifice of his glorified and deified humanity, which is the liturgy of the new covenant. And this in several ways: *First*, his is the body of our heavenly High Priest. *Second*, his body is our sanctuary (the true tent "not made with hands," 9:11). *Third*, his body is the sacrifice of the new covenant, which constitutes the everlasting liturgy in the heavenly Jerusalem (12:22–24). *Fourth*, this heavenly liturgy is what the church on earth enters through the Eucharist: "You *have come* to . . . the heavenly Jerusalem . . . and to Jesus, the mediator of a new covenant."

Hebrews thus echoes the gospels in proclaiming the new covenant: that is, how Jesus made his death and resurrection a perfect sacrifice and an everlasting liturgy. Thus, when we "do *this* in remembrance of him," we share in Jesus's sacrifice even as we renew our covenant with him in the Eucharist. We enter his real presence – by the eternal Spirit – to worship alongside the angels and saints in the heavenly liturgy of our *risen High Priest-King*. The Holy Spirit's action is the source and cause of Christ's *real* presence among us – in the sacrament of the Eucharist – as our High Priest, our Sanctuary, our Sacrifice, and our Liturgy. Jesus ordered his disciples to "do this as my memorial" (*anamnesis*), which implies their participation in his priestly sacrifice. Hebrews shows us how "this" is done after Jesus's resurrection and ascension, when he sent the Holy Spirit so that the redemption he *accomplished* so perfectly on our behalf might also be *applied* just as perfectly in perpetuity in the church.

Jesus's sacrifice is certainly not repeated; for how can you *repeat* what never ends? Rather, his self-offering is re-presented – continuously – on earth as in heaven. As "a priest forever" his sacrifice is "once for all," not in the sense of *termination* but as the *perpetuation* of his heavenly offering and its *prolongation* (extension) to us on earth. Hebrews shows us how Christ ratified the new covenant (the Eucharist) in his own body and blood as his sacrificial self-offering.[23]

---

23. See N. J. Moore, *Repetition in Hebrews* (Tübingen: Mohr Siebeck, 2015), 148–205, especially his treatment of the question of repetition: the "altar" (13:10) and "sacrifices" (13:15–16) of Christians (197–204).

CONCLUSION

In conclusion, Bruce and Williamson seem to have rejected a subtle but essential and strategic interpretive key to the epistle: Hebrews contrasts the old and new covenants *not* because the former has outward rites while the latter does not, but because the OT rites could not "perfect" or "cleanse the conscience" (9:9), whereas the NT rites *can* and *do*. It is not a contrast between a ritual cultus that is visible (OT) as opposed to invisible (NT), but one that is *prophetic yet ineffective* versus one that is *fulfilled and efficacious*. In other words, the author's typological use – and christological reading – of OT rites is radically incarnational and anagogical – not some form of Middle Platonism.[24]

It is likely that the earliest eucharistic traditions have not only provided the source of the author's identification of Jesus's death, resurrection, and ascension in terms of liturgical sacrifice, but also supplied some of the larger themes of the author's theology.[25] Thus, we side with those scholars from across the entire spectrum of Christian tradition[26] who acknowledge the presence of numerous allusions to the Eucharist, as well as sacramental influences in Hebrews.[27] More research in this area is warranted, for in pointing back to (and drawing from) eucharistic traditions in the early church, Hebrews may show scholars a way to trace the emergence of ancient sacramental customs. The varied strata and

---

24. See J. H. Davies, *A Letter to the Hebrews* (New York: CUP, 1967), 86.

25. For a more concentrated treatment of the presence and function of eucharistic allusions in the theological argument of Hebrews, see Daniel J. Brege, "Eucharistic Overtones Created by Sacrificial Concepts in the Epistle to the Hebrews," *Concordia Theological Quarterly* 66 (Jan 2002): 61–82, and J. Swetnam, "Christology and the Eucharist in the Epistle to the Hebrews," *Bib* 70 (1989): 75–78.

26. See especially, from a Baptist perspective, D. J. Pursiful, *The Cultic Motif in the Spirituality of the Book of Hebrews* (Lewiston, NY: Mellen Biblical Press, 1993). Likewise, from a Reformed/Calvinist tradition, Hughes, "Hebrews IX 15ff.," 51–57. From a Lutheran viewpoint, A. A. Just, "Entering Holiness: Christology and Eucharist in Hebrews," *Concordia Theological Quarterly* 69, no. 1 (2005): 75–95. J. Swetnam argues "the greater and more perfect tent" refers to the Eucharist in "'The Greater and More Perfect Tent': A Contribution to the Discussion of Hebrews 9,11," *Bib* 47 (1966): 91–106. He builds upon A. Vanhoye, "'Par la tente plus grande et plus parfaite. . . .' (Hé 9, 11)," *Bib* 46 (1965): 1–28, who argues the tent refers to the resurrected, glorified, and enthroned body of Christ. See also P. Andriessen, "L'Eucharistie dans l'Épître aux Hébreux," *NRTh* 94 (1972): 269–77; S. Aalen, "Das Abendmahl als Opfermahl im Neuen Testament," *NovT* 6 (1963): 128–52; and O. Moe, "Das Abendmahl im Hebräerbrief: Zur Auslegung von Hebr. 13,9—16," *StTh* 4 (1951): 102–8.

27. B. Lindars, *The Theology of the Letter to the Hebrews* (New York: CUP, 1981), 140–41: "Hebrews has constantly influenced the liturgical texts of the eucharist," even "in some of the earliest liturgies. . . . It has even been suggested that the liturgies came first, and that Hebrews is quoting from them." J. Gunther, *Paul's Opponents and Their Background: A Study of Apocalyptic and Jewish Sectarian Teachings* (Leiden: Brill, 1973), 149, takes 10:25 as a reference to the eucharistic assembly of the early Christians, absence from which was a grave offense (10:29). He concurs with J. Betz that there is "a liturgical import in all these passages": 10:19–35; 12:22–25; 12:28; 13:12–13, citing Betz, *Die Eucharistie in der Zeit der griechischen Väter*, Bd. II/I: *Die Realpräsenz des Leibes und Blutes Jesu im Abendmahl nach dem Neuen Testament* (Freiburg: Herder, 1961), 154–66.

sources of Christian antiquity bear witness to these customs, and at the same time they lead to greater insight into the cultic origins and theological reasons for the ancient church's appropriation and adaptation of the covenantal and sacrificial aspects and juridical-liturgical practices of Second Temple Judaism.

A CONCLUDING PATRISTIC POSTSCRIPT

What the first Christians knew as the New Testament/Covenant was not a book, but the Eucharist. In a cultic setting, at a solemn sacrificial banquet, Jesus made an offering of his "body" and "blood." He used traditional sacrificial language. He spoke of the action as his memorial. He told those who attended to repeat the action they had witnessed: "*do* this in remembrance of me" (Luke 22:19). Thus, he instituted the Christian priesthood and established the church's liturgy. He authorised the apostles, as his clergy, to *do* what he was doing: to make a memorial offering of his body and blood. He called his action the "new covenant in my blood" (Luke 22:20). He declared it to be the New Testament – and the New Testament was not a text but a sacramental action. He did not say "*write* this" or "*read* this," but rather "*do* this." By the time the Gospels and Epistles were written, the church had already been faithful to Jesus's instruction for decades. The New Testament was a sacrament at least a generation before it was a document. We learn this from the document itself, not excluding the book we call Hebrews.

Not surprisingly, what we find in all the Fathers, from the beginning, is the strong use of covenantal language employed to describe the Eucharist, the rite Jesus referred to as "the new covenant in my blood." Ignatius, bishop of Antioch, wrote seven letters around 107 AD as he was taken by military escort to his execution in Rome. Addressed to churches along his route, they are neither treatises nor essays, but rather exhortations. He urges Christians to be unified, obedient, and strong in the face of persecution. He assumes a common eucharistic practice, shared by all the churches, and a common eucharistic doctrine. He employs a complex sacrificial vocabulary when he speaks about liturgical matters. He repeatedly calls the church the *thusiastērion*, which is Greek for "altar" or "sanctuary" – literally, it is the "place of sacrifice."[28] Nor is Ignatius the first to apply such terms to the liturgy and its ministers. Preceding him by at least a decade

---

28. Ignatius of Antioch, *Ephesians* 5.2 (187), *Trallians* 7.2 (219), and *Philadelphians* 4 (239), in *The Apostolic Fathers: Greek Texts and English Translations*, 3rd ed., trans. M. W. Holmes (Grand Rapids: Baker Academic, 2007). Cf. F. C. Klawiter, *Martyrdom, Sacrificial Libation, and the Eucharist of Ignatius of Antioch* (Minneapolis: Fortress, 2022).

(and perhaps more) is Clement, bishop of Rome in the first century. He asserts that the bishop's work is to offer the oblation (*prospheretia*).[29]

An anonymous first-century document titled *The Didache* (or *Teaching of the Twelve Apostles*) also speaks of the Eucharist as "the sacrifice" in ch. 14, and invokes the oracle of the prophet Malachi as its witness: "For from the rising of the sun to its setting my name is great among the nations, and in every place incense is offered to my name, and a pure offering; for my name is great among the nations, says the LORD of hosts" (Mal 1:11). This is the prophecy most often applied to the Eucharist by the early Fathers. It is employed by Justin Martyr, Origen, John Chrysostom, and Augustine[30] – and it is profoundly sacrificial in character. Recent scholarship suggests that the ritual sections of the *Didache* may even predate the Gospels themselves.[31]

For the earliest Fathers, the Eucharist was simply "the sacrifice," the church's sacrifice. No one put this in more lapidary terms than Eusebius of Caesarea, the bishop and historian of the late third and early fourth centuries. In the years immediately before the Council of Nicaea (325 AD), he composed his *Proof of the Gospel*, in which he considered the Eucharist as it is foreshadowed in the old covenant and fulfilled in the new. He writes: "We sacrifice, therefore, to Almighty God a sacrifice of praise. We sacrifice the divine and holy and sacred offering. We sacrifice anew, according to the New Covenant, the pure sacrifice."[32]

This may sound remote or antiquarian, but it was not so to the early Christians. It was the substance of their new life in Christ. If this strikes us as little more than an exercise in semantics, perhaps it is because the primary sense of Christianity's most important words and practices have been obscured.

---

29. *1 Clement* 44 (Holmes, *Apostolic Fathers*, 105). On Clement's use of Hebrews, see D. Hagner, *The Use of the Old and New Testaments in Clement of Rome* (Leiden: Brill, 1973), 179–95. On the early dating of 1 Clement: T. Herron, *Clement and the Early Church of Rome* (Steubenville, OH: Emmaus Road, 2008); also, C. Jefford, *The Apostolic Fathers and the New Testament* (Peabody, MA: Hendrickson, 2006), 18; J. A. T. Robinson, *Redating the New Testament* (London: SCM, 1976), 327–35.

30. For these and others, see Albert Ferreiro, ed., *Ancient Christian Commentary on the Scriptures: Old Testament XIV* (Downers Grove: IVP, 2003), 288–96, and M. Aquilina, *The Eucharist Foretold: The Lost Prophecy of Malachi* (Steubenville, OH: Emmaus Road, 2019).

31. On the dating of the liturgical portions of the *Didache*, see E. Mazza, *The Origins of the Eucharistic Prayer* (Collegeville: Pueblo, 1995), 40–41; also, Jefford, *The Apostolic Fathers*, 20.

32. Eusebius, *Proof of the Gospel* 1.10, trans., W. J. Ferrar (Cascade, OR: Wipf and Stock, 2001), 62. It is also helpful to examine Cyril of Jerusalem's preaching in the fourth century, as he addresses new converts to Christianity who have just been baptised. Like Paul before him (see 1 Cor 8), Cyril contrasts the sacrificial meal of Christians with the ritual feasts of the pagans. In baptism, he explains, new Christians "renounce Satan, breaking all *covenant* with him, that ancient league with hell." He calls this pact *diathēkē*, which he identifies with ritual actions: "idol festivals," where "meat or bread or other such things are polluted by the invocation of the unclean spirits, are reckoned with the pomp of the devil." The neophytes had broken their former covenants with hell precisely "by *entering the New Covenant.*" *Catechetical Lecture* 19 1.7.9; *NPNF* 2/7, ed. Philip Schaff (Peabody, MA: Hendrickson, 1995), 146.

Interpreting the new covenant and Christ's high priesthood in Hebrews in view of the Eucharist might be a small step towards renewing our reading of sacred Scripture, both the OT and the NT.

SELECT BIBLIOGRAPHY

Aalen, S. "Das Abendmahl als Opfermahl im Neuen Testament." *NovT* 6 (1963): 128–52.

Abraham, William J. *Divine Agency and Divine Action*. Vols. 1–4. New York: OUP, 2017–2021.

Andriessen, P. "L'Eucharistie dans l'Épître aux Hébreux." *NRTh* 94 (1972): 269–77.

Aquilina, Mike. *The Eucharist Foretold: The Lost Prophecy of Malachi*. Steubenville, OH: Emmaus Road, 2019.

Aquinas, Thomas. *Commentary on the Epistle to the Hebrews*. South Bend, IN: St. Augustine's Press, 2006.

Arcadi, James M. *An Incarnational Model of the Eucharist*. New York: CUP, 2018.

Behm, J. "Diatheke." *TDNT* 2:131–132.

Bergsma, John. *Jesus and the Old Testament Roots of the Priesthood*. Steubenville, OH: Emmaus Road, 2021.

Betz, J. *Die Eucharistie in der Zeit der griechischen Väter*. Bd. II/I, *Die Realpräsenz des Leibes und Blutes Jesu im Abendmahl nach dem Neuen Testament*. Freiburg: Herder, 1961.

Brege, Daniel J. "Eucharistic Overtones Created by Sacrificial Concepts in the Epistle to the Hebrews." *CTQ* 66 (January 2002): 61–82.

Bruce, F. F. *Epistle to the Hebrews*. Rev. ed. Grand Rapids: Eerdmans, 1990.

Chenderlin, Fritz. *"Do This as My Memorial."* Analecta Biblica 99. Rome: Pontifical Biblical Institute, 1982.

Chester, A. N. "The Final Sacrifice." In *Sacrifice and Redemption*, edited by S. Sykes, 57–72. Cambridge: CUP, 1991.

Clement. *1 Clement*. In *The Apostolic Fathers: Greek Texts and English Translations*. 3rd ed. Translated by M. W. Holmes. Grand Rapids: Baker Academic, 2007.

Coppens, J. "The Church, The New Covenant of God with His People." In *The Birth of the Church: A Biblical Study*, 13–25. Staten Island, NY: Alba House, 1968.

Cyril of Jerusalem. *"Catechetical Lectures."* In *NPNF*, vol. 7, second series, edited by P. Schaff, 1–157. Peabody, MA: Hendrickson, 1995.

Davies, J. H. *A Letter to the Hebrews*. New York: CUP, 1967.

Dunnill, J. *Covenant and Sacrifice in the Letter to the Hebrews*. SNTSMS 75. Cambridge: CUP, 1993.

Eusebius. *Proof of the Gospel.* Translated by W. J. Ferrar. Cascade, OR: Wipf and Stock, 2001.

Fahrig, S. "The Context of the Text: Reading Hebrews as a Eucharistic Homily." Unpublished PhD. dissertation, Boston College, 2014.

Ferreiro, Albert, ed. *Ancient Christian Commentary on the Scriptures: Old Testament XIV.* Downers Grove: IVP, 2003.

Field, J. E. *The Apostolic Liturgy and the Epistle to the Hebrews.* London: Rivingtons, 1882.

Gunther, John J. *Paul's Opponents and Their Background: A Study of Apocalyptic and Jewish Sectarian Teachings.* NovTSup 35. Leiden: Brill, 1973.

Hagner, Donald A. *The Use of the Old and New Testaments in Clement of Rome.* NovTSup 34. Leiden: Brill, 1973.

Hahn, Scott W. *Kinship by Covenant.* AYBRL. New Haven: Yale University Press, 2009.

———. *Consuming the Word: The Eucharist and the New Testament in the Early Church.* New York: Doubleday, 2013.

Herron, Thomas J. *Clement and the Early Church of Rome.* Steubenville, OH: Emmaus Road, 2008.

Hughes, John J. "Hebrews IX 15ff. and Galatians III 15ff." *NovT* 21 (1976–77): 27–96.

Ignatius of Antioch. *Ephesians*; *Trallians*; *Philadelphians.* In *The Apostolic Fathers: Greek Texts and English Translations.* 3rd ed. Translated by M. W. Holmes, 182–247. Grand Rapids: Baker Academic, 2007.

Jefford, C. *The Apostolic Fathers and the New Testament.* Peabody, MA: Hendrickson, 2006.

Jeremias, Joachim. *The Eucharistic Words of Jesus.* New York: Scribner, 1966.

Klawiter, F. C. *Martyrdom, Sacrificial Libation, and the Eucharist of Ignatius of Antioch.* Minneapolis: Fortress, 2022.

Lane, William L. *Hebrews 9–13.* WBC 47b. Nashville: Thomas Nelson, 1991.

Lindars, B. *The Theology of the Letter to the Hebrews.* NTT. New York: CUP, 1981.

Mascall, E. L. *Corpus Christi.* London: Longmans, 1955.

Mazza, E. *The Origins of the Eucharistic Prayer.* Collegeville, MN: Pueblo, 1995.

McGrath, J. J. *"Through the Eternal Spirit": An Historical Study of the Exegesis of Hebrews 9:13–14.* Rome: Pontifical Gregorian University, 1961.

Milligan, William. *The Ascension and Heavenly Priesthood of Our Lord.* London: Macmillan, 1901.

Moe, O. "Das Abendmahl im Hebräerbrief Zur Auslegung von Hebr. 13,9—16." *StTh* 4 (1951): 102–8.

Moffitt, David M. *Atonement and the Logic of Resurrection in the Epistle to the Hebrews.* NovTSup 141. Leiden: Brill, 2011.

Moore, Nicholas J. *Repetition in Hebrews: Plurality and Singularity in the Letter to the Hebrews, Its Ancient Context, and the Early Church.* WUNT 2/388. Tübingen: Mohr Siebeck, 2015.

Nairne, Alexander. *The Epistle of Priesthood.* Edinburgh: T&T Clark, 1915.

Pitre, Brant. *Jesus and the Last Supper.* Grand Rapids: Eerdmans, 2015.

Pursiful, D. J. *The Cultic Motif in the Spirituality of the Book of Hebrews.* Lewiston, NY: Mellen Biblical Press, 1993.

Robinson, J. A. T. *Redating the New Testament.* London: SCM, 1976.

Swetnam, J. "Christology and the Eucharist in the Epistle to the Hebrews." *Bib* 70 (1989): 74–95.

———. "'The Greater and More Perfect Tent': A Contribution to the Discussion of Hebrews 9,11." *Bib* 47 (1966): 91–106.

———. "A Suggested Interpretation of Hebrews 9,15–18." *CBQ* 27 (1965): 373–90.

Vanhoye, Albert. "'Par la tente plus grande et plus parfaite....' (Hé 9, 11)." *Bib* 46 (1965): 1–28.

———. *Old Testament Priests and the New Priest.* Petersham, MA: St. Bede's, 1986.

Williamson, Ronald. "The Eucharist and the Epistle to the Hebrews." *NTS* 21 (1975): 300–312.

Wright, N. T. *The New Testament and the People of God.* Minneapolis: Fortress, 1992.

PART V

Divine Action and Hebrews Today

CHAPTER 14

Preaching Hebrews to Hear
God's Address Today[1]

Benjamin T. Quinn

INTRODUCTION

Anyone who has undertaken to teach or preach through the book of Hebrews knows well the sophistication and intricate beauty of this great sermon.[2] And yet we confess that the letter to the Hebrews is, as Christian Scripture, "living and active, sharper than any two-edged sword" (Heb 4:12). This confession is of utmost importance for preaching Hebrews. In fact, it is the starting point for hearing God's address in Hebrews today.

The burden of this chapter is to consider how to *preach* Hebrews in order to *hear* God's address *today* in light of the theme of divine action throughout Hebrews. Each italicised word – *preach, hear,* and *today* – is pivotal for properly addressing the task at hand. While there are many themes from Hebrews that deserve attention for contemporary preaching and application, space will limit my considerations to those that seem most pressing for our current cultural moment, especially in the West.

To begin, I invite the help of Jean-Louis Chrétien to help us understand what it means to *hear* the Bible *today* from his most insightful essay, "Reading

---

1. All Scripture quotations, unless otherwise indicated, are from the ESV.

2. For more on Hebrews as "sermon," see Jonathan I. Griffiths, *Hebrews and Divine Speech* (London, New York: T&T Clark, 2014); G. H. Guthrie, *Hebrews: The NIV Application Commentary* (Grand Rapids: Zondervan, 1998); G. Cockerill, *The Epistle to the Hebrews*, NICNT (Grand Rapids: Eerdmans, 2012).

the Bible Today." Having then attuned our ears to *hearing* for *today*, I will offer four exhortations for *preaching* God's address from Hebrews that aims to convert hearing into faithful, inside-out obedience in God's world. Each exhortation will consider the role divine action plays in our *hearing* and *preaching* of Hebrews and will engage insights from other chapters within this volume where possible to offer an overall coherence towards kerygmatic application.

HEARING GOD'S ADDRESS TODAY

In the opening chapter of his *Under the Gaze of the Bible*, Jean-Louis Chrétien reflects on what it means to read the Bible *today*. He quickly turns to Hebrews 3:13 and writes,

> The Letter to Hebrews offers us an indication of vital importance on what it is to read the Bible today. On two occasions, it indeed cites the words of a psalm, attributing them to the Holy Spirit: "Today, if you hear his voice," the voice of God, drawing from it the following lesson: "Exhort one another daily, while it is called *today*" (3:13), as long as there is what is called *today*.[3]

Chrétien notes that the context of this passage in Hebrews 3 is "human appeals that we send out to one another not to fall away from the living God, and hence to *listen to his voice in the Bible* . . ."[4]

A summary of Chrétien's chapter is helpful for our overall purpose here, and may be outlined as follows:

1. Chrétien considers the question, "***What*** is *today*?"
   a. Drawing upon Hebrews 3, "today" is a call to one another not to "fall away" from the living God but instead to *listen* to his voice in the Bible.
   b. The "today" of Scripture becomes our own "today" when we read with "attention, vigilance, and availability." It is God's gift for us to listen "contrary to the hardened pride in which I presume to know better than others what they're saying and what they mean, and better than God how he may act and how he may reveal himself."[5]

---

3. Jean-Louis Chrétien, *Under the Gaze of the Bible*, trans. John Marson Dunaway (New York: Fordham University Press, 2015), 1–2.

4. Chrétien, *Under the Gaze*, 2. Italics added.

5. Chrétien, *Under the Gaze*, 2.

    c. "Today" is the time in which it is still light, not dark – the time before death.

2. Then Chrétien asks, "***When*** is *today*?"

    a. The time of daylight when one may be changed by listening for understanding and discernment.

    b. The time of both urgency and of "God's patience toward humankind, the patience of apprenticeship in reading and listening."[6]

    c. The time to avoid the *idiocy* of merely privatised reading of the Bible. He writes, "The Greeks had a word for that which is only particular and private, that which is only my point of view. They called it *idiotic*." He continues, "We cannot without risk of idiocy dissociate the today of our reading from this tense history, passionate, violent, burning, and at the same time patient, which has made it possible for this writing to reach us."[7]

    d. The time of response, which is identical to listening. "That of the Word which sought our listening and our response is engendered in us when we listen to it and respond to it, which moreover is the same thing."

    e. The time of the humble spirit. As Bethlehem was the humble place of the nativity, "may each of us make of his spirit a Bethlehem, when he reads the Bible today. . . ."[8]

Though only five pages in length, Chrétien's essay brims with wisdom and we may glean three requirements from it concerning *hearing* the Bible for *today*.

REJECTING PRIDE

First, hearing God's voice today (Heb 3:7, 15, quoting Ps 95:7) requires rejecting pride and making "today" our own. In practice, this looks like a soft and confessing heart aimed towards perseverance and away from "falling away." For as long as it is "today," that time of life before death, we must *hear* the Bible with receptive and confessing hearts, avoiding the deceitfulness of sin. After all, the heart is the *place* for both wandering and worship.

The preacher, quoting Psalm 95, writes, "Therefore I was provoked with that generation, and said, 'They always go astray in their heart; they have not

---

6. Chrétien, *Under the Gaze*, 2.

7. Chrétien, *Under the Gaze*, 3.

8. Chrétien, *Under the Gaze*, 4–5.

known my ways.'" God was impatient with the first generation under Moses because they failed properly to align their time, place, and direction of life. In their heart (the place), they went astray (direction) during the day of testing (the time). "They have not known my ways," God commented. His desire was proper alignment of time, place, and direction – that in their heart (place) they might walk in his ways (direction), today and every day (time). This is *hearing* God's voice; this is participating in the Christ who is the Way.

This collection of time, place, and direction is the very stuff of God's creation, held together in Christ and delivered to us through an economic narrative; that is, a true narrative of *oikonomia* that relates all of time and space to the Creator and calls all creatures to *hear* (obey!) the voice of the living God. As Fellipe do Vale argues in the introduction to this volume, the theological task requires an organising principle to account for the many parts of the discipline and of Scripture. According to do Vale, theological work is thus "an economy of divine actions jointly arranged into a history of creation, redemption, sustenance, and perfection."[9] Our "today" is found within that economy of divine actions, a day of light and life during which we must remain soft in heart, ever preparing the way of the Lord.

APPRENTICESHIP IN *SHEMA*

Second, *hearing* God's voice *today* requires apprenticeship in *shema* – "Never the idiot!" The *shema* of Deut 6:4ff is arguably the most famous passage for the Jewish people in the Hebrew Bible – the John 3:16 of the OT, one might say. *Shema*, the Hebrew word for "Hear" or "Listen," is the first word in the passage that reads, "Hear, O Israel: the LORD our God, the LORD is one. You shall love the LORD your God with all your heart and with all your soul and with all your might." The passage continues insisting that this command remain on the heart of the hearers, and that they must "teach them diligently to your children, and shall talk of them when you sit in your house, and when you walk by the way, and when you lie down, and when you rise" (Deut 6:7). In other words, *shema* must be taught, practised, and learnt – much like an apprenticeship. It does not come naturally.

Such apprenticeship in *shema* must be recaptured in order to *hear* God's voice *today*. Too often we speak of the *shema* as a noun – simply that famous passage from Deuteronomy that the Jews recite daily. But Christians must

---

9. F. do Vale, "Divine Action, Theological Method, and Scripture's Narrative," 13.

acknowledge *shema* for the imperative that it is. To *hear* God's voice *today* requires active, verbal *shema* – listening with the intent of careful obedience. This is not an individual matter. Apprenticeship assumes community – a community who assists in tuning the ear of the apprentice towards *hearing* God's voice. As I noted in the list summary of his chapter, Chrétien warns against privatised approaches to reading the Bible, reminding us of the "idiotic" nature of isolation and individualism.[10] May our apprenticeship thus be well informed by that "cloud of witnesses" who have read and interpreted the Bible for centuries before us.

BECOMING BETHLEHEM

Third, *hearing* God's voice *today* requires becoming Bethlehem. Chrétien urges that when God speaks through Scripture, this Word seeks to become present in us. He writes, "If . . . I open my eyes, my ears, and my spirit, then it is every day, what can be each day, the Christmas of my reading, in which 'is born to us today a Savior' (Luke 2:11)." This beautiful and imaginative reading of Luke 2 leads Chrétien to insist: "When my life and my spirit open today to this Word, something of this Word is born in me; there is a nativity of meaning, a new dawn of the eternal truth, a humble and small Christmas that is nonetheless a real Christmas."[11] For this to happen, we must make our spirit "a Bethlehem" – a humble place to house the nativity, the birth of the Word.

PREACHING GOD'S ADDRESS *TODAY*

What, then, of *preaching* Hebrews for *today*? And how do the requirements for *hearing* relate to the task of *preaching*? This seems to be a conflicting assignment, for *preaching* assumes speaking while *hearing* assumes listening.

One might say that preaching is for the preacher and hearing is for the congregation, and certainly this is reasonable. But mustn't the preacher also *hear*? And mustn't the congregation also *proclaim* God's address in word and deed even if not from behind a pulpit? It would seem, then, that preaching Hebrews in order to hear God's address today is not for the preacher only, nor just the congregation, but for the whole of God's people. It is much like the prophet

---

10. Chrétien, *Under the Gaze*, 3.
11. Chrétien, *Under the Gaze*, 4–5.

Joel's opening address, "Hear this, you elders; give ear, all inhabitants of the land!" (Joel 1:2a).

And yet the link between *hearing* and *preaching* lies with the preacher him/herself. The three "requirements" for *hearing* – rejecting pride and making "today" our own, apprenticeship in *shema*, and becoming Bethlehem – must be exercised daily and embodied by those "leaders who speak the Word of God," such that we can call the congregation to "consider the outcome of our way of *listening*, and imitate our faith" (Heb 13:7, edited for emphasis). May such a person who proclaims this message serve to strengthen (13:9) and not harden (3:8) the heart of the hearers.

Such preaching of Hebrews, then, must stress at least the following five themes, each of which are undergirded by God's continued action through the Word, the priesthood of Christ, and the Spirit in the world.

GOD HAS SPOKEN

From its opening lines, the great sermon of Hebrews bursts forth with the unapologetic assertion that God speaks! Formerly he spoke to our fathers by the prophets, but "in these last days he has spoken to us by his Son" (1:2). Then at the end in 12:25, the preacher urges his listeners, "See that you do not refuse him who is speaking." This intentional *inclusio* marks divine speech arguably as the strongest feature of divine action in the entire letter.[12]

Jonathan Griffiths has recently argued, "As a discourse, Hebrews is intended to function as a means of delivering a divine word and, in the view of the writer, itself constitutes a form of divine word. The writer shows his conviction that this word will effect an encounter between God and his addressees that will achieve its intended results in the addressees."[13] This "effect" does

---

12. See George Guthrie's article in the present volume.
13. Griffiths, *Hebrews and Divine Speech*, 168. Griffiths also rightly stresses the nature of the book of Hebrews as sermon:

> Set against all the foregoing findings, the conclusion that the writer views his own sermon as a form of divine speech (knowing that, for him, an encounter with the divine word entails the opportunity to receive salvation, access to the heavenly rest, a personal encounter with Jesus Christ, and the obligation to respond appropriately) contributes substantially to contemporary discussion within the disciplines of biblical studies, Christian doctrine, and theologically informed homiletics concerning the theology of preaching. It establishes Hebrews as a sermon that was intended not only to communicate divine truth to its hearers, but to effect an encounter between them and the very word of God. Since Hebrews is the earliest extant complete Christian sermon, historical and theological investigations into the theology and practice of Christian preaching must take into account Hebrews's own robust theology of preaching. (169)

not stop with the original audience, but as divine speech it persists with power for every time, place, and people both now and into the future.[14] Ken Schenk also argues, "While we can thus say that the author interpreted the Scriptures Christologically, it is even more appropriate to deem his hermeneutic an *eschatological* hermeneutic. More than anything else, the author's interpretation was eschatologically driven." As such, Schenk continues, "The audience is understood to be the most important 'addressee' of the scriptural texts, that the Scriptures come to take on the meaning that they do."[15]

The contemporary preacher or teacher of Hebrews may – indeed, must! – therefore "boldly approach" the pulpit or lectern in the moment of proclamation. After all, God continues to speak through his "living and active Word" that divides between the marrow and bone of the one who truly *hears* and therefore obeys.

Kevin Vanhoozer said it well: "God's voice is unlike that of any other actor. Only his speaking sets the stage: 'Then God said, 'Let there be light'; and there was light' (Gen 1:3) . . . The word of God is 'living and active' (Heb 4:12), less a voice than an actor in its own right, doing things like healing and delivering (Ps 107:20)."[16] Later in the same chapter, Vanhoozer further stresses: "*Scripture not only conveys the content of the gospel but is itself caught up in the economy of the gospel, as the means by which God draws others into his communicative action.* Jesus is God's definitive Word, to be sure, but Scripture projects his voice and extends his action."[17] This last sentence by Vanhoozer drives home this all-too-brief emphasis that God has spoken. Yes, this is precisely where faithful preaching of Hebrews begins.

FAITH FOR TODAY

In a day when empiricism reigns supreme, talk of "faith" in things unseen seems futile. However, the author of Hebrews anticipates and even erodes this approach by claiming "faith" itself as a form of evidence for what is not seen. Thus, faith is also an assurance for hope.

---

14. See also Nick Brennan's chapter in the present volume for a compelling case on the important role of power and the abilities of the Son, especially how their unique role in identifying the Son as the locus of God's action in Hebrews.

15. Ken Schenk, "God Has Spoken," in *The Epistle to the Hebrews and Christian Theology*, ed. Richard Bauckham, Daniel R. Driver, Trevor A. Hart, and Nathan MacDonald (Grand Rapids: Eerdmans, 2009), 336. Emphasis original to the text.

16. Kevin Vanhoozer, *The Drama of Doctrine* (Louisville, KY: Westminster John Knox Press, 2005), 44.

17. Vanhoozer, *The Drama of Doctrine*, 48. Emphasis original to the text.

The language of "faith" or "faithfulness" appears almost forty times in Hebrews, surpassed only by Romans in the rest of the NT. Furthermore, Hebrews is home to a definition of faith in 11:1 and to the well-known "Hall of Faith" throughout the rest of chapter eleven, followed by the climactic chapter twelve wherein Jesus is declared "founder and perfecter of our faith" (12:2). Of these nearly forty occurrences throughout the book, thirty-one occur between chapters ten through thirteen, with twenty-three appearing in chapter eleven alone. Suffice it to say that the author of Hebrews means to make much of "faith" and "faithfulness" (πίστις and πιστὸς, respectively) with escalating importance as he approaches the climax of the message. Contemporary preaching of Hebrews does well to follow this scheme.

In 11:1–3, after declaring that "we are not of those who shrink back and are destroyed, but of those who have faith and preserve their souls" (10:39), the preacher explains,

> Now faith is the [reality of] things hoped for, the [evidence] of things not seen. For by it the people of old received their commendation. By faith we understand that the universe was created by the word of God, so that what is seen was not made out of things that are visible.[18]

From these verses we may briefly observe three things. First, faith fosters endurance and perseverance among God's people. This is how the preacher can declare that his audience has not shrunk back from their confession of 10:23 but rather perseveres through trial. As Mariam Kamell argues, "Believers must endure in active faith, trusting that God will fulfill his promises even if they die (or are killed) before they see the completion. Faith is the response to God's character that leads us inextricably into obedience and endurance, knowing that God himself will complete what he promised and bring us into perfection."[19]

Second, faith not only fosters perseverance but also carries a quality of preservation for the "souls" of God's people. Hence the preacher's emphasis on "those who have faith and *preserve* their souls." And, third, faith promotes confidence in our future hope despite a lack of sight in the present. For support, the preacher appeals to the Christian doctrine of *creatio ex nihilo*. Just as faith promotes the truth that the God whom we cannot see made all the things that we do see, so faith offers assurance of hope for the future. In other words, faith serves as an objective form of "evidence" for the promise to come. The author

---

18. Translation edited to stress the objective understanding of faith as "reality" and "evidence" rather than merely the subjective "assurance" and "conviction."

19. Mariam J. Kamell, "Reexamining Faith," in *The Epistle to the Hebrews and Christian Theology*, 431.

further appeals to the faithful obedience of Abel, Abraham, and Moses, who "all died in faith, not having received the things promised. . . ." (11:13).

What, then, of faith relative to preaching Hebrews to hear God's address today?

First, faith in Hebrews is *founded* on God's activity through the work of the Son: "Therefore [Christ] had to be made like his brothers in every respect, so that he might become a merciful and faithful high priest in the service of God, to make propitiation for the sins of the people" (2:17). This divine High Priest who was "made like his brothers in every respect" calls to mind and reinforces our Chalcedonian christological commitments. But, for more kerygmatic purposes, introducing the theme of "faith" in this way centres faith on God's work through Jesus and decentres the work of humankind. Further to Chrétien's exhortation to relinquish pride in our reading of the Bible, Hebrews reminds us that faith begins and ends with Jesus – the founder and perfecter of our faith (12:2).

Second, faith *forms* the people of God. Hebrews's heavy accent on faith speaks of more than a body of beliefs on the one hand or a personal experience on the other. Hebrews takes it further, exhorting God's people to cultivate faith like a virtue. As 10:23 exclaims, "Let us hold fast the confession of our hope without wavering, for he who promised is faithful." The link between "holding fast," "hope," and "faith" deserves deeper exploration, but here we simply note the integral connection between them. God's people are encouraged to "hold fast" (κατέχωμεν) to the confession of hope. Hope in what? Hope in *the promising one who is faithful* (πιστὸς γὰρ ὁ ἐπαγγειλάμενος). Without the faithfulness (πιστὸς) of Christ, the call to "hold fast" would be a call to hold on to an unsecured hope – an unreasonable hope, without grounds for confidence. Christ's faithfulness, however, grounds the promise and guarantees the hope to which we hold fast without question. This firm grip on hope is to be *unwavering* despite personal or cultural circumstances, and it leads God's people to consider how to stir one another up to love and good works and avoid neglecting gathering together "as is the habit of some" (10:25).

Such holding fast to the hope of Christ, the faithful one, thus has a virtue-forming – even habit-forming – effect, made possible by Christ the faithful one. Daniel Treier keenly observes the following concerning faith as virtue:

> Faith is a matter of time, for it is a virtue – not simply an internal property to be acquired, and then momentarily isolated when described or assessed – but an enduring pattern of action in a moral space marked by divine communication. Christian understanding of faith develops not by proof-texting biblical

definitions but from reading such texts within an anthropology and a narrative framework shaped by covenant.[20]

I must also note that the preacher returns to the virtue-forming nature of faith in chapter thirteen when he calls God's people to "imitate the faith" of their leaders (ἡγέομαι). He writes, "Remember your leaders, those who spoke to you the word of God. Consider the outcome of their way of life, and imitate their faith" (μιμεῖσθε τὴν πίστιν) (13:7). Also, ten verses later, "Obey your leaders and submit to them, for they are keeping watch over your souls, as those who will have to give an account" (13:17a). While much could be addressed from these verses, my concern is the emphasis on faith in the lives of church leaders. What must it mean to "imitate" the faith of a leader? So active and formative must such faith be in the life of a leader that church members should not only follow his or her example but imitate – literally, mimic – it. This leader is one who models the fruit of the Spirit that is "faithfulness" with regard to endurance and with regard to reliance on the Spirit of God rather than on oneself.

Third, faith *fuels* our future hope in God's promise. The author writes in 6:11–12, "And we desire each one of you to show the same earnestness to have the full assurance of *hope* until the end, so that you may not be sluggish, but imitators of those who through *faith* and patience inherit the *promises*" (emphasis added).

Following from my second point earlier that faith *forms* the people of God, this forming quality of faith is also linked both to hope and a future promise. Hope, we might say, is that theological virtue that is activated by faith and leans stubbornly forward towards God's promises of an eternal inheritance.[21] Hope cannot operate alone. Faith fuels hope towards this stubborn disposition of eternal confidence. But it not only fuels hope – it grounds it. Precisely here is where the embodied and in-creation work of Christ is of utmost importance. The Christian faith, founded on the activity of Jesus, God in the flesh, grounds this hope-filled future for those who believe.[22] This faith does not float aimlessly upon religious speculation or human emotion, but finds its footing in the work

---

20. Daniel J. Treier, "Faith," in *Dictionary of Theological Interpretation*, ed. Kevin J. Vanhoozer (Grand Rapids: Baker Academic, 2005), 228.

21. Stephen R. Spencer helpfully defines hope as, ". . . waiting in confident expectation for God's promises in Christ, summed up in the gospel." "Hope" in *Dictionary of Theological Interpretation*, 305.

22. Victor (Sung-Yul) Rhee has observed, "An examination of the major passages of Hebrews also indicated that faith is not only christological but also eschatological. . . . More specifically, the eschatological outlook of Hebrews is not simply futuristic; it also involves a present aspect." *Faith in Hebrews: Analysis within the Context of Christology, Eschatology, and Ethics* (New York: Peter Lang, 2001), 252.

of God in the flesh, who acted within the space and time of creation. Based on his promises, faith guarantees our hope for the future.

Such accents on faith in today's preaching of Hebrews must not end with mere information about God's work in Christ, how faith relates to formation, or an inspiring exposé about our future hope. Rather, it should first lead to deep reflection – *hearing* – taking internal inventory of the condition of one's soul, calling God's people towards confession and repentance. Then it needs to move from reflection to action – *obedience* – in the body, not just the soul, to manifest an active love for God and neighbor in the world.[23] Such a faith-fueled hope forms God's people from the inside out in ways that affect God's world. As Stephen Spencer suggests, "Hopeful Christians should be diligent servants in the world, manifesting the gospel's hope in their vocations. As new creations foreshadowing the new creation, Christians should be means of gracious change to the communities and structures of the age, calling others to join in mercy and justice now and hope for the culminative justice and renewal."[24]

Moreover, such preaching on faith for today must not be aimed only at the congregation. It must be reflexive, applying most especially to the leaders of the church. For these figures must set such an example of faith and faithfulness that they can humbly yet boldly invite congregants to *mimic* their way of life and faith.

ASSEMBLING TOGETHER

In his insightful book *Preaching Hebrews* Douglas D. Webster explains,

> Many Christians look upon the church as optional, as one of many weekend possibilities. If they're caught up with their work and sleep, and have nothing more pressing to do, they may attend to church....
>
> The [author] does not stop here to develop a theology of the church, partly because he cannot conceive of faith in Christ apart from the body of Christ. The obsolescence of Old Testament liturgical and priestly customs does not in any way diminish the importance of vital worship and fellowship among Christ's followers ... The supremacy of Christ over all things creates

---

23. A reminder of Chrétien's insight that "... the Word which sought our listening and our response is engendered in us when we listen to it and respond to it, *which moreover is the same thing*" (emphasis added), *Under the Gaze of the Bible*, 4–5.

24. Stephen R. Spencer, "Hope," 307.

a special identity and purpose for the church. Jesus is not only Lord of the universe but the head of the church and his presence fills not only the cosmos, but the church. This high view of the church and its impact on the world echoes Jesus' authoritative pronouncement in the Sermon on the Mount, when he declared to his disciples, "You are the salt of the earth," and "You are the light of the world (Matt 5:13, 14).[25]

Prior to global lockdowns in 2020–2021 due to the COVID-19 pandemic, emphasis on "assembling together" might have been a passing comment in a chapter such as the present one. Following lockdown restrictions, however, churches have struggled to return to pre-pandemic attendance and regular gathering rhythms. Reasons for this vary, but a common refrain from pastors and parishioners alike is that "people have learned they can worship from home," leaving many unmotivated to return to the corporate gathering, preferring instead the convenience of "online worship." While I do not mean to suggest that joining a worship service at home via technological means is of no value, especially for the elderly and infirm who have few other options, I do mean to stress that failure to gather with the people of God is to neglect the *ethos* of the confessing, hoping, and encouraging people of God.

Echoing the formative nature of faith discussed earlier, our current cultural moment demands attention to the importance of "assembling together." Excuses and failure for neglecting the corporate gathering are far from unique to our post-lockdown era. Even the original hearers of Hebrews needed a fresh reminder. Moreover, the author adds the passing comment that neglecting the assembly had become the "habit" or "custom" (ἔθος) of some.

What is so important about the *ethos* of God's gathered people? Hebrews associates gathering with confessing, hoping, and encouraging together.

> Let **us** hold fast the **confession of our hope** without wavering, for he who promised is faithful. And let **us** consider how to stir up **one another** to love and good works, not neglecting to meet **together**, as is the **habit** [ἔθος] of some, but **encouraging one another**, and all the more as you see the Day drawing near. (10:23–25, emphasis added)

At this point in the great sermon of Hebrews, we might imagine the volume of the preacher's emphasis on "us," "one another," and "together" to be almost

---

25. Douglas D. Webster, *Preaching Hebrews: The End of Religion and Faithfulness to the End* (Eugene, OR: Cascade Books, 2017), 128–29.

deafening Neither a priest nor parishioner of Israel was a freelancer.[26] The lone-ranger Christian walks a dangerous path, especially when in a persecuted context like the original audience of Hebrews. The path of aloneness lacks the much-needed reminder from others to "hold fast our confession of hope," lacks the provocation towards "love and good works," and lacks the much-needed "encouraging one another . . . as you see the Day drawing near."

Here the preacher returns to the notion of "day" found in chapter two. Hebrews employs the well-known motif of the day of the Lord specifically to highlight the time in which the original hearers lived – a time of suffering and trial yet a time ripe with opportunity for confession, hope, and "encouraging one another" in faithfulness to Christ. A time that while it is still day – that is, before the darkness of death comes – God's people must gather *together* in the confidence of Christ, our great High Priest (10:19–21).

CONSIDERING LOVE AND GOOD DEEDS – LIFE IN GOD'S WORLD TODAY

Craig Bartholomew's chapter in the present volume capably and convincingly argues for the essential role of the doctrine of creation both in the book of Hebrews and for a full understanding of divine action. As I highlighted earlier in connection with 11:3, Bartholomew also notes the role of faith in grasping a proper doctrine of creation and comments that this high view of creation is opposed to any background assumptions of a Platonic view of the natural world.[27] Moreover, he reminds us not only of the high view of creation in Hebrews, but also of the integral link between creation and eschatology. He argues,

> Are we to see the earth as secondary and heaven as our true home? Such a view is not uncommon, but it is damaging to the witness of the church. Far from a focus on our king in heaven making the things of the earth becoming strangely dim, as the chorus has it, earthly things come into proper focus as God's good creation. The world is not God – and nor, for that matter, is heaven – but it is his creation, and as such it bears witness to his glory. Heaven is his throne and earth his footstool, and thus in terms of priority the throne by far comes first. However, in terms of human beings, speaking of "the earth" as secondary

---

26. Thanks to Gareth Cockerill for this helpful insight.
27. C. Bartholomew, "Creation, Divine Action, and Hebrews," 153–54. Earlier in this chapter, Bartholomew cites Ceslas Spicq, *L'Épître aux Hébreux*, 2nd ed., 2 vols., Étude biblique (Paris: Gabalda, 1953), who argues for a Platonic background to the book of Hebrews.

is unhelpful. We only exist as part of the creation, of "the earth," and we live on the earth for God and seek to enhance his reputation. As such, we pray for the day when his kingdom will come *on earth*, just as it is in heaven.[28]

Following this exhortation, preaching Hebrews to hear God's address today must include a robust view of what it means to live faithfully day by day in God's world. While the world in its present form is not our ultimate end, nor do we ground our hope in the here and now, Hebrews urges that faithful daily living for the Christ-follower is ever aware of the goodness of God's created world and simultaneously the opposition that awaits those who believe. We are called to "hold fast" our confession "without wavering, for he who promised is faithful" (10:23). Nowhere does Hebrews urge us to abandon God's world or to abdicate our embodied responsibilities for loving God and neighbor. Quite the opposite. Rather, Hebrews expects those who have believed the promise to live evermore *into* this present world, sober to the reality of suffering yet committed to the vocation of love. This is why the author charges his audience to "consider how to stir up one another to love and good works" (10:24).

Preaching Hebrews today must then insist on the discipline of "considering" (κατανοέω). This "considering" is the act of careful reflection, which in this passage relies on the memory of the past – the promise of the Faithful One – in order to live rightly in the present. Memory is integral here, for it is that faculty of the soul that Israel so often neglected by failing to recall their God and his activity on their behalf, leading them to the unspeakable sin and injustice which the prophets described. And, just as in the new covenant the Lord will "remember [our] sins no more" (8:12; 10:17), the preacher of Hebrews must be diligent to *remind* God's people of his faithful action on their behalf as the stimulus for "considering" how to "stir up [literally, provoke] one another to love and good works."

Following the climactic discourse on faith in chapters eleven and twelve, the author of Hebrews returns to practical daily living with a string of imperatives and forceful rhetoric in chapter thirteen. "Considering" how to "stir up one another to love and good works" thus includes at least the following ten items:

- Brotherly love (13:1)
- Hospitality (13:2)
- Remembering the imprisoned (13:3)

---

28. Bartholomew, "Creation, Divine Action, and Hebrews," 164.

- Holding marriage in highest regard (13:4)
- Contentment (13:5)
- Remembering your leaders and imitating their faith (13:7)
- Turning from "diverse and strange" teaching (13:9)
- Doing good (13:16)
- Trusting and submitting to your leaders who keep watch over your souls (13:17)
- Praying for one another (13:18)

Space prevents in-depth attention to each of these (though much can and should be said especially about the important of a high view of marriage, sexual purity, and greed in contemporary society!), but a few brief and broad observations are in order. First, the place of these mostly neighborly virtues in the structure of Hebrews must not be overlooked. These imperatives are the right response of those who have believed in the past, present, and future work of Christ our Priest and King. Such "good works" do nothing to curry favor with God. Rather, they are the appropriate response of worship, the happy habits of those who delight in God's law of love.

Second, "brotherly love" (φιλαδελφία) functions as the fount for the subsequent acts of virtue. Since love is the greatest of the theological virtues (1 Cor 13:13), we should expect it to lead the list of virtuous activity in Hebrews's sermon application. But, like the fruit of the Spirit in Gal 5:22–23, love does not merely lead the list; it is the soil out of which the other fruit grows. For the preacher of Hebrews, then, such love immediately calls for the ministry of hospitality, which leads to remembering those in prison presumably for the Gospel's sake and then to holding the covenant of marriage in highest regard. Flowing from φιλαδελφία, these first three imperatives are exterior in nature – embodied and visible actions of God's faithful people that accord with the character of God, the gospel of the Son, and the ministry of the Spirit.

The remaining exhortations aim towards the interior life, with the expectation that proper interior cultivation manifests exterior virtue. Contentment, remembering and imitating our leaders, doctrinal discernment, the posture towards doing good, submitting to those who minister to us before God, and prayer – together these speak to a disposition of the soul: a soul that has tasted of the goodness of God and remained faithful; a soul that is keen to the dangers all around seeking to attack the mind through false teaching, the heart through discouragement and disbelief, and the body through immorality or defection from the faith; and a soul that daily confesses faith in God, looks to exercise good at all times, submits to authority, and remains fervent in prayer. Above all, this is the soul of one bent towards "lay[ing] aside every weight, and sin which clings so closely" and finishing the race.

THE *TELOS* OF TODAY: JESUS'S PRIESTHOOD AND THE *END* OF GOD'S PEOPLE

Each of the previous themes are, in my view, integral to the faithful preaching and teaching of Hebrews for today. But without a proper grounding in the priesthood of Jesus, one runs the risk of merely principlizing or moralizing the message of Hebrews. Moreover, failure to address the eschatology of Hebrews would also be a glaring mistake, especially given its radical and reorienting effect on the original audience. Thus, our final theme anchors the previous themes in Christ's priesthood with a view to its eschatological implications for today's audience.

For the original Jewish hearers of Hebrews, the person and work of Jesus radically altered eschatological expectations. Before Christ, even the most faithful Jewish followers assumed that the Messiah would reestablish the kingdom of God in full upon his arrival. While this remains the future hope and expectation of God's people, Christ did not reestablish the kingdom in full upon arrival – he inaugurated it.

From the opening lines, the author of Hebrews alerts his audience to the intersection of eschatology with Christ the creator of all things; for "in these last days [God] has spoken to us by his Son, whom he appointed the heir of all things, through whom also he created the world" (1:2b). And in 5:6, this Son is recognised as a "priest forever, after the order of Melchizedek." These three – eschatology, Christ as creator of all things, and his eternal priesthood – thus form a foundational and fertile seam in the sermon of Hebrews. It reoriented the expectations of early Jewish Christians away from an all-at-once kingdom establishment to a faith-forward, persevering-in-hope way of life.

At least two considerations are in order. First, the ongoing (eternal) priesthood of Jesus is the lynchpin of Christian hope. To remove, deny, or simply underemphasise the eternal priesthood of the Son is to weaken the inner logic of the message of Hebrews, thus undermining the overall supremacy of Jesus relative to the angels, to Moses, and to the old covenant.

Second, Jesus's ongoing priesthood reinforces God's commitment to creation. Because of the superior and eternally purifying work of Christ our High Priest, a "new and living way" is opened to us on earth through his flesh (10:20). In no way does Hebrews suggest that the original heavens and earth will be destroyed and a new heavens and earth created *ex nihilo* all over again. Rather, the imagery of Hebrews is that of purification (1:3, 9:13–23) wherein the grace of God through Christ restores creation unto a new heavens and earth, removing what is "shakable" while a "kingdom that cannot be shaken" remains (12:27–28). As Jihye Lee has recently argued,

> ... the author [of Hebrews] envisages the eschatological world that consists of not the heavenly world exclusively – as some scholars argue – but the renewed creation as well. God's rest, which Adam forfeited through his sin and which Israel were intended to enjoy when they were told to enter into the promised land, will finally be found in this unshakable kingdom where the renewed creation will be united with the revealed heaven.[29]

The precise how and when of this ultimate restoration and renewal is shrouded in mystery, but Christian confidence rides on the resurrected Christ, the "firstborn from the dead" (Col 1:18; Rev 1:5) who fills his followers with his Spirit and teaches us to pray, "Your Kingdom come, your will be done, *on earth as it is in heaven*" (Matt 6:10, emphasis added). Our sermonic accent, as modeled by the preacher of Hebrews, must address the "Why?" in the certainty of Christ's eternal priesthood and the "So what?" in the exhortation to faithful living. This is today's *telos*, the homing beacon of Christian hope, the true *end* for God's people.

CONCLUSION

Our considerations have merely scratched the surface of the many and important themes that inform contemporary preaching of Hebrews. In this vein, I join the author of Hebrews who urges, "bear with my word of exhortation, for I have written to you briefly" (13:22).

However, I trust that the themes considered in this chapter resonate with the heartbeat of the original preacher of Hebrews and warms and provokes the hearts of contemporary preachers and hearers of Hebrews. Further exploration of this great sermon would do well to attend more closely to Hebrews's

---

29. See Jihye Lee, *A Jewish Apocalyptic Framework of Eschatology in the Epistle to the Hebrews* (London; New York; Dublin: T&T Clark, 2022), 127. Following Koester and Cockerill, Lee denies any notion of Platonic dualism, urging instead that Jewish apocalyptic texts provide insight toward reading 12:26–29 as an "unshakable kingdom that will be established through the changing of the earth and heaven, which is called their shaking" (128).

rich Christology and to the many warning passages found throughout the book – especially with Jean-Louis Chrétien's suggestions for "hearing" in view. But positions notwithstanding, both preachers and hearers of God's word must ever remember to be a Bethlehem-kind of people apprenticed in *shema*. They must stress the God who speaks, the active faith of the faithful, and the discipline of assembling together; give careful attention to love and good deeds as shown in Hebrews's final chapter; and clarify eschatological expectations grounded in and reoriented by the eternal priesthood of Jesus.

SELECT BIBLIOGRAPHY

Bauckham, Richard, Daniel R. Driver, Trevor A. Hart, and Nathan MacDonald, eds. *The Epistle to the Hebrews and Christian Theology*. Grand Rapids: Eerdmans, 2009.

Chrétien, Jean-Louis. *Under the Gaze of the Bible*. Translated by John Marson Dunaway. New York: Fordham University Press, 2015.

Cockerill, Gareth Lee. *The Epistle to the Hebrews*. NICNT. Grand Rapids: Eerdmans, 2012.

Griffiths, Jonathan I. *Hebrews and Divine Speech*. London; New York: T&T Clark, 2014.

Guthrie, G. H. *Hebrews: The NIV Application Commentary*. Grand Rapids: Zondervan, 1998.

Lee, Jihye. *A Jewish Apocalyptic Framework of Eschatology in the Epistle to the Hebrews*. London; New York; Dublin: T&T Clark, 2022.

Rhee, Victor (Sung-Yul). *Faith in Hebrews: Analysis within the Context of Christology, Eschatology, and Ethics*. New York: Peter Lang, 2001.

Vanhoozer, Kevin, ed. *Dictionary of Theological Interpretation*. Grand Rapids: Baker Academic, 2005.

———. *The Drama of Doctrine: A Canonical Linguistic Approach to Christian Doctrine*. Louisville, KY: Westminster John Knox Press, 2005.

Webster, Douglas D. *Preaching Hebrews: The End of Religion and Faithfulness to the End*. Eugene, OR: Cascade Books, 2017.

CHAPTER 15

On the Road to Perfection

Divine Action, Human Agency, and Moral Transformation in the Epistle to the Hebrews

Michael J. Rhodes

INTRODUCTION

The author of Hebrews simply could not stop talking about transformation. Throughout the sermon, the preacher describes such transformation in varied and vivid language, speaking of Christians being brought to glory (cf. 2:10), being made holy (cf. 10:14), having the Lord's laws written on their hearts (cf. 10:16), having their consciences sprinkled clean, being purified (10:22), and, perhaps most strikingly, moving on to perfection or maturity (cf. 5:14–6:1). Such transformation frees God's people from acts that lead to death *so that* they might serve the living God (9:14).[1] Divine agency is emphasised in this process of human *transformation* throughout the letter. Intriguingly, however, human acts of moral and spiritual *formation* also play an essential and constitutive role in the process.[2]

In this chapter, I explore the interaction of divine and human agency in the

---

1. Thompson rightly translates "minister" here in order to "maintain cultic imagery" (James Thompson, *Hebrews*, Paideia Commentary on the New Testament [Grand Rapids: Baker Academic, 2008], 187).

2. In Michael J. Rhodes, *Just Discipleship: Biblical Justice in an Unjust World* (Downers Grove: IVP Academic, 2023), I make a similar theological case in regards to 1 John, and explore what this means for a biblical account of moral formation towards justice across the canon.

process of human transformation within Hebrews. I argue that the epistle commends character-forming practices of spiritual formation, growth in the virtues, and corporate gathering, and also understands such practices as human acts of *formation* that flow out of and participate in the triune God's *trans*formation of his people. Such an account not only clarifies aspects of the theology and ethics of Hebrews in relation to divine and human agency, but also contributes to a theological ethics concerned with issues of character, virtue, and formation.

WHAT IS MAN THAT YOU ARE MINDFUL OF HIM?: THE GOAL OF (TRANS)FORMATION IN HEBREWS

Shortly after the breathtaking introduction in 1:1–14, the author quotes portions of Ps 8:

> What is man that you are mindful of him,
> or a son of man that you care for him?
> You have made him a little lower than the angels;[3]
> you have crowned him with glory and honor
> subjecting all things under his feet. (2:6b–8a, author's translation)[4]

A major question that confronts interpreters at this point is the extent to which the author of Hebrews draws on the psalm's original meaning (the high calling of humanity) and to what extent the author applies the text to Jesus.[5]

Most likely, however, the ambiguity is intentional, with Ps 8 offering us "Hebrews' soteriology and anthropology"[6] simultaneously. In other words, Christ's incarnational ministry is the means by which the triune God leads many children to the glory and honor of their original human calling. The "glory of the Son is to become the glory of [humanity]."[7] Christ's vocation is to restore humans to their vocation.

---

3. Or perhaps, "you made him/them for a little while lower than the angels" (NRSV; ESV).

4. I have avoided the normally preferable use of gender-inclusive language here, because the use of singular masculine constructions that could be read as references to Jesus *or* to all of humanity (as Ps 8 clearly does) helps create a productive theological ambiguity.

5. Some argue for a heavy emphasis on Christ as the "man" referred to in 2:6b, such that the entire citation is about Jesus. Others see humanity as the referent up through 2:9. Interpreted thus, the meaning of 2:8b–9 would be something like "We do not yet see evidence of humanity fulfilling their high calling, but we do see Jesus doing so."

6. D. Stephen Long, *Hebrews*, Belief: A Theological Commentary on the Bible (Louisville, KY: Westminster John Knox Press, 2011), 58.

7. David Peterson, *Hebrews and Perfection: An Examination of the Concept of Perfection in the "Epistle to the Hebrews,"* SNTSMS 47 (New York: CUP, 1982), 56.

THE TRIUNE GOD ACTS TO TRANSFORM HIS PEOPLE

The rest of Hebrews will unpack in greater detail this story of the triune God's action to transform his people into a holy, perfected family freed *from* sin *for* service to the living God. Hebrews clearly emphasises divine agency in this transformation. Precisely because of this clear emphasis, for the purposes of this chapter, I will first very briefly summarise four ways Hebrews describes the triune God's action to transform humanity. I will then turn to a more thorough exploration of the somewhat surprising role human agency plays in this process.

First, the triune God acts to transform humans through divine speech. Such speaking occurs climactically through the Father's speaking "in one who is Son,"[8] but also includes the Scriptures themselves, which Hebrews refers to "as the words of God (1:5–13), of Christ (2:12–13), and of the Holy Spirit (3:7)."[9] In 4:11–13, the word of God is God-like: it is living, active, penetrating to the deepest interiority of human hearts, and filled with the "strength and effectiveness ... [of] a medicine."[10]

Second, the triune God transforms human lives through Jesus's embodiment of human virtue and perfection. Christ's moral character is emphasised throughout Hebrews in ways that underscore the nature of believers' own transformation. Jesus embodies moral dispositions and virtues such as mercy, faithfulness,[11] righteousness, "godly fear" (εὐλάβεια), and perseverance (ὑπομονή; 12:2–3). He is described as "holy, innocent, and undefiled" (cf. 7:26); indeed, he is a priest "according to the order of Melchizedek" (6:20), whose very name means king of righteousness and peace (7:2).[12] Moreover, Hebrews highlights Jesus's *spiritual* character in terms of his faithful orientation towards the Father, including in his earthly prayer life, heavenly intercession, and ongoing priesthood (cf. 3:2; 5:7; 7:25; 9:24; 10:5–10). Jason Whitlark argues compellingly that such descriptions present Jesus in ways that resonate with the ancient conception of the king as a living law who "embodied in himself all necessary virtue and conduct."[13] In any case, nearly every one of these moral and spiritual

---

8. This is Westcott's translation, quoted in H. W. Attridge, *The Epistle to the Hebrews: A Commentary on the Epistle to the Hebrews*, Hermeneia (Philadelphia: Fortress, 1989), 39.

9. Ben Witherington, *New Testament Theology and Ethics* (Downers Grove: IVP Academic, 2016), 393.

10. Luke Timothy Johnson, *Hebrews: A Commentary*, NTL (Louisville, KY: Westminster John Knox Press, 2006), 133.

11. Johnson, *Hebrews*, 103.

12. Unless otherwise noted, Scripture references are taken from the NRSV.

13. Jason A. Whitlark, "The Ideal King: The Exemplary and Empowering Role of the Son of God," in *"A Temple Not Made with Hands:" Essays in Honor of Naymond H. Keathley*, ed. Mikeal C. Parsons and Richard Walsh (Eugene, OR: Pickwick, 2018), 105.

dispositions ascribed to Jesus are presented in Hebrews as present or aspirational qualities in believers. Thus, the triune God transforms people in part through the provision of the ultimate *example* in Jesus.

Third, the triune God acts to transform humans through the Son's willing embrace of solidarity with his people. In Jesus we have one who, having been tempted in every way as we are yet without sin, can "sympathise" (συμπαθέω) with us (4:15). This language points to the "essentially familial bond of solidarity that Jesus shares with humanity."[14] Moreover, Jesus's *sharing* in human flesh – his μετέχω (2:14) – enables sinful humans to become sharers – μέτοχοι – in a heavenly calling (3:1), in Christ himself (3:14), and in the Holy Spirit (6:4). Stephen Long points out that such sharing language represents one of the two key ways the Orthodox tradition explains participation in Christ through the language of *theosis*.[15] Jesus's solidarity with humanity is the means by which Christians are united to Jesus by the power of the Spirit, becoming more of what he is by virtue of his becoming what we are.

Such transformative solidarity extends to Christ's faithfulness unto death, by which he destroyed the devil and the power of death. In this light, we can speak of the transforming solidarity of Jesus as also a liberating solidarity that establishes a radically new space within which human life can be lived, namely, one freed from the enslaving fear of death (2:15). Finally, the triune God transforms humans through the high priestly work of the Son. Christ, as Great High Priest and sacrificial victim, has once for all made the transforming power of the triune God available to humanity, and still lives to intercede on humanity's behalf (7:25). Christ abolishes the old covenant's sacrificial system[16] – which Hebrews consistently portrays as unable to provide for human transformation (7:19a) – and inaugurates a new covenant. This new covenant is new both "chronologically [and] ontologically" because "it essentially engages the internal dispositions of humans."[17]

This priestly work requires that Jesus serve as the representative of humanity who both "fulfills and displays" God's intention for humanity and "[suffers]

---

14. Kevin B. McCruden, "The Concept of Perfection in the Epistle to the Hebrews," in *Reading the Epistle to the Hebrews*, ed. Eric F. Mason and Kevin B. McCruden (Atlanta: SBL Press, 2011), 219.

15. Long, *Hebrews*, 101–4.

16. See Johnson, *Hebrews*, 210, 226, 239. While sufficient for creating some level of outward purity (9:13), the old covenant is explicitly or implicitly critiqued in Hebrews because it "made nothing perfect" (7:19a), could not cleanse the conscience of the worshiper (9:9b), failed to set worshipers free from "acts that lead to death, so that [they] may serve the living God" (9:14b), could not permanently remove the "sins of the people" (9:28; 10:3–4), could not make the people permanently holy (10:10) and pure (10:22), or write the law of God on the peoples' hearts (10:16). Yet at every point, the new covenant over which Christ is high priest, mediator, and sacrificial victim achieves precisely this needed transformation.

17. Johnson, *Hebrews*, 239.

on the behalf of humanity."[18] Jesus is "made perfect" (5:9) through his life, death, resurrection, and ascension, not in terms of an overcoming of character flaws, but in terms of his putting into human action his perfect character:

> [Christ] brings his perfection as the "exact imprint" of God into creation, into its space and time, and achieves it there. He becomes what he is. Because he achieves perfection, he then becomes the source for perfection, leading creation into it (5:9).[19]

And the blood Jesus spills in this journey of perfection is available for the cleansing of sin-corrupted human consciences,[20] thus sanctifying and perfecting for himself a people (cf. 10:14).

Indeed, Christ's high priestly work undergirds the other aspects of the triune God's transforming work. It is only the Son's offering in obedience to the Father by the power of the Spirit that allows humans to hear the God who speaks, imitate the example of the Son, or embrace the familial solidarity of Jesus.

HUMANITY PARTICIPATES IN THE TRANSFORMING WORK OF GOD THROUGH MORAL AND SPIRITUAL FORMATION

Given this emphasis on divine agency, we might assume Hebrews would downplay human agency in the process of transformation. Surprisingly, this is far from the case. Yes, Heb 10 declares that Christ has sanctified (v. 10) and perfected (v. 14) his people once for all. Nearly in the same breath, however, the preacher exhorts them to grow in love and good deeds (v. 24) and warns of the danger facing those who "willfully persist in sin after having received the knowledge of the truth" (v. 26) and "were sanctified" by "the blood of the covenant" (v. 29). Hebrews insists, in other words, that humans participate in God's *transformation* by exercising their renewed human agency in concrete acts of moral and spiritual *formation*. Such formation is the means "by which creatures . . . participate in the Holy Spirit's [*transforming*] work."[21] In this section, I will

---

18. Kevin B. McCruden, *Solidarity Perfected: Beneficent Christology in the Epistle to the Hebrews*, BZNW 159 (New York: De Gruyter, 2008), 48.

19. Long, *Hebrews*, 100.

20. Johnson, *Hebrews*, 238.

21. Long, *Hebrews*, 114.

consider such formative acts under the categories of spiritual formation, growth in the virtues, and corporate gathering.

SPIRITUAL FORMATION

The awe-inspiring depiction of the triune God's cosmos-rescuing action in and through the Son in 1:1–14 gives way to an exhortation to pay greater attention to what has been heard (2:1). This transition embodies the "close link between doctrine and ethics" visible throughout the sermon; what is heard is a "way of life. To hear [these words] is to be changed."[22]

But, apparently, it is possible to hear these words in such a way that one is *not* changed (cf. 4:2). The danger facing the listeners is neither that the triune God has not spoken nor that they have not heard, but, apparently, that the hearers are in danger of paying insufficient attention to what has been spoken. The solution to such inattention includes spiritual formation, by which I refer to practices that God's people actively use to orient themselves towards a transforming encounter with God.

Hebrews commends such practices repeatedly. God's people are called to an active listening that combines hearing with faith (4:2b). Three times the preacher quotes Ps 95:7's "Today, if you hear his voice, do not harden your hearts" (3:7–8, 15; 4:7), explicitly describing the active agency of the hearers in receiving what has been spoken.

Contemplation is another spiritual practice suggested by Hebrews. The preacher boldly proclaims that although we do not yet see Jesus and a renewed humanity ruling in glory over all things, *we do see Jesus* (2:9). This vision of Jesus that we see must lead to deeper contemplation. Therefore, just as the exalted speech about Jesus in Heb 1 gives way to the admonition to pay greater attention in Heb 2, Heb 2's exalted description of Jesus gives way to the admonition to "consider Jesus, the apostle and high priest of our confession" (3:1 RSV). The Greek word κατανοέω is "drawn from the visual sphere."[23] The language of sight gestures towards spiritual practices of deep contemplation of the triune God (cf. 12:2) and the destiny of the saints in the unshakeable kingdom (12:18–24).

Likewise, Hebrews also commends related acts of spiritual formation such as prayer, thanksgiving, and worship by which the people draw near to God (7:19; 10:22). This sermon, then, teaches that spiritual practices of attentiveness, contemplation, and "drawing near" in prayer and worship are truly human acts of formation that participate in the triune God's transformation of our lives.

---

22. Long, *Hebrews*, 52–53.
23. Thompson, *Hebrews*, 89.

GROWTH IN THE VIRTUES

Second, however, Hebrews depicts the cultivation of the virtues as essential "human acts by which creatures can participate in the Holy Spirit's work and thereby receive the promises."[24] Indeed, this can be seen by observing what gets in the way of the spiritual formation described in the previous section.

In 3:12, it is an evil, "unbelieving" or "faithless" (ἀπιστία) heart that causes us to turn away from God, just as our spiritual forefathers did in the wilderness (4:2). The repeated exhortation to refrain from actively hardening one's heart (cf. 3:8) should not be reduced to a warning about "unbelief" understood in a hypercognitive fashion. Instead, hardening one's heart occurs as one continues in sinful acts (3:13, 15–18) of *faithlessness* (3:19; 4:6).[25] This emphasis on pursuing a certain kind of heart is all the more remarkable given that the author can just as easily declare that Christ has already written the law on his new covenant people's hearts!

Hebrews, then, understands moral formation, including the active cultivation of virtue, as essential human activity necessary for believers to receive and appropriate Christ's transforming power. Intriguingly, such an account fits well with aspects of Aquinas's own overhaul of the Aristotelian virtue tradition. For Aquinas, unlike for Aristotle, the *source* of *true* or *infused* virtue is God himself, who works the virtues "in us, without us."[26]

Aquinas thus understands the truly virtuous life as a total gift from God. His understanding of the infused virtues, however, nevertheless includes human agency: infusion does not occur without the person's "consent";[27] contrary, habituated dispositions make the exercise of infused virtue difficult;[28] and acts produced by an infused virtue "strengthen the already existing [virtue]" just as medicine strengthens the health of an already healthy person.[29] This is true because the infused virtues take greater root in our souls through our practice of actions in line with those virtues.[30] Aquinas's infused virtues, in other words, act in ways that reflect the virtue tradition's insistence that moral formation includes habituation and practice.[31]

---

24. Long, *Hebrews*, 114.

25. Cf. Johnson, *Hebrews*, 119.

26. *Summa Theologiae* I–II, q. 62, a. 1.

27. *Summa Theologiae* I–II, q. 55, a. 4.

28. *Summa Theologiae* I–II, q. 65, a. 3.

29. Although here Aquinas refers to strengthening a "habit," because Aquinas sees virtue as a habit, I have substituted virtue language for ease of explanation. Cf. *Summa Theologiae* I–II, q. 51, a. 4.

30. *Summa Theologiae* II–II, q. 47, a. 14. Even this is the result of the Holy Spirit's work, as Aquinas makes clear in II–II, q. 24, a. 5.

31. On this point, see Jean Porter, "The Subversion of Virtue: Acquired and Infused Virtues in the Summa Theologiae," *The Annual of The Society of Christian Ethics* (1992): 41; William C. Mattison III,

Intriguingly for our purposes, in a discussion of this aspect of the infused virtues, Aquinas cites Heb 5:11–14 as evidence for his theological account of infused virtues.[32] In this passage, the author of Hebrews suggests his listeners struggle to understand the message because they have become sluggish in hearing. Though after so much time they should now be teaching others, they instead need to be taught the "ABCs" over again (5:12).[33] They are like infants who are unacquainted with the "word of righteousness."

"But," Hebrews continues, "solid food is for the mature/perfect (τελείων), who, on account of their mature state (διὰ τὴν ἕξιν), have had their faculties trained (γεγυμνασμένα) for distinguishing good and evil" (author's translation).

In his commentary on Hebrews, Aquinas suggests that the "mature state" or ἕξις referred to in 5:14 is that of one in whom the gift of virtue has grown through practice, both in terms of the exercise of the intellect and the exercise of the moral will.[34] Aristotle himself considered virtue a ἕξις, that is, a habituated disposition towards the good.[35] And while the "mature state" referred to by ἕξις need not refer specifically to a moral disposition appropriated through practice in the author of Hebrews's day, it certainly *could*. To take just one example, for Philo a ἕξις can refer to either virtuous or vicious dispositions (*Allegorical Interpretation* 2:18). The practice of vice leads to a vicious ἕξις or disposition (*On Agriculture* 101), while true blessedness occurs when actions are done from a fixed disposition to the good (*Allegorical Interpretation* 3:210).[36]

Moreover, Philo can deploy γυμνάζω language to speak of the acquisition of virtue through both teaching[37] and practising moral habituation. Thus, he speaks of Jacob as having attained the virtues through his training and exercise in wrestling with his passions (*On Sobriety* 1:65); of "training" in drinking wine as destroying virtue (*On Drunkenness* 1:22); and, maybe most tellingly, of those who have been made perfect still needing to "become strengthened . . . by

---

"Can Christians Possess the Acquired Cardinal Virtues?" *Theological Studies* 72, no. 3 (2011): 561; and Jennifer A. Herdt, *Putting on Virtue: The Legacy of the Splendid Vices* (Chicago: Chicago University Press, 2008), 88–91.

32. *Summa Theologiae* II–II, q. 24, a. 4. Although even this is the result of the Holy Spirit's work, as Aquinas makes clear in II–II, q. 24, a. 5.

33. Gareth L. Cockerill, *The Epistle to the Hebrews*, NIGTC (Grand Rapids: Eerdmans, 2012), 257.

34. See Thomas Aquinas, *Commentary on the Epistle to the Hebrews*, trans. Fabian R. Larcher, O.P., 273–74, accessed May 23, 2023, https://isidore.co/aquinas/english/SSHebrews.htm#52.

35. A point noted in Eric F. Mason and Kevin B. McCruden, *Reading the Epistle to the Hebrews: A Resource for Students*, Resources for Biblical Study 66 (Atlanta: SBL Press, 2011), 17.

36. See also the discussion in Thompson, *Hebrews*, 119–22. Thompson, however, overemphasises the way the language serves as a metaphorical reference to intellectual training. I see this as a mistake because it neglects the way ἕξις language points to habituation through practice and intellectual training.

37. *On the Posterity of Cain* 1:141; *On Giants* 1:60; *On the Change of Names* 1:17; *On Flight and Finding* 1:125.

continual study and incessant γυμνάσμασιν" (*On Agriculture* 160). This last idea is due to the fact that even the τέλειος is not yet "thoroughly *practiced* in virtue."

Philo's use of such language to describe growth in the virtues lends support to my argument that Heb 5:13–14 does in fact emphasise growth in the virtues as an important aspect of spiritual formation. Further evidence that Hebrews understands ἕξις as at least including virtuous character can be seen in the way 5:14b makes clear that the goal of this process of maturing includes moral discernment.[38] Indeed, both Aquinas and Chrysostom understood the "word of righteousness" (λόγου δικαιοσύνης; 5:13) as a reference to virtuous conduct, citing Matthew 5:20.[39]

I suggest, then, that the author of Hebrews would agree with Aquinas that the moral exercise of the virtues causes God's gracious gifts to take deeper root in the hearts of believers, and that such taking root would not only lead to a life of greater charity but also of wisdom.[40] Such growth in moral maturity would enable one to better grasp the necessary intellectual teaching. This is part and parcel of an understanding of character formation as both all gift *and* nevertheless bound up with human agency.

This interpretation is borne out elsewhere in Hebrews. The preacher describes the community's perseverance in suffering as participation in a divine "training" (παιδεία) that results in a harvest of the "peaceful fruit of righteousness" (12:11) and is itself a sign that they are already sons. Here again,

---

38. Aquinas, *Hebrews*, 274.

39. Aquinas, *Hebrews*, 269; John Chrysostom, *Homilies on the Gospel of St. John and the Epistle to the Hebrews*, trans. Philip Schaff, *NPNF* 1/14:406, https://www.ccel.org/ccel/schaff/npnf114; see also Attridge, *Hebrews*, 160. Thompson, however, argues that in Hebrews generally τέλειος does not refer to "moral perfection but of the right of access to God." In 5:14 he suggests the language simply contrasts a mature person with a child within the pedagogical metaphor (Thompson, *Hebrews*, 132). Thompson is no doubt right that being τέλειος is connected with access to God, but to eliminate the concept of moral maturity completely seems mistaken. Furthermore, even if the primary resonance here was in terms of the pedagogical metaphor, the references to the "word of righteousness" and "discerning good and evil" give it obvious ethical implications, as Thompson himself recognises (132). Cockerill suggests the phrase could even refer to the Christian faith more generally (Cockerill, *Hebrews*, 258–9).

40. I have drawn on Aquinas as a dialogue partner for exploring Hebrews's ethic of virtue formation. However, it's worth noting that Aquinas is by no means alone in claiming that the virtues that God gives the believer take greater root in their character through the believer's own acts of moral formation. Calvin likewise saw good works "as a pathway of transformation along which the goal of steady growth in sanctity throughout the Christian life is sought" (Stephen J. Chester, *Reading Paul with the Reformers: Reconciling Old and New Perspectives* [Grand Rapids: Eerdmans, 2017], 265). The authors of the Westminster Confession believed that sanctification was "the work of the Holy Spirit infusing a habit of holiness in the believer," so that "sanctification" included the "human pursuit of holiness subsequent to justification" (David B. Hunsicker, "Westminster Standards and the Possibility of a Reformed Virtue Ethic," *SJT* 71, no. 2 [2018]: 182, 184). And both Calvin and the Confession see the divine law as a summons that elicits character-forming acts of obedience (on which, see Michael J. Rhodes, *Formative Feasting: Practices and Virtue Ethics in Deuteronomy's Tithe Meal and the Corinthian Lord's Supper*, Studies in Biblical Literature [New York: Peter Lang, 2022], 26–35).

the required human formation through training in the virtues depends on and emerges out of the triune God's transforming work.

This idea of suffering as training is not limited to Hebrews; the concept also shows up in Philo, the Maccabean literature, and the Greco-Roman philosopher Seneca, among others.[41] Intriguingly for our purposes, this training through suffering is sometimes understood explicitly as training in virtue. In 4 Macc 10:10, for instance, one tortured Maccabean declares that his group is suffering "because of our godly training (παιδεία) and virtue (ἀρετή)."

The virtues developed through divine παιδεία include ὑπομονή. Christians require such "steadfast endurance" to do the will of God and receive the promise (10:36). Indeed, it is "steadfast endurance" which allows suffering to serve as effective training (12:7).[42] Thus, Christians must actively pursue and foster such ὑπομονή through concrete action that flows out of the triune God's loving offer of παιδεία (12:12–13).

Training in the virtues, however, also comes through imitation of Christ. The exhortation to imitate Jesus is more implicit than explicit. We see Hebrews present "Jesus as an example at the conclusion of a long line of Old Testament characters . . . [modeling] endurance in the face of shame and suffering."[43] Reflecting on his example enables us to persevere rather than give up (12:1–3). The parallel between the virtues of Christ and the exhortation for the saints to embody these same virtues also strongly suggests imitation is an aspect of discipleship. Indeed, while the sermon ascribes the wholly unique vocation of High Priest to Jesus, at the same time the preacher ascribes to humans an undeniably *priestly* vocation. This priestly vocation includes entering the holy place behind the curtain (10:19; cf. also 4:16; 7:1), serving the living God (9:14), and offering up sacrifices (θυσία) of praise (13:15). In any case, the summons to imitate Jesus becomes explicit in 13:12–14, which calls the saints to follow Jesus's example by joining him "outside the camp" and bearing the shame he bore.

All of this demonstrates the reality that Aquinas recognised, namely, that Christ is both "exemplar and example."[44] Christ "accomplishes in his own humanity the work of our salvation (exemplar), but also provides the model for

---

41. Thompson, *Hebrews*, 252.

42. Thompson rightly argues for substantial overlap between πίστις and ὑπομονή: "faith . . . is demonstrated through endurance" (Thompson, *Hebrews*, 253).

43. Jason Hood, *Imitating God in Christ: Recapturing a Biblical Pattern* (Downers Grove: IVP, 2013), 147.

44. Daniel Keating, "Thomas Aquinas and the Epistle to the Hebrews," in *Christology, Hermeneutics, and Hebrews: Profiles from the History of Interpretation*, ed. Jon C. Laansma and Daniel J. Treier, Library of Biblical Studies 423 (London: T&T Clark, 2012), 90.

us to follow (example)."[45] Because Jesus became *what we are*, his example of a life "eminently greater than our own" nevertheless is also "capable of being imitated."[46] We are to follow in his footsteps by approaching God "with the same [moral] dispositions that [Jesus] demonstrated."[47] Indeed, doing so is one way we become what he is, as we become united to him in his glorified, resurrected humanity. "Jesus' faithful endurance makes him a model for his brothers and sisters *and* inaugurates the context within which atonement can be effected."[48]

Whitlark's aforementioned argument that Hebrews draws on ancient discourse about the divine king as a "living law" strengthens this argument. Whitlark argues that in a tradition spanning both Greco-Roman and Jewish sources, the ideal king's "very presence" was understood to have "a powerful transformative effect on the lives of those under his rule." Indeed, the "presence of the ideal king cultivates virtuous inner dispositions among his subjects."[49] Notably, this tradition understands the transforming power of the king's presence to occur as his subjects *behold* the king.[50] Such a conception strengthens the connection in Hebrews between King Jesus's glorious example of perfect virtue and the exhortation that the community *fix their eyes* on Jesus (12:2; CEB).

But even as Hebrews creates resonances between the character to which we are called and the character of Christ, it also creates resonances between the character of Christ and the character of the saints. Indeed, "the similarity between the sacrifice of Jesus and the sacrifice of Old Testament saints makes them, like Jesus, models for perseverance and faithfulness in suffering and trial."[51] Hebrews explicitly connects growth in character that leads away from sluggishness to the imitation of the saints "who through faith and patience inherit the promises" (6:12). Between this command to imitate Abraham and 13:7's command to imitate the leaders of the church, Hebrews fills out this portrait of the "great cloud of witnesses" stretching across barriers of time and space in the justly legendary chapter 11.

The meaning of πίστις in chapter 11 indicates not faith in terms of mere belief, but rather as a "way of life . . . One might paraphrase it as 'living in accord with the reality of things hoped for.'"[52] Indeed, as can be seen through the

45. Keating, "Aquinas," 90.
46. Keating, "Aquinas," 98.
47. Johnson, *Hebrews*, 255.
48. David M. Moffitt, *Atonement and the Logic of Resurrection in the Epistle to the Hebrews*, NovTSup 141 (Leiden: Brill, 2011), 296.
49. Whitlark, "Ideal King," 107.
50. Whitlark, "Ideal King," 108–9.
51. Hood, *Imitating*, 159.
52. Cockerill, *Hebrews*, 520.

contrast between the *faithful* Christ (*pistos*; 3:6) and the unfaithful/unbelieving wilderness generation (*apistia*; 3:19), there is substantial overlap for the author in the idea of confidence in what is to come and active perseverance in line with that coming future.[53] The faith embodied by the heroes of faith in chapter 11, then, is an active exercise of faithfulness that overlaps with the preacher's understanding of patient endurance.[54] We, then, are called to actively imitate their faithfulness, for it is by such faith that "the people of old received God's commendation" (11:2 NET). Imitating the faithfulness and virtue of Christ *as it is encountered in the faithfulness and virtue of the saints*, then, is an essential human act of moral formation that flows out of the triune God's transformation of human character.

CORPORATE GATHERING

Finally, though, Hebrews emphasises the community of faith's corporate life together as essential for their "perfection" (5:14–6:1). Moral formation cannot be practised by lone wolves or solitary spiritual giants. Human formation is a team sport.

For instance, the metaphor of the community as a "house" for God's presence in 3:6 gives way to the exhortation that each member of the family ensures that no brick in that house crumbles through sin (3:12–18). The morally poignant language of sight is marshalled in 3:12 to remind the church to *pay attention* to the potential for faithless hearts – their own and their spiritual family members'. The daily, mutual exhortation that the preacher calls them to embrace serves as a defense against the corrupting power of sin that seems to threaten their very salvation (3:13–19).

In 10:24–25, the exhortation to spur one another on to love and good deeds provides the positive counterpoint to the warnings of 3:1–4:16.[55] The implication is that growth in virtue depends on a certain kind of community, a certain form of common life.[56] 10:25 emphasises one aspect of this life together: regular meetings with the saints lived in the shadow of the coming day of the Lord.

The alternative to such faithful gathering is an ἔθος or moral "habit" of neglecting such regular gatherings. ἔθος language in the virtue tradition often refers to moral habits. Philo, for instance, uses ἔθος language to speak of morally formative habits (cf. *Allegorical Interpretation* 4:218). Hebrews likewise uses this

---

53. See Johnson, *Hebrews*, 107–19.
54. Thompson, *Hebrews*, 93.
55. Warnings which are taken up again in 10:26–31.
56. Johnson, *Hebrews*, 260–61.

language to describe the problematic custom or habit developing among those whose "individualistic attitude" includes a rejection of the gatherings.[57]

In short, the community itself includes corporate acts of formation that depend on, participate in, and look forward to the *trans*forming work of the triune God. Indeed, the character of individual Christians and the community as a whole are both *God's gift* and the *community's task*.

THE SHAPE OF (TRANS)FORMED LIFE IN CHRIST

Before concluding, it is worth reflecting on the practical shape of transformed living as described in Hebrews. Far from being anticlimactic, the concluding ethical exhortations of Heb 13 provide just such a reflection.

The preacher begins with an exhortation to let familial love (φιλαδελφία) in the community remain, while also embracing hospitality – literally, "stranger love" (φιλοξενία). While such hospitality is often interpreted as offering welcome to other Christians and church leaders who were "regularly on the move,"[58] the alliterative connection between φιλαδελφία and φιλοξενία could just as easily highlight God's call for the faithful to lovingly welcome both those inside *and* those outside the community.[59] Indeed, the angelic visitors in the Abraham story referenced were actual strangers, rather than simply visitors from another Christian community.

Familial love means sharing in the sufferings of those in prison, an act of solidarity that resonates with Christ's own willingness to share humanity's sufferings (13:3). Sexual fidelity and a generosity empowered by contentment and resistance to greed come next (13:4–6). Perseverance in Christ as willing outcasts on the margins of society is exhorted in 13:11–14, while 13:15–16 refer to a worship that includes both praise and good deeds.

In short, the character of God's people, even amidst potentially horrendous suffering, shows forth in acts of love for the community, hospitable welcome for strangers, justice and righteousness in economic and sexual practices, perseverance in the face of suffering and shame, and worship that includes both the praise of lips and good deeds.

---

57. Johnson, *Hebrews*, 260–61.
58. Attridge, *Hebrews*, 386.
59. This argument rejects the idea that Hebrews only has an "insider ethic."

CONCLUSION

In conclusion, the triune God's transforming work both unleashes the possibility and demands the practice of human acts of moral and spiritual formation. This in *no way downplays* the essential uniqueness of and emphasis on the finished, definitive work of Christ.[60] Instead, human acts of formation are wholly dependent on and are themselves the gifts of God. Our intentions and abilities to engage in such actions are the result of God's grace.[61] God's action changes human lives by "altering the conditions they exist under."[62]

Indeed, because all human existence is grounded in the triune God who chooses to create space for human freedom, our formation can be said to occur through God's grace and through our action "without divine and human agency being in competition."[63] The very "'space' of moral selfhood and action" in Hebrews is set within the all-encompassing drama of the Father, Son, and Spirit's work.[64] Thus, as Michael Horton argues:

> Even when acting in the same sphere, or even in the same event, divine and human agency do not collide, because God is not simply one agent among others. To paraphrase St. Paul's citation of Epimenides, "In God we live and move and have our freedom."[65]

Such articulations stretch human understanding towards the breaking point, but the epistle to the Hebrews does not attempt to resolve the paradoxes. Instead, it invites its recipients to *live them*. Precisely *because* Hebrews holds such a high, all-encompassing view of the gracious transforming work of the triune God, it calls for God's people to actively and seriously embrace that transforming work through concrete, human acts of formation. May it be so in God's church, now and always. Or, as the author of Hebrews would have it:

---

60. Thus, Whitlark rightly argues that "'getting in' is grounded in God's gracious election while 'staying in' is grounded in God's enablement of fidelity..." (Jason Whitlark, "Fidelity and New Covenant Enablement in Hebrews," in *Getting 'Saved': The Whole Story of Salvation in the New Testament*, ed. Charles H. Talbert and Jason A. Whitlark [Grand Rapids: 2011], 72).

61. Nicholas M. Healy, "Practices and the New Ecclesiology: Misplaced Concreteness?," *International Journal of Systematic Theology* 5, no. 3 (2003): 305.

62. John Webster, "Eschatology, Ontology and Human Action," *Toronto Journal of Theology* 7, no. 1 (1991): 13.

63. D. Stephen Long, *Christian Ethics: A Very Short Introduction* (Oxford: OUP, 2010), 50.

64. This language is derived from John B. Webster, *Word and Church: Essays in Christian Dogmatics* (New York: T&T Clark, 2001), 283.

65. Michael Horton, "'Let the Earth Bring Forth...' The Spirit and Human Agency in Sanctification" in *Sanctification*, ed. Kelly Kapic (Downers Grove: Indiana University Press, 2014), 128.

... may the God of peace ... equip [us] with every good thing to do his will, working in us what is pleasing before him through Jesus Christ, to whom be glory forever. Amen. (13:20–21 NET)

SELECT BIBLIOGRAPHY

Aquinas, Thomas. *The Summa Theologica of St. Thomas Aquinas*. Translated by Fathers of the English Dominican Province. 2nd ed. 21 vols. London: Burns Oates & Washbourne, 1920–1935.

———. *Commentary on the Epistle to the Hebrews*. Translated by Fabian R. Larcher, OP. Accessed May 23, 2023. https://isidore.co/aquinas/english/SSHebrews.htm#52.

Attridge, H. W. *The Epistle to the Hebrews: A Commentary*. Hermeneia. Philadelphia: Fortress, 1989.

Chester, Stephen J. *Reading Paul with the Reformers: Reconciling Old and New Perspectives*. Grand Rapids: Eerdmans, 2017.

Chrysostom, John. *Homilies on the Gospel of St. John and the Epistle to the Hebrews*. Translated by Philip Schaff. *NPNF* 1/14. https://www.ccel.org/ccel/schaff/npnf114.

Cockerill, Gareth Lee. *The Epistle to the Hebrews*. NICNT. Grand Rapids: Eerdmans, 2012.

Healy, Nicholas M. "Practices and the New Ecclesiology: Misplaced Concreteness?" *International Journal of Systematic Theology* 5, no. 3 (2003): 287–308.

Herdt, Jennifer A. *Putting On Virtue: The Legacy of the Splendid Vices*. Chicago: Chicago University Press, 2008.

Hood, Jason. *Imitating God in Christ: Recapturing a Biblical Pattern*. Downers Grove: IVP Academic.

Horton, Michael. "'Let the Earth Bring Forth ...' The Spirit and Human Agency in Sanctification." In *Sanctification*, edited by Kelly Kapic, 127–49. Downers Grove: IVP Academic, 2014.

Hunsicker, David B. "Westminster Standards and the Possibility of a Reformed Virtue Ethic." *SJT* 71, no. 2 (2018): 179–94.

Johnson, Luke Timothy. *Hebrews: A Commentary*. NTL. Louisville, KY: Westminster John Knox Press, 2006.

Keating, Daniel. "Thomas Aquinas and the Epistle to the Hebrews." In *Christology, Hermeneutics, and Hebrews: Profiles from the History of Interpretation*, edited by Jon C. Laansma and Daniel J. Treier, 84–100. Library of Biblical Studies 423. London: T&T Clark, 2012.

Long, D. Stephen. *Christian Ethics: A Very Short Introduction*. Oxford: OUP, 2010.

————. *Hebrews*. Belief: A Theological Commentary on the Bible. Louisville, KY: Westminster John Knox Press, 2011.

Mattison, William C., III. "Can Christians Possess the Acquired Cardinal Virtues?" *Theological Studies* 72, no. 3 (2011): 558–85.

McCruden, Kevin B. "The Concept of Perfection in the Epistle to the Hebrews." In *Reading the Epistle to the Hebrews: A Resource for Students*, edited by Eric F. Mason and Kevin B. McCruden, 209–30. SBL Resources for Biblical Study. Atlanta: SBL Press, 2011.

————. *Solidarity Perfected: Beneficent Christology in the Epistle to the Hebrews.* BZNW 159. New York: De Gruyter, 2008.

Moffitt, David M. *Atonement and the Logic of Resurrection in the Epistle to the Hebrews.* NovTSup. Leiden: Brill, 2011.

Peterson, David. *Hebrews and Perfection: An Examination of the Concept of Perfection in the "Epistle to the Hebrews."* SNTSMS 47. New York: CUP, 1982.

Porter, Jean. "The Subversion of Virtue: Acquired and Infused Virtues in the Summa Theologiae." *The Annual of the Society of Christian Ethics* 12 (1992): 19–41.

Rhodes, Michael J. *Formative Feasting: Practices and Virtue Ethics in Deuteronomy's Tithe Meal and the Corinthian Lord's Supper.* Studies in Biblical Literature 176. New York: Peter Lang, 2022.

Thompson, James. *Hebrews.* Paideia Commentary on the New Testament. Grand Rapids: Baker Academic, 2008.

Webster, John B. "Eschatology, Ontology and Human Action." *Toronto Journal of Theology* 7, no. 1 (1991): 4–18.

————. *Word and Church: Essays in Christian Dogmatics.* New York: T&T Clark, 2001.

Whitlark, Jason A. "Fidelity and New Covenant Enablement in Hebrews." In *Getting 'Saved': The Whole Story of Salvation in the New Testament*, edited by Charles H. Talbert and Jason A. Whitlark, 72–94. Grand Rapids: 2011.

————. "The Ideal King: The Exemplary and Empowering Role of the Son of God." In *"A Temple Not Made with Hands:" Essays in Honor of Naymond H. Keathley*, edited by Mikeal C. Parsons and Richard Walsh, 103–17. Eugene, OR: Pickwick Publishers, 2018.

Witherington, Ben. *New Testament Theology and Ethics.* Downers Grove: IVP Academic, 2016.

PART VI

Concluding Reflections

CHAPTER 16

Reflections

"God Has Spoken"

Gareth Lee Cockerill

INTRODUCTION

"God . . . has spoken."[1] After reading the chapters in this book, and meditating once again on the letter to the Hebrews, I am convinced that speech is the primary way in which the pastor who wrote Hebrews describes divine action. It is appropriate, then, to use God's speech as the theme of these concluding reflections. After reviewing the role and nature of divine speech in Hebrews and taking note of the important implications that flow from its usage, I will look at how Hebrews depicts the role of divine speech in creation, at how God's word in the Son has fulfilled both the Sinai revelation and what God spoke in the "prophets" as a whole, at how God's word addresses his people today, and at the role of God's word in the final judgement. We are listening to discern the impact of God's speech "today."

---

1. Scripture quotations from Hebrews are taken from my own translation unless otherwise indicated. For that translation, see Gareth Lee Cockerill, *The Epistle to the Hebrews*, NICNT (Grand Rapids: Eerdmans, 2012).

THE ROLE, NATURE, AND SIGNIFICANCE
OF DIVINE SPEECH IN HEBREWS

THE FUNDAMENTAL ROLE OF GOD'S SPEECH
AND OF HIS SINAI REVELATION

Speech is the fundamental way in which Hebrews describes God's creation of, in the words of Fellipe do Vale in the essay that introduces this volume, "an economy of divine actions jointly arranged into a history of creation, redemption, sustenance, and perfection."[2] The author of Hebrews has shaped his description of this "economy" to address the pastoral needs of his hearers. He is not concerned with receiving salvation, but with the perseverance of a community that professes faith in Christ. Thus, he does not turn to the exodus from Egypt, however important that may be, but to God's provision at Sinai for faithful living in God's presence. That Sinai revelation is fulfilled by God's speech in his Son (2:1–4; 3:1–6). It provides the context for God's address to his people in the present. It is a model for the final judgement (12:25–29). God's people in the wilderness on pilgrimage from Sinai to God's promised "rest" is the paradigm for God's people throughout history. We who live after Christ join them in that pilgrimage as we journey between God's fulfillment of Sinai in his Son and the promised "rest" (4:1–11) – the "City that has foundations" anticipated by Abraham (11:8–10). As God's wilderness people approached him through the Levitical priesthood while on their journey, so we approach him through our "Great High Priest" "over the house of God" (4:14; 10:21).

Of course God's speech is a prominent biblical theme, beginning with the "let there be" of Genesis 1. However, the centrality of divine speech in Hebrews is closely related to this prominent role played by Sinai, the foundational self-revelation of God in the OT and the greatest disclosure of God before he spoke "in one who is Son."

An integral part of this "economy" is the way in which God's speech, through and on the basis of his speech in the Son, and in anticipation of his speech at the judgement, addresses the people of God "today." The sermon we call Hebrews ends with an invitation for God's people to respond to his speech with their own declaration of faith (13:6).

THE PERFORMATIVE NATURE OF GOD'S SPEECH

The speech by which God acts is performative. What God says comes into being, and what the word of God brings to reality is an integral part of the

---

2. Fellipe do Vale, "Divine Action, Theological Method, and Scripture's Narrative," 13.

message with which it addresses the people of God. This is especially true in regards to the eternal, incarnate Son of God seated at the Father's right hand. It is the scriptural divine Father-Son dialogue, as outlined in George Guthrie's chapter, that has established the Son in this position as "the Source of eternal salvation" (5:9), and it is as "the Source of eternal salvation" that he fulfills his role as "the radiance of God's glory and the exact reputation of God's very being" (Heb 1:3). The pastor relates the past acts of God's "economy" in order to focus his hearers on the present result of those acts – the Son seated at God's right hand who intercedes for the people of God. The "great salvation" (2:3) made available by the Son is the basis of the warnings and encouragements now addressed to the people of God in the "today" of their opportunity.

THE SIGNIFICANCE OF THE PASTOR'S USE OF DIVINE SPEECH

As just noted, speech is integral to the God of the Bible who communicates with his creation in order to accomplish its redemption. There is, therefore, nothing arbitrary or merely rhetorical about the way the pastor uses divine speech. Nevertheless, there are several significant implications of the prominent place given this motif.

- First, the ease with which God accomplishes his purposes with mere speech demonstrates the infinite power of God. In his chapter, Nick Brennan has shown that only the mighty power of God located in the Son delivers impotent human beings from sin, death, and alienation.[3]
- Second, the prominence of divine speech emphasises the interpersonal nature of divine revelation and the consequent necessity for God's people to respond with faithful obedience. Thus, by establishing the economy of salvation that addresses the people of God, divine speech provides the overall context for God's action in the lives of his people past (3:1–4:13; 11:1–40) and present ("Today, if his voice you hear," 3:7).
- Third, whether intentionally or incidentally, by this use of divine speech the pastor makes it clear that God's action is not restricted to the normal processes with which he endowed the world at creation. God's *speakings* at Sinai, in the prophets, and "in one who is Son" are divine interventions parallel with God's *speaking* creation into existence.[4] Furthermore, the Son "bears all to its intended end by the *word* of his power"

---

3. Nick Brennan, "Divine Power and the Priestly Abilities of the Son," 61–86.

4. Note Steve Motyer's statement in "Hebrews's Eschatology and the Action of God," 189: "The double use of the verb ποιεῖν in the preface (1:1–4) – the Son who 'made' the αἰῶνες (1:2) has now 'made' purification for sins (1:3) – introduces the work of salvation as a subsequent and parallel act of creation."

(1:3, emphasis added). The pastor is not deterred by the philosophers of his time, who believed that God was known through contemplation rather than through his actions in this world and its history.[5] He wastes no time arguing that God can act in creation: God fulfills his purpose for creation, in redemption, and in the lives of his people. The pastor affirms boldly that this speaking God has, does, and will act – especially in the Son seated "at the right hand of the Majesty on high" (1:3).

- Finally, God's speech is crucial for our day. "In *Waiting for Godot*, Samuel Beckett pictures the modern world waiting in vain for a word from God. The pastor who wrote Hebrews announces good news: 'God has spoken.' We are not left to grope our way through life. . . . 'without God in the world' (Eph 2:12 TNIV). There is a true north by which we can set our compass. God has spoken."[6]

THE WAYS IN WHICH GOD HAS SPOKEN ACCORDING TO HEBREWS

Hebrews begins by asserting that God spoke "in the prophets." The pastor uses "prophets" to cover all of the ways in which God spoke in the OT. "Prophets" also implies that all God had spoken was yet to be fulfilled – in what God has said, now says, and will say, "in one who is Son." I begin, then, by examining the significance of God's speaking creation into existence (1:3). Then I will review the way Hebrews describes how God's speech in the Son has fulfilled his speech at Sinai (2:1–4, 3:1–6). We will see how the members of the Trinity speak other passages from "the prophets," bringing them to fulfillment (1:1–2:18; 7:1–10:25). I will note how God's words to his people of old (3:7–4:13, etc.), and the examples of obedience and faithlessness recorded in them (11:1–38, etc.), continue to address the people of God in the present.[7] Finally, I will examine the role of divine speech in the final judgement (12:25–29).

---

5. Robert Louis Wilken, *The Spirit of Early Christian Thought* (New Haven; London: Yale University Press, 2003), 8–10.

6. Gareth Lee Cockerill, *Yesterday, Today, & Forever: Listening to Hebrews in the 21st Century* (Eugene, OR: Cascade Books, 2022), 2.

7. See Gareth Lee Cockerill, "The Sermon's Use of the Old Testament," in *The Letter to the Hebrews* (Grand Rapids: Eerdmans, 2012), 41–59.

GOD'S SPEECH IN CREATION – "THE WORLDS WERE ORDERED BY THE WORD OF GOD" (HEB 11:3)

Heb 11:3 presents faith in creation by the word of God as the foundation of all faith. God and his word, though invisible, are the fundamental reality behind the visible universe. Because God brought the universe into being by his invisible word, God's people can depend on him, in accord with his promises, to bring the universe to its intended goal by that same word. Furthermore, since the Son is also the creator (1:8–10), he shares in the power of God's word to accomplish God's purposes.[8]

Craig Bartholomew's chapter "Creation, Divine Action, and Hebrews" (pp. 148–67), along with Steve Motyer's chapter "Hebrews's Eschatology and the Action of God" (pp. 185–99), address the significance of creation and the divine purpose for it. Bartholomew underscores the foundational importance of creation not only for Hebrews but for the entire biblical narrative. Without creation there would be nothing to redeem. He insists that the creation is not destroyed but renewed in the unshakeable kingdom reserved for the faithful (12:25–29). Motyer is not quite as clear concerning this renewal; however, he gives no doubt that the divine "rest" of 3:7–4:11, the unshakeable kingdom of 12:25–29, and all of the other images Hebrews uses for this reality describe a concrete existence that is the fulfillment of God's intention for creation. Access to this renewed creation is provided by the Son who presides over it, and it is the inheritance of the resurrected people of God. The full significance of creation will not become evident until the final judgement, when creation reaches its God-intended end through the work of Christ.[9]

Before looking at God's speech by which he brings about redemption, it would be helpful to have a look at the way Hebrews describes the present situation of humanity within this creation. Human beings do not have the glory that God intended (2:5–10). They are bound by sin and thus threatened by the fear of death lest they experience the ultimate judgement of divine terror (2:14–18; 9:28). The people of God are encouraged to persevere through the work of Christ so that they escape this predicament, but are also urged to fear lest, if they abandon Christ, they experience the terror of exclusion from God's favor.[10]

---

8. Brennan, "Divine Power," 76–78.

9. Cockerill, *The Epistle to the Hebrews*, 95 on "bears all to its intended end by the word of his power" (1:3).

10. Brennan, "Divine Power," 73, describes the present state of human impotence characterised by sin and mortality.

GOD'S SPEECH AT SINAI – "A WITNESS OF
THINGS YET TO BE SPOKEN" (HEB 3:5)

I noted the importance of God's Sinai speech earlier and suggested why the pastor found it appropriate to give this foundational divine revelation such a prominent place in his sermon.[11] The Sinai covenant's condemnation of disobedience on the one hand, and its typological provision for cleansing and approach to God on the other, are both essential parts of this divine revelation. The first is introduced in 2:1–4, while the second is brought in with the statement in 3:5 that "Moses was faithful in all his house as a steward for a witness of things yet to be spoken." Moses bore witness to what God would say in "one who is Son" by establishing the Sinai covenant with its priesthood and sacrifice as a type or picture of the "great salvation" (2:3) that the Son would provide and "the Source of eternal salvation" (5:9) that he would become. This fulfillment of Sinai by the Son is described in 4:14–10:25.[12]

In order to be a type of what was to come, God's Sinai speech had to model the coming fulfillment yet also betray its own impotence to provide that fulfillment. This point is illustrated by the outline in 5:1–10 of the way in which Aaron illustrates, but cannot fulfill, the essentials of priesthood because his life is determined by human "weakness" characterised by sinfulness.[13] It is no surprise, then, that according to 7:1–19 the impotence of the Aaronic priests also consists in mortality. Heb 9:1–22, in particular, recounts many ways in which the descriptions of the old covenant and sacrificial system betrayed the priests' impotence.

The certainty of Sinai's condemnation of disobedience, and the reality of that condemnation as eternal loss, are only made clearer by the Son's gracious provision of the salvation that Sinai prefigured. Thus, in 12:18–24 both condemnation and provision come into clear focus in the description of what Sinai has become through the saving work of the Son. For the apostates who have rejected the Son's Sinai-fulfilling salvation, the word of God at Sinai has become sheer terror (12:18–21).[14] However, for the faithful Sinai has become, through God's gracious word, the glorious place of fellowship with God and his people on Mount Zion (12:22–24).[15] Both of these descriptions are a foretaste of the

---

11. The prominence given Sinai in Hebrews is appropriate in light of the fundamental place of Sinai in the Old Testament, on which see Craig G. Bartholomew, *The God Who Acts in History: The Significance of Sinai* (Grand Rapids: Eerdmans, 2020).

12. Gareth Lee Cockerill, "The Present Priesthood of the Son of God: '. . . he sat down . . .' (An Alternate to David M. Moffitt)," 211–12.

13. Cockerill, "Present Priesthood," 213–14.

14. On the use of fear in Hebrews, see Amy Peeler, "'A Fearful Thing to Fall into the Hands of a Living God': Divine Action in Human Salvation," 168–84.

15. For this interpretation of 12:18–24, see Cockerill, *The Epistle to the Hebrews*, 642–45.

ultimate Sinai pictured in 12:25–29, at which final judgement both the apostate and the faithful enter their ultimate destiny.

TRINITARIAN SPEECH FULFILLS GOD'S PROPHETIC WORD – "HE HAS SPOKEN TO US IN ONE WHO IS SON" (HEB 1:2)

The recognition of the Trinitarian nature of divine speech in Hebrews is one of the most fruitful recent developments in the study of this important biblical book.[16] In his chapter in this volume of essays, "Divine Action in the Jewish Scriptures according to Hebrews," George Guthrie ably develops these ideas pioneered by Matthew Malcolm and Madison Pierce.[17] The OT prophetic word finds its fulfillment in the dialogue between the Father and the Son that confirms the Son's fulfillment of the Sinai covenant and establishes him as High Priest, the "Source of eternal salvation," and thus as the ultimate revelation of God. It also finds fulfillment in the way in which the Holy Spirit addresses the OT to the contemporary people of God.

I am delighted to see this recognition of the fundamental way in which Hebrews supports and is in accord with the doctrine of the Trinity. The relationships between and functions performed by the members of the Trinity in Hebrews are in accord with these relationships and functions in the rest of the NT and in Christian theology in general.[18] This recognition of the Trinitarian character of Hebrews highlights the often-neglected role of the Holy Spirit and underscores the importance of the Son's deity for the pastor's theology.[19]

---

16. On pp. 32–33 of his chapter "Hebrews and Historical Theology: The Contours," Steven E. Harris notes that John Wesley "attends to the Trinitarian shape of divine action" in Hebrews, citing his interpretation of 9:14 as an example.

17. Matthew R. Malcolm, "God Has Spoken: The Renegotiation of Scripture in Hebrews," in *All That the Prophets Have Declared: The Appropriation of Scripture in the Emergence of Christianity*, ed. Matthew R. Malcolm (West Ryde, Australia: Paternoster, 2015), 174–81, and especially Madison N. Pierce, *Divine Discourse in the Epistle to the Hebrews: The Recontextualization of Spoken Quotations of Scripture*, SNTSMS 178 (Cambridge: CUP, 2020). For further comment on Pierce's groundbreaking work, see my chapter in this volume, Cockerill, "Present Priesthood," n. 19.

18. Guthrie's statement is helpful, but needs qualification: ". . . each member of the Trinity seems to direct his words *primarily* towards distinct parties. The Father speaks words to the Son. The Son speaks words to the Father. The Spirit *primarily* speaks words to human beings" ("Divine Action in the Jewish Scriptures according to Hebrews," 142, italics added). The Son speaks *only* to the Father and the Spirit *only* to humans. The Father speaks to the Son but also "in the prophets" (1:1), at Sinai (2:1–4), to Moses (8:5), Abraham (6:13-20), God's people (8:7–13; 10:37–38; 12:4–11; 12:26; 13:5), and at the judgement (12:26).

19. On the importance of the deity of the Son for the theology of Hebrews, see Nick Brennan, *Divine Christology in the Epistle to the Hebrews: The Son as God*, LNTS 656 (London; New York: T&T Clark, 2022), and his chapter in this volume, "Divine Power," 61–86. On the role of the Holy Spirit, see Mary Healy's chapter in this volume, "The Holy Spirit and Christ's Ongoing Priesthood in Hebrews," 227–41, and Steve Motyer, "The Spirit in Hebrews. No Longer Forgotten?," in *The Spirit and Christ in the New Testament and Christian Theology: Essays in Honor of Max Turner*, ed. I. Howard Marshall, Volker Rabens, and Cornelis Bennema (Grand Rapids: Eerdmans, 2012), 212–28. Mary Healy shows how the Spirit is

The Father-Son dialogue makes it quite clear that the Son delivers the people of God from sin and death through power properly exercised by God alone.[20]

The Scripture passages in the Father-Son dialogue are person-specific. The passages with which the Father addresses the Son affirm the Son's deity and establish his session as High Priest (1:4–14; 7:1–28). The Son responds with Scripture, affirming his identification with the people of God through the incarnation and the sacrifice of humble obedience through which he accepted God's invitation to sit at his right hand as High Priest and Mediator of the new covenant (2:11–13; 10:5–18). Thus, the quotations in this dialogue could not be reversed or attributed to the Holy Spirit. They affirm the Son's fulfillment of Sinai. They establish him as "the Source of eternal salvation" who is truly able to deliver God's people from sin and death, empower them for faithful living under the new covenant, and bring them at last to Mount Zion, the heavenly presence of God.

There is more flexibility, however, in regard to the speaker of the scriptural quotes addressed to God's people. Two of them (Ps 95:7–11 in Heb 3:7–11; Jer 31:33–34 in Heb 10:15–18) are attributed to the Spirit.[21] The rest are simply addressed to the people of God by God. The prologue of Hebrews (1:1–4) suggests that God the Father is the speaker. In the case of Prov 3:11–12 (Heb 12:4–11), the text identifies the Father as the one speaking. This situation reflects what we find in the OT, where God can speak directly to his people

---

involved in the atoning work of Christ (9:13–14), in the application of that work to believers (2:1–4; 6:4–8; 10:28–29), and in inspiring the author's christological interpretation of the Old Testament (3:7–8; 9:8–9; 10:15–17). As will be evident from the following comments, I believe that Healy makes more of the Spirit's role in christological interpretation than the author of Hebrews does. One does not have to accept all of her exegetical moves, however, to affirm the substance of her claims and the significance of the Holy Spirit's role in Hebrews. The climactic place given to "insulted the Spirit of grace" in the description of the apostate in 10:29 confirms the significance of the Holy Spirit and his work.

20. See Brennan, "Divine Power," 73, 74, 81, on the meaning of "the power of an indestructible life" (7:16).

21. In reference to these two texts (3:7–8; 10:14–17) plus 9:8–9, Mary Healy ("The Holy Spirit and Christ's Ongoing Priesthood in Hebrews," 236) writes: "In each of these passages (and, by extension, in the other biblical texts that are actualised in Hebrews), the Holy Spirit reveals to believers how Scripture is fulfilled in Christ and in their present life in him." In fact, 9:8–9 is the only one of these passages that clearly suggests that the Holy Spirit enlightens scriptural understanding in the wake of the Son's incarnation and session. I doubt that the author of Hebrews would have denied the Spirit's leading in his christological interpretation, but it is important to note that *the author* does *not* appeal to such inspiration for substantiation. Let's take Ps 95:7–11 in Heb 3:7–4:11 as an example. The author introduces this text in 3:7 with "the Spirit says." In light of this introduction, Healy (235–36) argues at some length that it is the Spirit who makes this text applicable to the present people of God. However, the author substantiates the application of this psalm to his hearers on the basis of clear argumentation. First, he shows that there is one people of God throughout history. He sights David's renewal of God's invitation to show that the "rest" was more than Canaan. Then he carefully defines God's "rest" on the basis of Gen 2:2. There is no arbitrary invoking of the Holy Spirit. At the very least, we might say that Healy makes more of the Holy Spirit's guiding this christological interpretation of Scripture than the author himself does.

or use his Spirit to convey his message.[22] Put another way, to affirm that the Spirit is the speaker of Scripture is not to deny, but to affirm, that the Scripture comes from God the Father.[23] Thus, we must resist the temptation to argue that because two Scriptures addressed to God's people are attributed to the Spirit, the other Scriptures addressed to God's people should be attributed to the Spirit. Nor, as the previous discussion shows, is this assertion necessary to protect the Trinitarian nature of divine speech in Hebrews.

Rather, we should ask why the writer of Hebrews describes the Spirit as addressing the people of God with these two Scriptures at two strategic locations in his sermon. The Spirit speaks Ps 95:7–11 in the long, terrifying warning passage (3:7–4:13) that precedes Hebrews's description of the Son's all-sufficient high priesthood (4:14–10:25). The Spirit "bears witness" to the effectiveness of Christ's sacrifice by addressing the new covenant blessings of Jer 31:33–34 to the people of God near the climax of that description.

Let's examine why the pastor associates Jer 31:33–34 with the Spirit in Heb 10:15–18. It is tempting to argue that the author intends for us to see the Holy Spirit as the speaker of Jer 31:31–34 in Heb 8:6–13 because he attributes the last half of that quotation to the Holy Spirit in 10:15–18 – despite the lack of any contextual clue in chapter 8 to alert listener (or reader) to this fact. In his insightful chapter mentioned earlier, George Guthrie yields to this temptation.[24] In fact, however, when analysed within context, Guthrie's own interpretation of Jer 31:33–34 in Heb 10:15–18 shows not only why attribution to the Spirit is *essential* to the author's intention in 10:15–18, but also why such attribution would have been *inappropriate* in 8:6–13.

Guthrie argues convincingly on the basis of the structure of this passage that the writer of Hebrews identifies the Spirit who "bears witness" in 10:16 with the "Lord" of Jer 31:33 (Heb 10:16) who puts into effect the benefits of the new covenant by writing God's "laws" on his people's hearts.[25] Mary Healy, following Steve Motyer, has also maintained that the Holy Spirit bears witness to the finality of Christ's sacrifice (affirmed in 10:15) by *applying* the benefits of the new covenant described in the quotation from Jer 31:33–34 in Heb 10:16–18.[26] Thus, the attribution of Jer 31:33–34 to the Holy Spirit in Heb 10:16–18

---

22. In this regard, note Healy's affirmation that "in those biblical texts that Hebrews attributes to the Spirit, God is the speaker; in those it attributes to Christ, a human interlocutor (the psalmist or the prophet) is the speaker" (n. 30 of "The Holy Spirit and Christ's Ongoing Priesthood in Hebrews").

23. In 2:1–4, the Spirit is the Father's agent.

24. Guthrie doesn't distinguish carefully between Jer 31:31–34 in Heb 8:6–13 and Jer 31:33–34 in Heb 10:15–18. However, Pierce, *Divine Discourse*, 85–86, attributes the Jeremiah passage to the Father in Heb 8.

25. Guthrie, "Divine Action in the Jewish Scriptures according to Hebrews," 141–42.

26. Healy, "The Holy Spirit and Christ's Ongoing Priesthood in Hebrews," 238–39.

is *essential* to the pastor's purpose of identifying the Holy Spirit as the one who applies the benefits of the new covenant by writing God's laws on our hearts.

However, a careful analysis of 8:6–13 and 10:15–18 within the context of 8:1–10:25 suggests that the author is intentional not only in his identification of the Holy Spirit as the speaker in chapter 10, but also in his refusal to identify the Holy Spirit as the speaker in chapter 8. First, 8:6–13 quotes the entire covenant passage from Jer 31:31–34. The first half of this quotation (Jer 31:31–32) describes the curse of the broken old covenant upon the people of God. The second half (Jer 31:33–34) describes God's promises of a new covenant that will remedy the defects of the old. The writer of Hebrews deals with the removal of the curse for covenant violation (Jer 31:31–34) in Heb 9:16–22, and then with the fulfillment of the new covenant promises (Jer 31:31–34) in Heb 10:15–18.[27] He associates the new covenant promises with the Holy Spirit in 10:15–18 in order to affirm that the Holy Spirit is the one who writes them on the heart. In fact, if Guthrie and Healy are correct, the Holy Spirit "bears witness" (10:16) to the sufficiency of Christ's sacrifice not merely by speaking but by *applying* the new covenant promises. Thus, it would have only been misleading to attribute the entire passage to the Holy Spirit in 8:6–15.[28] Moreover, in light of the flexibility just described, it was no problem to attribute the entire passage to the Father and then the new covenant promises to the Spirit.

I turn now to consider how other OT passages are addressed to the people of God today in the light of this Trinitarian affirmation of the Son's fulfillment of Sinai.

GOD'S SPEECH ADDRESSES HIS PEOPLE –
"TODAY, IF YOU HEAR HIS VOICE" (HEB 3:7)

According to the author of Hebrews there is one people of God throughout history – a people that responds to God's word with faith and obedience. We who trust in Christ are one "house" with the generation that stood before Sinai (3:1–6); those addressed by God's word in the Son are the spiritual descendants of those who heard God's word "in the prophets" (1:1–2).

Thus, the warnings (such as Ps 95:7–11 in Heb 3:7–4:11; Hab 2:3–4 in Heb 10:37–38; Hag 2:6 in Heb 12:25–29; Deut 31:6 in Heb 13:5), the promises

---

27. For this interpretation of 9:15–22, see the references to Scott Hahn's articles in n. 34 of my chapter, "Present Priesthood."

28. For a concise description of the important structural relationship between 8:6–13, 9:16(15)–22, and 10:15–18, see my chapter in this book, "Present Priesthood," 215–20, 224, and Gareth Lee Cockerill, *Yesterday, Today, & Forever*, 76.

(such as Jer 31:33–34 in Heb 10:15–18), and the exhortations (such as Prov 3:11–12 in Heb 12:5–6) addressed to the people of God in the OT, as well as the examples of faithfulness and faithlessness recorded there (such as the faithful of Heb 11:1–38 or unfaithful Esau in Heb 12:13–17), continue to address the people of God in the present. Yet they address us with much greater intensity in light of our "Great High Priest," the "Source of eternal salvation" who now sits at God's right hand, providing access to the presence of God for mercy and grace and guaranteeing the effectiveness of the new covenant. The "today" (3:7) of our obedient perseverance is the "today" (1:5) that began when our High Priest took his seat at God's right hand, and will last until his "enemies are made a stool for his feet" (1:13) at the judgement when he returns with "salvation" for those expecting him (9:28). Our resources are so much greater in him, and the magnitude of the promised reward and potential loss is so much clearer.

In summary: (1) The speech of God established the Sinai covenant as a type of the salvation the Son would provide as sacrifice, High Priest, and Guarantor of the new covenant. (2) Through the speech of God, in the form of the Father-Son dialogue, the Son fulfilled that type. (3) Now the speech of God addresses the people of God with eschatological intensity in the person of the "Great High Priest" seated at God's right hand and through the Spirit who applies the benefits of that High Priest to the people of God. God urges them to embrace the Son who provides "such a great salvation" (2:3) and warns them lest they abandon him.

Thus, the speech of God provides the context for the ongoing ministry of our "Great High Priest" and Mediator of the new covenant seated at the right hand of "the Majesty on high" (1:3). He saves "completely those who come to God through him, because he is always living to make intercession for them" (7:25). He ushers us into God's heavenly presence to receive the "mercy" of forgiveness and the "grace" for obedient perseverance (2:16–18). He has "cleansed" our "conscience from dead works to serve the living God" (9:13–14), thus "perfecting" us so that we can enter God's presence to receive what we need in order to persevere until we enter his presence once and for all at the Son's return (9:28; 12:25–29). The Holy Spirit applies the benefits of the new covenant, guaranteed by the Son, to the hearts of God's people so that they taste "the heavenly gift," partake of "the Holy Spirit," and experience "the good word of God and the powers of the age to come" (6:4–5).[29]

---

29. See Motyer, "Hebrews's Eschatology and the Action of God," 197.

GOD'S SPEECH AT THE FINAL JUDGEMENT –
"ONCE MORE I WILL SHAKE NOT ONLY THE EARTH,
BUT ALSO THE HEAVENS" (HEB 12:26)

Everything will climax in the final judgement (12:25–29) when the God who shook Sinai with his voice will shake the universe by speaking once again. The faithful enter the unshakeable kingdom and the apostate suffer ultimate loss. This event is intimated in Heb 1:3, 13 (Ps 110:1) as the time when the exalted Son's enemies will be made "a stool" for his feet. It is anticipated by all of the promises and warnings of Hebrews. It is the time when the Son will return with "salvation" for those awaiting him in faithful obedience (9:28). Thus, the day of judgement is the hope of the faithful in chapter 11 and of all who join their company (11:39–12:3). It is the ultimate tragedy for Esau (12:13–17). The destiny of both the faithless and the faithful is depicted in 12:18–24 and then finalised in the description of the last judgement in 12:25–29.[30]

This final judgement turns our focus back to the central story of Hebrews, to the account of the One who assumed the humanity of the people of God in order to save them from the sin and death that separated them from God (2:14–18) and thus enable them to escape judgement and enter their inheritance as the sons and daughters of God. He accomplished this through his divine power by offering his incarnate life as an obedient sacrifice (2:9–10; 10:5–10) and taking his seat at the Father's right hand.

There is, however, a more comprehensive though less prominent story that encompasses and reinforces this story of redemption. As is evident from both Craig Bartholomew and Steve Motyer's chapters, the story of what God has done to bring his people into their inheritance is also the story of the way he brings his creation to its intended end.[31] The pastor who wrote Hebrews could not tell the first story without introducing the second. Through his incarnate obedience the eternal Son took his seat at God's right hand as "the heir of all things," and from this position he "bears all to its intended end through the word of his power" (1:3). When he has brought God's "sons and daughters" into the "glory" for which they were created (2:5–10) and they have entered the "rest" that was the goal of creation, God's purpose for creation will reach its fulfillment in the unshakeable eternal kingdom (12:25–29) on Mount Zion (12:23–24).

---

30. See reference in n. 15 on p. 302.
31. Bartholomew, "Creation, Divine Action, and Hebrews," 148–67; Motyer, "Hebrews's Eschatology and the Action of God" 185–99.

CONCLUSION

I would grossly misrepresent the pastor if I did not conclude by reflecting on the importance of what God "speaks" to us in this sermon. Thus, I turn to issues of spiritual formation and preaching addressed in Michael Rhodes and Benjamin Quinn's helpful chapters.[32] Quinn appropriately concludes his chapter by urging us "to attend more closely to Hebrews's rich Christology."[33] The contemporary preacher will want to grasp the holistic way in which the author of Hebrews describes the person and work of Christ and the corresponding comprehensive description of the benefits he provides. By offering his obedient human life the Son of God made atonement for sin, was consecrated High Priest in heaven, and became the Guarantor of the new covenant. Through the cleansing from sin that he provides, his faithful people have access into the heavenly presence of God and enjoy the new covenant benefits of forgiveness, heart transformation, and intimacy with God.[34] Through this saving work the Son of God has become "the Pioneer and Perfecter of the faith" who empowers God's people for perseverance. Spiritual formation takes place when we follow the pastor's exhortations to give our full attention to and fully embrace this High Priest seated at God's right hand by drawing near to receive his benefits and persevering in faithful obedience. The resistance we encounter in an unbelieving world becomes God's means for reinforcing the character-shaping habit of obedience.

Although he was unfamiliar with our world, the pastor who wrote Hebrews addresses contemporary issues: (1) In his Son God has "spoken" to a confused and lost world with a sure word of direction and hope for the future. (2) In him God has provided the *only* all-sufficient "Source of eternal salvation" (5:9) for a pluralistic world trapped by the destructive nature of sin and terrorised by death, yet determined to go its own way. (3) In him God has provided "a new and living way" (10:20) for alienated people to come into the fellowship with God for which they were designed. (4) In him God has provided all that we need to live faithfully in a hostile world until we enter God's presence in "the City that has foundations, whose architect and builder is God" (11:10). And, finally, that (5) having been made "heir of all things" through his incarnate obedience the eternal, incarnate Son of God "bears all to its intended end by the word of his power" (1:3).

---

32. Michael J. Rhodes, "On the Road to Perfection: Divine Action, Human Agency, and Moral Transformation in the Epistle to the Hebrews," 279–94; Benjamin Quinn, "Preaching Hebrews," 261–78.

33. Quinn, "Preaching Hebrews," 277–78.

34. See Cockerill, "Present Priesthood," 218–21.

When we preach these truths, we point people to the Son in whom God has now *spoken* (1:1), "the Apostle and High Priest of our confession" (3:1), our "Great High Priest" (4:14), "the Source of eternal salvation" (5:9), our "Forerunner" (6:20), "the Guarantor of a better covenant" (7:20–22), a "Great Priest over the house of God" (10:21), and "the Pioneer and Perfecter of the faith, [the fully divine yet human] *Jesus*" (12:2, emphasis added) – who is thus "the radiance of God's glory and the exact representation of God's very being" (1:3). Amen.

Preaching Hebrews for All Its Worth[1]

Gareth Lee Cockerill's *The Epistle to the Hebrews* (NICNT, Eerdmans, 2012) is both scholarly and pastoral. Grant Osborne called this commentary "a first-rate work that is both readable and very deep" and asserted that those who read it would "gain a fine understanding of this incredibly important epistle and its place in the life of the church." Cockerill's commentary makes a special contribution to our understanding of the shape and pastoral purpose of Hebrews and to the relevance of the author's OT interpretation for the contemporary people of God. "Anyone planning to study, teach, or preach through Hebrews should have this commentary at their side" (*Denver Journal*).

John C. Laansma's *The Letter to the Hebrews: A Commentary for Preaching, Teaching, and Bible Study* (Cascade Books, 2017) is characterised by the balanced judgement that we have come to expect from its author. Laansma's interpretation of Hebrews is thorough, fresh, and pastoral without being idiosyncratic or superficial. This book may not address all the technical issues of the Greek text or interact with every competing interpretation, but it fulfills its title as *A Commentary for Preaching, Teaching, and Bible Study*. "Dr. Laansma has an intuitive grasp of the epistle's missional context and homiletical structure" (Philip Ryken).

Thomas R. Schreiner's *Commentary on Hebrews* (Biblical Theology for Christian Proclamation, Holman, 2015) is an accessible interpretation of Hebrews by a well-known evangelical biblical scholar. Its unique contribution is the way in which Schreiner begins by showing how Hebrews fits into the larger biblical story. His development of various theological themes at the end is also helpful. This commentary "manages to bridge the gap between the academy and the church in such a way that it is at home in both" (from a review by Alan S. Bandy Shawnee).

---

1. An edited and updated version of "Preaching the Bible for All Its Worth: *Hebrews*," *The Big Picture* (March, 2022): 46–47.

David G. Peterson, *Hebrews* (IVP, 2020) is a worthy addition to the Tyndale New Testament Commentary series. This volume provides us with a reliable interpretation of the text of Hebrews by a mature scholar known, among many other things, for his work on "perfection" in Hebrews. Each passage begins with a discussion of context and concludes with theological reflection. This is a solid meat, bread, and potatoes commentary.

Grant R. Osborne with George H. Guthrie, *Hebrews Verse by Verse* (Osborne New Testament Commentaries, Lexham, 2021) is clearly written and is vintage Osborne. The theological significance and contemporary relevance of the text arise directly out of the author's adequately thorough, though not overly technical, exposition. We are indebted to George Guthrie, Osborne's former student, for completing this commentary after the author's death.

George H. Guthrie's *Hebrews* (NIV Application Commentary, Zondervan, 1998), though a bit older than most of the books mentioned in this article, is a valuable addition to the libraries of both pastors and scholars. The NIV Application Commentary has the stated purpose of explaining both the original meaning and contemporary significance of the biblical text. Guthrie's explanations of the original meaning are adequately thorough, and his discussions of contemporary application are relevant without being faddish. Keep an eye out for his forthcoming *Theology of Hebrews* (Zondervan).

William L. Lane's *Hebrews 1–8* and *Hebrews 9–13* (Word Biblical Commentary, Word, 1991) is another older work that deserves mention. Those with command of the original language will want to take advantage of Lane's rich exposition of the Greek text. Everyone, however, can read his "Explanation" section at the end of each passage or consult his shorter work, *Hebrews: A Call to Commitment* (Hendrickson, 1985). That volume is a concise but accurate and readable exposition of Hebrews directed to serious laypeople; thus, it is also useful for pastors.

Some may like Herbert W. Bateman IV and Steven W. Smith's *Hebrews: A Commentary for Biblical Preaching and Teaching* (Kregel, 2021). The Kerux Commentary series, of which this volume is a part, boasts the advantages of combining the skills of an exegete and a homiletician. This volume makes a point of explaining Hebrews within the context of Second Temple Judaism. However, the abundant reference to background material tends, at times, to overwhelm rather than elucidate the passage in question, and some of the suggestions for preaching are only superficially related to the text.

Dana M. Harris's *Hebrews* (B&H Academic, 2019) in the Exegetical Guide to the Greek New Testament is worth mentioning, although its focused dedication on a close reading of the Greek text distinguishes it from most other commentaries mentioned in this article. Harris, however, is not insensitive to theological issues and she provides an extensive bibliography on each passage. Nevertheless, this commentary is for those who want a close structural, syntactical, grammatical, and linguistic (did I use enough adjectives?) reading of the Greek text.

Gareth Lee Cockerill's ***Yesterday, Today, and Forever: Listening to Hebrews in the 21st Century*** (Cascade Books, 2022). This seven-week (forty-nine-day) reading guide is an excellent foundation for preaching or teaching Hebrews because it immerses its reader in this profound biblical book. Each passage is clearly explained in light of the pastoral purpose and rhetorical structure of Hebrews as outlined in Cockerill's NICNT commentary discussed earlier. This book helps us to see Hebrews as a living, breathing organism rather than as an ancient artifact. "Cockerill puts his lifetime of studying and living Hebrews on the table in front of us and in a plate served just to us. This beautiful, timely book is what the church needs!" (Scot McKnight)

Herbert W. Bateman IV, editor, ***Four Views on the Warning Passages in Hebrews*** (Kregel, 2007). The way one understands the warning passages of Hebrews is closely tied to the way in which one understands the purpose and scope of the book as a whole. Thus it is appropriate, in conclusion, to mention this volume that provides a clear presentation of the various options. Several of the contributors to this project (Bateman, Osborne, Guthrie, and Cockerill) have written books mentioned earlier in this article. Buist Fanning is another contributor, whose position is fairly represented by both Schreiner and Peterson's commentaries.

Three Things That We Often Forget When Reading Hebrews

1. Salvation and revelation are intimately related in Hebrews. By becoming the "Source of eternal salvation" (5:9), the Son seated at God's right hand fulfills his role as the ultimate revelation of God.

2. Jesus's humanity is never discussed abstractly in separation from his deity. When the author addresses Jesus's humanity, he is always talking about the eternal Son who has *become* human – about the *incarnation*. Thus, it is less than accurate to say that Heb 1:1–14 is about the Son's deity and Heb 2:5–18 is about his humanity. Heb 1:1–14 is about the Son's eternal deity and exaltation, while Heb 2:5–18 is about the incarnation of the eternal Son, through which he has been exalted.

3. In Hebrews the earthly obedience of the Son of God has atoned for sin (5:7–9; 9:14; 10:5–10) and established a covenant that empowers the children of God for obedience. Consciences are "cleansed" (9:14) and God's law is written on the heart (10:14–18), enabling God's people to live faithful lives. Forgiveness is the door to obedient living.

Contributors

Craig G. Bartholomew is the director of the Kirby Laing Centre for Public Theology in Cambridge. Some twenty-five years ago he started the Scripture and Hermeneutics Seminar in partnership with the Bible Society when he was at the University of Gloucestershire. Craig is the author of many books, most recently *The Doctrine of Creation* (coauthored with Bruce Ashford), *The God Who Acts in History: The Significance of Sinai*, and *The Old Testament and God*.

Nick Brennan is lecturer in systematic theology at Reformed Theological College, Melbourne, Australia. He is author of *Divine Christology in the Epistle to the Hebrews*, and his research interests include Hebrews, Johannine literature, New Testament Christology, and theological retrieval.

Gareth Lee Cockerill is professor emeritus of New Testament and biblical theology at Wesley Biblical Seminary, Jackson, Mississippi, and an associate fellow of the Kirby Laing Centre for Public Theology in Cambridge. He is the author of *The Epistle to the Hebrews* (NICNT, Eerdmans, 2012), *Christian Faith in the Old Testament: The Bible of the Apostles* (Thomas Nelson, 2014), and *Yesterday, Today, and Forever: Listening to Hebrews in the 21st Century* (Cascade, 2022).

Fellipe do Vale (PhD, Southern Methodist University) is assistant professor and department chair of biblical and systematic theology at Trinity Evangelical Divinity School. His work focuses on the junction between theological anthropology and moral theology, and he has a forthcoming book entitled *Gender as Love: Human Identity, Embodied Desire, and Our Social World* from Baker Academic.

George H. Guthrie (PhD, Southwestern Baptist Theological Seminary) serves as professor of New Testament at Regent College in Vancouver, British Columbia.

He is the author of numerous books, including *The Structure of Hebrews: A Text-Linguistic Analysis* (Supplements to Novum Testamentum 73, E. J. Brill, 1994), *Hebrews* (NIV Application Commentary, Zondervan, 1998), and "Hebrews" in the *Commentary on the New Testament Use of the Old Testament* (Baker Academic, 2007).

Scott W. Hahn holds the Father Michael Scanlan, T.O.R., Chair of Biblical Theology and the New Evangelization at Franciscan University of Steubenville, Ohio, where he has taught since 1990, and is the founder and president of the Saint Paul Center for Biblical Theology. Scott is also the author of numerous books including *Romans: A Catholic Commentary on Sacred Scripture*, *The Creed*, *Evangelizing Catholics*, *Angels and Saints*, and *Joy to the World*.

Steven E. Harris is pastor of discipleship at Elim Church Saskatoon and adjunct professor of theology at Horizon College and Seminary. He works in systematic theology and the history of biblical interpretation, and is the author of *Resurrection from the Dead* (Baylor, forthcoming 2023) and *God and the Teaching of Theology* (Notre Dame, 2019).

Scott Leveille is a PhD candidate in theological studies at the University of Toronto, Wycliffe College and holds an MDiv from Beeson Divinity School. His research topic, "Coloring outside the Lines: Apophatic Trinitarian Anthropology in the Theology of Vladimir Lossky," combines his interests in theological anthropology, epistemology, and the Trinity. Scott has served in parish ministry for twenty years and is currently teacher in residence at Covenant Presbyterian Church in Birmingham, Alabama.

Mary Healy is professor of Scripture at Sacred Heart Major Seminary in Detroit, Michigan, is a general editor of the Catholic Commentary on Sacred Scripture, and is author of two of its volumes, *The Gospel of Mark* and *Hebrews*. Her other books include *The Spiritual Gifts Handbook* and *Healing*. She is one of the first three women ever to serve on the Pontifical Biblical Commission.

Scott D. Mackie teaches biblical studies at Chapman University, California, and has authored and/or edited *Eschatology and Exhortation in the Epistle to the Hebrews* (Tübingen: Mohr Siebeck, 2007), *The Letter to the Hebrews: Critical Readings* (London: Bloomsbury, 2018), and *Ancient Texts, Papyri, and Manuscripts* (Leiden: Brill, 2022).

Steve Motyer worked for many years at London School of Theology, where he taught New Testament and hermeneutics and ran the Theology and Counselling programme. Now retired, he is a full-time carer and (to his delight) manages to squeeze in bits of writing on the side.

Amy Peeler is associate professor of New Testament at Wheaton College, Illinois, and associate rector at St. Mark's Episcopal Church in Geneva, Illinois. She is author of *Women and the Gender of God* (Eerdmans, 2022), *Hebrews: An Introduction and Study Guide* with Patrick Gray (T&T Clark, 2020), and *"You Are My Son": The Family of God in the Epistle to the Hebrews* (T&T Clark, 2014).

Benjamin T. Quinn is associate professor of theology and history of ideas at Southeastern Baptist Theological Seminary/The College at Southeastern, associate director of the L. Russ Bush Center for Faith and Culture, and serves as director of partnerships for BibleMesh. Benjamin has authored several books, including his most recent volume, *Christ, the Way: Augustine's Theology of Wisdom*. Benjamin also serves as teaching pastor of Holly Grove Baptist Church in Spring Hope, North Carolina, near his home where he lives with his wife and four children.

Michael J. Rhodes is lecturer in Old Testament at Carey Baptist College and an ordained pastor in the Evangelical Presbyterian Church. His research focuses on the intersection of the Bible and ethics, especially in relation to matters of racial and economic justice. Michael is the author of *Practicing the King's Economy* (coauthored with Robby Holt and Brian Fikkert), *Formative Feasting*, and *Just Discipleship: Biblical Justice in an Unjust World*.

R. Lucas Stamps (PhD, The Southern Baptist Theological Seminary) serves as professor of Christian theology at Anderson University and Clamp Divinity School in Anderson, South Carolina. He is the author or editor of a number of published and forthcoming books, including *Thy Will Be Done: A Dogmatic Defense of Dyothelite Christology* and *Thomas F. Torrance and Evangelical Theology: A Critical Analysis* (edited with Myk Habets).

APPENDIX A

Kirby Laing Centre for Public Theology in Cambridge, UK

The Kirby Laing Centre (KLC) became a fully independent UK charity on 1 January 2021. We are a research centre in *public theology*, with the latter understood as Christian research across the disciplines oriented towards the question "How then should we live?" Our delightful offices are on the second floor of the old convent of Margaret Beaufort Institute, a Catholic women's house some fifteen minutes' walk from the centre of Cambridge. The KLC is an associate member of the Cambridge Theological Federation.

Our ethos is distinctive. Central to the KLC is intellectual community and we seek to ground this in Christian spirituality. Our desire is to do work for the glory of God and in the service of the church and the world.

In our view the Bible is central to public theology. This is reflected in our Scripture Collective, directed by Dr David Larsen and Rev Dr Craig G. Bartholomew. The Scripture Collective now houses four Seminars: the Scripture and Hermeneutics Seminar, the Scripture and Doctrine Seminar, the Scripture and Church Seminar (practical theology), and the Scripture and University Seminar. Each Seminar has its own committee and chair/s.

The origins of our Scripture Collective are found in the Scripture and Hermeneutics Seminar, which celebrated its twenty-fifth anniversary in 2022. This second volume in the KLC's new series with Zondervan Academic emerges from the work of our Scripture and Doctrine Seminar. We are delighted to have a formal publishing partnership with Zondervan Academic, and are excited about the potential of this series.

The KLC is a growing community, and we invite you to become part of it. You can sign up for our emails and see who we are and what we are up to on our website at www.kirbylaingcentre.co.uk.

Rev Dr Craig G. Bartholomew
Director, Kirby Laing Centre, October 2022

APPENDIX B

British and Foreign Bible Society

The British and Foreign Bible Society (BFBS) was founded in 1804 by Thomas Charles, William Wilberforce, and other members of the Clapham Sect. We exist to promote the widest possible distribution and use of the Bible throughout the world. We do this through translation, publishing, distribution, literacy, Bible engagement, and advocacy throughout all spheres of society. We work with all Christian traditions.

Throughout the nineteenth century, the BFBS helped establish a worldwide Bible Society network. Over 150 societies now operate in over 200 territories under the umbrella of United Bible Societies (UBS). The BFBS continues to operate worldwide in partnership with members of the UBS.

We believe that the global church faces a crisis of Bible confidence in the midst of a growing opportunity and openness to the Bible in multiple contexts. Our vision is to see Christians confident in the Bible in all aspects of life, to see a changed conversation about the Bible in wider society, and to see the transformation that the Bible brings when it is embodied in our lives, relationships, and communities.

We seek to work with the highest possible standards of academic and research excellence with respect to the Bible and to societies and cultures around the world. This requires an attitude of deep listening to Scripture as well as to our varied and distinctive audiences. Our interventions always seek to help people and communities engage the Bible more deeply for themselves and experience the reality of Jesus, to whom Scripture leads.

We are delighted to continue our association with the Scripture and Hermeneutics Seminar through an ongoing partnership with the Kirby Laing Centre for Public Theology. The KLC is now administering our research grant programme, intended to support research into the relationship between the Bible and contemporary life. For further information on the Bible Society's work, see www.biblesociety.org.uk.

Professor Paul S. Williams
Chief executive, British and Foreign Bible Society

The Scripture and Hermeneutics Seminar

Retrospect and Prospect

Craig G. Bartholomew, David J. H. Beldman, Amber L. Bowen, and William Olhausen, editors

For twenty-five years, the Scripture and Hermeneutics Seminar (SAHS) has produced a steady stream of influential, global, diverse, ecumenical, and world-class research and publications. This material has deeply influenced a generation of scholars now in mid-career, has resourced countless classrooms, and has been cited thousands of times in scholarly research as well as in pulpits and Bible studies worldwide.

This volume distills the work of the Seminar for a new generation of students, opening for them a gateway to the community and to the resources developed over the past two decades. Tightly organized, carefully arranged, and cross-referenced, this book:

- Highlights the work of a significant movement in biblical interpretation in the academy
- Charts a path of biblical interpretation from the past to the future
- Helps readers understand the philosophical and theological commitments that undergird biblical interpretation
- Helps readers construct a theological hermeneutics that yields a deeper, richer reading of Scripture
- Introduces readers to stories of the Seminar from scholars and ministers impacted by it

The volume features essays by Craig Bartholomew, David Beldman, Amber Bowen, Susan Bubbers, Jean-Louis Chrétien, Havilah Dharamraj, Bo Lim, Murray Rae, J. Aaron Simmons, Anthony Thiselton, and John Wyatt.

Available in stores and online!